National Association of Latino Independent Producers

the
latino
media
resource
guide
2004

National Association of Latino Independent Producers (NALIP)
P. O. Box 1247
Los Angeles, CA 90406
Phone 310.457.4445
www.nalip.org

Published in cooperation with the
Hollywood Creative Directory
1024 N. Orange Drive
Hollywood, CA 90038
Phone 323.308.3490
Toll-free 800.815.0503
www.hcdonline.com

Printed in the United States of America

Cover design by Jesus Garcia
Book design by Carla Green

"As broadcasters, we aim to ensure that our national viewing audience is reflected in our programming and our people.

We recognize that a work force comprised of a wide variety of perspectives, viewpoints and backgrounds is integral to our continued success.

This is not a campaign, but rather a fundamental way of how we do business, and we continue to be steadfast in our goal to become more diverse and more representative of the public we serve."

—LESLIE MOONVES

⦿CBS

Committed to Diversity

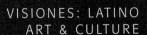

National Association of Latino Independent Producers

the latino media resource guide 2004

contents

DISCLAIMER
The information contained in this book is provided directly by the individuals, production companies, and all other resources listed. NALIP does not engage in editorializing and cannot be held responsible for the veracity of a particular listing or misrepresentation by a listee. NALIP is not responsible for information that has changed after the book has gone to press.

FOX ENTERTAINMENT GROUP

PROUDLY SUPPORTS THE NATIONAL ASSOCIATION OF LATINO INDEPENDENT PRODUCERS.

DIVERSITY DEVELOPMENT
www.fox.com/diversity

welcome from the NALIP Board Chair

Dear NALIP members, supporters and readers:

Welcome to the first edition of the National Association of Latino Independent Producers' **Latino Media Resource Guide**™.

Inclusion begins with information, communities with contact. Since the founding of NALIP, we have heard people say that they do not hire Latinos because they do not know any. We have also heard filmmakers express frustration at not being able to find each other to collaborate and work together. Thankfully, those days are over.

With the appearance of the Latino Media Resource Guide™, connecting to our community, locating each other, and finding resource information is as simple as picking up this book. By consulting this guide you will be able to identify Latino talent working in all aspects of media making in every part of the country. To facilitate access, the guide is available at no expense in hard copy and will be complemented with a web-based database that will provide continuous updated information.

The guide will certainly address the practical challenges of finding phone numbers and identifying which Latino writer is known for her comedic timing. But the guide is also important because, in enhancing the opportunities available to Latinos working in media, it contributes to the creation of a more inclusive media culture, a more equitable society.

NALIP is not alone in believing that inclusion begins with information. The project's funders, including the Rockefeller Foundation, the Ford Foundation, the MacArthur Foundation, Los Angeles Cultural Affairs Department, LA County Arts, Walt Disney Studios, Altria Group, MTV Networks, Univision, Workplace Hollywood, Corporation for Public Broadcasting, Fox Broadcasting, Latino Public Broadcasting, CBS and the SAG-Producers' IAC Fund, have made this their mission as well and we are grateful for their support.

Thank you for your contribution to the Latino Media Resource Guide™. We hope that you use it until it falls apart and you need a new one.

Warmly,
Frances Negrón-Muntaner, Chair

Sí what you've been missing!®

www.sitv.com

America's First Latino TV Network
IN ENGLISH

Launching 2.25.04

www.sitv.com

acknowledgments

We would like to acknowledge and extend our deepest appreciation and sincere friendship to all the wonderful people who contributed to making this book a reality.

First, the NALIP Board of Directors: J. George Cisneros, Moctesuma Esparza, Evy Ledesma-Galán, Sonia González, Evangeline Griego, Cynthia López, Frances Negrón-Muntaner, Dr. Chon A. Noriega, David Ortiz, Edwin Pagán, Sandra M. Pérez and Rick Ramírez.

Second, our Board of Trustees: Rudy Beserra, Carolyn Caldera, Dennis Leoni, Lisa Navarrete, David Valdés and Jeff Valdez.

Our research manager, Olga Arana, for her dedication and superb work, and our fearless research team and staff, Ismael Barrios Prado, Dolly Josette Espinal, Ann García-Romero, Abel Salas, Stephanie Martin, Paula Frye, José Carlos Mangual, Fernando Lebrija, Samuel Cordoba, Alberto González-Reyna and Irma Mangual.

Our partners and friends at Hollywood Creative Directory: Jeff Black, Lauren Rossini and production manager Carla Green.

And last but not least, our funders and supporters: The Rockefeller Foundation. The Ford Foundation. The John D. and Catherine T. MacArthur Foundation. The SAG-Producers' IAC Fund. Los Angeles Cultural Affairs Department. LA County Arts. Walt Disney Studios. Altria Group. MTV Networks. Univision. Latino Public Broadcasting. Workplace Hollywood. The Corporation for Public Broadcasting. Fox Broadcasting. CBS. The Coca Cola Company. American Airlines. NCLR. Kinko's Westwood Village. Packair. We appreciate your vision and commitment to this resource, and for sharing our commitment to advance the professional and creative endeavors of so many. Your generous participation will certainly make a difference.

Finally, to the many others who have so gracefully supported our efforts, thank you.

Kathryn F. Galán
Executive Director

Octavio Marin
Project Director

National Association of Latino Independent Producers

our mission

The National Association of Latino Independent Producers (NALIP) is a national membership organization that addresses the professional needs of Latino/Latina independent producers. Since its founding in 1999, NALIP has held five national Conferences, developed local chapters, plus hosted many regional workshops and networking events that develop the professional skills of film, television, documentary and new media makers. In 2003, we stepped into three new National Initiatives: a Latino Writer's Lab, a Latino Producers Academy™ and this published/on-line Latino Media Resource Guide™.

NALIP's mission is to promote the advancement, development and funding of Latino/Latina film and media arts in all genres. NALIP is the only national organization committed to supporting both grassroots and community-based producers/media makers along with publicly funded and industry-based producers.

NALIP's values are:
- Commitment to Latino/Latina media and filmmakers, regardless of the form or content of their work
- Commitment to respect for diversity based on a code of ethics open to and respectful of differences, including gender, geography, color, class, age, ethnicity, language, sexuality, religion, genre or physical abilities
- Commitment to solidarity and accountability, applying our code of ethics to the selection, funding and mentoring process
- Commitment to raise the question of historical and cultural relevance and awareness of Latinos and Latinas
- Commitment to solidarity, alliance building and multiple visions of Latina/Latino experiences within the local, national, international and global context

MEMBERSHIP BENEFITS
- Participation in the National Latino Media Agenda
- Discounts and scholarships to NALIP National Conference, LPA, LWL, regional seminars and workshops
- Trade discounts with Staples and other vendors
- Financial services and health insurance discounts
- Affiliate membership programs with AIVF, the IDA and others
- Web-based resource database and grants/events calendar at http://my.nalip.info
- Quarterly Board of Directors Minutes
- Annual NALIP financial report
- Copy of Latino Media Resource Guide™

ANNUAL MEMBERSHIP RATES

Student Membership (w/valid ID)	$10
Individual Membership	$40
Joint w/ AIVF	$85
Joint w/IDA	$110
Organizational Membership	$150

Make checks payable to NALIP and mail to:
NALIP Membership
P.O. Box 1247
Santa Monica, CA 90406
Tel: 310.857.1657
Fax: 310.453.5258
Email: abel@nalip.org
Or join online at www.nalip.org

NEW YORK CHAPTER
Perla de Leon
perlafotografica@aol.com

CHICAGO CHAPTER
Robert Leach
publisher@screenmag.com

FLORIDA CHAPTER
Martiza Guimet
maritza@cpeproduction.com

PUERTO RICO CHAPTER
Frances Lausell
isladigital@aol.com

SAN FRANCISCO CHAPTER
Monica Nañez
monanez@sbcglobal.net

SAN ANTONIO CHAPTER
Dora Peña
doralpena@hotmail.com

National Association of Latino Independent Producers

Salutes
the Corporation for Public Broadcasting
and its Efforts to Bring
the Work of Latino Producers
to Public Television

A private corporation funded by the American people. CPB.ORG

Vuelve al lugar donde el fútbol se juega con los pies.

Estar lejos cuesta mucho, volver cuesta poco.

American Airlines, la aerolínea más grande del mundo, tiene
más de 3,900 vuelos diarios a 250 ciudades en 40 países.
American Airlines. Más destinos, más vuelos, más razones.

Ponte cómodo

Latino Writers Lab™

APRIL 22 – 25, 2004 • NEW YORK CITY

This Lab is designed to assist NALIP members who aspire to work as professional writers in the film and television industry. This intensive four-day workshop will help identify concepts viable as films or shorts, will take treatments to first draft, and will develop scripts into polished drafts. It will also include introductions to agents, managers, producers and funders in order to expand a writer's network within the business of writing. This year's curriculum will be interactive and demanding, led by CBS story analyst Harrison Reiner.

The Writers Lab is specifically intended for producer/writers, director/writers and Latino/a screenwriters who are committed to writing well and writing more. Only 20 applicants will be accepted in the program.

LOCATION:
Roger Smith Hotel
501 Lexington, New York, NY
(@ 47th St. in
mid-town Manhattan)
212.755.1400

Applications available at www.nalip.org
Deadline: March 1, 2004
For more information please contact:
Octavio Marin, NALIP Signature
  Projects Director
310.208.1919 / octavio@nalip.org

Caldera/De Fanti Entertainment

A Production/Management Company
120 S. El Camino Dr.
Suite 116
Beverly Hills, CA 90212
(310) 281-6400 phone
(310) 281-6464 fax

Latino Producers Academy™

NALIP, in association with UCLA's School of Theater, Film and Television Professional Certificate Program, will hold the second year of our signature Latino Producers Academy™ in Tucson, Arizona, August 5–12, 2004. The purpose of this week-long intensive workshop is to provide Latino/a producers with the necessary tools to successfully advance their careers in the entertainment industry.

The Latino Producers Academy™ is developed for NALIP members who produce or intend to produce feature films, network television series or documentaries, either for public broadcasting or independently. "Producer" includes producer/writers and producer/directors; filmmakers who have worked locally as well as nationally, in all genres; professionals who work in video, film and interactive media; and those who work in studio-based as well as field production. This program is not for beginners: it has been designed as advanced training to hone and upgrade professional skills through classes and through direct contact with some of the industry's most talented and successful professionals, so that producers can apply these skills to works in progress. It is competitive and challenging: you won't want to miss it!

Applications available at www.nalip.org by **May 1, 2004**.
For more information please contact:
Octavio Marin, NALIP Signature Projects Director
310.208.1919 / octavio@nalip.org

National Association of Latino Independent Producers

production
companies

4 Elements Entertainment

P.O. Box 341784
Los Angeles, CA 90034
Tel 310-980-8906
Email ....shawnabaca@hotmail.com
Web ....www.shawnabaca.com

Shawna Baca, Writer/Director
Ryan Law

Credits
Rose's Garden, Impersonal Impression

In Development
3:52

Project Types
Short Films

Accent Media Productions, Inc.

1350 Beverly Road, #213
McLean, Virginia 22101
Tel ....703-356-9427 Ext. 26
Cell 703-477-0035
Fax 703-506-0643
Email ..jackjorgens@accentmediainc.com
Web ....www.accentmediainc.com

Cecilia Domeyko,President
Dr. Jack Jorgens, VP/Senior Producer

Credits
Magic Wool (Discovery), Portrait of Ana Maria
Vera (PBS), Uganda: Education for All,
Chilean Educational Reform

In Development
Cuba Mia: Portrait of An All Woman
Orchestra, Code Name: Butterflies

Project Types
Documentaries/ Training/ Promotions

Alexander-Orozco and Associates (AOA)

967 Lucile Ave.
Los Angeles, CA 90026
Tel 323-666-0690
Email ....info@alexander-orozco.com
Web ....www.alexander-orozco.com

Russell Alexander-Orozco,
  Producer/Writer
Daniel Foster, Director

Credits
Keepers of the Arts (National Geographic TV
Pilot), A Tu Salud (TV Pilot), The Wave
(Promotional Video)

In Development
Keepers of the Arts, Resolution,
The Acculturation of Indigenous Art

Project Types
Features/TV/Theater

Alpha Studios

3540 N. Southport, #157
Chicago, IL 60657
Tel 773-610-5407
Email..................rislas@alphaflicks.com
Web ....www.alphaflicks.com

Ricardo Islas, Producer/Director

Credits
Haciendo El Amor ...Brujo

Project Types
Tele-Films/TV/Mini-Series/Features

Alta Vista Films

6121 Santa Monica Blvd.
Los Angeles, CA 90038
Tel 323-461-0101
Fax 323-461-8181
Email..........altavistafilms@altavista.com
Web ....www.altavistafilms.com

David Lozano, Executive Producer

Amazonas Films, LLC

930 Euclid St., #207
Santa Monica, CA 90403
Tel 310-393-8636
Fax 310-899-1598
Email ....oarana@aol.com

Maureen Henry, Vice President/Founder
Olga Arana, Vice President/Founder

Credits
How The Garcia Girls Spent Their Summer
(Loosely Based Pictures), Biography of Mario
Vargas Llosa (Sogecable, Spain), What Really
Happened During the Cuban Missile Crisis
(Showtime/AFI), Saving The White Winged
Guan (Antena 3), Qoyllur Ritti: Mystery and
Legend (Antena 3)

In Development
24 Hours In..., Private Curator, America,
Animal Gods, Our Contact

Project Types
Features/Documentary/TV

American View Productions

586 Clinton Ave.
Bridgeport, CT 06605
Tel 203-366-5033
Fax 203-366-5044
Email.....................americanv@snet.net
Web ..www.americanviewproductions.com

Frank Borres, Executive Producer
Robert Alvarado, Creative Director

Credits
Celia Cruz and Friends; Puerto Rican
Messages; LottoMundo

Project Types
TV Commercials; Documentaries;
Entertainment Segments

Arenas Entertainment

100 N. Crescent Dr., Garden Level
Beverly Hills, CA 90210
Tel 310-385-4401
Fax 310-385-4402
Web ....www.arenasgroup.com

Santiago Pozo, CEO
David Acosta, Marketing & Distribution
Diana Lesmez, VP of Development &
   Production
Ivan de Paz, VP of Talent Management

Credits
Empire, Imagining Argentina

Project Types
Features

Anteros Films

P.O. Box 7083
Austin, TX 78713
Tel 512-576-9716
Email .... keiser_lupe@yahoo.com

Lupe Valdez, President and CEO

Credits
One Wish, Anteros

Project Types
Features

Athena Films

2973 Harbor Blvd., #461
Costa Mesa, CA 92626
Tel 714-343-3225
Email.................solis@athenafilms.com
Web ....www.athenafilms.com

Antonio Solis

Credits
Forever Yours, Travel Videos

In Development
December 32nd

Project Types
Features/TV

AZ Los Angeles

1657 12th St.
Santa Monica, CA 90404
Tel 310-581-8081
Fax 310-581-8091
Email..............alonzo@azlosangeles.com
Web ....www.azlosangeles.com

Alonzo Zevallos, President

Project Types
Publicist, Sound Design/Mixing,
DVD Authoring

Blind Ambition Films

P.O Box 1513
Venice, CA 90291-1513
Tel 323-460-2846
Email ....BAF@ureach.com
Web www.geocities.com/yazzie2000/
                    blindambitionfilms.html

Yazmin Ortiz
Jose Oscar Melendez
Kamala Lopez-Dawson

Credits
A Mother's Cry, El Baile, Mi Vida Con Danny,
Jamaican Market Woman, The Road to the
Oscars, LAPD, Just Another Skateboarder

In Development
American Contra, Redemption, La Ola,
Doradillo, Abigail, 1041, Dead Air

Project Types
Features/TV/Theater/Documentaries

Boricua Films

Warner Hollywood Studios
1041 N. Formosa Ave.
Formosa Blvd., #5
West Hollywood, CA 90046
Tel 323-850-2650
Fax 323-850-2650
Email ....bros@boricuafilms.com
Web ....www.boricuafilms.com

David and Erik Llauger-Maiselman,
    Executive Producers
Henry K. Priest, Producer

Credits
Urban Graffiti, Paris Falls, Ride the Spot,
Teva, TNK-Tomorrow Never Knows, The
Saving of Jesse O, The Bay School, LA River
Stories, Art Works

In Development
Development Hell, His Name Was Peres, Oh,
Mother Yemaña

Project Type
Features/TV

Broadcast Standards, Inc.

2044 Cotner Ave.
Los Angeles, CA 90025
Tel 310-312-9060
Fax 310-479-5771
Email ....sales@bsilab.tv
Web.............................. www.bsilab.tv

Rene Leda, CEO
Dolly Rosell, Sales VP

Project Types
Conversions, Duplications, Editing Non-
Linear/Linear Editing, Protools Editing, DVD
Authoring and Replication, Subtitling

Caldera/De Fanti Entertainment

120 El Camino Dr., #116
Beverly Hills, CA 90212
Tel 310-281-6400
Fax 310-281-6464

Carolyn Caldera, Partner
Jean-Luc DeFanti, Partner
Christopher Chang, Development
Gerardo Machado

Credits
Three Blind Mice

In Development
Diego Goes North

Project Types
Features/TV

Calla Productions

Tel 310-392-8055
Fax 310-399-5594
Email ....callaproductions@aol.com

Deborah Calla, Producer

Credits
Carnival In Rio-2003, Chicano Artists (HBO Latino), 500th Anniversary of Brazil (TNT Latin America), Ushi Goes USA (TV Endemol), Dream House, Lost Zweig

In Development
Miss Zacatecas, River City 106, Carnival In Rio-2004, Ted and Michael, Rio de Janeiro

Project Types
Features/TV/Documentaries

Carmona Entertainment

5400 E. Olympic Blvd., #227
Los Angeles, CA 90022
Tel 323-721-FILM
Fax 323-728-4045
Web ....www.carmona-entertainment.com

Gabriel Barbarena, CEO
Gabriel Carmona, President
Alfonso Espinosa, VP Production
Miguel Torres, VP Production Supervisor

Credits
Symbol of the Heart, In Search of Aztlan a Docu-Comedy, Resurrection Blvd., Behind-The-Scenes, Eva, Latinos: Lost In Translation (PBS)

In Development
Mexican in American Sports, God's Penitentiary, Lost Sounds...Forgotten Images, America's Hero

Project Types
Documentaries/TV

Casanova Pendrill

3333 Michelson Dr., #300
Irvine, CA 92612
Tel 949-474-5001
Fax 949-474-8407
Web ....www.casanova.com

Lora Marelle, Senior Vice President

Project Types
Ad Agency

Classified Films

P.O. Box 2006
Santa Ana, CA 92707-0006
Tel 310-980-9352
Fax 714-979-6107
Email ....classifiedfilms@yahoo.com

Alex D. Cortez, President
Quetzal Xavier, Executive Producer
Alfonso Alvarez, Executive Producer
Gerardo Briceno, Executive Producer
Toni Espiritu, Head of Commercial
  Production
Edilberto Calderon, CFO
Rocio M. Garcia, Entertainment Law
  Advisor

Credits
Sunshine Music, Nadie Sabe

In Development
Betrayal and Violations: Mexican Repatriation of the 1930's

Project Types
Music Videos/Commercials/TV/Documentaries

Cris Franco Entertainment (CFE)

5324 Kester Ave., #1
Sherman Oaks, CA 91411-4060
Tel 818-642-0935
Email ....me@crisfranco.com
Web ....www.crisfranco.com

Cris Franco, Producer

Credits
The Cris Franco Show, Café California Classics

In Development
Nacho

Project Types
Talk Shows/Sketch Comedy

Cuentos del Pueblo Productions

P.O. Box 10746
Beverly Hills, CA 90213
Email..cuentos_del_pueblo@hotmail.com
Web ....www.cuentosdelpueblo.com

Alejandro J. Diaz, Writer/Director
Adriana E. Padilla, Writer/Producer

Credits
Pan Dulce y Chocolate

In Development
Cuentos del Pueblo TV Series, Open Swim,
By the Light of the Moon

Project Type
Features/TV

Daniel Hernandez Productions

P.O. Box 90
Montebello, CA 90640
Tel 562-634-3448
Fax 562-634-5131
Email ....sptfishing@aol.com
Web ....www.sport-fishing.com

Daniel Hernandez, Executive Producer

Credits
Sport Fishing with Dan Hernandez, Angler's
Journal, Life of a Mariachi

Project Types
Features/TV

Diva Digital Pictures

3020 SW 28th St.
Coconut Grove, FL 33133
Tel 305-445-1898
Fax 305-445-1557
Email ....gerardo@divadigitalpictures.com

Gerardo Cabrera

Credits
Soccer with Mayte, Solo en Miami,
Informalmente Formal, El Libro Mágico, Una
Noche Con...Las Estrellas

Project Type
TV/Corporate Videos/Commercials

D-No Entertainment

6565 Sunset Blvd., #415
Los Angeles, CA 90028
Tel 323-856-5060
Fax 323-856-5061

Darlene Caamano Loquet,
  Producer/Partner
Noah Rosen, Manager/Partner

Credits
Last Night In East LA, The Chuco Brothers,
Jumped In, Next Door, Nos Miran, On 2,
Just the Beginning, Love Simple

In Development
Lowrider

Project Type
Features/TV

production companies

Edge Entertainment

1571 Irving St.
Rahway, NJ 07065
Tel 732-669-0112
Fax 732-669-0217
Email ....CEERB@aol.com
Web ....www.ceetv.com

Rey Blanco, CEO/Executive Producer

Credits
Gloria and Emilio Estefan: Made For Each Other (A&E), Oscar de la Hoya: Body and Soul (A&E), Broadway's Best (Tribune), America Eats (Tribune), Viva! (SYN) Black and White in Exile (PBS), Orozco in Gringoland (PBS)

In Development
Wifredo and Me (PBS), Star Models: The Audition, Opening Night

Project Type
Documentaries/TV

El Norte Productions

Los Angeles, CA
Tel 213-253-0825
Fax 213-625-2492
Email ....bmjelnorte@hotmail.com

Gregory Nava, Producer/Director
Barbara Martinez-Jitner, Producer

Credits
American Family, Selena, Why Do Fools Fall In Love

Project Types
Features/TV

Empire Pictures

595 Madison Ave., 39th Fl.
New York, NY 10022
Tel 212-629-3097
Fax 212-629-3629
Web ....empirepicturesusa.com

Armando Schwartz, CEO

Credits
Las Tres Marias, Tan De Repente

Project Types
Features

Encantado Films

217 Camino del Las Colinas
Redondo Beach, CA 90277
Tel 310-373-0324
Fax 310-373-3749
Web ....www.encantadofilms.com

Don Henry
Lisa Henry
Candice Rosales
Cristian Rosales

In development
Desert of Blood, Something to Believe

Project Types
Features/Suspense, Thriller, Horror, Drama

Ex-Bo Productions, Inc.

580 8th Ave., 8th Fl.
New York, NY 10018
Tel 646-366-0018
Fax 212-921-0456
Email.......................exboprod@aol.com

Joseph La Morte, Director/Executive Producer
Gloria La Morte, Executive Producer

Credits
Washington Heights, Details (HBO), What's for Dinner

Project Types
Features

Eye On the Ball Films, Inc.

P.O. Box 46877
Los Angeles, CA 90046
Tel 323-935-0634
Fax 323-935-4188
Email ....keepyoureye@aol.com
Web ....www.sergioarau.com
Web ....www.yareli.com

Sergio Arau, Executive Producer/Director
Yareli Arizmendi, Producer

Credits
A Day Without A Mexican, El Muro, Café Tacuba

Project Types
Features/Music Videos

Farmore Casting and Production

Tel 213-840-4738
Fax 530-325-4738
Email ....farmorecasting@earthlink.net

Rosalinda Morales, Casting Director
Adriana Millan, Casting Director

Credits
El Padrino, Bread and Roses (Lions Gate
Films), Reyes y Rey

Project Type
Features/TV/Theater

Fawn Mountain Creative Media

26763 Fawn Mountain Rd.
Boerne, TX 78015
Tel 210-698-1191
Fax 210-698-5390
Email ....contact@fawnmountain.com
Web.................www.fawnmountain.com

Roger Castillo, Owner/Executive
  Producer

Project Type
Commercials/Industrial/Features/Video

Fiesta Studios

6777 Hollywood Blvd., Fl. 4
Los Angeles, CA 90028
Tel 323-314-5647

Jon Mercedes, Producer

Flip Films

1617 Broadway St.
Santa Monica, CA 90404
Tel 310-401-6140
Fax 310-401-6149
Web..........................www.flipfilms.com

Adrian Castagna, Executive Producer

Project Types
TV Commercials

Galán Entertainment

523 Victoria Ave.
Venice, CA 90291
Tel 310-823-2822
Fax 310-823-7361
Email ....info@galanent.com
Web.........................www.galanent.com

Nely Galán, CEO
Diana R. Mogollon, Director of Development

Credits
Padre Alberto, Los Beltran, Viva Las Vegas,
La Cenicienta

Project Types
TV/Cable

Galán Productions

5524 Bee Caves Rd., #B5
Austin, TX 78746
Tel 512-327-1333
Email ....galan@galaninc.com
Web.........................www.galaninc.com

Hector Galán, President
Evy Ledesma Galán, Vice President
Gustavo Aguilar, Production Manager
Marta Aguayo, Production Coordinator

Credits
Visiones, Accordian Dreams, The Forgotten
Americans, Chicano! The History of the
Mexican/American Civil Rights Movement,
Numerous Frontline and American Experience
Documentaries

Project Types
Documentaries/CD-ROM Production/TV

Garcia Weiss Productions

118 Broadway, #525
San Antonio, TX 78205
Tel 210-224-2400
Fax 210-224-9618
Email........................garcia9@juno.com

David Garcia, Partner
Fred A. Weiss, Partner

Credits
The Last Carpa, Salt and Earth

In Development
Fausto-A Dark Comedy, Wifey Dearest

Project Types
Features/TV

Gaucho Productions

920 W. 25th St.
Houston, TX 77008
Tel 281-620-9696
Fax 713-937-9309
Email ....martin@gouchop.com
Web ....www.gauchop.com

Martin Delon
Andrea Elustondo-Sanchez

Credits
La Taqueria (York Latino)

In Development
Pizza Boy

Project Types
Features/TV

Green Moon Productions

11718 Barrington Crt., #827
Los Angeles, CA 90004
Tel 310-471-8800
Fax 310-471-8022
Email...........catherine@greenmoon.com

Antonio Banderas
Melanie Griffith
Diane Sellan Isaacs

Credits
Imagining Argentina (Arenas Entertainment),
Tart (Lions Gate Films), Forever Lulu (Starz!
Movie Channel), Crazy in Alabama (Columbia
Tri Star)

Project Types
Features

Ground Zero Latino

6701 Center Dr. West, #655
Los Angeles, CA 90045
Tel 310-410-3030
Fax 310-410-3003
Email ....tony@ground-zero-ent.com
Web ....www.groundzeroent.com

Anthony Perez, Executive Producer
Nestor Miranda, Producer/Director

Credits
Destination Unknown, Blazin', Big Pun Live,

In Development
Shiver

Project Types
Features/Marketing/Distribution

Hope Street Productions, LLC

1800 E. Ft. Lowell Rd., #126-186
Tucson, AZ 85719
Tel 520-319-2613
Fax 520-797-0356
Email.................hsp2@mindspring.com
Email ....hopestreet601@hotmail.com
Web ....www.runninatmidnite.com

Pablo Toledo
Lawrence R. Toledo

Credits
Runnin' at Midnite

In Development
Crossover

Project Types
Commercials/PSA/Music Videos/Features

Humo Films

3270 Oakshire Dr., #14
Los Angeles, CA 90068
Tel..................323-481-5914 (Gustavo)
Tel ....323-708-1452 (Adam)
Email........humo@sbglobal.net (Gustavo)
Email....Adimafilm@hotmail.com (Adam)
Web ....www.humofilms.com

Gustavo Hernandez Perez,
  Director/Writer
Adam Schlachter, Writer/Producer

Credits
The Mexican Dream (AFI), Gentleman, Solo,
Coming Undone, Beware of You, Zero Miles,
XZC637

In Development
Los Bullet

Project Types
Features

Imagentertainment

2706 W. Burbank Blvd.
Burbank, CA 91505
Tel 818-845-1524
Fax 818-845-1113
Email............info@imagentertainment.tv
Web ....www.imagentertainment.tv

Walter Carasco, Founder/CEO
Marvin Acuna, Producer
Jacob Mosler, Producer
Daniel Faraldo, Writer/Director

Credits
Te Amare en Silencio (Univision), How Did It
Feel

Project Types
Features/TV

Impacto Films

3300 Marathon St., #5
Los Angeles, CA 90026
Tel 323-251-7787
Email ....impactofilm@hotmail.com
Web ....www.impactofilms.com

Anayansi Prado, President

Credits
Maid in America

Project Types
Documentary

Jacobi Entertainment

P.O. Box 8088
Universal City, CA 91618
Tel 818-615-6973
Email ....GiGiFilms@aol.com
Web ....www.GIGIERNETA.com

Gigi Erneta

Credits
Crossed

Project Types
Features/TV

Jakmar Entertainment

P.O. Box 8776
Universal City Station
Universal City, CA 91618
Tel 818-761-5725
Fax 818-761-5725
Email ....jakmar@jackietorres.com
Email ....jakmar@marioramirez.com
Web.....................www.jackietorres.com
Web ....www.marioramirez.com

Jackie Torres, Director/Writer/Producer
Mario Ramirez, Director/Writer/Producer
Janet Torres, Marketing Director

Credits
The Price of the American Dream, La Hora
Lunatica

In Development
King of East LA, Afterlife, The Fourth
Dimension

Project Types
Features/TV/Theater

Kendalec Film and Media Productions

1905 S. Broadway
Santa Ana, CA 92707
Tel 323-496-0328
Tel 562-678-3332
Tel 714-540-1964
Fax 714-979-6107
Email ....kendalec99@hotmail.com

Jim Martinez, CEO
Oscar Trotter, VP Production

In Development
Can You Hear Me Now

Project Type
Features/Music Videos/TV

La Banda Films

329 N. Wetherly Dr., #205
Beverly Hills, CA 90211
Tel 310-858-7204
Fax 310-858-7206
Email ....labanda@labandafilms.com
Web ....wwwafilms.com

Francisco Cossio, Producer
Roberto Snider, Producer/Director

Project Types
TV Commercials

La Negrita Productions, LLC

P.O. Box 1888
New York, NY 10021
Tel 212-502-0316
Tel 347-739-1720
Fax 212-772-1506
Email ..LaNegritaProductions@yahoo.com

Sandra Duque, Writer/Producer

Credits
Dear Abigail

Project Types
Short Films/TV

Latin Hollywood Films

Email ....latinafilm@aol.com
Web...........................www.kikikiss.com

Christian "Kiki" Melendez, CEO
Eva Longoria, Producer
David Baum, Vice President
Anthony Lopez, Head Writer

Credits
Salsa desde Hollywood, Kiki desde
Hollywood, Hot Tamales Live!

In Development
Hot Tamales Live! Television Show

Project Types
Features/TV

Latino Flavored Productions

185A Lamped Loop
Staten Island, NY 10314
Tel 212-971-1954
Fax 509-693-1758
Email ....latinoflavored@aol.com
Web ....www.latinoflavored.com

Linda Nieves-Powell

Credits
HBO New Writer's Project, Yo Soy Latina!,
Soul Latina!

Project Types
Features/TV/Theater

Los Hooligans Productions

Austin, TX
Web ....www.loshooligans.com

Robert Rodriguez,
   Director/Producer/Writer
Elizabeth Avellan, Producer

Credits
Spy Kids 3D: Game Over (Dimension Films),
From Dusk 'til Dawn 3 (Buena Vista
Distribution), From Dusk 'til Dawn 2
(Dimension Films), Desperado (Columbia Tri
Star), El Mariachi (Columbia Pictures)

Project Types
Features

Lower East Side Films

443 Broadway, 5th Fl.
New York, NY 10013
Tel 212-966-0111
Fax 212-966-0555
Email ....lesfilms@aol.com

Kathy de Marco, Producer
John Leguizamo, Producer

Credits
Pinero, Undefeated, Joe the King

Project Types
Features/TV/Documentary

Magia Uno Inc.

930 Euclid St., #207
Santa Monica, CA 90403
Tel 310-393-8636
Fax 310-899-1598
Email ....mangual1@msn.com

Jose Carlos Mangual, President/Producer
Jadit de Brito, Vice President/Director

Credits
How the Garcia Girls Spent Their Summer
(Loosely Based Pictures LLC), Anima (AFI)

In Development
La Gran Batalla de Aimee

Project Types
Features

Marilyn Atlas Management

8899 Beverly Blvd., #704
Los Angeles, CA 90048
Tel 310-278-5047
Fax 310-278-5289
Email................rosie91754@yahoo.com

Marilyn R. Atlas, Producer
S. Rosenthal, Literary Manager
Elizabeth Lopez, Literary Development

Credits
Real Women Have Curves (HBO Films),
A Certain Desire, Echoes

In Development
En El Corazon de las Montañas, Suburban
Turban, MacArthur Park (Showtime Pilot)

Project Types
Features

Material Productions

3000 W. Olympic Blvd.
Santa Monica, CA 90404
Tel 310-998-5828
Fax 310-998-5827
Email ....nicole.terry@verizon.net

Jorge Saralegui, Producer/Executive
  Producer

Credits
Queen of the Damned (Warner Bros.), The
Time Machine (Warner Bros.), Showtime
(Warner Bros.), The Big Bounce (Warner
Bros.)

Project Types
Features

Maya Pictures

3030 Andrita St., Bldg. D, Fl. 2
Los Angeles, CA 90065
Tel 310-281-3770
Fax 310-281-3777
Web ....www.maya-pictures.com

Moctesuma Esparza, Executive Producer
Kim Meyers, Director of Development
Tery Lopez, Creative Development
Greg Gomez, Creative Development
Andre Orci, Creative Development
Tonantzin Esparza, Creative
  Development
Luis Guerrero, Executive Assistant
Erick Garcia, Office Manager

Credits
Selena, Introducing Dorothy Dandridge,
Price of Glory

Project Types
Features/TV

Monsoon Entertainment

6100 Wilshire Blvd., #1640
Los Angeles, CA 90048
Tel 323-525-2720
Fax 323-525-2721
Email.........monsoon@monsoon-ent.com

Alfonso Cuaron, Partner
Jorge Vergara, Partner
Arnaud Duteil, President/COO

Credits
The Assassination of Richard Nixon,
Speed Queen, Y Tu Mama Tambien

Project Types
Features

Montebello Entertainment

12423 Ventura Ct.
Studio City, CA 91604
Tel 818-506-7887
Fax 818-506-8822

Steven Peña
Tom Flores

In Development
Skin Deep

Project Types
Features/TV

Morningside Movies Inc.

70 La Salle, #14G
New York, NY 10027
Tel 212-866-5332
Fax 212-665-4779
Email ....la@morningsidemovies.com

Luis Argueta, Producer/Director

Credits
Llamada Por Cobrar, El Silencio de Neto

Project Types
Feature

Narrow Bridge Films

4077 Tujunga Ave., #201
Studio City, CA 91604
Tel 818-766-1582
Fax 818-766-1582
Email ..narrowbridgefilms@sbcglobal.net

Roni Eguia Menendez, Producer

Credits
Hunting Of Man

Project Types
Feature

Noovision Entertainment

P.O. Box 191524
Dallas, TX 75219-1524
Tel 214-521-8357
Fax 214-521-0272

Jose Luis Partida, Executive Producer

Credits
Just For You

Project Type
Features/Commercials/Documentaries

Nuyorikan Productions

1100 Glendon Ave., Suite 920
Los Angeles, CA 90024
Tel 310-209-6055
Fax 310-943-6639

Julio Caro, Producer
Jennifer Lopez, President/Producer

Credits
Carmen, Monster-in-Law

Olmos Productions

500 S. Buena Vista St.
Old Animation Bldg. 1G2 Code 1675
Burbank, CA 91521-1675
Tel 818-560-8651
Fax 818-560-8655
Email ....olmosonline@earthlink.net

Edward James Olmos, Chairman
Lea Ybarra, Executive VP, Publishing Div.
Nick Athas, Producer
Javier Varon, Dir. Development
Martha Hernandez, Office Manager

Credits
American Family, Stand and Deliver,
Lives in Hazard, Americanos

Project Types
Features/TV/MOWs

Patagonia House

Chatsworth, CA 91311
Tel 661-254-0979
Fax 661-253-1763
Email ....patagoniahouse@aol.com

Dennis Leoni, Writer/Producer

Credits
Resurrection Blvd. (Showtime)

In Development
Black and White

Project Type
TV/Features

Phil Roman Entertainment

4450 W. Lakeside Dr., #250
Burbank, CA 91505
Tel 818-985-1200
Fax 818-985-2668
Email ....sales@romanent.com
Web ....www.philromanent.com

Phil Roman, President/CEO

Credits
King of the Hill, Tom & Jerry Movie, Garfield,
Grandma Got Run Over By a Reindeer,
The Simpsons

Project Types
Animation/TV/Features

Pigeon Productions

1267 Coral Way
Miami, FL 33145
Tel 305-856-2929
Fax 305-858-0357
Web ....www.pigeonprod.com

Mercedes Palomo, President
Luisa Correa, Producer/Sales Director
Maria Burés, Executive Producer/
   Pigeon TV
John Hamlet, Controller

Project Types
Film/TV/Commercials/Production Services

Premiere Films

614 Hipodromo St.
San Juan, PR 00909
Tel 787-724-0762
Fax 787-723-4562
Email ....vasco@muvifilms.com

Elba Luis-Lugo, Producer

Credits
12 Horas

Project Types
Feature

Producciones Copelar

313 Eleonor Roosevelt
San Juan, PR 00918
Tel 787-279-6407
Fax 787-754-2809
Email ....copelar@copelar.com
Web ....www.copelar.com

Sonia Valentin, President

Credits
Sudor Amargo, Psycosis, Plaza Vacante, Y Si
Cristobal Despierta

Project Types
Features/TV/Commercials

production companies

Rain Forest Films, Inc.
45 N. Station Plaza, #313
Great Neck, NY 11021
Tel 718-279-0273
Fax 718-423-1157

Maria Escobedo, Writer/Director
Charles Gherardt, Producer

Credits
Rum and Coke, La Cocina

Project Types
Features/TV/Commercials

Raven's Call Productions
P.O. Box 410772
San Francisco, CA 94141
Tel 415-821-7012
Email ....info@hiddeninplainsight.org
Web ....www.hiddeninplainsight.org

Vivi Letsou, Writer/Director

Credits
Hidden in Plain Sight, Skeleton Woman

Project Types
Features/Documentaries

Rebel Crew Films, Inc.
468 N. Camden Dr., 2nd Fl.
Beverly Hills, CA 90210
Tel 310-860-7408
Fax 310-860-7400
Email ....cesar@rcfhomevideo.com
Web ....www.rcfhomevideo.com

Cesar Chatel, President
Robert Arevalo, CEO
Jay Scott Lowry, Chief Counsel

Credits
Infraterrestre, Santo and Blue Demon vs.
Dr. Frankenstein, Santo en La Venganza de
la Momia, El Tesoro de Dracula, Frontera
Sin Ley

In Development
Blue Demon (Animated TV Series)

Project Types
Features

Republica Trading Company
51 MacDougal St., #405
New York, NY 10012
Tel 212-795-1067
Email ..production@republicatrading.com
Web ....www.republicatrading.com

Rafael Jimenez, Founder
Renzo Devia, Director of Production

Credits
Teen People's Top 25 Under 25, Ricky Martin,
Loaded Live (Sony International/MTV), The
Blaze, Battle World Championship (HBO),
MTV's Smokin' Grooves Countdown

Project Types
Music Videos/Commercials/Industrial
Videos/Features

Safada y Sano Productions, LLC
P.O. Box 573
La Puente, CA 91747
Tel 323-445-0939
Email ....info@safadaysano.com
Web ....www.safadaysano.com
Web ....www.passthemic.net

Richard Montes
Jessica Martinez-Puga

Credits
Pass the Mick, Toci: A Mexican Tail

Project Type
Features/Documentaries/Shorts/Music Videos

SI-TV

3030 Andrita St., Bldg. D, Fl. 2
Los Angeles, CA 90065
Tel 323-256-8900
Fax 323-256-9888
Web...............................www.SiTV.com

Jeff Valdez, Co-Chairman
Leo Perez, COO
Rita Morales, Development & Production

Credits
Comedy Compadres, Café Ole with Gisele
Fernandez, The Brothers Garcia

Project Types
Cable/Network

Sleeping Giant Productions

1635 Angelus Ave.
Los Angeles, CA 90026
Tel 323-887-0665, 323-667-3390
Fax 323-887-9600, 323-667-3392
Email ....SGPProductions@aol.com
Web ....www.sleepinggiantpro.com

Evelina Fernandez, Partner/Writer
Sal Lopez, Partner/Producer
Jose Luis Valenzuela, Partner/Director

Credits
Luminarias, Dementia

Project Types
Features/TV/Theatre

Spank Monkey Productions

1125 Crowne Dr., #1135
Pasadena, CA 91107
Tel 818-415-4434
Fax 626-797-5519
Email ....spankmonkeyfilms@aol.com
Web.....................www.joeymedina.com

Joey Medina
Jason Rohrbacker

Credits
El Matador, LA Limo, Below the Belt

Project Types
Features/TV

Three Moons Entertainment, Inc.

7040-F W. Sunset Blvd., #206
Los Angeles, CA 90028
Tel 323-890-1969
Fax 323-890-1990
Email.......................treslunas3@aol.com
Web ..www.threemoonsentertainment.com

Xavier C. Salinas, Manager/Producer

Credits
Making of a Calendar Girls, Calendar Angels,
Sunset Park, Asthma: Fighting to Breathe, Un
Titan, Hot Babes, Hot Cars, The Silent Crisis
Diabetes Among Us, The Kiss, Ratas,
Ratones, Rateros

In Development
Rocket Girl, Dark Days, There She Goes,
Morales, My Brother Is a Girl, Laughing Aztec

Project Types
Features/TV/Talent Management

Total Axis

9899 Santa Monica Blvd., #340
Beverly Hills, CA 90212
Tel 310-925-4415
Email ....info@totalaxis.com
Web ....www.totalaxis.com

Benjamin Torres, CEO

Project Types
Promotion

Velasco and Associates

650 N. Bronson Ave., #102
Hollywood, CA 90004
Tel 323-466-8566
Fax 323-466-8540
Email ....velascojgv@aol.com

Jerry Velasco

Credits
Nosotros Golden Eagle Awards, World Vision
Telethons, Navidad en Barrio Telethons

Project Types
Award Shows/Public Relations/Management

Ventanarosa Productions

Los Angeles, CA

Salma Hayek, Senior Executive Producer

Credits
The Maldonado Miracle, Frida, In the Time of the Butterflies, No One Writes to the Colonel, The Velocity of Gary

Project Types
Features

Agent
Michelle Stern Boaz, William Morris Agency, 310-274-7451

World Film Magic Dist. Corp.

1149 N. Gower, #210
Hollywood, CA 90038
Tel 323-785-2118
Web ....www.worldfilmmagic.com

Roman Alvarado
Jose Gonzalez
Francisco Olea

In Development
A Fool's Plan

Project Types
Film Distribution

ZGS Communications, Inc.

2000 N. 14th St., #400
Arlington, VA 22201
Tel 703-528-5656
Fax 703-528-6566
Web ....www.zgsonline.com

Ron Gordon, President
Eduardo Zavala, Vice President

Credits
Viva Hollywood, True Champions, Latino Athletes and Their Stories

Project Types
Features/TV

Zokalo Entertainment, Cartel

2118 Wilshire Blvd., #1105
Santa Monica, CA 90403
Tel 310-478-0770
Fax 310-496-2772
Email ....info@zokalo.com

Jesus Nebot, Producer

Credits
No Way Out

Project Types
Feature

National Association of Latino Independent Producers

film
schools

Note: 2003 dates are included in this section as reference only. Please contact individual listings for current deadlines.

Academy of Art College

Motion Pictures & Television Program:
  BFA, MFA

Mailing Address
79 New Montgomery St.
San Francisco, CA 94105

Physical Address
79 New Montgomery St.
San Francisco, CA 94105

Organization Tel 415-274-2219
Program Tel 1-800-544-ARTS
Email ....admissions@academyart.edu
Web ....www.academyart.edu

Application Available
Online

Application Deadline 2004
Open admissions

Cost of Program
$16,000 - $20,000

American Film Institute

Cinematography: MFA
Directing: MFA
Producing: MFA
Production Design: MFA
Screenwriting: MFA
Editing: MFA

Mailing Address
2021 North Western Ave.
Los Angeles, CA 90027

Physical Address
2021 North Western Ave.
Los Angeles, CA 90027

Organization Tel 323-856-7600
Program Tel 323-856-7600
Fax 323-467-4578
Email ....shardman@AFIonline.org
Web ....www.afi.com

Application Available
Online

Application Deadline 2004
Early January, 2004

Cost of Program
$21,000 - $25,000

American University

Visual Media: BA
Film and Video: BA; MA
Film and Electronic Media: MFA
Producing Film and Video
  (Weekend Program): MA

Mailing Address
4400 Massachusetts Ave., NW
Washington, DC 20016

Physical Address
Graduate Admissions
School of Communication
American University
4400 Massachusetts Ave. NW
Washington, DC 20016-8017

Organization Tel 202-885-1000
Program Tel 202-885-2060
Email ......communication@american.edu
  ....undergradcomm@american.edu
  ....gradcomm@american.edu
Web ....www.soc.american.edu

Application Available
Online

Application Deadline 2004
Early Decision Freshman Fall Admission
Nov. 15
Regular Freshman Fall Admission Feb. 1
Graduate Spring Admission Nov. 15
Graduate Fall Admission June 1

Cost of Program
$25,000+
Average Non-Res. Tuition

Contact
Kurt Gunderson, Academic Advisor

film schools

Arizona State University West

Interdisciplinary Arts and Performance
  with a Concentration on Media Arts: BA
Interdisciplinary Arts and Performance
  with a Concentration on Visual Arts: BA
Interdisciplinary Arts and Performance
  with a Minor in Film and Video: BA
Film and Video: Certificate

Mailing Address
4701 W. Thunderbird Rd.
P.O. Box 37100
Phoenix, AZ   85069-7100

Organization Tel 602-543-6000
Program Tel 602-543-6132
Fax 602-543-6004
Email ....coas@asu.edu
Web ....www.west.asu.edu

Application Available
Online

Application Deadline 2004
December 1

Cost of Program
$12,113

Bard College

Film and Electronic Arts: BA
Integrated Arts: BA

Mailing Address
Office of Admission, Bard College,
30 Annandale Rd.
Annandale-on-Hudson, NY 12504-5000

Physical Address
School of Communications
Annandale-on-Hudson, NY 12504-5000

Organization Tel 845-758-7472
Fax 845-758-5208
Email ....admission@bard.edu
Web ....www.bard.edu

Application Available
Online

Application Deadline 2004
January 15

Cost of Program
$25,000+

Biola University

Radio/Television/Film: BA
Motion Picture Production: BA
Motion Picture and Television Directing:
  BA
Screenwriting: BA
Television/Video Production: BA
Audio Production: BA
Media Management: BA

Mailing Address
13800 Biola Ave.
La Mirada, CA 90639-0001

Physical Address
La Mirada, CA 90639-0001

Organization Tel 562-903-6000
Program Tel 1-800-OK-BIOLA
                                    (Admissions)
Web ....www.biola.edu

Application Available
Online

Application Deadline 2004
Fall Early Action 1: Dec. 2
Fall Early Action 2: Jan. 15
Fall Regular: March 1

Cost of Program
$25,000+ Average Non-Res Tuition

Boston University

Film Program: BS
Television Program: BS
Film Production: MFA
Screenwriting: MFA
Film Studies: MFA
Television Production: MS
Television Management: MS, MFA

Mailing Address
Department of Film & Television
121 Bay State Rd.
Boston, MA 2215

Physical Address
4400 Massachusetts Ave. NW
Boston, MA 02215

Organization Tel 617-353-2300
Fax 617-353-9695
Email ....admissions@bu.edu
Web ....www.bu.edu

Application Available
Online

Application Deadline 2004
November 1
January 1

Cost of Program
$21,000 - $25,000

Bringham Young University

Visual Arts: BA

Mailing Address
Admissions, A-153 ASB
Provo, UT 84604

Physical Address
Theatre and Media Arts, D-551
Brigham Young University
Provo, UT 84604

Organization Tel 801-422-2507
Program Tel 801-422-2997
Fax 801-422-0005
Email ....admissions@byu.edu or
                    cfacadvise@byu.edu
Web..................................www.byu.edu

Application Available
Online

Application Deadline 2004
October 3

Brooks Institute of Photography

Motion Picture/Video: BA
Photographic/Filmmaking
   Studies: Diploma
Visual Journalism: AAD

Mailing Address
5301 North Ventura Ave.
Ventura, CA 93001

Physical Address
5301 North Ventura Ave.
Ventura, CA 93001

Organization Tel 805-585-8000
Email ....admissions@brooks.edu
Web.............................www.brooks.edu

Application Available
Online

Application Deadline 2004
On-going

Cost of Program
$16,000 - $20,000

California Institute of the Arts (CalArts)

Film and Video: BFA
Experimental Animation: BFA
Character Animation: BFA
Film Directing: BFA
Integrated Media Program in
   Experimental Animation: BFA
Integrated Media Program in Film and
   Video: BFA

Mailing Address
School of Film/Video
24700 McBean Parkway
Valencia, CA 91355

Physical Address
School of Film/Video
24700 McBean Parkway
Valencia, CA 91355

Organization Tel 661-255-1050
Email ....admiss@calarts.edu
Web ....www.calarts.edu

Application Available
Request Online

Application Deadline 2004
Starts October 15

Cost of Program
$22,190

film schools

California State University Fullerton

Radio-TV-Film: BA
Communications with Concentration on
  Entertainment Studies: BA, MA

Physical Address
Communications College
800 N. State College Blvd.
Fullerton, CA 92834

Organization Tel 714-278-3517
Email ....rtvf@fullerton.edu
Web ....www.fullerton.edu

Application Available
Online: www.csumentor.edu

Application Deadline 2004
August 1
October 1

Cost of Program
Up to $5,000

California State University, Northridge

Cinema & Television Arts: BA
Mass Communication with an Option in
  Screenwriting: MA

Mailing Address
18111 Nordhoff
Northridge, CA 91330-8207

Physical Address
Admissions and Records
18111 Nordhoff
Northridge, CA 91330-8207

Organization Tel 818-677-3700
Fax 818-677-3766
Email ......admissions.records@csun.edu
Web ....www.csun.edu
Web ....www.cinemaandtelevision.com

Application Available
Online

Cost of Program
$6,000 - $10,000

Chapman University

Film Studies: BA, MA
Screenwriting: BA
Film Production: BFA, MFA
Television: BFA
Broadcast Journalism: BFA
Screenwriting: MFA
Producing for Film and Television: MFA

Mailing Address
Cecil B. DeMille Hall
333 North Glassell St.
Orange, CA 92866

Physical Address
Cecil B. DeMille Hall
One University Dr.
Orange, CA 92866

Organization Tel 714-997-6765
Fax 714-997-6700
Email ....ftvinfo@chapman.edu
Web..........................www.chapman.edu

Application Available
Online

Application Deadline 2004
Spring: November 1
Fall: January 31

Cost of Program
$25,000+

Columbia College, Chicago

Alternative Forms: BA
Film and Video: MFA
Film and Video with a Concentration in
  Audio: BA
Film and Video with a Concentration in
  Cinematography: BA
Film and Video with a Concentration in
  Critical Studies: BA
Film and Video with a Concentration in
  Directing: BA
Film and Video with a Concentration in
  Documentary: BA
Film and Video with a Concentration in
  Editing: BA
Film and Video with a Concentration in
  Editing: BA

Film and Video with a Concentration in
Producing: BA
Film and Video with a Concentration in
Screenwriting: BA
Film and Video with a Concentration in
Animation: BA

Mailing Address
600 S. Michigan Ave.
Chicago, IL 60605

Physical Address
600 S. Michigan Ave.
Chicago, IL 60605

Organization Tel 312-663-1600
Web ....www.colum.edu

Application Available
Online

Application Deadline 2004
July 15
December 15
May 1

Cost of Program
$16,000 - $20,000

Columbia University
Screenwriting: MFA
Directing: MFA
Producing: MFA
Film Studies: BA, MA

Mailing Address
School of the Arts
305 Dodge Hall
Mail Code 1808
2960 Broadway
New York, NY 10027

Physical Address
School of the Arts
305 Dodge Hall
2960 Broadway
New York, NY 10027

Organization Tel 212-854-2314
Email ......admissions-arts@columbia.edu
Web..........................www.columbia.edu

Application Available
Online

Application Deadline 2004
Film: December
Theater: January 2
Visual Arts: February 1
Writing: January 2

Cost of Program
$25,000+

De Sales University
Television & Film: BA
Communications: BA

Mailing Address
2755 Station Ave.
Center Valley, PA 18034

Physical Address
2755 Station Ave.
Center Valley, PA 18034

Organization Tel 610-282-1100
Email ....Caryn.Lee@desales.edu
Web ....www.desales.edu

Application Available
Online

Cost of Program
$21,000 - $25,000

Contact
Caryn Lee, Admissions Counselor

Emerson College
Visual and Media Arts: BA

Mailing Address
Visual & Media Arts
120 Boylston St.
Boston, MA 02116-4624

Physical Address
Visual & Media Arts
120 Boylston St.
Boston, MA 02116-4624

Organization Tel 617-824-8500
Web ....www.emerson.edu

Application Available
Online

film schools

Application Deadline 2004
January 15
November 1

Cost of Program
$25,000+

Florida State University
Film: BFA
Film Production: MFA

Mailing Address
110 Longmire Building
Tallahassee, FL 32306-1280

Physical Address
College of Arts and Sciences
Florida State University
110 Longmire Building
Tallahassee, FL 32306-21280

Organization Tel 850-644-5034
Program Tel 850-644-1081
Fax 850-644-8642
Email ....mbehm@filmschool.fsu.edu
..................admissions@admin.fsu.edu
Web ....www.filmschool.fsu.edu

Application Available
Online

Application Deadline 2004
November 3, 2003
March 1, 2004

Cost of Program
$11,000 - $15,000

Howard University
Film and Television: BA

Mailing Address
2400 Sixth St., NW
Washington, DC 20059

Physical Address
2400 Sixth St. NW
Washington, DC 20059

Organization Tel 202-806-6100
Email ....jdates@howard.edu
Web ....www.howard.edu

Application Available
Online

Hunter College - City University of New York
Film: BA
Media: BA
Integrated Media Arts: MFA

Mailing Address
The Department of Film and Media
Studies at Hunter College
695 Park Avenue
Room 433 Hunter North
New York, NY 10021

Physical Address
The Department of Film and Media
Studies at Hunter College
695 Park Avenue
Room 433 Hunter North
New York, NY 10021

Organization Tel 212-772-4949
Fax 212-650-3619
Web ....www.cuny.edu

Application Available
Online

Application Deadline 2004
Undergraduate Fall: March 1
Undergraduate Spring: Oct. 1
Graduate: Feb. 1

Cost of Program
$2,800+

Los Angeles Film School
1 Year Filmmaking Program: Certificate
6-Week Digital Filmmaking Program:
  Certificate
8-Month Feature Development Program:
  Certificate

Mailing Address
6363 Sunset Blvd., #400
Hollywood, CA 90028

Physical Address
6363 Sunset Blvd., #400
Hollywood, CA 90028

Organization Tel 323-860-0789
Program Tel 877-9LA-FILM
Email ....info@lafilm.com
Web..............................www.lafilm.com

Application Available
Online

Application Deadline 2004
Rolling Admissions

Cost of Program
$25,400; $4,500; $15,000

Loyola Marymount University
Los Angeles

Animation: BA, MFA
Film Production: BA, MFA
Recording Arts: BA
Screenwriting: BA
Television Production: BA, MFA

Mailing Address
7900 Loyola Blvd.
Los Angeles, CA 90045-8347

Physical Address
Office of Admission Loyola Marymount
University One LMU Drive
Los Angeles, CA 90045-8350

Organization Tel 310-338-3750
Program Tel 800-568-4636
Fax 310-338-2797
Email ....admissions@lmu.edu
Web ....www.lmu.edu

Application Available
Online

Application Deadline 2004
February 1st
Spring priority: December 1st

Cost of Program
$23,934

New York Film Academy -
New York and Universal Studios

One Year Filmmaking: Certificate
One Year Acting for Film: Certificate
4,6,and 8 week Filmmaking: Certificate
4 week Digital Editing – Final Cut Pro
  & AVID: Certificate
5 Week Digital Filmmaking: Certificate
4 Week Acting for Film: Certificate
Screenwriting: Certificate
3D Animation: Certificate
Advanced Film Directing Workshop:
  Certificate
Evening Sync Sound: Certificate
One Year Screenwriting: Certificate
One Year Producing: Certificate
High School Film Camp – Ages 14-17:
  Certificate
AMC 1 Week Movie Camp: Certificate

Mailing Address
NY: 100 East 17th St.
    New York, NY 10003
LA: 3801 Barham Blvd.
     Bldg. 9128, Ste. 179
     Los Angeles, CA 91608

Physical Address
NY: 100 East 17th St.
    New York, NY 10003
LA: 3801 Barham Blvd.
     Bldg. 9128, Ste. 179
     Los Angeles, CA 91608

Organization Tel ......NY: 212-674-4300
..............................LA: 818-733-2600
Fax ....NY: 212-477-1414
..............................LA: 818-733-4074
Email ....film@nyfa.com
Web ....www.nyfa.com

Application Available
Online

Application Deadline 2004
Ongoing

Cost of Program
$3,500 - $25,000+

film schools

film schools

New York University

Film & Television: BFA, MFA
Cinema Studies: BFA, MA, PhD
Design for Stage and Film: MFA

Mailing Address
Department of Film & TV
70 Washington Square South
New York, NY 10012

Physical Address
721 Broadway, 9th Floor
New York, NY 10012

Organization Tel 212-229-5150
Program Tel 212-998-1702
Web..........................www.nyu.edu/tisch

Application Available
Online

Application Deadline 2004
December and April

Cost of Program
$21,000-$25,000+

North Carolina School of the Arts

Filmmaking: BFA, Diploma
Design and Production: BFA, MFA,
  Diploma

Mailing Address
School of Filmmaking
1533 South Main St.
Winston-Salem, NC 27127-2188

Physical Address
School of Filmmaking
1533 South Main St.
Winston-Salem, NC 27127-2188

Organization Tel 336-770-3290
Fax 336-770-3370
Email ....admissions@ncarts.edu
Web.............................www.ncarts.edu

Application Available
Online

Application Deadline 2004
Call for an Inverview.
Deadlines Nov 8th-Jan 31st

Cost of Program
$11,000 - $15,000

Northwestern University

Radio/Television/Film: BA, MFA, PhD

Mailing Address
Department of Radio, Television and Film
633 Clark St.
Evanston, IL 60208

Physical Address
2240 Campus Dr.
Evanston, IL 60208

Organization Tel 847-491-7214
Fax 847-467-1464
Email ....dear-sam@northwestern.edu
Web www.communication.northwestern.edu

Application Available
Online

Application Deadline 2004
Early Decision: November 1st
January 1st

Cost of Program
$25,000+

Ohio University

International Film Scholarship: MA
Film Production and Scholarship: BA, MFA

Mailing Address
School of Film
Lindley Hall 378
Athens, OH 45701

Physical Address
School of Film
Lindley Hall 378
Athens, OH 45701

Organization Tel 740-593-1323
Fax 740-593-1328
Email.....................filmdept@ohiou.edu
Web ....www.ohiou.edu

Application Available
Online

Application Deadline 2004
January 15th

Rochester Institute of Technology

Film & Animation: BFA, MFA

Mailing Address
School of Photographic Arts & Sciences
One Lomb Memorial Dr.
Rochester, NY 14623

Physical Address
School of Photographic Arts & Sciences
One Lomb Memorial Dr.
Rochester, NY 14623

Organization Tel 585-475-2411
Program Tel 585-475-6736
Fax 585-475-7424
Email ....admissions@rit.edu
Web...................................www.rit.edu

Application Available
Online

Application Deadline 2004
February 2nd
February 15th

Cost of Program
$25,000+

Rockport College - International Film Workshops

Photography: MFA, AAD, Certificate
Digital Media: Certificate
Filmmaking: Certificate
Film and Video: AAD
New Media: MFA, AAD
Film: MFA

Mailing Address
P.O. Box 200
Rockport, ME 4856

Organization Tel 877-577-7700
Email................info@theWorkshops.com
Web ..www.RockportCollege.edu/pcert.asp

San Diego State University

Communications with Specialization in
  New Media Studies: MA
Communications with Specialization in
  Telecommunications and Media
  Management: MA
Communication: BA

Physical Address
One Washington Square
San Jose, CA 95192-0055

Organization Tel 408-924-3240
Fax 408-924-3229
Email................cbaldwin@casa.sjsu.edu
Web ....www.sdsu.edu

Application Available
Online

Application Deadline 2004
Fall: March 1
Spring: October 1

San Francisco Art Institute

Film: BFA

Mailing Address
800 Chestnut St.
San Francisco, CA 94133

Physical Address
800 Chestnut St.
San Francisco, CA 94133

Organization Tel 415-771-7020
Email ....admissions@sfai.edu
Web..................................www.sfai.edu

Application Available
Online

Application Deadline 2004
September 1st
January 15th

film schools

San Francisco State University

Cinema: BA, MFA
Cinema Studies: MA
Cinema with Emphasis on Animation: BA

Mailing Address
1600 Holloway Ave.
San Francisco, CA 94132

Physical Address
1600 Holloway Ave.
San Francisco, CA 94132

Organization Tel 415-338-1111
Program Tel 415-338-1629
Email ....cinedept@sfsu.edu
Web ....www.sfsu.edu

Application Available
Online

Application Deadline 2004
August 1st

Cost of Program
Depends on Residency

Savannah College of Art and Design

Film and Television: BFA, MA, MFA
Animation: BFA, MA, MFA
Sound Design: BFA
Visual Effects: BFA, MA, MFA

Mailing Address
Hamilton Hall
Indian Ave.
Savannah, GA 31401

Physical Address
Film and Television Department
P.O. Box 3146
Savannah, GA 31402-3146

Organization Tel 912-525-6479
Fax 912-525-6459
Email ....admission@scad.edu
Web ....www.scad.edu/dept/film

Application Available
Online

Application Deadline 2004
Rolling admissions

School of the Art Institute of Chicago

Film, Video and New Media: BA, MFA
Visual and Critical Studies: BA

Mailing Address
37 South Wabash
Chicago, IL 60603-3103

Physical Address
37 South Wabash
Chicago, IL 60603-3103

Organization Tel 312-899-5219
Email ....admissions@artic.edu
Web ....www.artic.edu

Application Available
Online

Application Deadline 2004
November 15, 2003 for priority
financial aid consideration
or January 15, 2004

School of Visual Arts

Film and Video: BFA
Photography & Related Media: MFA
Film and Video: screenwriting,
    production, cinematography, acting,
    directing, producing, the digital image,
    sound design, editing and marketing:
    Certificate

Mailing Address
209 East 23rd St.
New York, NY 10010

Physical Address
209 East 23rd St.
New York, NY 10010

Organization Tel 202-592-2000
Program Tel 212-592-2100
Email...............................admissions@
                adm.schoolofvisualarts.edu
Web ....www.schoolofvisualarts.edu

Application Available
Online

Application Deadline 2004
Undergraduate: Feb. 2
Graduate: Feb. 1

Southwest Texas State University

Department of Communication Studies:
BA, MA

Mailing Address
601 University Dr.
San Marcos, TX 78666

Physical Address
Department of Communication Studies
205 Centennial Hall
San Marcos, TX 78666-4616

Organization Tel 512-245-2111
Program Tel 512-245-2165
Email ....admissions@swt.edu
Web ....www.swt.edu

Application Available
Online

Application Deadline 2004
Undergrad. Fall: June 1
Undergrad. Spring: Dec. 1
Grad. Fall: June 15
Grad. Spring: Oct. 15

Cost of Program
$11,393

Stanford University

Documentary Film and Video: MA
Communication: BA, MA, PhD
Media Studies: MA

Mailing Address
Department of Communication
Stanford, CA 94305-2050

Physical Address
Department of Communication
Stanford, CA 94305-2050

Organization Tel 650-723-1941
Fax 650-725-2472
Email..........krawitz@stanford.edu comm
..............inforequest@lists.stanford.edu
Web ....www.stanford.edu

Application Available
Online

Application Deadline 2004
Undergrad Early Decision: November 1st
Undergrad: December 1st
Graduate: December 16th

Cost of Program
$25,000+

Syracuse University

Film Art: MFA

Mailing Address
Syracuse University
Syracuse, NY 13244

Physical Address
Syracuse University
Syracuse, NY 13244

Organization Tel 315-443-1870
Email ....orange@syr.edu
Web ....www.syr.edu

Application Available
Online

Application Deadline 2004
Graduate: Dec. 1
Undergrad. Early Decision: Nov. 15
Undergrad. Regular: Jan. 1

Cost of Program
$25,000+

Temple University

Film and Media Arts: BFA, MFA
Broadcasting, Telecommunications &
Mass Media: BFA, MFA
Media Production and Theory: BA

Mailing Address
Department of Film and Media Arts
09 Annenberg Hall
Temple University 011-00
Philadelphia, PA 19122

Physical Address
Department of Film and Media Arts
09 Annenberg Hall
Temple University 011-00
Philadelphia, PA 19122

Organization Tel 215-204-5273
Program Tel 215-204-7000
Fax 215-204-6641
Email ....tuadm@mail.temple.edu
Web ....www.temple.edu

Application Available
Online

Application Deadline 2004
Graduate: Dec. 1
Undergraduate: Spring – Nov. 1
Fall – April 1

Cost of Program
$12,000

University of Arizona

Media Arts: BA, BFA, MA

Mailing Address
The University of Arizona
Tucson, AZ 85721

Physical Address
P.O. Box 210076
Harvill Bldg. Rm. 226
Tucson, AZ 85721

Organization Tel 520-621-1778
Fax 520-621-1307
Email ....marinfo@email.arizona.edu
Web ....www.arizona.edu

Application Available
Online

Application Deadline 2004
Graduate: Aug. 1
Media Arts: Feb. 15

Cost of Program
$22,814

Contact
Dr. Daniel Bernardi

University of California at Irvine

Department of Film and
  Media Studies: BA

Mailing Address
Office of Admissions and
Relations with Schools
204 Administration
Irvine, CA 92697-1075

Physical Address
Undergraduate Counseling Office
University of California
Irvine, CA 92697-2775

Organization Tel 949-824-5386
Program Tel 949-824-6703
Fax 949-824-2464
Web ....www.uci.edu

Application Available
Online

Application Deadline 2004
Fall: Nov. 1-30

Cost of Program
$17,840

University of California at Los Angeles

Film and Television: BA, MA, PhD
Animation: MFA
Production/Directing: MFA
Production/Cinematography: MFA
Screenwriting: MFA
Producers Program: MFA
Moving Image Archive Studies: MA

Mailing Address
School of Theater, Film and Television
405 Hilgard Ave.
Box 951361
Los Angeles, CA 90095-1361

Physical Address
UCLA Undergraduate Admissions, and
Relations with Schools
1147 Murphy Hall
Box 951436
Los Angeles, CA 90095-1436

Organization Tel 310-825-5761
Program Tel 310-825-8764
Fax 310-825-3383
Email..........................info@tft.ucla.edu
Web ....www.ucla.edu

Application Available
Online

Application Deadline 2004
Undergrad.: Nov. 15
MFA: Nov. 1
Animation MFA: Feb. 28
PhD: Dec. 15

Cost of Program
$16,000 - $20,000

University of California at Los Angeles - Professional Program in Producing

School of Theater, Film and Television:
  Certificate

Mailing Address
102B East Melnitz
Los Angeles, CA 90095-1622

Organization Tel 310-825-6124
Program Tel 310-825-3383
Email ....professionalprogram@tft.ucla.edu
Web ....www.filmprograms.ucla.edu

Application Available
Online

Application Deadline 2004
Summer: June 21st
Fall, Winter & Spring: 30 days prior to
start of quarter

Cost of Program
$3,950

Contact
Stephanie Moore
Denise Mann

University of California at Los Angeles - Professional Program in Screenwriting

School of Theater, Film and Television:
  Certificate

Mailing Address
102B East Melnitz
Los Angeles, CA 90095-1622

Organization Tel 310-825-6827
Program Tel 310-825-3383
Email ....professionalprogram@tft.ucla.edu
Web ....www.filmprograms.ucla.edu

Application Available
Online

Application Deadline 2004
July 30

Cost of Program
$3,950

Contact
Stephanie Moore
Denise Mann

University of California at San Diego

Film, Video, Photography: BFA, MFA

Mailing Address
Visual Arts – Media
9500 Gilman Dr.
La Jolla, CA 92093-0327

Physical Address
9500 Gilman Dr.
La Jolla, CA 92093-0003

Organization Tel 858-534-2860
Fax 858-534-8651
Email ....vis-ug@ucsd.edu
Web ....www.ucsd.edu

Application Available
Online

Application Deadline 2004
Grad: December 1
Undergrad. Early Decision: Nov. 15
Undergrad. Regular: January

film schools

University of California at Santa Barbara

Film Studies: BA, MA

Mailing Address
UCSB
Santa Barbara, CA 93106

Physical Address
Ellison Hall 1720
Santa Barbara, CA 93106

Organization Tel 805-893-8000
Program Tel 805-893-2347
Fax 805-893-8630
Email ....fsoadmin@filmstudies.ucsb.edu
Web ....www.ucsb.edu

Application Available
Online

Application Deadline 2004
Fall: Nov.1-30
Winter: July 1-31
Fall: Nov.1-30

Cost of Program
$18,083

University of Iowa

Communication Studies: BA
Cinema: BA
Film Studies: MA, PhD
Film and Video Production: MFA

Mailing Address
University of Iowa
Iowa City, IO 52442

Physical Address
105 Becker Communication
Studies Building
The University of Iowa
Iowa City, IA 52242-1498

Program Tel 319-335-0575
Fax 319-335-0575
Email ....Carol-Schrage@uiowa.edu
Web ....www.uiowa.edu

Application Available
Online

Application Deadline 2004
Undergrad. Fall: April 1
Undergrad. Spring: Nov.15
Grad. Fall: July 15
Grad. Spring: Dec. 1

Cost of Program
Online

University of Massachusetts

Communication Studies: MA

Mailing Address
UMass Boston
100 Morrissey Blvd.
Boston, MA 02125-3393

Physical Address
Undergraduate Admissions
Quinn Building, 1st Fl.
100 Morrissey Blvd.
Boston, MA 02125-3393

Organization Tel 617-287-6000
Fax 617-287-5999
Web ....www.umb.edu

Application Available
Online

Application Deadline 2004
January

Cost of Program
$16,887

University of Miami

Motion Pictures:
   Production/Producing: MFA
Motion Pictures:
   Production/Scriptwriting: MA
Film Studies: MA
Communication Studies: PhD
Visual Communication: BA
Film-Video: BA

Mailing Address
Coral Gables
Miami, FL 33124

Physical Address
5100 Brunson Drive
Frances L. Wolfson Bldg. 3005
Coral Gables, FL 33124

Organization Tel 305-284-2265
Program Tel 800-577-8133
Fax 305-284-3648
Email ....communication@miami.edu
.............................lherrera@miami.edu
Web.............................www.miami.edu

Application Available
Online

Application Deadline 2004
Undergrad Early Decision/Action: Nov. 1
Undergrad Regular Decision: Feb. 1
All Graduate: March 1

Cost of Program
$25,000+

Contact
George Fernandez
Luis Herrera, Director of Student Services

University of New Mexico

Communication: BA, MA, PhD
Media Arts: BA

Mailing Address
The University of New Mexico
Albuquerque, NM 87131

Organization Tel 505-277-0111
Program Tel 505-277-2446
Email ....apply@unm.edu
Web ....www.unm.edu

Application Available
Online

Application Deadline 2004
Undergrad. Spring: Nov. 15
Undergrad. Fall: June 15
MA: Oct. 31
PhD: Feb. 11

Cost of Program
$14,846

University of New Orleans

Film/Video: BA
Film Production/Directing: MFA
Film Production/Production Design: MFA
Film Production/ Creative Writing: MFA

Mailing Address
University of New Orleans
Lakefront
2000 Lakeshore Dr.
New Orleans, LA 70148

Physical Address
Department of Drama and
Communications,
Performing Arts Center
New Orleans, LA 70148

Organization Tel 504-280-6595
Program Tel 504-280-6317
Fax 504-280-5522
Email ....admissions@uno.edu
Web................................www.uno.edu

Application Available
Online

Application Deadline 2004
Undergrad. and Grad. Fall: July 1st
Undergrad. and Grad. Spring: Nov. 15th
International Students have different
dates and therefore should consult
Admissions

University of Southern California

Animation and Digital Arts: BA, MFA
Critical Studies: BA, MA, PhD
Film/Televsion Production: BA, MFA
Interactive Media: MFA
Writing for Screen and Television:
   BA, MFA
Peter Stark Producing Program: MFA
The Business of Entertainment:
   BS, MBA
Summer Production Workshop:
   Certificate

Mailing Address
School of Cinema-Television
University Park Campus
Los Angeles, CA 90089

film schools

Physical Address
University Park Campus,
University of Southern California
Los Angeles, CA 90089

Organization Tel 213-740-8358
Program Tel 213-740-2804
Fax 213-740-7682
Email ....admissions@cinema.usc.edu
Web................................www.usc.edu

Application Available
Online

Application Deadline 2004
Animation and Digital Arts:
   Undergrad: Oct. 15, MFA: Nov. 15
Critical Studies, Writing for Screen and
   TV: Undergrad: Oct. 15,
   MA, PhD: Dec. 10
Film/Televsion Production:
   Undergrad: Oct. 15, MFA: Nov. 15
Interactive Media: MFA Program: Jan. 30
Peter Stark Program: Dec. 10
The Business of Entertainment: Must be
   in MBA Program
Summer Production Workshop: Rolling
   Admissions January 10 – June 23

Cost of Program
$25,000+

University of Texas at Austin

Radio/Television/Film: BA
Screenwriting: MA
Production: MFA
Ethnic and Minority Issues and the
   Media: MA, PhD
Gender and Sexuality Issues and the
   Media: MA, PhD
International Communication Issues:
   MA, PhD
Media, Culture and Society: MA, PhD
Technology, Culture and Society:
   MA, PhD

Mailing Address
Department of Radio-Television-Film
CMA 6.118
Austin, TX 78712-1091

Physical Address
Office of Admissions
P.O. Box 8058
Austin, TX 78713-8058

Organization Tel 512-475-7399
Fax 512-475-7478
Web..............................www.utexas.edu

Application Available
Online

Application Deadline 2004
Grad: December 1
Undergrad. Early Decision: Nov. 15
Undergrad. Regular: January

Cost of Program
$25,000+

film schools

National Association of Latino Independent Producers

diversity
programs

Note: 2003 dates are included in this section as reference only. Please contact individual listings for current deadlines.

ABC Talent Development Programs
The Walt Disney Studios and ABC Entertainment Writing Fellowship Program
500 South Buena Vista Street
Burbank, CA 91521-4389
Tel 818-560-6894
Tel 818-460-6452
Email..............abc.fellowships@abc.com
Web ......www.abctalentdevelopment.com

Application Available
Online

Description
Writing Fellowship Program

Support Provided
Fellows receive a flat weekly salary of $961.54 ($50,000 for one year) for a one-year period. Workshops & seminars, and personalized mentorship with creative executives from ABC, Touchstone and the Buena Vista Motion Picture Group for one year.

Deadline
June 1-27, 2003

Contact
Carmen Smith, VP Talent Development
  Programs
Frank Gonzalez, Director, Talent
  Development

ABC Scholarship Grant Program
500 South Buena Vista Street
Burbank, CA 91521-4389
Tel 818-560-6894
Tel 818-460-6452
Email..............abc.fellowships@abc.com
Web ......www.abctalentdevelopment.com

Application Available
Online

Description
Scholarship Grant Program

Support Provided
Grants/scholarships support new writing, filmmaking and directing talent. Scholarships and grants help finance creative efforts. For one year, grantees are paired with a mentor. Needs to be nominated by a nonprofit organization. Grant of $20,000 to help finance the completion of a screenplay or directing sample.

Deadline
February 1 – Check nominating nonprofit deadline

Contact
Carmen Smith, VP Talent Development
  Programs
Frank Gonzalez, Director, Talent
  Development

ABC Television Directing Fellowship Program
500 South Buena Vista Street
Burbank, CA 91521-4389
Tel 818-560-6894
Tel 818-460-6452
Email..............abc.fellowships@abc.com
Web ......www.abctalentdevelopment.com

Application Available
Online

Description
TV Directing Fellowship Program

Support Provided
The Directing Initiative is not employment and there is no monetary compensation. It is a program of personal exposure to the process of television directing, career development and access to executives and decision-making processes. The goal of the Directing Initiative is to prepare aspiring directors for later employment opportunities in television

Deadline
February 28, 2003

Contact
Carmen Smith, VP Talent Development
  Programs
Frank Gonzalez, Director, Talent
  Development

ABC Casting Project
500 South Buena Vista Street
Burbank, CA 91521-4389
Tel 818-560-6894
Email..............abc.fellowships@abc.com
Web ......www.abctalentdevelopment.com

Application Available
Online

Description
Opportunities for actors
(SAG/Professional theater companies) of
diverse backgrounds.

Support Provided
Allows actors exposure, direction and
feedback from creative and casting
executives of ABC Entertainment,
Touchstone Television, as well as writers
and executive producers from the
entertainment industry.

Deadline
Ongoing

Contact
Carmen Smith, VP Talent Development
  Programs
Frank Gonzalez, Director, Talent
  Development

ABC Micro-Mini Series Development
500 South Buena Vista Street
Burbank, CA 91521-4395
Tel 818-560-6894
Email .... abc.fellowships@abc.com
Web ......www.abctalentdevelopment.com

Application Available
Online

Description
Series of interstitial short programs
integrated into ABC's primetime and/or
late-night lineup. Each Micro-Mini
program will be three minutes in length.

Support Provided
Three one-minute interstitial acts to
be aired over the course of a single
evening. The Micro-Mini Series may be
repurposed on ABC Family or other
distribution platforms.

Deadline
June 30th, 2003

Contact
Carmen Smith, VP Talent Development
  Programs
Frank Gonzalez, Director, Talent
  Development

ABC Daytime Writing Program
500 South Buena Vista Street
Burbank, CA 91521-4389
Tel 818-560-6894
Email .... abc.fellowships@abc.com
Web ......www.abctalentdevelopment.com

Application Available
Online

Description
Discovers and employs creative talent,
mainly writers of culturally and ethnically
diverse backgrounds interested in
Daytime programming writing.

Support Provided
Workshops, seminars, and personalized
mentorship with creative executives from
ABC, Touchtone and the Buena Vista
Motion Picture Group.

Deadline
Summer 2004

Contact
Carmen Smith, VP Talent Development
  Programs
Frank Gonzalez, Director, Talent
  Development

ABC Associate Programs

500 South Buena Vista Street
Burbank, CA 91521-4389
Tel 818-560-6894
Email .... abc.fellowships@abc.com
Web ......www.abctalentdevelopment.com

Application Available
Online

Description
Management internships in the
television industry.

Support Provided
Provides a broad overview of the
Entertainment Division, also permits
time for exploration of specific areas of
interest.

Deadline
Contact Human Resources on March
31st, 2003

Contact
Carmen Smith, VP Talent Development
Programs
Frank Gonzalez, Director, Talent
Development

ABC Internship Programs

500 South Buena Vista Street
Burbank, CA 91521-4389
Tel 818-560-6894
Email..............abc.fellowships@abc.com
Web ......www.abctalentdevelopment.com

Application Available
Online

Description
Paid internships to eligible college
juniors, seniors and graduate students.

Support Provided
Exposes students to a variety of job
duties, provides valuable hands-on
experience and increases knowledge of
the industry. Summer internships work
full-time at ABC. 10-15 hours per week
are expected of each student intern
during terms.

Deadline
Ongoing

Contact
Carmen Smith, VP Talent Development
Programs
Frank Gonzalez, Director, Talent
Development

ABC Production Associate Program

500 South Buena Vista Street
Burbank, CA 91521-4389
Tel 818-560-6894
Email..............abc.fellowships@abc.com
Web ......www.abctalentdevelopment.com

Application Available
Online

Description
12-month paid program for individuals
with diverse backgrounds placed in
entry-level positions in the production
areas of Touchstone Television.

Deadline
Between Dec. 1st, 2002 and March
15th, 2003

Contact
Carmen Smith, VP Talent Development
Programs
Frank Gonzalez, Director, Talent
Development

Academy of Television Arts & Sciences

Education Programs & Services

5220 Lankershim Blvd.
N. Hollywood, CA 91601-3109
Tel 818-754-2830
Fax 818-761-2827
Web ....www.emmys.com

Description
The Academy Foundation offers various
programs for college students and
professors, as well as informational
opportunities for the telecommunications
and general community.

diversity programs

41

Support Provided
The Student Internship Program offers thirty-one 8-week paid summer internships in 27 categories of telecommunications work. The Academy of Television Arts & Sciences Foundation awards $4,000 to each intern accepted into the program—half to be paid at the mid-point of the internship and half upon successful completion of the program.

Deadline
2004 Internship deadlines will be posted in January 2004

American Cinema Editors
ACE Internship Program
100 Universal City Plaza,
Ross Hunter Building B, Room 202
Universal City, CA 91608
Tel 818-777-2900
Fax 818-733-5023
Email .... amercinema@earthlink.net
Web ......www.ace-filmeditors.org/educate

Application Available
By Request

Description
A yearly internship program for college graduates seeking a career in film editing.

Support Provided
Each intern spends one week with three editors—one episodic, one long form television and one feature. There are also field trips to post-production related facilities.

Deadline
November 3, 2004

Contact
Lory Coleman, Head of Internship Program

ACE 2004 Student Editing Competition
100 Universal City Plaza, Ross Hunter Building B, Room 202
Universal City, CA 91608
Tel 818-777-2900
Fax 818-733-5023
Email .... amercinema@earthlink.net
Web ......www.ace-filmeditors.org/educate

Application Available
By Request

Description
Participating students edit a set of video dailies. Three finalists will be guests at the annual ACE Eddie Awards in February.

Support Provided
The winner receives a special Student Award and publicity in the Hollywood trade papers.

Deadline
October 3, 2004

Contact
Lory Coleman, Head of Internship Program

American Federation of Television and Radio Artists (AFTRA)
AFTRA Performer Mentor Program
5757 Wilshire Blvd., Suite 900
Los Angeles, CA 90036-3689
Tel 323-634-8181
Tel 323-634-8175
Fax 323-634-8190
Email ....plopez@aftra.com
Web ....www.aftra.org

Application Available
By request.

Description
Performer program for students at 2 or 4 year colleges or graduate schools in the fields of television and cinema, or broadcast journalism.

Support Provided
Sponsored tape critiques, shadowing days and special events with feature professional performers and journalists.

Deadline
Rolling

Contact
John Russum, Executive Director

AFTRA Broadcast Mentor Program
5757 Wilshire Blvd., Suite 900
Los Angeles, CA 90036-3689
Tel 323-634-8181
Tel 323-634-8119
Fax 323-634-8190
Email ....ranosa@aftra.com
Web ....www.aftra.org

Application Available
By request.

Description
The Broadcast Mentor Program is for students of Broadcast Journalism.

Support Provided
Sponsored tape critiques, shadowing days and special events with professional performers and journalists.

Deadline
Rolling

Contact
Jean Frost, Director of Agency and
  Mentor Programs

Broadcast Training Program/MIBTP

Broadcast Training Program/MIBTP
P.O. Box 67132
Century City, CA 90067
Tel 310-551-1035
Fax 310-388-1383
Email ....ContactUs@theBroadcaster.com
Web ....www.TheBroadcaster.com

Application Available
Online

Description
Provides training opportunities to minority college graduates in radio/TV news reporting and news management, and TV/film production. Training includes the development of writing, editing, producing and reporting skills.

Support Provided
For TV/radio reporter trainees, stations will pay minimum wage to $6.50 an hour for duration; news management trainees' salary arrangements vary for each station.

Deadline
July 30, 2004

Contact
Patrice Williams, CEO

CBS

CBS Diversity Institute
51 West 52nd Street
New York, NY 10019
Tel 212-975-8941
Fax 212-975-9174
Email........................Diversity@cbs.com
Web......................www.cbsdiversity.com

Application Available
Online

Description
Designed to identify and develop diversity within the writing and directing community.

Support Provided
The Institute combines three programs: the CBS Directing Initiative, the Writers Mentoring Program and the Talent Showcase

Deadline
October 1, 2003

diversity programs

CBS Directing Initiative
51 West 52nd Street
New York, NY 10019
Tel 212-975-8941
Fax 212-975-9174
Email........................Diversity@cbs.com
Web.....................www.cbsdiversity.com

Application Available
Online

Description
The program identifies promising directing candidates and matches them with directors of CBS Television Network drama and comedy series. Aspiring directors of diverse backgrounds with a strong desire to direct on a CBS television series are encouraged to apply. You must be 21 or older to be eligible.

Support Provided
There is no monetary compensation, instead a program of personal exposure to the process of television directing, career development and access to executives and decision making process.

Deadline
Ongoing

CBS Writing Mentoring Program
51 West 52nd Street
New York, NY 10019
Tel 212-975-8941
Fax 212-975-9174
Email........................Diversity@cbs.com
Web.....................www.cbsdiversity.com

Application Available
Online

Description
Each participant will be teamed with a mentor—a network executive with whom they will meet on a regular basis, to discuss their work and get advice and support in furthering their career. There will be a series of small networking gatherings with various CBS show runners, in order to gain a better understanding of the show-making process and to begin to form relationships.

Support Provided
The Writers Mentoring Program is not employment and there is no monetary compensation. It is, instead, a structured program of career development, support, and personal access to executives and decision-making processes, with the goal of preparing aspiring writers for later employment opportunities in television.

Deadline
October 1, 2003

CBS Talent Program
51 West 52nd Street
New York, NY 10019
Tel 212-975-8941
Fax 212-975-9174
Email........................Diversity@cbs.com
Web.....................www.cbsdiversity.com

Application Available
Online

Description
CBS television will sponsor its second Latino talent showcase, at the Court Theatre in Los Angeles, in association with NOSOTROS, AFTRA and SAG.

Deadline
August 20 and 29, 2003

Comedy Central
Comedy Central Learning Groups Mentoring Program New York
1775 Broadway, 10th Fl.
New York, NY 10019
Tel 212-767-8600

DGA—Directors Guild of America
New York DGA Assistant Director Training Program
1697 Broadway
New York, NY 10019
Tel 212-397-0930
Email ....info@dgatrainingprogram.org
Web ....www.DGATrainingProgram.org

Application Available
By request online

Description
Provides opportunities for a limited number of individuals to become assistant directors in film, television and commercials

Support Provided
350 days of on-the-job training, combined with seminars and special assignments. After completion, trainees are eligible to join the DGA as second assistant directors.

Deadline
November 7, 2003

Contact
Sandy Forman, Administrator

Assistant Directors Training Program
14724 Ventura Blvd., Suite 775
Sherman Oaks, CA 91403
Tel 818-386-2545
Email ....traningprogram@dgptp.org
Web ....www.trainingplan.org

Application Available
Online

Description
The program provides an inside look at the organization and logistics of motion picture and TV production.

Support Provided
Upon competition, trainees' names are placed in the Southern California Area Qualification making them eligible for employment as Second Assistant Directors.

Deadline
November 7, 2004

Contact
Janet Dyer, Administrator

Fox Diversity Development
Fox Writers Program
Fox Broadcasting Program,
89/3027
P.O. Box 900
Beverly Hills, CA 90213-0900
Tel 310-369-2976
Tel 310-369-5838
Email ....diversity_program@fox.com
Web ....www.fox.com/diversity

Application Available
Online

Description
A Writers Initiative designed to identify diverse writers for various staff positions on Fox series.

Support Provided
Writers are called in to Fox for initial assessment meetings, and have their scripts read by Fox Creative Executives Writers from this pool are interviewed for positions as Writers and Writers Assistants on Fox network television series.

Deadline
Between December and March

Contact
Mina Taylor, Senior Vice President,
　Legal Affairs

Fox Diversity Casting Festival
10201 W. Pico Blvd.
Bldg. 88 / Room 233
Los Angeles, CA 90035
Tel 310-369-2213
Email ....diversity_program@fox.com
Web ....www.fox.com/diversity

Application Available
Online

Description
African American, Asian American, Native American and American Latino talent to showcase before Fox network executives and studio casting directors.

Support Provided
Casting showcases. One-on-one follow-up session with a Fox Broadcasting Company or 20th Century Fox Television casting executive with feedback on actor's scene.

Deadline
December

Contact
Rachel Tenner

Dorsey High School Mentor Program
10201 W. Pico Blvd.
Bldg. 88 / Room 233
Los Angeles, CA 90035
Tel 310-369-2976
Email ....diversity_program@fox.com
Web ....www.fox.com/diversity

Application Available
Online

Description
The Fox S.T.A.R. Mentor Program, bridging the school-to-career gap.

Support Provided
One-on-one mentoring sessions between a high school student and a Fox employee; workshops for students on personal development, higher education planning, career choices and life skills.

Contact
Rachel Tenner

Fox Searchlight
Fox Search Lab
10201 W Pico Blvd., Building 667
Suite #5
Los Angeles, CA 90035
Tel 310-396-1000
Web ....www.foxsearchlight.com

Application Available
Send required material

Description
Encourges new voices and ideas. The Lab is open to international submissions.

Support Provided
The Lab works with selected filmmakers each year to create digital shorts. Each Lab Filmmaker receives a first look deal with Fox Searchlight Pictures.

Deadline
Ongoing

IFP/Los Angeles
Independent Feature Project/ Los Angeles
Project Involve
8750 Wilshire Blvd., Fl. 2
Beverly Hills, CA 90211
Tel 310-432-1280
Tel 310-432-1200
Fax 310-432-1206
Email ....projectinv@ifp.org
Web ....www.ifp.org

Application Available
Online

Description
Mentoring, training and job placement program that provides diverse filmmakers with exposure, experience and connections in the film industry. Two cycles (Fall & Spring) per year for four months each. Twenty participants are selected for each cycle.

Support Provided
Career workshops, individual counseling and access to quality job listings and referrals.

Deadline
October 23, 2003
April 2004

Contact
Pamela Tom, Project: Involve Director

Inner-City Filmmakers Los Angeles
Inner-City Filmmakers Summer Program
3000 W. Olympic Blvd.
Santa Monica, CA 90404
Tel 310-264-3992
Email ....innercity@earthlink.net
Web ....www.InnerCityFilmmakers.com

Application Available
Online

Description
Trains inner-city youth in all aspects of filmmaking and helps them to find industry jobs when they graduate from the eight-week summer program.

Support Provided
Hands-on training with the latest in technology—digital cameras, lighting and sound equipment, Final Cut Pro editing and professional Avid editing systems—to further prepare students for the professional world.

Deadline
April 16th, 2003

Contact
Fred Heinrich, Founder

Inner-City Filmmakers Job Programs
3000 W. Olympic Blvd.
Santa Monica, CA 90404
Tel 310-264-3992
Email ....innercity@earthlink.net
Web ....www.InnerCityFilmmakers.com

Application Available
Online

Description
The Inner-City Filmmakers Jobs Program places qualified ICF graduates in paying entry-level jobs at film studios and production companies.

Support Provided
Helps the development of careers in production and postproduction as students build relationships and advance their careers.

Contact
Fred Heinrich, Founder

MTV Network
MTV Internship Program
1515 Broadway 16th Floor
New York, NY 10036
Tel 212-258-8000
Email..................internships@mtvn.com
Web ....www.MTVNCareers.com

Application Available
Online

Description
An MTV Networks Internship allows college students to work in an innovative, progressive, fast-paced and professional environment.

Support Provided
Students are exposed to all levels of MTV Networks.

Deadline
Ongoing

MTV Network Huddle
MTV Network Internship Program
1515 Broadway 16th Floor
New York, NY 10036
Tel 212-258-8000
Email .... careers@mtvstaff.com.
Web ....www.MTVNCareers.com

Application Available
Online

Description
Mentors (at the manager level or above) establish relationships with employees who wish to advance their careers.

Support Provided
Participants meet one on one for approx-imately nine months and often keep up communication beyond that time, occasionally after the mentored partici-pants have left the company.

Deadline
Contact local Human Resources department and complete an application. March 31st, 2004

diversity programs

National Association of Minorities in Communication

National Association of Minorities in Communication / L. Patrick Mellon Mentorship Program
600 Anton Blvd., 11th Fl.
Costa Mesa, CA 92626
Tel 714-371-4077
Fax 714-371-2103
Email .... info@namic.com
Web ....www.namic.com

Application Available
Online

Description
Making mentors available for career advancement strategies in the Cable and Telecommunications industry.

Support Provided
Top-level industry professionals. Mentor for nine months. One-to-one sessions, support, guidance and career advice and up to two hours per month.

Deadline
Ongoing

Contact
Kathy Johnson, President

NBC

NBC Entertainment Associate Program
Human Resources
3000 W. Alameda Ave.
Burbank, CA 91523
Tel 818-840-4444
Tel 202-885-4445
Email .... epgmassoc@nbc.com
Web ....www.nbcjobs.com

Application Available
Online

Description
Hands-on experience in the development and management of entertainment programming. Program Associates will analyze/develop scripts and provide creative input to writers and producers on review of scripts, stories, casting and scheduling of programs.

Support Provided
Successful graduates of the program move into Creative Executive positions within the NBC Network or NBC Studios. The program offers competitive compensation including benefits.

Deadline
May 31, 2003

Contact
Michael Jack, General Manager in Washington, D.C.

NBC News Associate Program
Human Resources
3000 W. Alameda Ave.
Burbank, CA 91523
Tel 818-840-4444
Tel 202-885-4445
Email .... news.associate@nbc.com
Web ....www.nbcjobs.com

Application Available
Online

Description
Fast-track opportunity for people with the goal to learn news gathering and production skills.

Support Provided
News Associates gain real-world experience honing research skills, developing news stories working in a news bureau, participating in field and studio show production, on the nightly news, a morning news program, or on a magazine program. Salary: $33,600

Deadline
February 1, 2003

Contact
Michael Jack, General Manager in Washington, D.C.

NBC Sales Associate Program
Human Resources
30 Rockefeller Plaza
New York, NY 10112
Tel 818-840-4444
Tel 202-885-4445
Email ....Nysales@nbc.com
Web ....www.nbcjobs.com

Application Available
Online

Description
Rotations in all aspects of the field of Sales and Marketing. Areas covered during rotations include research, customer service, advertising agencies, business development, technology, Internet and desk experience across NBC, Telemundo and Paxson.

Support Provided
After training, fellows will be eligible for employment at NBC and Telemundo owned and operated stations or national sales offices.

Deadline
Periodically

Contact
Michael Jack, General Manager in Washington, D.C.

NBC Internship Program
Human Resources
3000 W. Alameda Ave.
Burbank, CA 91523
Tel 818-840-4444
Tel 202-885-4445
Email ....NYintern@nbc.com or
                             CAintern@nbc.com
Web ....www.nbcjobs.com

Application Available
Online

Description
Students are placed in television broadcast/production areas, business operations and NBC interactive positions related to their major and career goals.

Support Provided
The Internship program offers college students the opportunity to take a first step into the broadcasting industry.

Deadline
Fall: May, June, July, August
Spring: September, November, December
Summer: January, February, March

Contact
Michael Jack, General Manager in Washington, D.C.

NBC Page Program
Human Resources
3000 W. Alameda Ave.
Burbank, CA 91523
Tel 818-840-4444
Tel 202-885-4445
Email........................NYpage@nbc.com
Email ....CApage@nbc.com
Web ....www.nbcjobs.com

Application Available
Online

Description
Applicants will be given the chance to learn about many aspects of network television from the ground up. Primary function is to act as a liaison between NBC and the general public. You will conduct guided tours and perform various audience services for NBC shows.

Support Provided
Applicants have the opportunity to work in different departments within the company on either short or long term assignments.

Deadline
Periodically

diversity programs

Emma Bowen Program

Human Resources
3000 W. Alameda Ave.
Burbank, CA 91523
Tel 818-840-4444
Tel 202-885-4445
Email ....Contact the local NBC TV Station
listed online
Web ....www.nbcjobs.com

Application Available
Online

Description
Students work for a partner company during summers and school breaks from the end of their junior year in high school until they graduate from college.

Support Provided
Students learn many aspects of corporate operations and develop company-specific skills. Students in the program receive an hourly wage, as well as matching compensation to help pay for college tuition and expenses.

Deadline
Periodically

Minority Writers Program/network writing

Human Resources
3000 W. Alameda Ave.
Burbank, CA 91523
Tel 818-840-4444
Tel 202-885-4445
Email ....www.wga.org
Web ....www.nbcjobs.com

Application Available
Online

Description
NBC provides funding for a minority staff writer position for all scripted Primetime Series, Daytime and Late Night Programming (including non-NBC Studio produced series).

Support Provided
Funds a staff writer position on all new and returning Primetime Series for up to a total of three seasons for each minority staff writer so hired.

Deadline
Between mid-January and March each year

The NBC Agency Associates Program

Human Resources
3000 W. Alameda Ave.
Burbank, CA 91523
Tel 818-840-4444
Tel 202-885-4445
Email...........AGENCYASSOC@NBC.com
Web ....www.nbcjobs.com

Application Available
Online

Description
Hands-on experience while writing and editing on-air promos for NBC's prime time line-up of shows as well as for the various clients of the NBC Agency.

Support Provided
Successful graduates of the program move into Writer/Producer positions within the NBC Agency.

Deadline
July

Nickelodeon

Nickelodeon Animation Studio Internship Program

231 West Olive Ave.
Burbank, CA 91502
Tel 818-736-3673
Fax 818-736-3539
Email.................katie.fiedler@nick.com

Application Available
Please fax cover letter and resume.

Description
Internships offered in all areas of animation production.

Support Provided
For school credit only. Non-paid.

Deadline
Ongoing. Programs start September, January and June.

Contact
Kate Fiedler-Garcia, Human Resources Assistant

Showtime Networks
Showtime Latino Filmmaker Showcase
10880 Wilshire Blvd., Suite 1600
Los Angeles, CA 90024
Tel 310-234-5300
Fax 310-234-5391
Email...........sandra.avila@showtime.net
Web ....www.sho.com

Description
Selects 30-minute shorts produced or directed by a Latino to be showcased on Showtime during Hispanic Heritage month.

Support Provided
There is a license fee for each short selected and the winner gets a $30,000 grant to produce a short film in association with Showtime.

Deadline
May 16, 2003

Contact
Sandra Avila, Program Coordinator

Step Up Women's Network
Step Up Women's Network Professional Mentorship Program
8424 A Santa Monica Blvd., #857
West Hollywood, CA 90069
Tel 323-549-5347
Email.................stepupla@hotmail.com
Web ......www.stepupwomensnetwork.org

Application Available
Online

Description
Empowers women and girls as activists and advocates for positive social change.

Support Provided
Places women in volunteer oportunities in the entertainment and media industries.

Deadline
Ongoing

Contact
Traci Fleming, President

Streetlights
Production Assistant Program
650 N. Bronson Ave., Suite B108
Hollywood, CA 90004
Tel 323-960-4540
Fax 323-960-4546
Email ....streetlights@streetlights.org
Web ....www.Streetlights.org

Description
Designed to help minorities establish careers in the entertainment industry.

Support Provided
240 hours of classroom work and paid on-the-job training that prepares graduates for entry-level jobs as production assistants in film, TV and commercials.

Deadline
Deadline Online

Contact
Dorothy Thompson, Executive Director

diversity programs

Sundance Institute
The Screenwriters Lab
8857 W. Olympic Blvd.
Beverly Hills, CA 90211
Tel 310-360-1981
Email ....info@sundance.org
Web ....www.sundance.org

Application Available
Online

Description
The program offers ten to twelve emerging artists the opportunity to work intensively on their feature film scripts with the support of established screen-writers. January and June sessions at Sundance.

Support Provided
One-on-one problem solving story sessions with Creative Advisors, engaging in individual dialogues that combine life lessons in craft with practical suggestions to be explored in the next drafts.

Deadline
May 1, 2003

Contact
Jason Shinder (CA), Writers Fellowship Program

Filmmakers Lab
8857 W. Olympic Blvd.
Beverly Hills, CA 90211
Tel 310-360-1981
Email ....info@sundance.org
Web ....www.sundance.org

Application Available
Online

Description
Three-week long hands-on workshop for writers and directors that takes place each June at Sundance.

Support Provided
Participants gain experience rehearsing, shooting and editing scenes from their screenplays on videotape under the mentorship of accomplished directors, editors, cinematographers and actors.

Deadline
May 1, 2003

Composer's Lab
8857 W. Olympic Blvd.
Beverly Hills, CA 90211
Tel 310-360-1981
Email ....info@sundance.org
Web ....www.sundance.org

Application Available
Online

Description
The Sundance Composers Lab, a two-week training program for film composers that is run in conjunction with the Sundance Filmmakers Lab.

Deadline
April 1, 2003

Contact
Larin Sullivan (CA), Programming and Composers Lab Coordinator

Sundance Institute's Native American Initiative
8857 W. Olympic Blvd.
Beverly Hills, CA 90211
Tel 310-360-1981
Email ....info@sundance.org
Web ....www.sundance.org

Application Available
Online

Description
Supports Native American writers and directors through the Institute's Feature Film Program, which operates the Institute's Screenwriters and Directors Labs.

Support Provided
Designed to offer emerging screenwriters and directors the opportunity to develop new work.

Deadline
Ongoing

Sundance Arts Writing Program
8857 W. Olympic Blvd.
Beverly Hills, CA 90211
Tel 310-360-1981
Email ....info@sundance.org
Web ....www.sundance.org

Application Available
Online

Description
The Arts Writing Program supports arts writing and writers by offering annual fellowships to select authors, and by sponsoring public forums and publications, among other activities.

Support Provided
Offers California-based writers an opportunity to work intensively on a new and challenging arts writing project with the support of creative advisors and workshops, and to participate in select Sundance programs such as the film festival.

Deadline
Deadline Online

Contact
Amaya Cervino, Program Coordinator

Warner Bros.
Animation Internship Program
Attention: Recruitment
4000 Warner Blvd.
Burbank, CA 91522-0001
Tel 818-954-3550
Web ....www.WBJobs.com

Application Available
Online

Description
Internship that develops applicant pool for Animation positions and helps the selected candidates adapt their skills to this unique art form.

Support Provided
The internship provides training to develop a career path for entry-level animation artists, animation writers and production personnel.

Deadline
Positions become available based on business unit's needs.

Time Warner STARS Program (Summer)
Attention: Recruitment
4000 Warner Blvd.
Burbank, CA 91522-0001
Tel 818-954-3550
Web ....www.WBJobs.com

Application Available
Online

Description
Provides college students with a real-life business environment and encourages them to discover their own interests and capacities.

Support Provided
Paid program that exposes college students to career opportunities in the entertainment industry.

Deadline
Positions become available based on business unit's needs.

diversity programs

Collegiate Internship Program

Attention: Recruitment
4000 Warner Blvd.
Burbank, CA 91522-0001
Tel 818-954-3550
Web ....www.WBJobs.com

Application Available
Online

Description
Gives college students educational-related work experience during the academic year for specific disciplines within participating divisions.

Deadline
Positions become available based on business unit's needs.

Corporate Legal Clerkship Program (Available for credit only)

Attention: Recruitment
4000 Warner Blvd.
Burbank, CA 91522-0001
Tel 818-954-3550
Web ....www.WBJobs.com

Application Available
Online

Description
Identifies 1st year Law Students with a strong interest in Entertainment Law and assigns them professional-level projects in various legal divisions.

Deadline
Positions become available based on business unit's needs.

Credit-Only Internship Program (Available for credit only)

Attention: Recruitment
4000 Warner Blvd.
Burbank, CA 91522-0001
Tel 818-954-3550
Web ....www.WBJobs.com

Application Available
Online

Description
Gives college students educational-related work experience during the academic year while gaining course credit towards their area of study.

Deadline
Positions become available based on business unit's needs.

Feature Production Management Trainee Program

Attention: Recruitment
4000 Warner Blvd.
Burbank, CA 91522-0001
Tel 818-954-3550
Web ....www.WBJobs.com

Application Available
Online

Description
Provides individuals with the exposure to all facets of the production process.

Deadline
Positions become available based on business unit's needs.

Global Trainee Program

Attention: Recruitment
4000 Warner Blvd.
Burbank, CA 91522-0001
Tel 818-954-3550
Web ....www.WBJobs.com

Application Available
Online

Description
Yearlong training both on the job and in a classroom setting within a division in specific disciplines such as Marketing, Sales, Accounting, Production and more.

Deadline
Positions become available based on business unit's needs.

Production Assistant Trainee Program

4000 Warner Blvd.
Burbank, CA 91522-0001
Tel 818-954-3550
Web ....www.WBJobs.com

Application Available
Online

Description
Offers the opportunity for individuals who have been historically underrepresented within the industry, a chance to explore the Production arena.

Deadline
Positions become available based on business unit's needs.

Writegirl

Writegirl
Tel 323-363-1287
Email ....info@writegirl.org
Web ....www.writegirl.org

Description
Matches high school girls from underprivileged communities in Los Angeles with professional women writers who mentor them on a weekly basis in creative writing, journalism and other styles of writing.

Support Provided
Mentors and students meet one on one once a week to develop writing skills and attend monthly full-day creative writing workshops.

Contact
Keren Taylor, Executive Director

Youth Mentoring Connection (YMC)

Youth Mentoring Connection (YMC)
1316 Keniston Avenue
Los Angeles, CA 90019
Tel 323-525-1049
Fax 323-525-1048
Email ....ymc@youthmentoring.org
Web ....www.youthmentoring.org

Application Available
By Request

Description
Mentoring program that matches companies such as HBO, Endeavor and Warner Bros. with at-risk youth.

Support Provided
Matches companies with a school or youth center; their employees mentor the youth at their corporate office.

Contact
Tony LoRe, President

diversity programs

National Association of Latino Independent Producers

**funding
resources**

Note: 2003 dates are included in this section as reference only. Please contact individual listings for current deadlines.

Academy of Motion Picture Arts and Sciences Film Scholarship

8949 Wilshire Blvd.
Beverly Hills, CA 90211

Tel 310-247-3000
Email..........................gbeal@oscars.org
Web ....www.oscars.org/foundation/grants/

Support Provided
Supports the creation of innovative and significant works of film scholarship about aesthetic, cultural, educational, historical, theatrical and scientific aspects of motion pictures. Proposed projects may be books, multimedia presentations, curatorial projects, CD-ROMs and internet sites. Projects cannot be film, television or video productions. Two grants of $25,000.

Deadline
8/29/03

Program Officer
Greg Beal

The Adolph and Esther Gottlieb Society Foundation

380 West Broadway
New York, NY 10012

Tel 212-226-0581

Support Provided
Funding for visual artists who incorporate video and film in their work. Mature film and video artists whose work can be directly interpreted as painting or sculpture may be eligible to apply for the programs. Or an artist who works in a combination of performance art, film or video and installation may also qualify. Ten grants of $20,000.

Deadline
12/15/03

Program Officer
Sheila Ross

American Antiquarian Society (AAS)

185 Salisbury St.
Worcester, MA 01605-1634

Tel 508-471-2131
Tel 506-471-2139
Fax 508-754-6069
Email ....jmorgan@mva.org
Web ..www.americanantiquarian.org/artist-fellowship.htm

Support Provided
Applications for visiting fellowships for historical research by creative and performing artists, writers, filmmakers, journalists and other persons whose goals are to produce imaginative, non-formulaic works dealing with pre-twentieth-century American history. Projects may include documentary films, television programs, screenplays. Grants $1,200 plus travel expenses.

Deadline
10/05/03

Program Officer
James David Moran

Aperture Film Grant

1040 North Fairfax Avenue #230
Los Angeles, CA 90046

Tel 310-772-8294

Support Provided
For Film or Video Projects costing
$20,000 or less. Pre-production through
post-production. No finishing funds.
Narrative applicants are required to
shoot 16mm, while documentary
applicants may shoot 16mm or video.
Funding must be used within six months
of awarding the grant. The grant is open
to U.S. residents over the age of 21.

Deadline
9/30/03

Program Officer
Leslie Nia Lewis

Arizona Humanities Council

1242 N. Central Ave.
Phoenix, AZ 85004-1887

Tel...........................602-257-0335 x25
Fax 602-257-0392
Email ....lstone@azhumanities.org
Web ....www.azhumanities.org

Support Provided
General Grants are available for
community-initiated projects that help
Arizonans understand and appreciate
the humanities. AHC is especially
interested in funding projects that
bring good humanities scholarship to
out-of-school audiences in Arizona.
Format may includes radio, CD and
video productions. Grants up to $3,000.
Applicant must have a 501(c)(3)
designation or be governmental entities.

Deadline
Proposal deadlines are the first business
day of every fourth month.

Program Officer
Elizabeth Larson-Keagy

Arkansas Humanities Council: Media Projects

10800 Financial Centre Pky., Ste. 465
Little Rock, AK 72211

Tel 501-221-0091
Email ....lavonawilson@sbcglobal.net
Web...........................www.arkhums.org

Support Provided
Funds media projects that result in the
development of humanities audiovisual
resources, including film and video
productions, exhibits, audio productions,
slide-tape programs, and websites.
Preference given to media projects that
focus on Arkansas prehistory, history and
culture. Major grants of up to $25,000
for film and video preproduction,
including development of scripts and
production treatments. Funds all format
shorts, documentaries, features.

Deadline
2/15/04 and 9/15/04 deadlines.
Applications for major grants of up to
$25,000 for film and video production
are accepted only at the 9/15 deadline.

Program Officer
Lavona Wilson

Arthur Vinning Davis Foundations

111 Riverside Ave., Ste 130
Jacksonville, FL 32202-4921

Tel 904-359-0670
Fax 904-359-0675
Email............arthurvining@bellsouth.net
Web ....www.jvm.com/davis

Support Provided
Grants primarily provide partial support
for major educational series assured of
national airing by PBS. Children's series
are of particular interest. Consideration
also will be given to innovative uses of
public television (including online
efforts) to enhance educational outreach
in schools and communities. Grants
$100,000 to $500,000.

Deadline
Rolling

Program Officer
Dr. Jonathan T. Howe

Astrea National Lesbian Action Foundation

116 E. 16 St., 7th Fl.
New York, NY 10003

Tel 212-529-8021
Fax 212-982-3321
Email ....grants@astraea.org
Web.............................www.astraea.org

Support Provided
Support provided for lesbian-led
film/video projects that explicitly
address lesbian of color issues $1,000-
$6,000; the average is near $3,000.
Funds short, features, documentaries.

Deadline
11/1/03

Program Officer
Christine Lipat

California Council For The Humanities: The California Documentary Project

312 Sutter St., Suite 601
San Francisco, CA 94108

Tel ....415-391-1474 (SF)
Tel ....213-623-5993 (LA)
Email ....info@calhum.org
Web ....www.calhum.org

Support Provided
Encourages documentaries to
create enduring images and text of
contemporary California life. For video
documentaries or any digital media.
Must involve at least two humanities
experts in the design and implementa-
tion of the project. Have a total budget
of no more than $20,000. May request up
to $5,000.

Deadline
12/1/03

Program Officer
Felicia Kelley

Center For Alternative Media and Culture

P.O. Box 0832, Radio City Station
New York, NY 10101

Tel 212-977-2096
Email ....tvnatfans@aol.com

Support Provided
Supports independent media projects in
post-production that address the econo-
my, class issues, poverty, women, war
and peace, race and labor. Grants range
$100-$10,000.

Center For Independent Documentary

1608 Beacon St.
Waban, MA 01268

Tel 781-784-3627
Email ....info@documentaries.org
Web ....www.documentaries.org

Support Provided
Seeks proposals from independent producers for the production of documentaries on contemporary issues. Applicants receive a variety of services and resources.

Deadline
Rolling

Program Officer
Susan Walsh

Colorado Endowment For The Humanities

1490 Lafayette St., Ste. 101
Denver, CO 80218

Tel..........................303-894-7951 x15
Fax 303-864-9361
Email ....mskinner@ceh.org
Web ....www.ceh.org

Support Provided
Awards pre-production development of script and narrative treatments for all media formats, including films and video tapes. Must be centered on one or more disciplines of the humanities. Applicants may request up to $5,000.

Deadline
9/16/04 Research grant;
9/16/04 Program and Planning

Program Officer
Mark Skinner

Connecticut Humanities Council Cultural Heritage Development Fund

955 S. Main St., Ste. E
Middletown, CT 06457

Tel 800-628-8272
Fax 860-704-0429
Email .... info@ctculture.org
Web ....www.ctculture.org

Connecticut Non-Profit Grants

Support Provided
Awards grants to Connecticut-based nonprofit organizations, including educational television stations, for public projects in the humanities.

Deadline
11/1/03

Program Officer
Bruce Fraser

Exhibition Grants

Support Provided
Grants support research and scripting of temporary, traveling and permanent exhibitions (both traditional and online); creation of living history programs of significant aspects of Connecticut history and heritage (includes catalogues, interpretive brochures, walking tours and guidebooks, audiovisual presentations, interactive computer/videodisc displays and online exhibitions and tours). Grants $15,500.

Deadline
1. For proposals seeking more than $5,000: 2/1/04, 5/1/04, 8/1/04, 11/1/04 or the first working day thereafter.
2. For proposals under $5,000: The first day of every month or the first working day thereafter.
3. For proposals seeking $2,500 or less: Rolling deadline.

Program Officer
Bruce Fraser

Implementation Grants

Support Provided
Actual production of heritage programs once planning is complete. Applications should reflect thoughtful humanities content, well-developed project scripts, clear work-plans and detailed production budgets and comprehensive plans for project marketing. Grants $67,000.

Deadline
1. For proposals seeking more than $5,000: 2/1/04, 5/1/04, 8/1/04, 11/1/04 or the first working day thereafter.
2. For proposals under $5,000: The first day of every month or the first working day thereafter.
3. For proposals seeking $2,500 or less: Rolling deadline.

Program Officer
Bruce Fraser

Corporation For Public Broadcasting:
New Voices, New Media Fund

901 E St. NW
Washington, DC 20004-2037

Tel 202-879-9734
Tel 202-879-9839
Fax 202-783-1019
Email ....programming@cpb.org
Web ....www.cpb.org

Support Provided
Funding for innovative, educational and informational public television programming. Documentary programs and series, children programming, news programming.

Deadline
Please check the website for information on 2004 funding.

Program Officer
Cheryl Head

Corporation of Public Broadcasting Diverse Voices

401 Ninth Street, NW
Washington, DC 20004-2129

Tel 1-800-272-2190
Web ....www.cpb.org/grants

Support Provided
This program development and mentoring project is a strategic and focused expansion of previous P.O.V. efforts to showcase emerging media makers of diverse backgrounds for public broadcasting's national audience. In collaboration with stations and the Minority Consortia, P.O.V. will seek out and mentor minority producers to bring multicultural programming to the series. A CPB Diversity Fund Project. Grants around $500,000.00.

Creative Capital Foundation

65 Bleecker Street, 7th Fl.
New York, NY 10013

Tel 212-598-9900
Fax 212-598-4934
Email ..submissions @creative-capital.org
Web ....www.creative-capital.org

Support Provided
Revolving fund supporting artists pursuing innovative, experimental approaches. All forms of film and video, including experimental documentary, animation, experimental media, non-traditional narrative in all formats and interdisciplinary projects. Most initial grants (about 15 in each discipline) will be in the $5,000 range, with a few (about five) in the $15-20,000 range for projects further along in their development.

Deadline
Early 2004

Program Officer
Ruby Lerner

funding resources

Delaware Division of The Arts Individual Artists Fellowships

820 North French St.
Wilmington, DE 19801

Tel 302-577-8278
Fax 302-739-5304
Web ....www.artsdel.org

Support Provided
Provides funding to Delaware creative artists working in the visual, performing, media, interdisciplinary, folk and literary arts.

Deadline
8/1/04

Program Officer
Kristen Pleasanton

Delaware Humanities Forum

100 West 10th St., Ste. 1009
Wilmington, DE 19801

Tel 302-657-0650
Fax 302-657-0655
Email ....dhdirector@dhf.org
Web ....www.dhf.org/grants.htm

Support Provided
Supports humanities program for the public sponsored by nonprofit organizations. Average grants is $5,500 up to $35,000. Supports media projects. Teachers and scholars in the humanities must be involved in planning, presenting and evaluating the project.

Deadline
1/1/04, 4/1/04, 7/1/04, 10/1/04

Program Officer
Jean Sadot

Digital Media Educational Center

5201 SW Westgate Dr., Ste. 114
Portland, OR 97221

Email ....kate@filmcamp.com
Web ....www.filmcamp.com

Support Provided
Supports independent feature directors looking for means to complete their films, while offering Avid-authorized training to career editors.

The Durfee Foundation Artists: Resource for Completion

1453 3rd St., Ste. 312
Santa Monica, CA 90401

Tel 310-899-5120
Fax 310-899-5121
Email ....admin@durfee.org
Web ....www.durfee.org

Support Provided
The ARC (Artists' Resource for Completion) grants provide rapid, short-term assistance to individual artists in Los Angeles County who wish to complete work for a specific, imminent opportunity that may significantly benefit their career. Artists in any discipline are eligible to apply. The applicant must already have secured an invitation from an established organization to present the proposed work.

Deadline
Fourth Quarter - We are currently accepting applications from this deadline. November 4, 2003 (presentation start date: between December 4, 2003 and May 4, 2004)

Program Officer
Caroline D. Avery

Echo Lake Fund

213 Rose Av., 2nd Fl.
Venice, CA 90291

Tel 310-399-9164
Fax 310-399-9278
Email contact@echolakeproductions.com

Support Provided
Film fund for independent narrative features, not documentaries. For both producing and financing projects, the script and the director are crucial. Grants range $500,000 - $1,000,000.

Deadline
Rolling

Program Officer
Mark Dempsey

Experimental Television Center

109 Lower Fairfield Rd.
Newark Valley, NY 13811

Tel 607-687-4341
Email ....etc@experimentaltvcenter.org
Web ....www.experimentaltvcenter.org

Completion Grants

Support Provided
Grants up to $2,000 to help with the completion of works-in-progress. Funds electronic media, film, video, digital, sonic work, and work for the Internet and new technologies. All genres are eligible, from documentary to narrative and experimental work. Funds only to New York State individual artists.

Deadline
3/15/04

Program Officer
Sherry Miller Hocking

New York Non-Profit Grants

Support Provided
Grants to nonprofit organizations throughout New York State. Provides fees to electronic media and film artists for personal appearances. All genres eligible. Up to $1,000.

Deadline
Rolling

Program Officer
Sherry Miller Hocking

Film Arts Foundation

145 9th Street, Suite 101
San Francisco, CA 94103

Tel 415-552-8760
Fax 415-552-0882
Web ....www.filmarts.org

Support Provided
Funds different projects, from documentaries, experimental, features, educational videos. Grants from $1,000 to $4,000 for residents of the Bay Area.

Deadline
Check Website

Program Officer
Gail Silva

Fleischhacker Foundation

P.O. Box 29918
San Francisco, CA 94129-0918

Fax 415-561-5350

Support Provided
Offers grants for Arts & Culture and Collegiate (K-12) Education. Grants between $1,000 and $10,000 for dance, film/video and media, music, theatre and visual arts. For organizations in the greater San Francisco Bay area.

Deadline
1/15/04

Program Officer
Christine Ebel

funding resources

Flintridge Foundation

1040 Lincoln Ave., Ste. 100
Pasadena, CA 91103

Tel 626-744-9256
Tel 800-303-2139
Email ....FFAVA@JLMoseleyCo.com
Web ....www.flintridgefoundation.org

Support Provided
Awards support artists working in fine
arts and crafts media, which could
include jewelry, ceramics, glass, fiber,
multimedia installation and
performance, in addition to film and
video. Artists may use video and film
as elements of sculpture or installations,
or they may extend their artistic
explorations into single-channel media.
Program doesn't support artists who
work primarily in film and video as a
single-channel medium. Applicants must
live in California, Oregon or Washington
at least nine months per year, for the
last three years. $5,000-$30,000.

Deadline
9/17/03

Program Officer
Pam Wolkoff

Ford Foundation

320 E. 43rd St.
New York, NY 10017

Tel 212-573-5000
Fax 212-351-3677
Email...............secretary@fordfound.org
Web ....www.fordfound.org/grant/
                                    guidelines.html

Support Provided
Supports public broadcasting and the
independent production of film, video
and radio programming; and supports
efforts to engage diverse groups in work
related to the media and to analyze the
media's effect on society. Supports high-
quality productions that enrich public
dialogue on such core issues as building
democratic values and pluralism. Grants
vary from case to case. All formats are
accepted.

Deadline
Rolling

Program Officer
Pamela Meyer, Orlando Bagwell

The Foundation Center

79 5th Avenue
New York, NY 10003

Web ....www.fdncenter.org/onlib

Support Provided
Online resource for researching funders,
with tips on proposal writing.

The Fund for Jewish Documentary Filmmaking

330 Seventh Avenue, 21st Fl.
New York, NY 10001

Tel 212-629-0500
Email ....Grants@JewishCulture.org
Web ....www.jewishculture.org

Support Provided
Supports original documentary films
and videos by American documentarians
that promote thoughtful consideration
of Jewish history, culture, identity and
contemporary issues. Grants range from
$20,000-30,000.

Deadline
3/4/04

Program Officer
Nancy Schwartzman

Funding Exchange/Paul Robeson Fund for Independent Media

666 Broadway, Room 500
New York, NY 10012

Tel 212-529-5300
Fax 212-982-9272
Email ....grants@fex.org
Web...................................www.fex.org

Support Provided
Grants film and video projects of all
genres that address critical social and
political issues; that will reach a broad
audience; that include a progressive
political analysis combining intellectual
clarity with creative use of the medium.
Prioritizes projects that give voice to
marginalized communities and to those
traditionally excluded from mainstream
media. Funds all formats' documentaries, shorts, features, all media.
Projects only in preproduction or distribution. Grants range $5,000-$15,000.

Deadline
5/15/04

Program Officer
Trinh Duong

HBO America Undercover

1100 Sixth Ave.
New York, NY 10036

Tel 212-512-1670
Fax 212-512-8051
Email ....grhem@hbo.com
Web ....www.hbo.com

Support Provided
Provide production funds for American
Indie documentaries.

Program Officer
Greg Rhem

Hollywood Film Foundation

433 Camden Dr., Ste. 600
Beverly Hills, CA 90210

Tel 310-288-1882
Web ..www.hff.org/grants/application.html

Support Provided
Awards grants in the following categories:
Experimental, Digital Moviemaking,
Post-production and Partial Budget.
Grants for up to 50 percent of budget.

Deadline
Please call for '04 deadlines and grants

IFP/Chicago Production Fund

Chicago, IL

Tel 312-485-1825
Fax 312-435-1828
Email ....infoifpmw@aol.com
Web...................................www.ifp.org

Support Provided
In-kind donation of production equipment and services, up to $85,000 for
the next short film.

Deadline
10/14/03

Program Officer
Rebekah Cowling

Illinois Humanities Council Media Grants

203 N. Wabash Ave., Ste. 2020
Chicago, IL 60601-2417

Tel 312-422-5580
Fax 312-422-5588
Email ....ihc@prairie.org
Web ....www.prairie.org

Support Provided
Funding for development, research of scripts (up to $4,000) or production and post production (up to $10,000). Projects must relate to the humanities. Production company must be based in Illinois, or the theme be related to Illinois. Funds documentaries and narratives in film and video.

Deadline
2/15/04 and 7/15/04. Recommends submitting 3 weeks in advance

Program Officer
Luis Ramiro

Independent Television Service (ITVS)

501 York St.
San Francisco, CA 94110

Tel.......................415-356-8383 x232
Email..............marlene_velasco@itvs.org
Web ....www.itvs.org

Open Call

Support Provided
Provides production license agreements for public television programs.
Production funds for documentaries and narratives. Funds provided will cover the production or post-production budget, or portion; must be last funds in.

Deadline
2/1/04 and mid-8/04

Program Officer
Marlene Velasco

Lincs

Support Provided
Co-production funds for independent producers who partner with a local PBS station. Provides production license agreements for public television documentaries and narratives. Funds provided will cover the production budget.

Deadline
3/1/04

Program Officer
Marlene Velasco

Jerome Foundation

125 Park Square Ct.
St. Paul, MN 55101-1928

Tel 651-224-9431
Fax 651-224-3439
Email..............mediaarts@jeromefdn.org
Web ....www.jeromefdn.org

Support Provided
Grant program for individual media artists living and working in the five boroughs of New York City and the State of Minnesota. (Anything but commercials, promotional, industrial and education.) Funds documentaries, feature, shorts for all media. Grants for budgets $200,000 or under, not including in-kind donation for New York and $175,000 budgets for Minnesota.

Deadline
NY: Ongoing, Minnesota: 5/04

Program Officer
Robert Byrd

John D. and Catherine T. MacArthur Foundation

140 S. Dearborn St.
Chicago, IL 60603

Tel 312-726-8000
Email ....4answers@macfdn.org
Web ....www.macfdn.org

Support Provided
Provides partial support for selected documentary series and independent films intended for national and international broadcast; community outreach related to media; community based centers and public radio. Grant awards for production typically range from $50,000 to $300,000.

Deadline
Rolling

Program Officer
Kathy Im

Kansas Arts Commission

700 SW Jackson St. Ste 1004
Topeka, KS 66603-3761

Tel 785-296-3335
Fax 785-296-4989
Email ....KAC@arts.state.ks.us
Web.......................www.arts.state.ks.us

Support Provided
Limited number of Kansas Artist Fellowships in various disciplines. Awards $5,000. Disciplines include film and video.

Deadline
9/04

Program Officer
Lindsay Howgill

Latino Public Broadcasting

6777 Hollywood Blvd., Ste. 500
Los Angeles, CA 90028

Tel 323-466-7110
Web ....www.lpbp.org

Support Provided
Supports the development, production, acquisition and distribution of non-commercial educational and cultural television programming that is representative of Latino people, or addresses issues of particular interest to Latino Americans. Funds range from $5,000 to $100,000 for programs of most genres, including drama, comedy, animation, documentary or mixed genre. Considers projects at any production stage.

Deadline
6/2/03

Program Officer
Luca Bentivoglio

Louisiana Division of The Arts: Artists Fellowship

P.O. Box 44247
Baton Rouge, LA 70804-4247

Tel 225-342-8180
Fax 225-342-8173
Email ....arts@crt.state.la.us
Web ....www.crt.state.la.us/arts

Support Provided
Fellowship award for $1,000 depending on the artist work. Artists must submit sample of their work. Project Assistance program grants $1,000-$20,000 to artists in different discipline including documentary films.

Deadline
Fellowship—9/1/04
Project Assistance—3/1/04

Program Officer
Anne Russo

funding resources

Maine Humanities Council

674 Brighton Ave.
Portland, ME 04102

Tel 207-773-5051
Fax 207-773-2416
Email ......ejorgens@mainehumanities.org
Web ....www.mainehumanities.com

Support Provided
Films that have a humanities content and are related to Maine. Awards scripting or post-production grants. Documentaries and narratives film and video. Grant normally not more than $3,000. Requires draft proposal before deadline.

Deadline
4/10/04

Program Officer
Victoria Bonebakker or Erik Jorgensen

Maryland Humanities Council

Executive Plaza One, Ste. 503
11350 McCormick Rd.
Hunt Valley, MD 21031-1002

Tel 410-771-0650
Fax 410-771-0655
Email ....shardy@mdhc.org
Web...............................www.mdhc.org

Support Provided
Considers regular grants ($1,200-$10,000) for funding twice a year. Projects must be a public program, the disciplines of the humanities must be central to the project, humanities scholars must be involved in the project and funding must support projects that would not normally occur without council support. Maryland topics priorities. All formats.

Deadline
First draft: Late 10/03, Final Proposal Early 12/03. Decision Late 1/04, First Draft Late 6/04, Final Prop Early 8/04. Decision date late 9/04.

Program Officer
Steven Hardy

Massachusetts Foundation for the Humanities

66 Bridge St.
Northampton, MA 01060

Tel 413-584-8440
Fax 413-585-8454
Email......................ekrothman@mfh.org
Web ....www.mfh.org

Support Provided
Films and videos that explore humanities themes, documentaries and narratives. Grant up to $5,000.

Deadline
5/04 and 11/04

Program Officer
Ellen Rothman

Minnesota Independent Film Fund

401 North Third Street, Suite 450
Minneapolis, MN 55401

Tel 612-338-0871
Fax 612-338-4747
Email ....jobrien@ifpmsp.org
Web.............................www.ifpmsp.org

McKnight Artists Fellowship

Support Provided
McKnight Artists Fellowship for film-makers. Awards two $25,000 grants for documentaries, narrative, animation and multimedia. Open to Minnesota residents. Applicants must have at least 5 years experience.

Deadline
3/2/04

Program Officer
Jeanne O'Brien

Screenwriting Grant

Support Provided
Grants two $25,000. Funds only narrative features for theatrical release. Minnesota residents. (Need to live at least one continuous year in the state.)

Deadline
2/3/04

Program Officer
Jeanne O'brien

Minnesota State Arts Board Artist Fellowship

400 Sibley St., Ste. 200
Saint Paul, MN 55101-1928

Tel 651-215-1600
Web ....www.arts.state.mn.us

Support Provided
Rewards outstanding individual artists who are Minnesota residents.

Deadline
11/3/03

National Asian American TV Communications Association (NAATA)

145 9th St., Ste. 350
San Francisco, CA 94103

Tel 415-863-0814
Fax 415-863-7428
Email ....mediafund@naatanet.org
Web ....www.naatanet.org

Open Call For Production Fund

Support Provided
For Asian Pacific American programming for public TV. All formats are considered: features, shorts, documentaries for public television programming. Funds range from $20,000-$50,000.

Deadline
Please check for '04 deadlines

Program Officer
Pia Shaa

Open Door Completion Fund

145 9th St., Ste. 350
San Francisco, CA 94103

Tel 415-863-0814
Fax 415-863-7428
Email ....mediafund@naatanet.org
Web ....www.naatanet.org

Support Provided
Finishing funds for all formats: features, shorts, documentaries for public television programming. Funds range from $20,000-$50,000 for post production.

Deadline
Rolling

Program Officer
Pia Shaa

National Black Programming Consortium

145 East 125th Street, Suite 3R
New York, NY 10035

Tel 212-828-7588
Email................................info@nbpc.tv
Web ....www.nbpc.tv

Support Provided
NBPC funds, commissions, acquires and awards talented makers of quality African American film and video projects.Through annual open solicitations and requests for proposals, NBPC awards grants ranging from $1,000 to $50,000.

Deadline
10/30/03

Program Officer
Leslie Fields-Cruz

funding resources

The National Endowment for the Humanities: Planning, Scripting and Production Grant

1100 Pennsylvania Ave. NW
Washington, DC 20506

Tel 202-606-8269
Email ....publicpgms@neh.gov
Web ....www.neh.gov

Support Provided
NEH supports projects that use the medium of television to address significant figures, events or developments in the humanities and that draw their content from humanities scholarship. Projects may be in the form of either documentary programs or historical dramatizations and must be intended for national distribution during prime time on either broadcast or cable networks. Grants up to $30,000 for planning, $60,000 to $70,000 for scripting and $40,000 to $800,000 for production.

Deadline
11/3/03

Program Officer
David Weinstein

National Science Foundation

4201 Wilson Blvd.
Arlington, VA 22230

Tel 703-292-5090
Email ....info@nsf.gov
Web ....www.nsf.gov

Support Provided
Supports media projects designed to deepen the appreciation of science and technology and the understanding of the impact science and technology have on today's society.

Nevada Humanities Committee

P.O. Box 8029
Reno, NV 89154-5080

Tel 702-895-1878
Web ....www.nevadahumanities.org

Support Provided
Media grants used to support the production of films, videos, radio programs or educational Web-based projects. Grants up to $10,000.

Deadline
3/10/04 and 10/10/04

Program Officer
Mary Toleno

New Hampshire Humanities Council

19 Pillsbury St., P.O. Box 2228
Concord, NH 03302-2228

Tel 603-224-4071
Fax 603-224-4072
Web ....www.nhhc.org

Support Provided
Awards grants to public programs in the humanities, such as film viewing and discussion series, and script development for documentary films.

Deadline
1/1/04, 4/1/04, 6/1/04, 10/1/04

Program Officer
Laurie Quinn

New York Foundation For The Arts

155 Avenue of the Americas, 14th Floor
New York, NY 10013-1507

Tel 212-366-6900
Tel........................212-366-6900 x217
Email........................ nyfaafp@nyfa.org.
Web..................................www.nyfa.org

Support Provided

Artists' Fellowships are $7,000 cash awards made to individual originating artists living and working in the state of New York for use in career development. Grants are awarded in 16 artistic disciplines, with applications accepted in eight categories each year. Comprehensive online resource for researching grants and funding opportunities.

Deadline
10/1/03

Program Officer
Margie Lempert

New York State Council on the Arts

175 Varick Street
New York, NY 10014-4604

Tel 212-627-4455
Web...............................www.nysca.org

Distribution

Support Provided

Funding is available to organizations that distribute film, new media, sound art or video work. Organizations may request support for core distribution activities, expanding a collection into new formats, marketing, closed captioning and subtitling, or packaging of titles into collections. The program encourages projects that address changing trends for radio distribution and experiments in distributing Web-based art or using the Internet for delivery or marketing of film and electronic media.

Deadline
5/1/04 and 7/1/04

Program Officer
Karen Helmerson

Exhibitions

Support Provided

Exhibition support is available for the public presentation of film, video, sound art, new electronic media, and installation work offered on-site (in cinemas, community centers, galleries, libraries, or museums) or via broadcast, cable, radio, satellite, or Internet dissemination. Funding is available for projects on a variety of scales and design, including festivals, series, installations, and touring programs, as well as for year-round programming. The presentation of work by independent artists is strongly encouraged.

Deadline
5/1/04 and 7/1/04

Program Officer
Karen Helmerson

General Support Program

Support Provided

General Program Support (GPS) offers unrestricted support for ongoing media arts programming. GPS is designed to support qualifying organizations that have a consistent track record of artistic achievement, public service, and managerial competence in their media art programming. GPS support reflects NYSCA's recognition of the artistic and programmatic capabilities of qualified arts and cultural organizations.

Deadline
3/21/04 and 7/21/04

Program Officer
Karen Helmerson

funding resources

Newton Television Foundation

1608 Beacon St.
Waban, MA 02168

Tel 617-965-8477

Support Provided
Collaborates with independent producers
on documentaries concerning contemporary issues.

NEXTPIX

295 Greenwich St., Ste. 348
New York, NY 10007

Tel 212-465-3125
Fax 212-658-9627
Email ....info@nextpix.com
Web............................www.nextpix.com

Support Provided
Seeks to foster the best and brightest
new talent in digital video, film and
animation, and to help promote that
talent by providing supplemental
post-production funds in all formats:
documentary, narrative. Budget cannot
exceed $250,000. The DV/film should
have a positive humanitarian message.

Deadline
9/16/03

Program Officer
Diana Takata

Ohio Humanities Council

471 E. Broad St., Ste. 1620
Columbus, OH 43215-3857

Tel 614-461-7802
Fax 614-461-4651
Email ....ohc@ohiohumanities.org
Web.................www.ohiohumanities.org

Support Provided
Supports media projects when they
convey the humanities effectively to
large, diverse audiences. Any nonprofit
organization operating in Ohio may
apply. The disciplines of the humanities
must be central to the project, humanities scholars must be involved in the
project. Up to $20,000.

Deadline
7/15/04 and 12/15/04

Program Officer
Jack Shortlidge

Oklahoma Humanities Council

428 W. California, Ste. 270
Oklahoma City, OK 73102

Tel 405-235-0280
Email........ohc@okhumanitiescouncil.org
Web ....www.okhumanitiescouncil.org

Support Provided
Awards mini grants (up to $1,500)
and major grants ($1,501-$5,000) to
support projects, including film and
video production, designed to increase
public understanding and appreciation
of the humanities.

Deadline
8/1/03 and 9/5/03

Program Officer
Jennifer Kidney

The Open Society Institute's Youth Media Program

400 West 59th Street
New York, NY 10019

Tel 212-548-0127
Email .... lmcdermott@sorosny.org
Web........................www.soros.org/youth

Support Provided
Youth Media Program engages youth in community based settings and provides them with the means and tools to present their viewpoints. The program operates under the premise that authentic youth-produced media can educate and inform local communities and the general public about young people's concerns and perspectives.

Program Officer
Lee McDermott

Oppenheimer Camera New Filmmaker Equipment Grant Program

666 S. Plummer St.
Seattle, WA 98134

Tel 206-467-8666
Fax 206-467-9156
Email..filmgrant@oppenheimercamera.com
Web ....www.oppenheimercamera.com

Support Provided
Gives new filmmakers access to a professional 16 mm camera system for their first serious new production in the dramatic, narrative, documentary or experimental form. Program does not support commercials, industrials, PSAs, music video or pornography.

Deadline
Rolling

Program Officer
Marty Oppenheimer

Pacific Pioneer Film Fund

P.O. Box 20504
Stanford, CA 94309

Tel 650-996-3122
Email......................armin@stanford.edu
Web ....www.pacificpioneerfund.com

Support Provided
To support emerging documentary filmmakers. The term emerging is intended to denote a person committed to the craft of making documentaries, who has demonstrated that commitment by several years of practical film or video experience. Grants limited to filmmakers or videographers who live and work in California, Oregon and Washington. Grant Range $1,000-$10,000. All subjects.

Deadline
Applications are accepted on an ongoing basis. Application deadlines in 2003-04 are 5/15/03, 9/15/03, 12/15/03, 5/1/04 and 10/1/04. Rejected applicants must wait one year to reapply

Program Officer
Armin Rosencranz

Panavision New Filmmakers Program

6219 DeSoto Ave.
Woodland Hills, CA 91367-2602

Tel 818-316-1000
Tel 818-316-1111
Web ....www.panavision.com

Support Provided
Panavision's New Filmmakers Program donates 16mm camera packages to short, nonprofit film projects, including graduate student thesis films, of any genre. Highly competitive—only two packages available. Filmmakers must secure equipment and liability insurance.

funding resources

Deadline
Submit proposals five to six months before you intend to shoot.

Program Officer
Kelly Simpson

Paul Robeson Fund For Independent Media

666 Broadway, #500
New York, NY 10012

Tel 212-529-5300
Tel ....212- 529-5356 x 307
Email......................trinh.duong@fex.org
Web....................................www.fex.org

Support Provided
Supports media activism and grassroots organizing by funding the pre-production and distribution of social issue film and video projects, and the production and distribution of radio projects. Grants range from $5,000-$15,000.

Deadline
5/15/04

Program Officer
Trinh Duong

Pen Writers Fund and Fund For Writers and Editors With AIDS

568 Broadway
New York, NY 10012

Tel 212-334-1660
Tel........................212-334-1660 x116
Email ....victoria@pen.org
Web ....www.pen.org

Support Provided
The PEN Fund for Writers and Editors with HIV/AIDS, administered under the PEN Writers Fund, gives grants of up to $1,000 to professional writers and editors who face serious financial difficulties because of HIV or AIDS-related illness.

Deadline
The Writers Fund Committee meets approximately every two months to review applications.

Program Officer
Victoria Kupchinetsky

Pennsylvania Council On The Arts Fellowships

216 Finance Bldg.
Harrisburg, PA 17120

Tel 717-787-6883
Email ....csavage@mailnet.state.pa.us
Web ....www.artsnet.org/pca/

Support Provided
The PCA supports outstanding Pennsylvania artists by awarding Fellowships on an annual basis. The range of awards is $5,000 to $10,000. Disciplines funded are Documentary and Experimental.

Deadline
8/1/04

Program Officer
Carolyn Savage

Playboy Foundation Media Grants

680 North Lake Shore Drive
Chicago, IL 60611

Tel 312-373-2435
Web ....www.playboy.com/corporate/
foundation/index.html

Support Provided
Charitable giving program of Playboy Enterprises that provides funding to documentary film and video projects. Grants range from $1,000 to $5,000.

Deadline
Please write for application

POV/American Documentary

32 Broadway, Fl. 14
New York, NY 10004

Tel 212-989-8121
Fax 212-989-8230
Web ....www.pbs.org/pov

Support Provided
PBS's premiere showcase for independent point of view non-fiction films. Through summer series and year-round specials, POV brings 12-16 new films each year to public television viewers, publishing non-fiction work of diverse voices. Filmmakers must be U.S. citizens and must provide broadcast premiere of the program. Considers primarily completed work for standard acquisitions. Occasionally provides funds for completion costs such as: sound editing, mixing, negative cutting, online editing, etc. Completion funding will be applied towards the acquisition fee for broadcast rights. POV is continuing the Diverse Voices Project (DVP) and provides co-production financing up to $80,000 for 4-5 selected non-fiction projects for POV/PBS.

Deadline
May 2004

Program Officer
Cara Mertes

Roy W. Dean Film and Video Grants

1455 Mandalay Beach Road
Oxnard, CA 93035-2845

Tel 866-689-5150
Email ....caroleedean@worldnet.att.net
Web ..www.fromtheheartproductions.com

Editing Grant
Support Provided
Takes filmmakers to New Zealand and offers off-line editing for the editing grants. Available for shorts and low budget features as well as documentary.

Deadline
9/30/04

Program Officer
Carole E. Dean

LA Film Grant
Support Provided
Grant for Los Angeles shorts and low budget independents as well as documentary filmmakers. Grants for student filmmakers, independent producers and independent production companies producing documentaries or other socially aware film projects for television, film or video. Goods and services around $50,000.

Deadline
6/1/04

Program Officer
Carole E. Dean

LA Video Grant

Support Provided
Grant for Los Angeles shorts and low budget independents as well as documentary filmmakers. Grants for student filmmakers, independent producers and independent production companies producing documentaries or other socially aware video projects for television, film or video. Goods and services around $50,000.

Deadline
6/30/04

Program Officer
Carole E. Dean

NY Film Grant

Support Provided
Grant for New York shorts and low budget independents as well as documentary filmmakers. Grants for student filmmakers, independent producers and independent production companies producing documentaries or other socially aware projects for television, film or video. Goods and services around $50,000.

Deadline
4/30/04

Program Officer
Carole E. Dean

Writing Grant

Support Provided
Takes filmmakers to New Zealand to write in a beautiful setting and offers off-line editing for the editing grants. Available for shorts and low budget features as well as documentary.

Deadline
4/1/04

Program Officer
Carole E. Dean

The Soros Justice Media Fellowship
400 West 59th St. 3rd fl.
New York, NY 10019

Tel 212-548-0170
Email ....kblack@sorosny.org
Web ....www.soros.org/crime

Support Provided
Seeks dynamic journalists working in media, photography, radio and documentary film and video to improve the quality of media coverage of incarceration and criminal justice issues. Must be a 501(c)(3) tax-exempt organization, or have a tax-exempt fiscal agent.

Deadline
9/26/03

Program Officer
Kate Black

South Carolina Arts Commission Quarterly Grants
1800 Gervais St.
Columbia, SC 29201

Tel 803-734-8681
Fax 803-734-8526
Web.......................www.state.sc.us/arts

Support Provided
Provides grants for projects for organizations, cultural visions for rural communities and quarterly projects for artists. Nonprofit organizations must be incorporated and registered in the state of South Carolina. Individuals must maintain a permanent residence in South Carolina prior to the application date and throughout the grant period.

Deadline
Depends on specific grant

Program Officer
Susan Leonard

Sundance Documentary Fund

8857 W. Olympic Blvd.
Beverly Hills, CA 90211

Tel 310-360-1981
Email .... sdf@sundance.org
Web ....www.institute.sundance.org

Support Provided
Grant-giving program available to film-makers around the world to support full length documentaries in development and production of contemporary human rights, freedom of expression, social justice and civil liberties issues. Does not accept historical projects, biographies or series. Documentary film or video projects that range in length from full broadcast hour to long format feature. Development funds up to $15,000. Production funds up to $75,000.

Deadline
Rolling

Program Officer
Diane Weyermann

Texas Filmmakers Production Fund

1901 E. 51st St.
Austin, TX 78723

Tel 512-322-0145
Email ....elisabeth@austinfilm.org
Web ....www.austinfilm.org

Support Provided
The Texas Filmmakers' Production Fund is an annual grant awarded to emerging film and video artists in the state of Texas. We fund all genres (narrative, documentary, experimental, animation) and hybrids thereof. All variety of projects, multimedia projects or television series. $1000 to $5000 in a cash award, up to $5000 in Kodak film stock, and up to $500 in videotape stock.

Deadline
7/1/04

Program Officer
Elisabeth Sikes

Utah Humanities Council: Research Fellowship Grants

202 West 300 North
Salt Lake City, UT 84103

Tel 801-359-9670
Email ....black@utahhumanities.org
Web ....www.utahhumanities.org

Annual Fellowships

Support Provided
Two annual fellowships are offered to humanities scholars:

- The Albert J. Colton Fellowship supports a research project on a topic of national or international significance.
- The Delmont R. Oswald Fellowship supports a research project in Utah studies. Research fellowships, which provide a $3,000 stipend, are evaluated and approved by UHC's Board of Directors.

Awards Mini-grants (up to $1,500) and Major Grants (1,501-$5000) to support projects, including film and video production, designed to increase public understanding and appreciation for the humanities.

Deadline
Deadline: 9/15/03, drafts received prior to 8/15 will receive staff comments

Program Officer
Marisa Black

Quick Grants

Support Provided
Quick Grants support direct program costs of smaller projects, with a simplified and expedited process. Eligible requests include:
- small projects using proven formats and scholars
- film, video, exhibit or book programs with discussion led by a humanities scholar
- planning or consultant grants, hiring a consultant to plan and help prepare a competitive grant application.

Quick Grants, which provide up to $400, are reviewed year-round and are approved by the Executive Director.

Deadline
Deadline: application must be received 4-6 weeks prior to need

Program Officer
Marisa Black

Visual Studies Workshop Media Center

31 Prince Street
Rochester, NY 14607

Tel 585-442-8676
Email ....info@vsw.org
Web ....www.vsw.org

Support Provided
The Media Center supports film- and video-making through its low-cost equipment rental to independent producers and members of the community, training workshops and its screening and exhibition programs. Awards artists, independent producers and nonprofits working on non-commercial projects reduced rates for production and post production equipment.

Deadline
Rolling

The Wallace Alexander Gerbode Foundation

470 Columbus Ave., #209
San Francisco, CA 94133

Tel 415-391-0911
Email ....maildesk@gerbode.org
Web ....www.fdncenter.org/
grantmaker/gerbode/

Support Provided
Grants for media projects proposed by 501(3) organizations. Focused in San Francisco Bay Area and Hawaii.

Deadline
Ongoing

National Association of Latino Independent Producers

filmmakers

Note: Names marked with an asterisk (*) indicate a NALIP member. To update and/or submit new information, please email directly to LMRG@nalip.info.

Luis Cady Abarca*
New York, NY 10012
Tel 212-529-3977
Email...........................Cadab@aol.com

Bonnie Abaunza*
Director of Artist Relations
Amnesty International
Culver City, CA 90232
Tel 310-815-0450
Tel 310-815-0457
Email ....babaunza@yahoo.com

Beatriz Acevedo
President
Hip TV
Hollywood, CA 90038
Tel 323-993-0904
Email ....beatrizacevedo@worldnet.att.net

Stephen Acevedo*
San Antonio, TX 78230
Tel 210-492-5301
Email ....Sacevedo@aol.com

Belinda Acosta*
Columnist
Austin Chronicle
Austin, TX 78751
Tel 512-653-3918
Fax 512-458-6910
Email............tveye@austinchronicle.com

Mark Acosta
Reporter
The Press-Enterprise
Miami, FL 33185
Tel 909-737-1366

Carlos Acuña*
Tucson, AZ 85746
Tel 520-889-0088
Email ......ollinentertainment@yahoo.com

Marvin Acuña*
Manager
Acuña Entertainment
Sherman Oaks, CA 91423
Tel 818-501-1072
Fax 818-501-1072
Email ..marvin@acunaentertainment.com
Web ....www.acunaentertainment.com

Producer, HOW DID IT FEEL, 2004, Feature
Producer, TWO DAYS, 2003, Feature

Ricardo Acuña
Los Angeles, CA 90041
Tel 323-478-1928
Email ......writericardoacuna@yahoo.com

Writer

Alejandro Agresti
Agresti Films S.R.L.
Buenos Aires,   Argentina
Tel 5411-4384-5883

Director, VALENTIN, 2002, Miramax Films, Feature
Director, A NIGHT WITH SABRINA LOVE, 2000, Buena Vista International, Feature
Director, WIND WITH THE GONE, 1998, Nirvana Films S.A., Feature
Producer, WIND WITH THE GONE, 1998, Nirvana Films S.A., Feature
Producer, BUENOS AIRES VICE VERSA, 1996, Agresti Films, Feature

Sergio Aguero*
Executive Producer
Apuesta Pictures
Los Angeles, CA 90048
Tel 323-936-2110
Fax 323-525-2721
Email ....saguero@3monkeysla.com

Executive Producer, Y TU MAMA
    TAMBIEN, 2001, IFC Films, Feature
Executive Producer, LET THE DEVIL
    WEAR BLACK, 1999, A-Pix
    Entertainment, Inc., Feature

Maria Agui-Carter*
Iguana Films
Cambridge, MA 02138
Tel 617-429-1258
Email ....iguanafilms@earthlink.net

Producer, RUMBLE OVER WEST SIDE
    STORY, 2001, PBS, Documentary
Director, RUMBLE OVER WEST SIDE
    STORY, 2001, PBS, Documentary
Producer, TANGO: DUEL OR DANCE,
    2000, PBS, Documentary
Director, TANGO: DUEL OR DANCE,
    2000, PBS, Documentary
Producer, THE DEVIL'S MUSIC, 2000,
    PBS, Documentary
Director, THE DEVIL'S MUSIC, 2000,
    PBS, Documentary

Carolina Aguilera*
Author
New York, NY 10009
Tel 212-253-7076
Email......................aguilerac@aol.com

Jorge Aguirre*
Maldito Perrito Prod. Co.
New York, NY 10002
Tel 212-477-3143
Cell 917-687-2674
Fax 305-448-4761
Email ....jaguirre1@earthlink.net

*Agent: ICM, Eddie Borges,
310-550-4266*

Director, HISTORY DETECTIVES, 2003,
    PBS, TV Series
Director, IS MY NEIGHBOR LATINO?,
    2002, Latino Public Broadcasting,
    Interstitial
Producer, A MORE PERFECT UNION,
    2001, Broadcast: MPT, Short
Writer, IF YOU WERE THERE, 2001,
    Noggin Television, TV Series,
    Animated
Director, THE ABSENTEE FATHER,
    2001, Sundance Channel, Short
Producer, PANCHO'S REVENGE, 1999,
    Broadcast: WNET/MPT, Short

Margarita D. Aguirre*
Abrazo Productions
Yorba Linda, CA 92887
Tel 714-777-6810
Email ....mareflections@aol.com

Valentin Aguirre*
San Francisco, CA 94114
Tel 415-644-9610
Email ....tinobear@hotmail.com

Omonike Akinyemi*
Image Quilt Productions
New York, NY 10012
Email ....abike_99@yahoo.com

Writer, HOW TO STAY SANE IN PARIS,
    2003, Maurits Binger Film Institute,
    Feature
Writer, NELLY'S BODEGA, 2000,
    Coalition of Mental Health
    Professionals, Short

Noemi Alarcon

Reporter Liaison
The Miami Herald
Miami, FL 33156
Tel 305-376-2124
Fax 305-789-8265
Email...................nalarcon@herald.com

Victor Albarran

Marina Del Rey, CA 90272
Tel 310-993-6843

Line Producer, DREAMING OF JULIA,
  2003, Arza-Gerard, Feature
Line Producer, MERRY CHRISTMAS,
  2002, Lolafilms S.A., Feature
Line Producer, NATALE SUL NILO,
  2002, Lolafilms S.A., Feature

Carlos Alberto*

Fuerza Films
North Hollywood, CA 91606
Tel 818-764-6534
Fax 818-764-6534
Email ....largelatinlead@netscape.net
Web www.my8by10.com/carlosalberto

Actor, ARRESTED DEVELOPMENT,
  2004, FOX, TV Series
Actor, BOLD AND THE BEAUTIFUL,
  2003, Bell-Phillips TV Productions, TV
  Series
Actor, SAMMY'S NEW LIFE, 2003,
  BWCT Productions, Short
Producer, I NEVER WANT TO WORK
  FOR JOHN WOO, 2002, Fuerza Films,
  Short

Magdalena Albizu*

Brooklyn, NY 11205
Tel 718-622-0083
Email ....nubianlatina@aol.com

Producer
Media Advocate

Felix Alcala

FLX Entertainment
Burbank, CA 91505
Tel 818-954-7419

Director, FLASHPOINT, 2002,
  Touchstone Television, TV Series
Director, FOR THE PEOPLE, 2002,
  Lifetime Television, TV Series
Director, HACK, 2002, CBS, TV Series
Director, JOHN DOE, 2002, Fox
  Network, TV Series
Director, TAKEN, 2002, Dreamworks, TV
  Series
Director, THE SHIELD, 2002, Fox
  Network, TV Series
Director, CSI, 2000, CBS Television, TV
  Series
Director, THE STRIP, 1999, United
  Paramount Network, TV Series
Director, THIRD WATCH, 1999, NBC, TV
  Series

Martin Alcala

Simi Valley, CA 93063
Tel 310-369-5868
Email.......handsofwisdom@earthlink.net

Production Accountant, JUSTIN TO
  KELLY, 2003, J2K Prods., Inc.,
  Feature
Production Accountant, COAL MINER'S
  STORY, 2002, Touchstone, TV Movie
Supervising Producer, DAWG, 2001,
  Gold Circle Films, Feature
Production Accountant, INSOMINA,
  2001, Warner Bros., Feature

Felipe Alejandro*

Glendale, CA 91206
Tel 323-466-8566
Email ....andro71f@yahoo.com

Russell Alexander-Orozco

Alexander-Orozco and Associates (ADA)
Los Angeles, CA 90026
Tel 323-666-0690
Email ....info@alexander-orozco.com
Web ....Alexander-orozco.com

Producer
Writer

Fabio Alexandre da Silva

Manager
TV Globo Ltda
Rio de Janeiro, Rio 22790735 Brazil
Tel 55-21-2444-4660
Tel 55-21-2444-5041
Cell...........................55-21-9384-2216
Fax 55-21-2444-5883
Email ....fabio.alexandre@tvglobo.com.br
Web ....www.globo.com/agrandefamilia

Production Manager, TO THE LEFT OF
   THE FATHER, 1997, Videofilms
   Production Company, Feature
Production Coordinator, THE
   CANGACEIRO REVENGE, 1991, TV
   Globo Ltda, TV Episode
Production Coordinator, THE MASTER
   OF THE WORLD, 1991, TV Globo
   Ltda, TV Soap Opera
Production Coordinator, THE CARRIER,
   1990, TV Globo Ltda, TV Series

Yolanda Alindor

Kahlo Group
Balacynwyd, PA 19004
Tel 650-637-9676

Natalia Almada*

Editor, Documentary Director
Brooklyn, NY 11201
Tel 718-782-4501
Email.........nataliaalmada@hotmail.com

Producer, AL OTRO LADO, 2004,
   Documentary
Director, AL OTRO LADO, 2004,
   Documentary
Editor, AL OTRO LADO, 2004,
   Documentary
Associate Producer, REVOLUCION,
   2004, Documentary
Editor, REVOLUCION, 2004,
   Documentary
Director, ALL WATER HAS PERFECT
   MEMORY , 2001, Sundance Channel,
   Documentary Short
Producer, ALL WATER HAS PERFECT
   MEMORY , 2001, Sundance Channel,
   Documentary Short
Editor, ALL WATER HAS PERFECT
   MEMORY, 2001, Documentary Short

Raquel Almazan*

La Lucha Arts Company
Miami, FL 33143
Tel 305-527-3395
Email ....raquelalmazan@hotmail.com

Diane Almodovar

Music Executive
BMI
Miami, FL 33126
Tel 305-266-3636
Fax 305-266-2442
Email ....dalmodovar@bmi.com

Elizabeth Almonte

Business Director
Rage Productions
Collinsville, OK 74021
Tel 212-591-0295

German Alonso*
South El Monte, CA 91733
Tel 626-401-2571
Email...............jalonso11@earthlink.net

Roxana Altamirano*
West Hills, CA 91307
Tel 310-502-4279
Email ....maltami@hotmail.com

Carlos Alvarado
Agent
Alvarado Rey Agency
Los Angeles, CA 90048
Tel 323-655-7978
Fax 323-655-2777

Juan Manuel Alvarado
Infinity Video Poductions
Chestnutridge, NY 10977
Tel 510-657-8315
Email ....jm_alvarado04@hotmail.com

Patricia Alvarado*
La Plaza - WGBH
Boston, MA 02134
Tel 617-300-2289
Email ....patricia_alvarado@wgbh.org

Robert Alvarado*
President
Westport Filmworks
Westport, CT 06880
Tel 203-226-4817
Email ....alvarado@optonline.net
Web............................www.jcorona.com

Barbara Alvarez*
New York, NY 10032
Email...........................sis7ta@aol.com

Miguel Alvarez*
Austin, TX 78751
Tel 512-791-9134
Email ....flaco2k1@yahoo.com

E. Alvarez-Abogyewa
True Roots Productions
Atlanta, GA 30312
Tel 404-572-6210
Email....................blkhrtwom@tbwt.com

Gonzalo Amat
21st. Century Aztlan Productions
San Francisco, CA 94114
Fax 323-899-3376
Email ....tinobear@hotmail.com

Director of Photography

Abel Amaya*
Professor
Cal State Dominguez Hills
Carson, CA 90747
Tel 909-593-8330

Claudia Amaya*
Co-Executive Director
The Latin American Cinema Festival of
New York
Bronx, NY 10468
Tel 917-353-2290
Fax 718-228-3540
Email ....claudia_lacinemafe@yahoo.com
Web ....www.cinemafe.org

Producer, AMY IN THE CAFÉ, 2000,
City College of New York-City Visions,
Short
Producer, BECOMING AMERICAN,
2000, City College of New York, Short
Director, SILENT DAWN, 2000, City
College of New York, Documentary
Producer, SILENT DAWN, 2000, City
College of New York, Short
Writer, SILENT DAWN, 2000, City
College of New York, Documentary

Juanita Anderson

Legacy Productions, Inc.
Boston, MA 02119
Tel 617-427-5595
Fax 617-427-0150
Email ....legacypro@earthlink.com

Executive Producer, FAVORITE POEM
  PROJECT, 1997, Library of
  Congress/Boston University,
  Documentary

Rafael Andreu*

Director of Animation Films
Ramm Animation
Miami Beach, FL 33140
Tel 305-532-1575
Fax 305-532-4491
Email ....randreu@rammprod.com
Web ....www.rammprod.com

Director, GUGULAND, 2004, TV Series,
  Animated
Director, FLORUS, 2003, TV Series,
  Animated
Director, PLAZA SESAMO, 2002,
  Televisa, TV Series

Cruz Angeles*

Writer/Director
Brooklyn, NY 11234
Tel 718-252-1272
Email...............cruzangeles@yahoo.com

Director, ABUELA'S REVOLT, 2001,
  Short
Writer, ABUELA'S REVOLT, 2001, Short
Producer, ABUELA'S REVOLT, 2001,
  Short
Editor, ABUELA'S REVOLT, 2001, Short

Abdiel Anglero

Marketing Director
WNTJ TV Ch. 40
San Francisco, CA 94114
Tel 787-766-2600

Fernando Anguita

Merlin Features
Los Angeles, CA 90026
Tel 310-551-4973

Emilia Anguita Huerta*

Andromeda Productions, Inc.
Coral Gables, Fl 33146
Tel 305-447-8578
Fax 305-447-8579
Email........emilia@andromedavisual.com

Writer, SOMBRAS Y BARRO, 1995,
  Short
Director, SÍNTOMA: MADRE - NIÑA,
  1994, Andromeda/USB, Venezuela,
  Documentary
Writer, SÍNTOMA: MADRE - NIÑA,
  1994, Andromeda/USB, Venezuela,
  Documentary
Producer, SÍNTOMA: MADRE - NIÑA,
  1994, Andromeda/USB, Venezuela,
  Documentary
Director, CARIBE, 1992, Radio Caracas
  Television, TV
Director, DE MUJERES, 1991-1992,
  Radio Caracas Television, Venezuela ,
  TV
Producer, ENTRE LÍNEAS, 1990, Short
Writer, PERFILES EN EL TIEMPO,
  1986, Andromeda Productions,
  Documentary
Producer, PERFILES EN EL TIEMPO,
  1986, Andromeda Productions,
  Documentary

Jaime Angulo

Festival Director
Miami Latin Film Festival
Miami, FL 33176
Tel 305-279-1809
Email ....jangulo@hispanicfilm.com
Web ....www.hispanicfilmcom.

Kary Antholis

VP of Development and Production
HBO Films
Los Angeles, CA 90067
Tel 310-201-9200
Web ....www.hbo.com/films

Executive Producer, THE CAPE, 1996,
    MTM ENterprises Inc., TV Series
Director, ONE SURVIVOR REMEMBERS,
    1995, HBO, Documentary
Producer, THE SHADOW OF HATE,
    1995, Guggenheim Productions,
    Documentary

Rene Anthony Torres

Director of Sales
Alpine Pictures International
Van Nuys, CA 91406
Tel 818-909-5207
Web ....www.alpinepix.com

Alex Anton*

Forever Present Prod.
Miami, FL
Tel 305-299-9310

Richard Apodaca*

Lakewood, CA 90712
Tel 562-423-1997
Email ....lkwdrich@hotmail.com

Ruben Apodaca*

Digitoon Comp Animation Unlimited
Barstow, CA 92311
Tel 888-646-4610
Email ....ruapodaca@yahoo.com

Ray Aragon

Woodland Hills, CA 91367
Tel 818-347-3958

Tania Araiza*

San Jose, CA 95127
Tel 408-729-7871
Email ....taraiza@hotmail.com

Olga Arana*

Amazonas Films, LLC
Santa Monica, CA 90404
Tel 310-393-8636
Fax 310-899-1598
Email ....OArana@aol.com

Producer, HOW THE GARCIA GIRLS
    SPENT THEIR SUMMER, 2004,
    Loosely Based Pictures, LLC, Feature
Producer, BIOGRAPHY OF MARIO
    VARGAS LLOSA, 2003,
    Sogecable-Canal Plus Spain,
    Documentary
Researcher, MOSTLY TRUE STORIES,
    2003, The Learning Channel, TV
    Series
Producer, WHAT REALLY HAPPENED
    DURING THE CUBAN MISSILE
    CRISIS, 2002, AFI & Showtime, Short
Director, SAVING THE WHITE WINGED
    GUAN, 2000, Antena 3, Documentary
Producer, SAVING THE WHITE WINGED
    GUAN, 2000, Antena 3, Documentary
Director, QOYLLUR RITTI: MYSTERY
    AND LEGEND, 1999, Antena 3,
    Documentary
Producer, QOYLLUR RITTI: MYSTERY
    AND LEGEND, 1999, Antena 3,
    Documentary

Jesse Aranda*

Los Angeles, CA 90028
Tel 310-480-6028
Email ....jar_anda@yahoo.com

filmmakers

Alfonso Arau

Mexico, DF Mexico
Tel 011-5255-10890626

Agent: ICM, Nick Reed, 310-550-4000

Producer, LOS HIJOS DEL TOPO, 2004, Titan Producciones, Feature
Director, ZAPATA, 2004, Latin Arts LLC, Feature
Producer, ZAPATA, 2004, Latin Arts LLC, Feature
Director, A PAINTED HOUSE, 2003, CBS, TV Movie
Director, THE MAGNIFICENT AMBERSONS, 2002, A&E, TV Movie
Producer, PICKING UP THE PIECES, 2000, Cinemax, Feature
Director, A WALK IN THE CLOUDS, 1995, 20th Century Fox, Feature
Director, LIKE WATER FOR CHOCOLATE, 1992, Miramax, Feature
Director, TACOS DE ORO, 1985, Hermes Films International, Feature

Sergio Arau

Eye On The Ball Films
Los Angeles, CA 90046
Tel 323-935-0634
Fax 323-935-4188
Email ....keepyoureye@aol.com

Director, A DAY WITHOUT A MEXICAN, 2004, Alta Vista, Feature
Writer, A DAY WITHOUT A MEXICAN, 2004, Alta Vista, Feature
Director, A DAY WITHOUT A MEXICAN, 1998, Short
Director, EL MURO, 1998, Short

José Araujo*

Tupa Films
Brooklyn, NY 11215
Tel 718-768-0358
Fax 718-832-5766
Email ....araujo@tupafilms.com
Web ....www.tupafilms.com

Director, O SERTAO DAS MEMÓRIAS/LANDSCAPES OF MEMORY, 1996, Tupa Films, Feature
Writer, O SERTAO DAS MEMÓRIAS/LANDSCAPES OF MEMORY, 1996, Tupa Films, Feature
Producer, O SERTAO DAS MEMÓRIAS/LANDSCAPES OF MEMORY, 1996, Tupa Films, Feature
Director, SALVE A UMBANDA/HAIL UMBANDA, 1987, Tupa Films, Documentary
Writer, SALVE A UMBANDA/HAIL UMBANDA, 1987, Tupa Films, Documentary
Producer, SALVE A UMBANDA/HAIL UMBANDA, 1987, Tupa Films, Documentary
Director, UNA FAMILIA MEXICANA 14 AÑOS DESPUES, 1980, Tupa Films, Documentary
Writer, UNA FAMILIA MEXICANA 14 AÑOS DESPUES, 1980, Tupa Films, Documentary
Producer, UNA FAMILIA MEXICANA 14 AÑOS DESPUES, 1980, Tupa Films, Documentary

Leida Arce*

COS Enterprises, Inc.
Studio City, CA 91604
Tel 818-985-7031
Email ....leidaarce@hotmail.com

Alicia Arden*
Los Angeles, CA 90048
Tel 323-850-8086
Email ....missusa@earthlink.net

Lucero Arellano*
California Arts Council
Sacramento, CA
Tel 916-322-6588
Fax 916-322-6567
Email..........larellano@caartscouncil.com

Roberto Arevalo*
The Mirror Project
Decatur, GA 30030
Tel 404-373-0779
Fax 404-651-0574
Email..............roberto@mirrorproject.org
Web ....www.mirrorproject.org

Producer, UNDERSTANDING VIOLENCE, 2003, The Mirror Project, Short
Educator, WE GROW UP SO FAST, 2003, The Mirror Project, Short
Producer, PORVENIR, 2000, The Mirror Project, Short
Producer, WITHOUT MAKE-UP, 1999, The Mirror Project, Short
Educator, I'M THE MAN, 1995, The Mirror Project, Short
Educator, IT'S TOUGH, 1995, The Mirror Project, Short

Edward Arguelles*
Trecena Entertainment
Los Angeles, CA 90027
Tel 323-660-7074
Email.....................trecena@excite.com

Luis Argueta
New York, NY 10027
Tel 212-866-5332
Tel 212-316-3760
Fax 212-316-3926

Director, COLLECT CALL, 2002, Maya Media Corp., Feature
Writer, COLLECT CALL, 2002, Maya Media Corp., Feature
Executive Producer, COLLECT CALL, 2002, Maya Media Corp., Feature
Writer, EL SILENCIO DE NETO, 1994, Buenos Dias, Feature
Director, EL SILENCIO DE NETO, 1994, Buenos Dias, Feature
Director, THE COST OF COTTON, 1978, PBS, Documentary

Eva S. Aridjis
Brooklyn, NY 11215
Tel 718-623-2405
Email ....earidjis@nyc.rr.com

Director, CHILDREN OF THE STREET, 2003, Documentary
Director, BILLY TWIST, 1998, Documentary
Writer, BILLY TWIST, 1998, Documentary
Editor, BILLY TWIST, 1998, Documentary
Director, TAXIDERMY, 1998, Short

Catherine Armas-Matsumoto*
SDSU
Vista, CA 92084
Tel 760-598-7450
Fax 760-598-8446
Email.....................matsumoto@fda.net

Sergio Armendariz*
Fiesta Studios
Los Angeles, CA 90026
Tel 213-384-5069
Email............fiestastudios@hotmail.com

filmmakers

Eddie Arnold*
Communications Counsel
Nielsen Media Research
Washington, DC 20006
Tel 202-296-9733
Fax 202-296-7908
Email.................arnolde@tvratings.com
Web ......www.nielsenmediaresearch.com

Media Advocate

Rosa Arredondo*
Astoria, NY 11106
Tel 718-204-4962
Email...............cavewomantoo@aol.com

Ishmael Arredondo Henriquez*
Codices Entertainment
Hollywood, CA 90078
Tel 323-462-5448
Fax 323-462-5448
Email ....ishmaelo@pacbell.net

Producer, THE SPIRIT OF MY MOTHER,
   2001, Codices Entertainment, Feature
Producer, SIN PAPELES, 1997, Codices
   Entertainment, Short

Guillermo Arriaga
*Agent: United Talent Agency, Shana
Eddy, 310-273-6700*

Writer, 21 GRAMS, 2003, Focus
   Features, Feature
Associate Producer, 21 GRAMS, 2003,
   Focus Features, Feature
Writer, THE HIRE: POWDER KEG, 2001,
   Films, Short
Associate Producer, AMORES PERROS,
   2000, Lion's Gate Films, Feature

Diego Arsuaga
Montevideo, Uruguay

Writer, CORAZON DEL FUEGO (LAST
   TRAIN), 2002, Buena Vista
   International, Feature
Director, CORAZON DEL FUEGO (LAST
   TRAIN), 2002, Buena Vista
   International, Feature
Producer, EN TRANSITO, 2001,
   Documentary
Director, OTARIO, 1997, Feature
Director of Photography, OTARIO, 1997,
   Feature

Isaac Artenstein
Cinewest
Hollywood, CA
Tel 323-295-0773
Email ....cinewest@aol.com

Producer, A DAY WITHOUT A MEXICAN,
   2004, Eye on the Ball Films, Feature
Co-Producer, EL GRITO, 2000, Beret
   Films, Feature
Producer, LOVE ALWAYS, 1997, Legacy
   Releasing Corporation, Feature

Miguel Arteta
Flan de Coco Films
Los Angeles, CA 90040
Tel 323-666-8485

*Agent: William Morris Agency, David
Lubliner, 310-274-7451*

Director, THE GOOD GIRL, 2002, Fox
   Searchlight, Feature
Director, PASADENA, 2001, Columbia
   Tri Star/Fox, TV Series
Director, SIX FEET UNDER, 2001, HBO,
   TV Series
Director, CHUCK & BUCK, 2000,
   Artisan Entertainment, Feature
Writer, LIVIN' THING, 1998,
   Filmmakers Forum, Feature
Director, STAR MAPS, 1997, 20th
   Century Fox, Feature
Writer, STAR MAPS, 1997, 20th
   Century Fox, Feature

Marilyn Atlas*

Manager
Marilyn Atlas Management
Los Angeles, CA 90048
Tel 310-278-5047
Fax 310-278-5289
Email ....matlas704@yahoo.com

Producer, REAL WOMEN HAVE CURVES, 2002, HBO Films, Feature
Producer, ECHOES, 1991, Short
Producer, A CERTAIN DESIRE, 1986, Feature

Bernadette Aulestia

Marketing Executive
HBO Pictures
New York, NY
Tel 212-512-1000
Email ....bernadette.aulestia@hbo.com

Elizabeth Avellan

Los Hooligans Productions
Austin, TX 78746
Email ....rn_gomez@hotmail.com

Publicist: Sandra Condito,
323-822-4336

Producer, ONCE UPON A TIME IN MEXICO, 2003, Sony Pictures Entertainment, Feature
Producer, SECUESTRO EXPRESS, 2003, Feature
Producer, SPY KIDS 3D: GAME OVER, 2003, Miramax Films, Feature
Producer, SPY KIDS 2: ISLAND OF THE LOST DREAMS 2002, 2002, Dimension Films, Feature
Producer, SPY KIDS, 2001, Dimension Films, Feature
Producer, THE FACULTY, 1998, Dimension Films, Feature
Producer, FROM DUSK TILL DAWN, 1996, Miramax Films, Feature
Producer, DESPERADO, 1995, Columbia TriStar, Feature
Producer, EL MARIACHI, 1992, Feature

Davah Avena*

Los Angeles, CA 90027
Tel 323-662-5281
Email ....guavis@hotmail.com
Web ....http://www.inhotpursuit.com

Director, IN HOT PURSUIT, 2003, Short

Carlos Avila

Echo Park Films
Glendale, CA 91202
Tel 818-773-7846
Fax 818-242-7234
Email ....echoparkfilms@aol.com

Agent: Broder • Webb • Chervin •
Silbermann Agency, Rhonda Gomez,
310-281-3400

Director, FOTO NOVELAS 2: JUNKYARD SAINTS, 2003, PBS, TV Series
Executive Producer, FOTO NOVELAS 2: JUNKYARD SAINTS, 2003, PBS, TV Series
Writer, FOTO NOVELAS 2: JUNKYARD SAINTS, 2003, PBS, TV Series
Director, PRICE OF GLORY, 2000, New Line Cinema, Feature
Director, FOTO NOVELAS: IN THE MIRROR, 1997, PBS, TV Series
Executive Producer, FOTO NOVELAS: IN THE MIRROR, 1997, PBS, TV Series
Writer, FOTO NOVELAS: IN THE MIRROR, 1997, PBS, TV Series
Executive Producer, LA CARPA, 1993, American Playhouse, TV Series
Writer, LA CARPA, 1993, American Playhouse, TV Series

filmmakers

Isaac Avila
Aztlan Entertainment M.P
Los Angeles, CA 90015
Tel 213-738-7917
Fax 213-738-7918
Email ......info@aztlanentertainment.com
Web ....http://aztlanentertainment.com

Production Facilities & Services, THE
LOWRIDER SHOW, Charter
Communications, TV Special

José Avila*
San Diego, CA 92168
Email bonovoxproductions@sbcglobal.net

Mario Avila
Midcoast Pictures
Collinsville, OK 74021
Tel 918-527-8796
Email ......mario@midcoast-pictures.com
Web ....www.midcoast-pictures.com

Producer, CHOICES, 2003, Midcoast
Pictures, Short
Writer, OKLAHOMA TRAGEDY, 2003,
Midcoast Pictures, Feature
Producer, DOWN THE ROAD, 2002,
Road Pictures, Feature
Writer, LA CABANA (THE CABIN), 2002,
Midcoast Pictures, Feature
Director, NELLY DVD, 2001, Universal
Records, Music Video
Director, OKLAHOMA TRAGEDY, 2001,
Midcoast Pictures, Short
Producer, GRAND THEFT AUTO 2,
2000, Sony Plastation, Short

Sabrina Avila*
New York, NY 10025
Tel 212-496-0552
Email ....savilany@earthlink.net

Producer

Sandra Avila
Coordinator
Showtime Networks, Inc.
Los Angeles, CA 90024
Fax 310-234-5259
Email...........sandra.avila@showtime.net
Web ....www.sho.com

Coordinator, LATINO FILMMAKER
SHOWCASE, 2004, Showtime, TV
Series

Sabrina Aviles*
Boston, MA 02131
Tel 617-640-8919
Fax 617-323-0598
Email...................sabaviles@yahoo.com

Producer

Shawn Baca
4 Element Entertainment
Los Angeles, CA 90034
Tel 310-980-8906
Email ....shawnabaca@hotmail.com
Web ....www.shawnabaca.com

Writer, ROSE'S GARDEN, Impersonal
Impression
Director, ROSE'S GARDEN, Impersonal
Impression

Monica Bacigaluppi
Marketing Manager
Accent Media
McLean, VA
Tel 703-356-9427

Evelyn Badia*

Evebad Productions, Inc.
Brooklyn, NY 11215
Tel 917-539-1677
Tel 718-768-7483
Email ....evebad@aol.com

Director, GONNA GET CONTEST, 2003,
Commercial
Director, SAY WHAT, 2003, Toyblue
Productions, TV Series
Producer, AMTRAK CAMPAIGN, 2002,
The Chisholm Mingo Group,
Commercial
Producer, THE BOX, 2000, Karma Films,
Short
Director, THE BOX, 2000, Karma
Productions, Short
Writer, THE BOX, 2000, Karma
Productions, Short
Producer, FOREVER, 1997, NYU, Short

Michael Baez*

Hollywood, CA 90078
Tel 323-244-1737
Email ....Baezent@yahoo.com

Director, DEVIL'S KISS, 2002, Baez
Entertainment, Short
Writer, NUDE IN NY, 2000-2001, TV
Director, LIGHTS, CAMERA, ACTION,
1997, TV
Director, SPANISH HARLEM, 1997,
Boricua Film Works, Feature
Director, CONSEQUENCES, 1996,
Latino Jams Filmworks, Feature

Jaime Baker*

Manager
Baker Management
New York, NY 10021
Tel 212-262-4234
Cell 917-627-7764
Fax 212-262-4235
Email ....jbakermanagement@aol.com

Producer

Peter Bandera

Bandera Productions
Santa Monica, CA 90403
Tel 310-474-1712

Executive Producer

Antonio Banderas

Green Moon Productions
Los Angeles, CA 90041
Tel 310-471-8800

*Agent: Creative Artists Agency, Emanuel
Nunez, 310-288-4545*

Actor, AND STARRING PANCHO VILLA
AS HIMSELF, 2003, HBO Films, TV
Movie
Actor, ONCE UPON A TIME IN MEXICO,
2003, Sony Pictures Entertainment,
Feature
Actor, SPY KIDS 3-D: GAME OVER,
2003, Dimension Films, Feature
Actor, SPY KIDS 2: ISLAND OF LOST
DREAMS, 2002, Dimension Films,
Feature
Actor, SPY KIDS, 2001, Dimension
Films, Feature
Director, CRAZY IN ALABAMA, 1998,
Hatbox Productions/TriStar, Feature
Actor, THE MASK OF ZORRO, 1998,
Columbia Tristar, Feature

filmmakers

Norbeto Barba

Los Angeles, CA
Tel 310-578-9530

Agent: Diverse Talent Group, Susan
Sussman, 310-201-6565

Director, AMERICAN DREAMS, 2003,
  NBC, TV Series
Director, LEVEL 9, 2000, Paramount TV,
  TV Series
Director, RESURRECTION BLVD., 2000,
  Showtime, TV Series
Director, TERROR IN THE MALL, 1998,
  Warner Bros. Television, TV Movie
Director, NEW YORK UNDERCOVER,
  1996, Fox Network, TV Series
Director, SOLO, 1996, Sony Pictures
  Video, Feature

Gabriel Barbarena

CEO
Carmona Entertainment
Los Angeles, CA 90022
Tel 323-721-FILM
Fax 323-728-4045
Web ....www.carmona-entertainment.com

Producer

Alberto Barboza*

Los Angeles, CA 90032
Tel 323-343-9037
Email ....abarboza@ucla.edu

Lisset Barcellos*

Solaris Films
San Francisco, CA 94114
Tel 415-861-2609
Fax 415-861-2609

Trina Bardusco

BaMo Productions
New York, NY 10009
Tel 347-837-1542
Email.............elturistasoy@hotmail.com

Director, EL TURISTA SOY: LUIS
  AGUJETA Y SU CANTE GITANO,
  2003, HBO Latino, Documentary
Producer, HBO LATINO ON-AIR
  PROMOTIONS

Frank Barrera*

Long Island City, NY 11105
Email...............eganbarrera@yahoo.com

Producer

Rick Barreras*

Anchorage, AK 99521
Tel 907-830-0845
Email ....aserb6@uaa.alaska.edu

Actor

Alicia Barron*

Production Assistant
Tucson, AZ 85745
Tel 520-884-7590
Email ....Shab28@aol.com

Frank Barron*

KOCE-TV
Huntington Beach, CA 92647
Tel 949-581-6703
Email................................fb@cccd.edu

Marta Bautis*

Tiempo Azul Productions
New York, NY 10009
Tel 212-673-8065
Fax 212-673-8065
Email ....mbautis@nyc.rr.com

Director, NICARAGUA: THE CHILDREN
    ARE WAITING, 2002, Tiempo Azul
    Productions, Documentary
Producer, NICARAGUA: THE CHILDREN
    ARE WAITING, 2002, Tiempo Azul
    Productions, Documentary
Director, THE MOTHER: MITOS
    MATERNOS, 1994, Women Make
    Movies, Documentary
Producer, THE MOTHER: MITOS
    MATERNOS, 1994, Women Make
    Movies, Documentary
Director, HOME IS THE STRUGGLE,
    1991, Women Make Movies,
    Documentary
Producer, HOME IS THE STRUGGLE,
    1991, Women Make Movies,
    Documentary

José Bayona*

Unicorn Films
Corona, NY 11368
Tel 347-351-0207
Fax 718-305-8458
Email ....josebayona@yahoo.com

Director
Writer
Director of Photography

Richard Beaumont*

New York, NY 10029
Tel 212-426-9212
Email ....vagabond96@aol.com

Alfredo Bejar*

Brooklyn, NY 11238

Director, GETTING TO HEAVEN, 1996,
    Facets Multimedia, Documentary
Director, ONCE UPON A TIME IN THE
    BRONX, 1994, Subcine, Short

Ivonne Belen

Miramar San Juan, PR 00907
Email ....ibelen@caribe.net

Director, JULIA, TODO EN MI, 2002,
    Documentary

Mary Beltran*

Austin, TX 78704
Tel 512-912-9571
Fax 512-471-4077
Email ....em78704@earthlink.net

Jellybean Benitez

Jellybean Recording, Inc.
New York, NY 10003
Tel 212-777-5678
Fax 212-777-7788
Web ....www.Jellybean-recordings.com

Associate Producer, DUMMY, 2002,
    Artisan Entertainment, Feature
Associate Producer, ANGEL EYES,
    2001, Warner Bros., Feature
Executive Producer, FOR LOVE OR
    COUNTRY: THE ARTURO SANDOVAL
    STORY, 2000, HBO, TV Movie
Co-Producer, TAINA, 2000,
    Nickelodeon, TV Series
Executive Producer, NUYORICAN
    DREAM, 1999, Big Mouth
    Productions, Documentary

filmmakers

Frank Bennett Gonzalez
Senior Manager, Talent Development
Programs
ABC Entertainment Television Group
Burbank, CA 91521
Tel 818-460-6452
Fax 818-460-5292
Email ....Frank.B.Gonzalez@abc.com
Web ....www.abcnewtalent.disney.com

Luca Bentivoglio
Executive Director
Latino Public Broadcasting
Los Angeles, CA 90028
Tel 323-466-7110
Fax 323-466-7521
Email ....lucabenti@lpbp.org

Producer

Victoria Bernal*
On Ramp Arts
Los Angeles, CA 90026
Tel 213-481-2395
Email.......................V_Bernal@msn.com

Daniel Bernardi*
Associate Professor
University of Arizona
Tucson, AZ 85745
Tel 520-971-8075
Fax 520-621-9661
Email ....bernardi@email.arizona.edu

Writer
Producer

Enrique Berumen*
Rasquachi CineDigital
Los Angeles, CA 90031
Tel 323-254-0666
Fax 323-343-6035
Email ....eberume@calstatela.edu

Nelson Betancourt*
Leafstorm Pictures
Orlando, FL 32812
Tel 407-273-4079
Fax 407-273-4079
Email........nelson@forevermorefilms.com
Web ....www.forevermorefilms.com

Producer, THE FIRST OF MAY, 1997,
WIN, Feature

James Blancarte
Los Angeles, CA 90067
Tel 310-788-2760
Fax 310-788-2764
Email ....jblancarte@aol.com

Attorney

Elisa Blatteis*
New York, NY 10023
Tel 212-496-0227
Email ....elisab@mindspring.com

Carlos Bolado*
Sincronia/BBM Productions
Berkeley, CA 94709
Tel 505-525-8998
Email ....bolex@pobox.com

Director, PROMESAS, 2001,
PBS/POV/IVTS, Documentary
Editor, POR LA LIBRE, 2000, Fox Home
Entertainment, Feature
Director, BAJO CALIFORNIA, THE LIMIT
OF TIME, 1998, Columbia Pictures
Mexico, Feature
Writer, BAJO CALIFORNIA, THE LIMIT
OF TIME, 1998, Columbia Pictures
Mexico, Feature
Editor, COMA AGUA PARA CHOCOLATE,
1992, Miramax, Feature

Angelo Bolaños*
Paterson, NJ 07522
Tel 973-904-0062
Email ....bpa7@yahoo.com

Blanca Bonilla*
Fe Productions
Jamaica Plain, MA 02130
Tel 617-524-8154
Email ....bblinkie@aol.com

Piedad Bonilla*
Talent Manager
Pinata Productions & Management
Beverly Hills, CA 90212
Tel 310-358-1943
Email ....pinatamgmt@aol.com

Margarita Borda*
Miami, FL 33155
Tel 305-667-4887
Cell 305-898-6607
Email ....marborda_2000@yahoo.com
Web ....www.connexusconsulting.com

Writer
Producer

Eddie Borges*
Agent
International Creative Management
Beverly Hills, CA 90211
Tel 310-550-4000
Fax 310-550-4100
Email ....eborges@icmtalent.com
Web ....www.icmagency.com

Frank Borres*
American View Productions
Bridgeport, CT 06604
Tel 203-366-5033
Fax 203-366-5044
Email.....................americanv@snet.net
Web ..www.americanviewproductions.com

Producer/Director, YOU'RE ON THE AIR,
   2002, PBS, Documentary
Producer/Director, CELIA CRUZ AND
   FRIENDS, 2000, PBS, TV Special
Producer/Director, PUERTO RICAN
   PASSAGES, 1993, PBS, Documentary

Maria Bozzi
Programs Director
IFP-LA
Beverly Hills, CA 90211
Tel 310-432-1200
Email ....mbozzi@ifp.org

Vanessa Braccini*
Staten Island, NY 10307
Fax 718-967-6617
Email ....vnyce30@hotmail.com

Dean Anthony Bradford*
Abrad Entertainment, Inc.
Pasadena, CA 91104
Tel 323-839-3115
Email.........................dean@abrad.com

Margot Bradley*
Togram Productions, Inc.
Miami, FL
Tel 305-279-8912
Email...............margotb@bigplanet.com

Carla Brandon*
SDSU
San Diego, CA 92108
Tel 619-297-0013
Email ....tictac@san.rr.com

Charles Branson Guevara*
Austin, TX
Tel 512-478-2058
Email ....charliebranson@email.com

Pablo Bressan*
Miami Beach, FL 33139
Tel 305-458-0197
Fax 305-532-8621
Email pablo@goinggoingproductions.com

Producer, LOS DUROS, 2004,
   Going-Going Productions,
   Documentary

filmmakers

filmmakers

Abraham Brown*
Santa Monica, CA 90404
Tel 310-829-3948
Email ....sarcasm4all@aol.com

Sarah Brown-Gonzales*
American Cinema Editors Internship
Program
Universal City, CA 91608
Tel 818-777-2900
Email ....sbbg@earthlink.net

Cynthia Buchanan*
Assistant Directors Training Program
Sherman Oaks, CA 91403
Tel 830-876-3034
Fax 830-876-3034
Email...........trainingprogram@dgptp.org

Writer

Juan Carlos Buitron
Founder & CEO
Genuine Productions, Inc.
Los Angeles, CA 90036
Tel 773-728-9677

Efraim Burdeinick*
Stevenson Ranch, CA 91381
Tel 661-255-5079
Email ....efri@rocketmail.com

Maria Bures*
Pigeon Productions
Miami, FL 33134
Tel 305-856-2929
Fax 305-858-0357
Email ....maria@pigeonprod.com

Director, SOMOS, 2004, Documentary
Producer, SOMOS, 2004, Documentary

Paris Bustillos
Animator
Pachango Animation
Washington, DC 20009
Tel 202-518-8257

Barbara Bustillos-Cogswell*
Bustillos & Co.
Tempe, AZ 85282
Tel 480-768-1561
Email ....bbustillos@aol.com

Frank Bustoz*
Oso Negro Productions
Austin, TX 78751
Tel 512-323-5886
Email...................bustozf@hotmail.com

Darlene Caamano-Loquet
Producer Partner
D-No Entertainment
Los Angeles, CA 90028
Tel 323-856-5060
Fax 323-856-5061

Producer

Agustin & Alicia Caballero
AC Talent Agency
Baldwin Park, CA 91706
Tel 213-381-8774

Alberto Caballero*
Knightmare Pictures
Los Angeles, CA 90069
Tel 310-854-6518
Fax 928-395-9180
Email ....acabal@adelphia.net

Technical Director, DELILAH'S NIGHT
    CLUB, 2003-2004, Electrosonic
    Themed Systems, Industrial
Producer, MI ABUELA, 1999,
    KnightMare Pictures, Feature

Producer, THE LIGHT HOUSE, 1996,
  Water Mark Productions, Feature
Producer, THROUGH THE NARROW
  GATE, 1995, Changing Images
BORN TO LOSE, 1994, TV
THE NOVICE, 1994, TV

Gerardo Cabrera
Diva Digital Pictures
Coconut Grove, FL 33133
Tel 305-445-1898
Fax 305-445-1557
Email ..Gerardo@divadigitalpictures.com

Vic Cabrera*
Fiesta Studios
Los Angeles, CA 90026
Tel 213-384-5069
Email.................vicwrites@hotmail.com

Writer

Juan Caceres*
New York, NY 10031
Tel 212-491-3892
Fax 212-926-7030
Email ....SUPAJUAN@aol.com
Web ....www.nuevayorkfilms.com

Producer
Writer
Director, ROCK STEADY, JUICY

Jorge Cadena*
Miami, FL 33015
Email................jcadena@talkvisual.com

Nora I. Cadena
Nov. 20 Productions
Austin, TX 78757
Tel 512-380-0229
Email ....noracadena@earthlink.net

Paul F. Cajero
Los Angeles, CA
Tel 323-667-3454

Production Manager, KAREN SISCO,
  2003, Universal Network Television,
  TV Series
Producer, KINGPIN, 2003, NBC, TV
  Series
Production Manager, UNDECLARED,
  2001, Fox, TV Series
Producer, MANHATTAN, AZ, 2000, USA
  Networks, TV Series
Producer, AVALON, 1999, UPN
  Network, TV Movie
Producer, GOOD VS. EVIL, 1999, SciFi
  Channel, TV Series

Roma Calatayud*
Los Angeles Mentoring Partnership
Los Angeles, CA 90014
Tel 323-634-4151
Email ....tstocks835@aol.com

Carolyn Caldera*
Manager
Caldera/De Fanti Entertainment
Beverly Hills, CA 90212
Tel 310-281-6400
Fax 310-281-6464
Email.................ccaldera@earthlink.net

Producer, THREE BLIND MICE, 2002,
  Feature

Julio Calderon
Los Angeles, CA
Agent: Genesis, Michael Margules,
310-967-0200

Writer, THE ORTEGAS, 2003, Fox
  Broadcasting, TV Series
Writer, BROTHERS GARCIA, 2001,
  Nickelodeon Networks, TV Series

Elizabeth Calienes*

Creative Director
Sak Studios
Los Angeles, CA 90064
Tel 310-709-7418
Cell 310-709-7418
Fax 928-222-5209
Email...............calienes@sakonline.com
Web ....www.sakonline.com

Production Designer, HOW THE GARCIA
GIRLS SPENT THEIR SUMMER,
2004, Loosely Based Pictures, LLC.,
Feature
Production Designer, FIGHT OR FLIGHT,
2003, Red Demon Productions, Short
Art Director, LETHAL, 2003, Silverline
Pictures, Feature
Production Designer, SHUI HEN, 2003,
AFI & Sugar Cane Productions, Short
Art Director, SINGULARITY, 2003, Fox
Searchlab, Short
Art Director, WISHING TIME, 2003,
Schmidt/Rosenzweig, Short

Deborah Calla*

Calla Productions
Santa Monica, CA 90405
Tel 310-392-3775
Fax 310-399-5594
Email ......callaproductions@adelphia.net

*Agent: ICM, Tanya Lopez/Eddie Borges,
310-550-4000*

Attorney: Darrell Miller, 310-826-0300

Producer, CARNIVAL IN RIO - 2003,
2003, Travel Channel, Documentary
Producer, LEHI'S WIFE, 2002,
AFI-Special Projects, Short
Producer, LOST ZWEIG, 2002, Grupo
Novo, Feature
Producer, USHI GOES USA, 2002,
Endemol, TV Series
Producer, CHICANO ARTISTS, 2001,
HBO Latino, Documentary
Line Producer, FOX KIDS CLUB, 1998,
Fox Kids, TV Series
Producer, DREAM HOUSE, 1997,
American Image, Feature

Michael Camacho

Agent
Creative Artists Agency
Beverly Hills, CA 90212
Tel 310-288-4545
Fax 310-288-4800
Email ....mcamacho@caa.com

Juan Jose Campanella

Los Angeles, CA

Manager: John Ufland, 310-550-9600

Director, DRAGNET, 2002, ABC, TV
Series
Director, EL HIJO DE LA NOVIA, 2001,
Columbia TriStar, Feature
Writer, EL HIJO DE LA NOVIA, 2001,
Columbia Tri Star, Feature
Director, LAW & ORDER CRIMINAL
INTENT, 2001, NBC, TV Series
Director, LAW & ORDER SVU, 2000,
NBC, TV Series
Director, EL MISMO AMOR, LA MISMA
LLUVIA, 1999, Warner Bros., Feature
Writer, EL MISMO AMOR, LA MISMA
LLUVIA, 1999, Warner Bros., Feature
Director, UPRIGHT CITIZENS BRIGADE,
1999, Comedy Central, TV Series

Felix Leo Campos*

After Dark CATV Productions, Inc
Bronx, NY 10459
Tel 718-842-4460
Fax 718-842-4480
Email ....nochecera2000@yahoo.com

AMERICAN JUSTICE, 2003, A&E, TV
SIGNAL TO NOISE, 1997, PBS, TV
P.E.G. Access TV, TV

Marlon Cantillano*

Animator
Ft. Wayne, IN 46802
Tel 219-426-7226
Fax 219-426-2408
Email.................macpro4@comcast.net

Ralph Cantu*
Houston, TX 77096
Tel 713-668-6605
Email ....rcantu@houston.rr.com

Rocky Capella
RCP Group
Foster City, CA 94404
Tel 800-400-3124
Tel 323-462-2301
Email ....rcpstunts@aol.com
Web ....www.rockycapella.com

Stunt Coordinator, BLACKOUT, 2004
Stunt Coordinator, MONK, 2004, ABC,
   TV Series
Stunt Coordinator, HENRY LEE, 2003,
   CBS, TV Movie
Stunt Man, THE HULK, 2003, Universal
   Pictures, Feature
Stunt Coordinator, ED TV, 2002,
   Universal, Feature
Stunt Coordinator, HIGH CRIMES, 2002,
   20th Century Fox, Feature
Stunt Man, MATRIX, 1999, Warner
   Bros., Feature
Stunt Man, TERMINATOR, 1984, MGM,
   Feature

David Capurso
Warner Bros. Global Trainee Program
Brooklyn, NY 11222
Tel 917-748-7436
Fax 718-398-6446
Email...........................capu5@aol.com

Walter Carasco
CEO/Founder
ImagenEntertainment
Burbank, CA 91505
Tel 818-845-1424
Fax 818-845-1113
Email............info@imagentertainment.tv
Web ....www.imagentertainment.tv

Johnny Carbajal*
Primo Entertainment
Los Angeles, CA 90032
Tel 323-227-5581
Email ....johnnycarbajal@hotmail.com

Alejandro Cardenas*
Los Angeles, CA 90036
Tel 323-653-0908
Email ....acardsoto@yahoo.com

Laura Cardona*
New York, NY 10003
Tel 646-924-9267
Email......................tislaura@yahoo.com

Editor, Assistant, JOE REDNER
   CAMPAIGN COMMERCIALS, 2003,
   TV
Editor, Assistant, WALT DISNEY WORLD
   HIGHLIGHT VIDEO, 2003, Action
   Sports International, TV
Editor, Assistant, FIGHTING FOR LIFE
   IN THE DEATH BELT, 2002-2003, TV
Producer, 143 MILES, 2002, FSU Film
   School, Feature
Producer, THE ORGANIC HOUR, 2002,
   Public Access National Syndication,
   TV

filmmakers

Patricia Cardoso
Santa Monica, CA 90406
Tel 310-850-2107
Fax 310-450-4677
Email ....lechuga@earthlink.net

Agent: ICM, Barbara Mandell,
310-550-4000

Manager: Rosalie Swedlin,
323-964-9220

Director, NAPPILY EVER AFTER, 2004,
    Universal Pictures, Feature
Director, REAL WOMEN HAVE CURVES,
    2002, HBO, Feature
Director, EL REINO DE LOS CIELOS:
    THE WATER CARRIER, 1996, UCLA
Writer, EL REINO DE LOS CIELOS: THE
    WATER CARRIER, 1996, UCLA
Director, AIR GLOBE, 1990, UCLA,
    Short
Writer, AIR GLOBE, 1990, UCLA, Short

Gabriel Carmona
Carmona Entertainment
Los Angeles, CA 90022
Tel 323-721-FILM
Fax 323-728-4045
Web ....www.carmona-entertainment.com

Producer

Julissa Carmona*
Yonkers, NY 10705
Tel 914-423-1001
Email ....julissacarmona@hotmail.com

Carlos Caro*
Fluxus Imagination
Huntington Beach, CA 92646
Tel 714-206-0306
Email ....fluxus_imagination@netzero.net

Loreto Caro
Radio-TV-Film at UT-Austin
Austin, TX 78705
Tel 512-380-9513
Email ....lcaro@mail.utexas.edu

Supervising Producer, GUM, 2003, RTF
    at UT-Austin, Short
Camera Assistant, INGRID, 2003, RTF
    at UT-Austin, Short
Camera Assistant, EMMA'S VISIT, 2002,
    RTF at UT-Austin, Short
Director, I JUST KNOW, 2002, RTF at
    UT-Austin, Experimental
Director, SOME DAY, 2002, RTF at
    UT-Austin, Short
Director, I, SOR JUANA, 2001, RTF at
    UT-Austin, Documentary Short

Michael Caro*
Regional Manager, San Diego
Latin Style Magazine
San Diego, CA 92108
Tel 619-934-8768
Email ....latinstyle3@cox.net

Octavio Carranza*
Carranza Brothers
Los Angeles, CA 90294
Tel 323-650-6649
Cell 310-699-5273
Email ....Octavio@LAart.com

Writer, ARTURO - EL SONADOR, 2002,
    Film Festival Circuit, Short
Producer, ARTURO - EL SONADOR,
    2002, Film Festival Circuit, Short

Salvador Carrasco*

Salvastian Pictures
Santa Monica, CA 90403
Tel 310-576-6785
Email ....SalvastianPics@aol.com
Web ....www.theotherconquest.com

Agent: The Bohrman Agency, Caren Bohrman, 310-550-5443

Director, THE BROTHERS GARCIA, 2000, Nickelodeon, TV Series
Director, LA OTRA CONQUISTA, 1998, Carrasco & Domingo Films, Feature
Writer, LA OTRA CONQUISTA, 1998, Carrasco & Domingo Films, Feature
Editor, LA OTRA CONQUISTA, 1998, Carrasco & Domingo Films, Feature

David Carrera

Carrera Productions
E. Hampton, CT 06424
Tel 860-690-2636
Email ..carreraproductions@hotmail.com

Producer

James Carrera*

Carpinteria, CA 93013
Email ....jlj@terranigrausa.com

Carlos Carreras

Agent
United Talent Agency
Beverly Hills, CA 90212
Tel 310-273-6700
Email ....carrerasc@unitedtalent.com

Juliette Carrillo

Venice, CA
Tel 310-664-0778
Email ....cilantro@earthlink.net

Director, ANNA IN THE TROPICS, 2003, South Coast Repertory, Stage Play
Director, SPIRAL, 2002, AFI, Short
Writer, SPIRAL, 2002, AFI, Short
Producer, HISPANIC PLAYWRIGHTS PROJECT, 1997-present, South Coast Repertory, Stage Play Festival
Director, HISPANIC PLAYWRIGHTS PROJECT, 1997-present, South Coast Repertory, Stage Play Festival

Elvira Carrizal*

New York, NY 10025
Email ....elvirac1@yahoo.com

Angel Carrizosa*

Queens, NY 11370
Tel 718-478-1517
Email ....carrizosa777@yahoo.com

Raesha Cartagena*

New York, NY 10010
Tel 212-686-5098
Email ....cartagena211@aol.com

Lupe Casares

HCCTV
New York, NY 10013
Tel 713-718-6312

Producer

Pauline Cashion*

Bulverde, TX 78163
Tel 210-385-8109
Email ....pauline_cashion@yahoo.com

Production Assistant
Publicist, Commercial Copywriting

Claudia Casillas*

Executive Assistant
Arenas Entertainment
Beverly Hills, CA 90210
Tel 310-385-4401
Email ....cclaudia@attbi.com

Rudy Casillas

Program Manager
PBS KUAT-TV
Tucson, AZ 85721
Tel 520-621-7368
Fax 520-621-3360
Email ....rcasillas@kuat.arizona.edu
Web...............................www.kuat.org

Producer

Adrian Castagna

Flip Films
Santa Monica, CA 90404
Tel 310-401-6140
Fax 310-401-6149

Producer

Al Castañeda

3rd Millennium Films
Los Angeles, CA 90024
Tel 818-807-2546
Fax 818-886-6891
Email ....AlcFilmmaker@Netscape.net

Producer

Carlos Castañeda

Independent
San Antonio, TX 78216
Tel 210-344-6378
Email ....ccastanedatx@sbcglobal.net
Web ....www.geocities.com

Director, THE MESTIZO VIRGIN, 2003
Producer
Editor, CAMINANTE

Laura Castañeda

Press Pass International
San Diego, CA 92103
Tel 619-585-3359
Email ....Presspasslc@aol.com

Producer, CUNA: MEDICINE MAN,
   2003, UCSD-TV, TV Series
Producer, LA CUCARACHA, 2003, Cox
   Communications, TV Series
Producer, AMERICA'S MOST WANTED,
   2001, Fox TV, TV Series
Production Company, TOLERANCE FOR
   KIDS, 2001, American Bar
   Association, Educational/Industrial
Production Company, CHICANO
   FEDERATION HISTORY, 2000, The
   Chicano Federation SD County,
   Corporate Training

Laura Castañeda

Reporter
Channel 4
San Diego, CA 92114
Tel 619-266-5631
Email ....laura.castaneda@cox.com

Marisa Castañeda*

University of New Mexico - Albuquerque
Albuquerque, NM 87197
Tel 505-268-0987
Email ....mcastan@unm.edu

Producer, ICARUS HAS FALLEN
   SUMMER, 2002, Flicks on 66 Film
   Festival, Short
Producer, RIDE SUMMER, 2001, Flicks
   on 66 Film Festival, Short

Richard Castaniero

Chicano Studies Research Center
Oxnard, CA 93033
Tel 213-483-8353
Email.............................cast@ucla.edu

Jesús Castellanos*

Union City, CA 94587
Tel 510-673-0238
Email ....Jcscribbler@aol.com

Liliana Castellanos*

New York, NY 10002
Tel 212-505-0344
Email ....liliprisas@yahoo.com

Eloisa Castillo*

Houston, TX 77087
Tel 713-540-8618

Gina Castillo*

Cinegold Pictures
Austin, TX 78749
Tel 512-891-7624
Email ....moviechick@collegeclub.com

Juan Castillo*

New York, NY
Tel 212-431-2950

Ramon Castillo

Tu Musica TV
Los Angeles, CA 90048
Tel 323-269-5134

Raul Castillo*

Brooklyn, NY 11205
Tel 917-804-7434
Email ....odioelinternet@hotmail.com

Roger Castillo*

Boerne, TX 78015
Tel 210-698-1191
Email ....roger@fawnmountain.com

Thomas Javier Castillo*

Tucson, AZ 85701
Tel 520-622-2358
Email ....tjc@email.arizona.edu

Producer, CANOA, 2003, University of
   Arizona, Documentary Short
Sound, A VICIOUS LICK, 2002,
   Aaquinas Productions, Feature

Karina Castorena*

Los Angeles, CA 90005
Tel 213-381-1245
Email ....karinastarr@yahoo.com

Gabriel Castro*

Executive Assistant
Ground Zero Entertainment
Los Angeles, CA 90045
Tel 310-410-3003
Email ....castro@groundzeroent.com
Web ....www.groundzeroent.com

Fernando Alberto Castroman

Playa del Rey, CA 90293
Tel 310-822-2281
Cell 310-874-4062
Email ....nando@earthlink.net

1st Assistant Director, ER, 2003, NBC, TV Series
1st Assistant Director, RESURRECTION BLVD., 2000, Showtime, TV Series
1st Assistant Director, AVALON: BEYOND THE ABYSS, 1999, UPN, TV Movie
1st Assistant Director, BAYWATCH "WHITE THUNDER AT GLACIER BAY", 1998, Trimark Pictures, TV Series
1st Assistant Director, THE VIVERO LETTER, 1998, York Entertainment, Feature
1st Assistant Director, ASSAULT ON DEVIL'S ISLAND, 1997, TNT, TV Movie
2nd Assistant Director, RAPA NUI, 1994, Warner Bros., Feature
2nd Assistant Director, AIRBORNE, 1993, Warner Bros., Feature
2nd Assistant Director, HOFFA, 1992, 20th Century Fox, Feature

Veronica Cavazos*

Laredo, TX 78041
Tel 956-753-3032
Email ....vjcavasos@yahoo.com

Iris Cegarra*

La Jolla, CA 92037
Tel 305-461-2030
Email ....irisb@electro-dziska.com

Pedro Celedon*

Barefoot Productions
Hollywood, CA 90028
Tel 323-461-9773
Fax 323-913-1331
Email ....pceledon@e-nfomercial.com

Producer, A CONTINENT ENFLAMED, 2004, NEH, Documentary
Producer, FULL BLOOM, 2002, Michelle Mattei Productions, Documentary
Producer, A TALE OF THREE LIVES, 1999, KCET-TV, TV
Producer, BILL VIOLA, A TWENTY-YEAR RETROSPECTIVE, 1998, KCET-TV, Documentary
Producer, THE CROSSING OF THE ATLANTIC, 1992, TVN Chile, TV
Producer, HISTORY TOLD ON WALLS, 1991, The Getty Trust, Documentary
Producer, AUF ACSHE, 1987, Bavaria Studios, Feature
Producer, LAWLESS LAND, 1987, New Line Cinema, Feature

Michael Centeno*

Elusive Minds Productions
Sylmar, CA 91342
Tel 818-362-5753
Email........elusivemindsprod@yahoo.com

Leticia Cervantes-Lopez*

Whittier, CA 90604
Fax 562-692-9194

Ivan Cevallos

Ethos Group, Inc.
S. Pasadena, CA 91030
Tel 626-388-2100
Email ....icevallos@ethosagency.com

Director, PIÑATA STAND, 2003, Commercial
Producer, 14 WAYS TO WEAR LIPSTICK, 1999, Feature
Publicist

Mike & Gibby Cevallos

Cevallos Brothers Productions
Sherman Oaks, CA 91403
Tel 818-380-8128
Fax 818-380-8125

Director, THE BROTHERS GARCIA,
  2000, Nickelodeon, TV Series
Creator, THE BROTHERS GARCIA,
  2000, Nickelodeon, TV Series
Writer, THE BROTHERS GARCIA, 2000,
  Nickelodeon, TV Series
Director, BARBACOA THE MOVIE, 1998,
  Feature
Writer, BARBACOA THE MOVIE, 1998,
  Feature

Teofilo Chacin

Armadillo Entertainment
Miami, FL 33138
Tel 770-451-6154
Email ....teofilochacin@yahoo.com

Producer

Daniel Chacon*

Los Angeles, CA 90034
Tel 310-815-8139
Email ....chacon22@yahoo.com

Nancy Chaidez

Agent
Nancy Chaidez Agency & Associates, Inc.
Los Angeles, CA 90048
Tel 323-655-6455
Fax 323-655-1255
Email ....talria@aol.com

Natalie Chaidez

Los Angeles, CA

*Agent: United Talent Agency, Peter
Benedek, 310-273-6700*

Executive Producer, Co-, SKIN, 2003,
  Fox Film Corporation, TV Series
Writer, SKIN, 2003, Fox Film
  Corporation, TV Series
Producer, THE WARDEN, 2001, Turner
  Network Television, TV Movie
Writer, THE WARDEN, 2001, Turner
  Network Television, TV Movie
Producer, JUDGING AMY, 1999, CBS
  Television, TV Series
Writer, JUDGING AMY, 1999, CBS
  Television, TV Series
Producer, TRINITY, 1998, NBC

Daniel Chairez*

Bakersfield, CA 93301
Email ....DChairez@hotmail.com

Arcie Chapa

KNME-TV
Albuquerque, NM 87102
Tel 505-277-1242
Fax 505-277-2191
Email ....achapa@unm.edu

Barry Chase*

Miami, FL 33131
Tel 305-373-7665
Fax 305-373-7668
Email ....loboc@aol.com
Web ....backlands@earthlink.net

Joaquin Chavez*

San Ysidro, CA 92173
Tel 526-803-8526
Email ....lobotmex@mailcity.com

filmmakers

Maria Chavez

We Shoot 'Em
Fresno, CA 93725
Tel 305-442-0048

Producer

Calixto Chinchilla

Festival Director
New York International Latino Film
Festival
New York, NY 10019
Tel 212-265-8452
Email ....calixto@nylatinofilm.com

Jose Ciccone*

Three Piece Scandal Films
Chula Vista, CA 91913
Tel 619-482-0343
Email......................pepe711@aol.com

Ileana Ciena

Miramar San Juan, PR 00907

Producer, JULIA, TODO EN MI, 2002,
Documentary

George Cisneros*

Owner/Manager
VuTure Arts
San Antonio, TX 78207
Tel 210-527-0377
Fax 877-842-0329
Email ....gcisneros@dcci.com

Evelyn Collazo*

Administrative Assistant to Chief
Administrator
Henry Street Settlement
New York, NY 10024
Tel 212-874-7587
Fax 212-505-8329
Email ....emcfoto@aol.com

Jose Colomer

Colomer Productions
Los Angeles, CA
Tel 310-713-4059
Email ....colomerproductions@yahoo.com

Director, AL DÍA CON MARÍA
  CONCHITA, 1998, Telemundo, TV
Director, REAL T.V., 1997, 20th.
  Century Fox, TV Series
Director, A PERFECT SCORE, CBS
Director, EL NUEVO SHOW DE PAUL
  RODRIGUEZ, Univision
Director, LIFE CAMERA ACTION, Fox
  Family Channel
Director, LIVE FROM THE ACADEMY
  AWARDS, Tribune Entertainment

Dianet Colon*

Jersey City, NJ
Tel 201-951-6538
Fax 201-434-2440
Email ....lopezdi@aol.com

Ezequiel Colon-Rivera*

Jersey City, NJ
Email ....ecolonrivera@hotmail.com

Dolores Colunga-Stawitz

Story Makers, Inc.
Houston, TX 77037
Tel 281-591-7479
Email ....stmkr@aol.com

Producer

Denise Contreras

CBS Telenoticias
Hialeah, FL 33010
Tel 305-889-6995

Diana Contreras*
Diosa Productions
Northridge, CA 91326
Tel 818-360-0813
Email ....diana.shakti@verizon.net

Director, POR UN AMOR, 1999, Diosa
    Productions, Short
Director, LUMINARY, 1998, Diosa
    Productions, Short
Director, PORTRAIT OF LIGHT, 1996,
    Diosa Productions, Short

Ernie Contreras*
Los Angeles, CA 90068
Tel 323-876-3424
Cell 323-447-4069
Fax 323-876-3424
Email ....cemtr@sbcglobal.net

Agent: Paradigm, Mark Ross,
310-277-4400

Writer, FAIRY TALE: A TRUE STORY,
    1997, Paramount, Feature
Writer, THE PAGEMASTER, 1994, 20th
    Century Fox, Feature
Writer, THE SMURFS, 1990,
    Hanna-Barbera/Turner, TV Series,
    Animated
Camera Assistant, TELEVISION
    ANIMATION, 1988-1993,
    Hanna-Barbera, TV Animation

Rosemary Contreras*
Los Angeles, CA 90048
Tel 310-474-6054
Email ....rosemarycontreras@hotmail.com

James Cooper*
San Diego, CA 92101
Tel 619-525-1430
Email ....jcooper@swsl.edu

Roberto Coppola*
Los Angeles, CA 90039
Tel 310-770-4945
Email...................uroboros@pacbell.net

Samuel Cordoba
Look Pictures, LLC
Los Angeles, CA 90027
Tel 323-667-2072
Cell 213-840-6847
Fax 323-667-2072
Email ....samuel@lookpictures.net
Web ....www.lookpictures.net

Production Designer, THE TREE

Carlene Cordova*
Planet BB Entertainment
Los Angeles, CA 90027
Tel 310-738-5363
Email ....carlene@mac.com

Lori Cordova
Owner
Catering By Lori Cordova
Santa Barbara, CA
Tel 805-733-3141
Fax 805-733-3142

Caterer, HOW THE GARCIA GIRLS
    SPENT THEIR SUMMER, 2003,
    Loosely Based Pictures LLC., Feature
Caterer, ANIMA, 2002, AFI, Short

Roberta Cordova*
Alzada Productions
North Hills, CA 91343
Tel 818-895-0631
Fax 818-895-9933
Email.............roberta007@earthlink.net

Gilbert Cordova III*
W. Hartford, CT

filmmakers

Sergio Coronado*
Tarzana, CA 91356
Tel 818-415-3056
Email ....sergiocoronado@msn.com

Manuel de Seixas Correa
Strictly Kings Productions
New York, NY 10023
Cell 646-209-0177
Email ....
contact@strictlykingsproductions.com

Writer, PEOPLES, 2003, Strictly Kings
  Productions, Feature
Producer, PEOPLES, 2003, Strictly
  Kings Productions, Feature
Production Manager, LOVE SONG -
  HARVEY MILK, 2001, Hypnotic, Short
Writer, WUNDER, 2001, Jetlag
  Productions, Short
Director, WUNDER, 2001, Jetlag
  Productions, Short

Marisol Correa
Centauro Comunicaciones
Salinas, CA 93905
Tel 800-644-9205

Alex D. Cortez*
Santa Ana, CA 92701
Tel 714-587-0692
Email ....adcortez@hotmail.com

David Cortez*
McAllen, TX 78501
Tel 202 425 5435
Tel 956-212-1896
Email ....cortezdl@mac.com

Claudia Cosio
Chairperson
Promotora La Vida es Bella
Mexico, DF 6760 Mexico
Tel 52-55-55251183
Tel 52-55-52076803
Cell 52-55-19002660
Fax 52-55-55251183
Email..........claudia_cosio@terra.com.mx
Web ....www.mazatlanfilmfest.com.mx

Production Manager, ENTRE LA TARDE
  Y LA NOCHE, 2000, Imcine, Feature
Writer, UN BOLETO PARA SOÑAR,
  1998, Septimo Arte, Short
Production Manager, ONDAS
  HERTZIANAS, 1997, CUEC, Short

Valintino Costa*
Tucson, AZ 85704
Tel 520-292-2035
Cell 520-235-1862
Email ....tinoc72@yahoo.com

2nd 2nd Assistant Director, HOW THE
  GARCIA GIRLS SPENT THEIR
  SUMMER, 2003, Loosely Based
  Pictures, LLC., Feature
2nd Assistant Director, THE
  CONNECTICUT KID, 2003, TCK
  Productions, Feature

Oscar Luis Costo
Vice President
MARdeORO Film Inc.
San Marino, CA 91108
Tel 626-799-1388
Fax 626-799-2388
Email ....mardeoro@earthlink.net
*Agent: Innovative Artists, Jack Leighton,
310-656-0400*

Director, ENCRYPT, 2003, USA Films,
  TV Movie
Producer, STEALING CHRISTMAS,
  2003, USA Films, TV Movie
Producer, SAINT/SINNER, 2002, USA
  Films, TV Movie

Producer, HITCHED, 2001, USA Films,
TV Movie
Director, SPECIAL UNIT 2, 2001,
United Paramount Network, TV Series
Director, MY FUNNY VALENTINE, 2000,
Rainbow Media Inc., TV Movie
Producer, THE CHIPPENDALE MURDER,
2000, USA Network, TV Movie
Producer, SINS OF THE CITY, 1998,
Alliance Entertainment, TV Series

Manny Coto
Hollywood, CA
Tel 323-667-3003

*Agent: Endeavor, David Greenblatt,
310-248-2000*

Writer, ODYSSEY 5, 2002, Columbia
TriStar, TV Series
Executive Producer, ODYSSEY 5, 2002,
Columbia TriStar, TV Series
Writer, ENTERPRISE, 2001, Paramount
Pictures, TV Series
Executive Producer, ENTERPRISE,
2001, Paramount Pictures, TV Series
Director, ZENON: THE SEQUEL, 2001,
The Disney Channel, TV Movie
Director, THE OTHER ME, 2000, The
Disney Channel, TV Movie
Writer, STRANGE WORLD, 1999, 20th
Century Fox, TV Series
Director, STAR KID, 1997, Trimark
Pictures, Feature

Elika Crespo*
Wilshire Stages
Los Angeles, CA 90048
Tel 323-951-1700
Email..........ecrespo@wilshirestages.com

Production Facilities and Services

Greg Crowder*
6 Reel Pictures
Los Angeles, CA 90049
Tel 310-472-1515
Fax 310-471-2457
Email ....gcrowder@6reel.com

Ricardo Crudo*
Los Angeles, CA 90049
Tel 310-288-1125
Tel 310-471-1004
Email ....rpcarn@aol.com

Director of Photography, GRIND, 2003,
Warner Bros., Feature
Director of Photography, DOWN TO
EARTH, 2001, Paramount Pictures,
Feature
Director of Photography, AMERICAN
PIE, 1999, Universal Pictures,
Feature

Brad Cruz*
Newhall, CA 91321
Email ....cruzfilms@aol.com

Kaye Cruz
24 Hour Entertainment
San Antonio, TX
Tel 210-573-6990
Email ....onair@juno.com

Nilo Cruz
New York, NY 10021

*Agent: Peregrine Whittlesey Agency,
212-737-0153*

Writer, ANNA IN THE TROPICS, 2003,
Royale Theater (Broadway), Stage
Play, 2003 Pulitzer Prize Winner in
Drama

Ray Cruz
WLRN, Instructional TV
Los Angeles, CA 90012

Rene Simon Cruz*

Esperanza Films, Inc.
Santa Monica, CA 90404
Tel 310-899-9336
Fax 310-899-9007
Email ....renecruz@esperanza.com
Web ....www.esperanza.com

Attorney: Michael Morales,
310-278-0066

Producer, CROSS THE LINE, 2003,
  Feature
Producer, DR. TIME, 2003, Independent
  Film Channel, TV Series
Producer, BEYOND BORDERS: JOHN
  SAYLES IN MEXICO, 2002,
  Independent Film Channel,
  Documentary
Director, THEY SPEAK OF HOPE, 1986,
  Lutheran World Ministries,
  Documentary

Alfonso Cuaron

Monsoon Entertainment
Los Angeles, CA
Tel 323-525-2721

Agent: William Morris Agency, Steve
Rabineau, 310-274-7451

Producer, THE ASSASSINATION OF
  RICHARD NIXON, 2004, Monsoon
  Pictures, Feature
Producer, CRONICAS, 2004,
  Producciones Anhelo, Feature
Director, HARRY POTTER AND THE
  PRISONER OF AZKABAN, 2004,
  Warner Bros., Feature
Director, THE CHILDREN OF MEN,
  2003, Beacon Communications,
  Feature
Director, Y TU MAMA TAMBIEN, 2001,
  IFC, Feature
Producer, Y TU MAMA TAMBIEN, 2001,
  IFC, Feature
Director, GREAT EXPECTATIONS, 1998,
  20th Century Fox, Feature
Director, LITTLE PRINCESS, 1995,
  Warner Bros., Feature
Director, FALLEN ANGELS, 1993,
  Showtime, TV Series

Carmen Cuba

Tel 213-503-4405
Email ....cubaahse@aol.com

Agent: Endeavor, Sean Elliott,
310-248-2000

Casting Director, 1.0, 2004, Armada
  Films, Feature
Casting Director, BUTTERFLY EFFECT,
  2004, New Line Cinema, Feature
Casting Director, BULLY, 2001, Lions
  Gate Films, Feature

Alfredo Cubiña*

Miami, FL
Tel 787-748-5390
Email ....acubina@hotmail.com

Writer

Michael Cuesta

New York, NY
Tel 516-909-4787
Email ....howie516@aol.com

Agent: ICM, 310-550-4000

Director, L.I.E., 2001, Lot 47 Films,
  Feature
Writer, L.I.E., 2001, Lot 47 Films,
  Feature
Producer, L.I.E., 2001, Lot 47 Films,
  Feature
Director, SIX FEET UNDER, 2001, HBO,
  TV Series

Tania Cuevas Martinez

Expansion Films/H2O International Film
Festival 2002
Tel 718-953-1107
Email ....tania@expandingthereal.com

Director
Producer

Yuri Cunza*

Nashville, TN 37204
Tel 615-386-3667

Tania Cypriano*
Viva! Pictures
New York, NY 10014
Tel 212-691-5303
Fax 212-604-9158
Email ....backlands@earthlink.net

DAME LA MANO, 2001, PVH Films-the
Netherlands, Feature
Producer, DESTINO EXPORTADOR,
2001, TV Cultura-Brazil, TV
NO MIRROR, 1991, Viva! Pictures,
Feature
Director, VIVA EU!, 1989, Feature

Ignacio Darnaude
Executive Vice President,
International Creative Advertising
Columbia TriStar
Culver City, CA 90232
Tel 310-244-4000

Angel David*
Flights of Angel
New York, NY 10024
Tel 212-769-1137
Email ....nyangeldavid@aol.com

Director, THE LONG GOODNIGHT, 2004,
Short
Writer, THE LONG GOODNIGHT, 2004,
Short
Director, CUCHIFRITO, 2003, INTAR
Theatre, Stage Play
Director, EL SALVADOR, 2002, Legend
Theatre Co., Stage Play
Writer, BY REASON OF..., 1994, INTAR
Theatre, Stage Play

Gilbert Davila
VP, Multicultural Marketing
Walt Disney Company
Burbank, CA 91521
Tel 818-560-6905
Email ....gilbert.davila@disney.com

Carlos de Jesus
Valley Cottage, NY 10989
Tel 212-691-4930

Victor de Jesus*
Passion Entertainment
Los Angeles, CA 90026
Tel 213-250-3889
Tel 310-390-2935
Email ....vdejesus@aol.com

Writer, BOSTON PUBLIC, 2003, Spec
Script: FOX, TV Series
Writer, SIX FEET UNDER, 2003, Spec:
Showtime, TV Series
Writer, THIRD WATCH, 2003, NBC, TV
Series

Maggie de la Cuesta
Polymorphous Pictures
New York, NY 10027
Tel 212-222-4134

Writer

Ana Marie de la Peña Portela*
San Antonio, TX 78209
Tel 210-669-9935
Tel 212-313-6850
Email...............adep78209@yahoo.com
Web....................www.anadeportela.com

*Manager: George & Liz Ozuna,
210-669-9935, cineman@ev1.net*

Writer, I LIKE EUROPE AND EUROPE
LIKES ME, 2003, Experimental
Writer, LAST TANGO IN SAN ANTONIO,
2003, Ozuna Digital, Short
Writer, SHAVING FOR THE CITY, 2003,
Ozuna Digital, Short
Writer, COMPOSITION FOR HAND AND
ORGAN, 1999, Cine Festival,
Experimental
Actor, DIVA, 1993, Club Berlin, Short
Writer, THE SECRET CURL, 1993,
Friesenwall 120, Documentary

filmmakers

Roberto de la Rosa*
Santa Cruz, CA 95060
Email ....delarosa@ebold.com

Deborah de la Torre*
Festival Director
Tulipanes Latino Art & Film Festival
Holland, MI 49423
Tel 616-355-2121
Fax 616-355-2123
Email ....info@tlaff.org
Web ....www.tulipanes.org

Margie de la Torre Aguirre*
Abrazo Productions
Yorba Linda, CA 92887
Fax 714-773-0986
Email ....mareflections@aol.com

Rafael de la Uz*
Brooklyn, NY 11225
Email ....rafadelauz@earthlink.net

Mario de la Vega*
Studio City, CA 91604
Tel 818-985-2630
Email ....mariodlv@access1.net

David de Leon*
Millennium Crop Entertainment
Los Angeles, CA 90018
Tel 323-737-6332

Dita de Leon
Muevete Entertainment, Inc.
Beverly Hills, CA 90212
Tel 917-587-4203
Tel 973-484-5161
Email ....mueveteUSA@aol.com
Web.....................www.DitadeLeon.com

Actor
Producer

Eloisa de Leon*
San Diego, CA 92102
Tel 619-595-1448

Perla de Leon*
New York, NY 10036
Tel 212-244-5182
Fax 212-244-5182
Email ....perlafotografica@aol.com

Nancy de los Santos*
Bronze Screen Productions Company
Los Angeles, CA 90027
Tel 818-551-9619
Email ....LaNancyD@sbcglobal.net

Producer, LALO GUERRENO: THE
ORIGINAL CHICANO, 2004, LPB,
Documentary
Writer, AMERICAN FAMILY, 2002, PBS,
TV Series
Director, BRONZE SCREEN: ONE
HUNDRED YEARS OF THE LATINO
IMAGE IN AMERICAN CINEMA,
2002, Bronze Screen Productions,
Documentary
Writer, BRONZE SCREEN: ONE
HUNDRED YEARS OF THE LATINO
IMAGE IN AMERICAN CINEMA,
2002, Bronze Screen Productions,
Documentary
Writer, GOTTA KICK IT UP!, 2002,
Disney Channel, TV Movie
Writer, RESURRECTION BLVD., 2002,
Showtime, TV Series
Associate Producer, SELENA, 1997,
Warner Bros., Feature
Associate Producer, MI FAMILIA/MY
FAMILY, 1995, New Line, Feature
Director, BREAKING PAN WITH SOL,
1993, Universal Television, TV Movie

Ron de Moraes
Los Angeles, CA

Agent: William Morris Agency, John Ferritere, 310-859-4000

Director, EMMY AWARDS PRE-SHOW, 2003, Fox Film Corp., TV Special
Director, PRIMETIME CREATIVE ARTS EMMY AWARDS, 2003, E! Entertainment Television, TV Special
Director, 2002 WINTER OLYMPICS OPENING & CLOSING CERMONIES & MEDAL CONCERTS, 2002, TV Special
Director, WORLD'S GREATEST COMMERCIALS, 2002, CBS, TV Special
Director, MICHELLE KWAN: PRINCESS ON ICE, 2001, Disney, TV Special
Director, SUPER BOWL'S GREATEST COMMERCIALS, 2001, CBS, TV Special
Director, CANDID CAMERA, 1998, CBS, TV Series
Director, WHOSE LINE IS IT ANYWAY?, 1998, ABC, TV Series
Director, ENTERTAINMENT TONIGHT, 1981, Paramount Television, TV Series

Ivan de Paz
Agent
Arenas Group
Beverly Hills, CA 90210
Tel 310-385-4401
Fax 310-385-4402
Email.................ivan@arenasgroup.com

Alfredo de Villa*
Miami Beach, FL 33139
Tel 917-749-2244
Fax 305-666-2101
Email ....bunuelhitch@earthlink.net

Agent: United Talent Agency, Stuart Manashil, 310-273-6700, smanashil@unitedtalent.com

Director, WASHINGTON HEIGHTS, 2002, Mac Releasing, Feature
Director, THE DOORMAN, 1999, Documentary
Director, NETO'S RUN, 1998, Atom Films, Short
Producer, TV COMMERCIALS, 1997-Present, Y&R, DDB, TV
Director, TV COMMERCIALS, 1997-Present, Y&R, DDB, TV

Dan del Campo
Publicist
401 Productions/DDC Publicity and Communications
Los Angeles, CA 90036
Tel 310-314-2790
Fax 310-314-2790
Email ....dan@indiefilter.net

Publicist, HEALTHY LIVING, 2001, PBS Series with Actor, Jane Seymour, TV
Publicist, THE WOMAN CHASER, 2001, Patrick Warburton, Feature

Celeste del Gado
Miami New Times
Miami, FL
Tel 305-571-7569

Ignacio del Moral

Marina Del Rey, CA 90292
Tel 310-396-6041
Email ....lsosin@igecorp.com

Writer, LOS LUNES AL SOL, 2002,
Feature

Guillermo del Toro

Austin, TX

*Agent: William Morris Agency, Mike
Simpson, 310-214-7451*

Director, HELLBOY, 2004, Columbia
Pictures, Feature
Writer, HELLBOY, 2004, Columbia
Pictures, Feature
Director, BLADE II, 2002, New Line
Cinema, Feature
Producer, I MURDER SERIOUSLY, 2002,
Magna Films S.L., Feature
Director, MIMIC, 1997, Dimension
Films, Feature
Writer, MIMIC, 1997, Dimension Films,
Feature
Writer, CRONOS, 1993, October Films,
Feature

Rafael del Toro*

Brooklyn, NY 11226
Tel 917-406-3320
Email ......brownbull@industryfreaks.com
Web ....www.brownbullfilms.com

Editor, DOS MINUTOS, 2003, TuTV, TV
Series
Editor, 25TH HOUR, 2002, Touchstone,
Feature
Director, THE SILENCE BEFORE, 2002,
NYU, Short
Writer, THE SILENCE BEFORE, 2002,
NYU, Short
Editor, THE SILENCE BEFORE, 2002,
NYU, Short
Director, MUST BE LOVE, 2001, NYU,
Short
Writer, MUST BE LOVE, 2001, NYU,
Short
Director, PLAYROOM, 1999, NYU,
Documentary Short

Margarita del Valle*

BnA Productions
Santa Barbara, CA
Tel 805-948-2949
Email ....mdelvallebnaproductions@earth-
link.net

Andrew Delaplaine*

Shallow Beach Entertaiment
Miami Beach, FL 33139
Tel 305-535-6522
Fax 305-868-4477
Email ....andrew@shallowbeach.tv
Web..............................shallowbeach.tv

Director, MIDNIGHT NEWS, 2003,
Short
Director, THE MORNING NEWS, 2003,
Short
Director, PRODUCT PLACEMENT, 2002,
Short

Laura Delgado*

Pacoima, CA 91331
Email ....delgadolaura1@msn.com

Cos Delli*

COS Enterprises, Inc.
Studio City, CA 91604
Tel 818-985-7031

Nelson Denis*

New York, NY 10032
Tel 212-568-0230
Cell 917-325-0453
Email..............nelsondenis248@aol.com
Web ....voteformemovie.com

Director, VOTE FOR ME!, 2002, Feature
Writer, VOTE FOR ME!, 2002, Feature
Producer, VOTE FOR ME!, 2002,
Feature
Director, HOUND DOG, 1987, Short
Director, EAST MEETS WEST, 1986,
Short

Marlene Dermer

Festival Director
Los Angeles Latino International Film
Festival
Los Angeles, CA 90028
Tel 323-466-7110
Fax 323-466-7521
Email ....mdermer@earthlink.net

Yaquelin Di Crystal*

Van Nuys, CA 91408
Tel 818-617-4110

Alejandro Diaz

Cuentos del Pueblo Productions
Beverly Hills, CA 90213
Tel 323-883-1600
Email..cuentos_del_pueblo@hotmail.com
Web ....www.cuentosdelpueblo.com

Writer, PAN DULCE Y CHOCOLATE,
   Short
Director, PAN DULCE Y CHOCOLATE,
   Short

Marissa Diaz Granados*

London, SW3 4DY England
Tel 212-512-5337
Email ....mdiazgr@aol.com

Alejandro Diaz Jr.*

Panorama City, CA 91402
Tel 818-988-1391
Email ....aalexjdiaz@aol.com

Cecilia Domeyko

Accent Media Productions Inc.
McLean, VA 22101
Tel ....703-356-9427, Et. 26
Cell 703-477-0035
Fax 703-506-0643
Email ..jackjorgens@accentmediainc.com

Writer, CUBA MIA, 2002, Retrato de
   Una Orquestra de Mujeres
Director, CUBA MIA, 2002, Retrato de
   Una Orquestra de Mujeres
Producer, CUBA MIA, 2002, Retrato de
   Una Orquestra de Mujeres
Producer, MAGIC WOOL, Discovery
   Communications
Producer, PORTRAIT OF ANA MARIA
   VERA
Producer, UGANDA: EDUCATION FOR
   ALL

Alberto Dominguez

Glendale, CA 91206
Tel 818-662-8009
Fax 818-662-0109
Email.........hollywoodcom@earthlink.net

Director, THE BRONZE SCREEN: 100
   YEARS OF THE LATINO IMAGE IN
   AMERICAN CINEMA, 2002,
   Documentary
Producer, THE BRONZE SCREEN: 100
   YEARS OF THE LATINO IMAGE IN
   AMERICAN CINEMA, 2002,
   Documentary

Denise Dorn

New York, NY 10014
Tel 646-638-4364
Cell 646-250-0537
Email ....dedorn@yahoo.com

Writer, DORA THE EXPLORER, 2000,
   Nickelodeon, TV Series, Animated
Audio Supervisor, DORA THE
   EXPLORER, 2000, Nickelodeon, TV
   Series, Animated

filmmakers

Xochitl Dorsey*
Brooklyn, NY
Tel 718-623-2690
Email..........xochitl_dorsey@hotmail.com

Maria Dupont*
Hollywood, CA 91601
Tel 818-980-9754
Email ....luisita18@earthlink.net

Sandra Duque
La Negrita Productions
New York, NY 10021
Tel 212-502-0316
Tel 347-739-1720
Fax 212-772-1506
Email..LaNegritaProductions@yahoo.com

Writer, DEAR ABIGAIL
Producer, DEAR ABIGAIL

Eddy Duran*
Brooklyn, NY 11208
Tel 212-727-5766
Fax 718-277-2655
Email ....duranfilms@hotmail.com

Ester Duran*
New York, NY
Tel 212-315-5607
Email ....ED90@columbia.edu

Juan Carlos (JC) Duran*
Pepe & Elmer Media, Inc
Los Angeles, CA 90048
Tel 323-960-5520
Fax 818-986-8582
Email ....jcduran@pepe-elmer.com
Web ....www.pepeandelmer.com

Producer, EPK

Joe Eckardt*
Tarzana, CA 91357
Tel 818-708-7166
Fax 212-315-5607
Email......................joeeckardt@aol.com

Joseph Edo*
Advent Entertainment
Pasadena, CA 91107
Tel 626-281-0274
Email ....jettafilm@juno.com

Writer

Roni Eguia Menendez
Narrow Bridge Films
Studio City, CA 91604
Tel 818-766-1582
Fax 818-766-1882
Email ..narrowbridgefilms@sbcglobal.net

Producer, HUNTING OF MAN, 2003,
   Feature
Producer, BAD SEED, 2001, New City
   Releasing, Feature
Producer, SCRAPBOOK, 1999,
   PorchLight Entertainment, Feature
Associate Producer, AFTER SUNSET:
   THE LIFE & TIMES OF THE DRIVE-IN
   THEATER, 1995, Moonshadow
   Entertainment, Documentary
Producer, REMEMBRANCES, 1995,
   Feature

Daniel Eilemberg*
MGM
Los Angeles, CA 90035
Tel 310-586-8106
Email ....daniel_eilemberg@yahoo.com

Katrina Elias*
Jude Shaw Co.
N. Hollywood, CA 91606
Tel 818-766-3766
Fax 818-766-3766
Email ....kelias1056@aol.com

Writer, ABUELO'S LEGACY, 2001, Stage
　Play
Writer, DEAD HEAT FILM, 2001, Feature

Hector Elizondo
Shanti Productions
Sherman Oaks, CA 91403

Agent: William Morris, 310-274-7451

Manager: Gail Nachlis

Actor, MIRACLES, 2003, ABC, TV Series
Actor, HOW HIGH, 2001, Universal,
　Feature
Actor, TORTILLA SOUP, 2001, Samuel
　Goldwyn Films, Feature

James Encinas
Latino Writers Workshop
Venice, CA 90291
Tel 310-450-4814
Fax 310-859-2778
Email ....nora@bdhc.usa.com

Edgar Endress
MCCC
Lynchburg, VA 24503
Tel 609-586-4801
Email ....endresse@mccc.edu
Web www.eendress1.com

Media Advocate, MCCC
Director, THE MEMORY OF THE SNAILS

Alberto Enriquez
CNN en Español
N. Miami Beach, FL 33160

Serge Ernandez*
Miami, FL 33319
Tel 305-535-2940
Email ....auteurauthor@aol.com
Web ....www.rsbsfilms.com

Laura Escamilla
San Antonio, TX 78212
Tel 210-736-1473
Fax 210-696-4299
Email ....loride@sbcglobal.net

Geno Escarrega
Top Boss Productions, Inc.
Santa Monica, CA 90406
Tel 310-393-9308

Producer, PASADENA, 2001, Columbia
　TriStar, TV Series
Producer, CHINA BEACH, 1988, ABC,
　TV Series

Juan Carlos Escobedo*
New York, NY 10035
Tel 212-426-2700
Email ....carlos@rojaproductions.com

Maria Escobedo*
Rain Forest Films
Great Neck, NY 11021
Tel 718-279-0273
Email ....cghera1801@aol.com

Writer, RUM AND COKE, 2000,
　Delta/MCI Video, Feature
Director, RUM AND COKE, 2000,
　Delta/MCI video, Feature

filmmakers

Moctesuma Esparza*

Executive Producer
Maya Pictures
Los Angeles, CA 90065
Tel 310-281-3770
Fax 310-281-3777
Web ....www.maya-pictures.com

Executive Producer, GODS AND
  GENERALS, 2003, Warner Bros.,
  Feature
Executive Producer, PRICE OF GLORY,
  2002, New Line Cinema, Feature
Executive Producer, INTRODUCING
  DOROTHY DANDRIDGE, 1999, HBO,
  Feature
Executive Producer, SELMA, LORD,
  SELMA, 1999, Buena Vista Television,
  TV Movie
Executive Producer, BUTTER, 1998, Life
  Entertainment, Feature
Executive Producer, ROUGH RIDERS,
  1997, TNT, TV Movie
Producer, SELENA, 1997, Warner Bros.,
  Feature
Producer, THE DISAPPEARANCE OF
  GARCIA LORCA, 1997, Columbia
  TriStar, Feature
Producer, GETTYSBURG, 1993, New
  Line Cinema, Feature

Tonantzin Esparza*

Creative Development
Maya Pictures
Los Angeles, CA 90038
Tel 310-281-3770
Fax 310-281-3777
Email ....tonantzin_e@hotmail.com
Web ....www.maya-pictures.com

Actor

Dolly Josette Espinal*

Los Angeles, CA 90028
Tel 323-962-6809
Cell 213-840-7451
Fax 323-962-6809
Email.......................dllyjosett@aol.com

Attorney: Stephen Espinoza,
310-552-6506, stephene@2bbfgs.com

Supervisor, Cultural Content , DORA
  THE EXPLORER, 1999, Nickelodeon,
  TV
Producer, BODY TALK, 1994, Skyline
  Features, TV Series
Assignment Editor, GOOD DAY NY,
  1994, WNYW-Fox Affiliate, TV Series
Assignment Editor, STREET TALK,
  1994, WNYW-Fox Affiliate, TV Series

Alfonso Espinosa

VP, Production
Carmona Entertainment
Los Angeles, CA 90022
Tel 323-721-FILM
Fax 323-728-4045
Web ....www.carmona-entertainment.com

Producer
Writer

Elizabeth Espinosa

General Assignments Reporter
KTTV Fox 11 News
Los Angeles, CA 90025
Tel 310-584-2369
Web www.fox11la.com

Paul Espinosa*
Espinosa Productions
San Diego, CA 92116
Tel 619-220-6893
Fax 619-220-6895
Email ....espinosa@electriciti.com
Web ....www.EspinosaProductions.com

Producer, BEYOND THE DREAM, 2004, LPB, Documentary
Producer, TV Series, VISIONES, 2004, PBS, Documentary
Producer, TACO SHOP POETS, 2003, PBS, Documentary
Producer, BORDER, 2001, PBS, Documentary
Producer, THE U.S. - MEXICAN WAR:1846-1848, 1992, PBS, Documentary

Carlos Espinoza*
Yuma, AZ 85364
Tel 928-782-3228
Email ....nito_ent03@yahoo.com

Production Assistant, HOW THE GARCIA GIRLS SPENT THEIR SUMMER, 2003, Loosely Based Pictures, LLC, Feature

Freddie Espinoza
West Coast Bureau Producer
Univision Network
Los Angeles, CA 90093

Richard Espinoza
Saugus, CA 91390
Tel 661-296-6362
Fax 661-296-1984
Email.....................palomapic@aol.com

1st Assistant Director, KINGPIN, 2003, NBC, TV Movie
1st Assistant Director, UNDECLARED, 2001, Fox Network, TV Series
1st Assistant Director, RESURRECTION BLVD., 2000, Showtime, TV Series

1st Assistant Director, GANGS, 1998, CBS, TV Movie
1st Assistant Director, DR. QUINN MEDICINE WOMAN, 1993, CBS, TV Series
1st Assistant Director, DR. GIGGLES, 1992, Universal, Feature
1st Assistant Director, BAYWATCH, 1989, NBC, TV Series
1st Assistant Director, JUDGEMENT, 1989, Vidmark Entertainment, Feature
1st Assistant Director, THE CHAINSAW MASSACRE II, 1986, MGM, Feature

Sonny Richard E. Espinoza*
Assistant Professor of Chicano Studies
Loyola Marymount University
Los Angeles, CA 90045
Tel 310-313-5259
Fax 310-338-2356
Email ....respinoz@lmu.edu

Producer, RAZA SI, GUERRA NO, 2003, LMU Dept. of Chicana/o Studies, Documentary
Director, BROWN BERETS RETURN TO CATALINA ISLAND, 1996, Brown Beret National Organization, TV
Director, LA RAZA DE UCLA, 1995, UCLA Academic Advancement Program, Short

Stephen Espinoza
Entertainment Attorney
Los Angeles, CA
Tel 310-552-3388
Email ....stephen@zbbfgs.com

Stephen Espinoza
Attorney
CA
Tel 310-552-6506
Email ....stephene@2bbgs.com

Stephen Espinoza

Attorney
Ziffren, Brittenham, Branca, Fischer,
Gilbert-Lurie & Stiffelman LLP
Los Angeles, CA 90067
Tel 310-552-6506
Email....................Stephen@zbbfgs.com

Mario Esquer*

Glendale Community College
Scottsdale, AZ 85253
Tel 480-483-8473
Emailmario.esquer@gcmail.maricopa.edu

Melinda Esquibel*

Mundo Maravilla
Beverly Hills, CA 90213
Tel 323-654-9874
Email ......melinda@mundomaravilla.com

Melinda Esquivel

Black Monkey Suit Prods
Hollywood, CA 90069
Tel 310-235-5838

Cari Esta Albert

Noon Attack
Los Angeles, CA 90035
Tel 310-278-7477
Email....................NoonAttack@aol.com

Executive Producer, LOVE IS STRANGE,
   1999, Lifetime Television, TV Movie
Producer, THE TRUTH ABOUT CATS &
   DOGS, 1996, 20th Century Fox,
   Feature
Executive Producer, HEART AND SOULS,
   1993, MCA/Universal Pictures,
   Feature

Natatcha Estebanez*

Belmont, MA 02478
Tel 617-484-1325
Fax 617-484-2383
Email ....natatcha@aol.com
Web ....bluediner.com

Writer, BLUE DINER, 2002, First Look
   Home Entertainment, Feature
Director, BLUE DINER, 2002, First Look
   Home Entertainment, Feature
Producer, BLUE DINER, 2002, First
   Look Home Entertainment, Feature
Writer, BREAKTHROUGH: THE
   CHANGING FACE OF SCIENCE
   AMERICA, 1996, Black Site Inc.,
   Documentary
Producer, BREAKTHROUGH: THE
   CHANGING FACE OF SCIENCE
   AMERICA, 1996, Black Site Inc.,
   Documentary

John Estrada*

Los Angeles, CA 90018
Tel 818-777-3270
Email ....jfe@estradaproductions.com

Supervising Producer, FRANKENCHOLO
Supervising Producer, SPACE BANDA

Elliott Estrine*

SDSU
Poway, CA 92064
Tel 858-646-4861

James Evans*

Diamond Bar, CA 91765
Tel 888-699-6949
Fax 909-861-8008
Email ....evansactor@aol.com

Errol Falcon

Falcon Film
Miami, FL
Tel 305-442-1318
Email ....falconfilm@aol.com

Producer, LOS TEENS, 2002, Mund Z, TV Series

Daniel Faraldo

ImagenEntertainment
Burbank, CA 91505
Tel 818-845-1424
Fax 818-845-1113
Email............info@imagentertainment.tv
Web ....www.imagentertainment.tv

Writer, HOW DID IT FEEL
Director, HOW DID IT FEEL

Ricardo Favela*

Mexicanos Unidos Por La Defensa del Pueblo
Fallbrook, CA
Tel 760-451-1754
Email ....ricardo@mudp.org

Joao Fernandes

Los Angeles, CA
Tel 323-664-8464
Email ....jferna2501@aol.com

Director of Photography, BETRAYAL, 2003, American World Pictures, Feature
Director of Photography, ONE MAN'S HERO, 1999, MGM - Orion, Feature
Director, WALKER TEXAS RANGER, 1996, CBS, TV Series

Richard Fernandes

Los Angeles, CA
Tel 888-688-9821
Email ....rick@fernandes.net

Producer, THE PET PSYCHIC, 2002, A & R Media Group, TV Series
Director, THE PET PSYCHIC, 2002, A & G Media Group, TV Series
Producer, BOOK OF POOH, 2001, Buena Vista Television, TV Series
Editor, TAINA, 2001, Nickelodeon Networks, TV Series
Director, BETWEEN THE LIONS, 2000, PBS/WBGH-Boston, TV Series
Producer, TAINA, 2000, Nickelodeon, TV Series
Director, BEAR IN THE BIG BLUE HOUSE, 1997, Disney Channel, TV Series
Editor, THE PUZZLE PLACE, 1994, KCET, TV Series

Evelina Fernandez

Sleeping Giant Productions
Los Angeles, CA 90026
Tel 323-667-3390
Fax 323-887-9600
Email............SleepingGiantPro@aol.com
Web ....www.sleepinggiantpro.com

Agent: The Artists Agency, Jimmy Cota, 310-277-7779

Manager: Maggie Roithe, 310-876-1561

Writer, DEMENTIA, 2003, Latino Theatre Company, Stage Play
Writer, LUMINARIAS, 2000, New Latin Pictures, Feature
Producer, LUMINARIAS, 2000, New Latin Pictures, Feature
Writer, PREMEDITATION, 1995, Stage Play

George Fernandez
Professor
Florida State University
Tallahassee, FL 32306
Tel 850-644-3592
Fax 305-626-9711
Email ....gefern@bellS..net

Ilse Fernandez*
Staff
Lion Television
New York, NY 10012
Tel 646-729-8482
Tel 212-533-5592
Email..........................ifnyc@yahoo.com

Producer, PROS/CONS: THE GOOD, THE BAD, & THE UGLY, 2003, BBC, TV Series
THE SEQUOIA PRESIDENTIAL YACHT, 2002, History Channel, Documentary

Luis Fernandez
Plural Entertainment
Miami Beach, FL 33139
Tel 305-538-3100
Fax 305-531-1354
Email ....lfernandez@pluralent.com
Web ....www.pluralent.com

Richard A. Fernandez
Los Angeles, CA

Production Designer, HERE ON EARTH, 2000, Twentieth Century Fox, Feature
Production Designer, US MARSHALS, 1998, Warner Bros., Feature
Production Designer, ALIEN: RESURRECTION, 1997, 20th Century Fox

Ron Fernandez*
Casting Associate
CBS
Santa Monica, CA 90405
Tel 310-428-2126
Email ....treasure88@yahoo.com

Ivonne Fernandez-Jack
Marketing Dept.
Showtime Network
New York, NY 10019
Tel 212-708-7306
Email ivon.fernandez-jack@showtime.net

Jaime Ferrer
Affirmative Action
Screen Actors Guild
Los Angeles, CA 90036
Tel 323-549-6644

Marisa Ferrey
Los Angeles, CA 90025
Tel 310-966-9927
Cell 310-922-6794

2nd 2nd Assistant Director, SURVIVING CHRISTMAS, 2004, Columbia Pictures, Feature
2nd 2nd Assistant Director, DADDY DAY CARE, 2003, Columbia Pictures, Feature
2nd 2nd Assistant Director, AUSTIN POWERS IN GOLDMEMBER, 2002, New Line Cinema, Feature
2nd Assistant Director, SHOWTIME, 2002, Warner Bros., Feature
2nd 2nd Assistant Director, JOY RIDE, 2001, 20th Century Fox, Feature
2nd 2nd Assistant Director, LEGALLY BLONDE, 2001, MGM, Feature
2nd 2nd Assistant Director, IF THESE WALLS COULD TALK 2, 2000, HBO, TV Movie
2nd Assistant Director, RESURRECTION BLVD., 2000, Showtime, TV Series

Drew Figueroa
Moxie Films
New York, NY 10002
Tel 212-982-5008

Edwin Figueroa
Los Angeles, CA
Tel 310-666-5290

Writer
Director

Noemi Figueroa Soulet
Executive Producer
El Pozo Productions
Yonkers, NY 10703
Tel 914-969-0118
Fax 914-969-0118
Email ....prsoldiers@aol.com
Web.........................www.prsoldier.com

Stephanie Fische
Executive Producer
RiverFish Productions
Miami Beach, FL
Cell 305-790-4515
Email ....sfisch@riverfishproductions.com
Web.........www.riverfishproductions.com

Executive Producer, LATIN ACCESS,
    2002, NBC, TV Series
Creator, LATIN ACCESS, 2002, NBC, TV
    Series
Executive Producer, NEW YORK
    MAGAZINE AWARDS SHOW, 2001,
    NBC, TV Special
Executive Producer, PUERTO RICAN DAY
    PARADE, 2000, NBC, TV Special

Albert Flores*
VP, Marketing
Diverse Media
Boerne, TX 78006
Tel 210-364-2684
Fax 830-981-4667
Email ....aflores1@satx.rr.com

Alex Flores*
Albuquerque, NM 87196
Email ....lxflores@earthlink.net

Alicia Flores*
S. El Monte, CA 90733
Tel 626-374-3619
Email ....a_flores79@yahoo.com

Camera Operator, LATV LIVE, 2003,
    LATV, TV
Line Producer, MEX 2 THE MAX, 2003,
    LATV, TV
Camera Assistant, KING OF THE MOON,
    2002, Short
Camera Assistant, PACO'S SUITCASE
    BOMB, 2002, Short

Benny Flores*
Benny Flores Creations
San Antonio, TX 78247
Tel 210-325-6724
Email ....bennyflorez@yahoo.com
Web.........................www.whatsuptv.com

Producer, WHATSUP TEXAS!, 2003,
    PBS, TV
Producer, MAXIMUM OUTDOORS,
    2002, La Familia , international and
    national network, TV
Camera Operator, MAXIMUM
    OUTDOORS, 2002, La Familia
    Network, TV
Producer, THE EDGE, 1998, CTSA
    Television, TV
Camera Operator, THE EDGE, 1998,
    CTSA, TV

Claudia Flores*

Director of Operations
National Hispanic Media Coalition
Downey, CA 90242
Tel 213-746-6988
Email ....shadow021@yahoo.com
Web.................................www.nhmc.org

Consuelo Flores

Diversity Department
Writers Guild of America
Los Angeles, CA 90048
Tel 323-782-4589
Fax 323-782-4807

Nubia Flores

Slamdance
Los Angeles, CA 90038
Tel 323-466-1786
Email ....nubia@slamdance.com

Tom Flores

West Covina, CA 91791
Tel 818-259-6989
Email ....flores626@hotmail.com

Producer

Lorena Flores Chatterjee*

San Carlos, CA 94070
Tel 650-631-0000
Email.........lorenachatterjee@yahoo.com

Roberto Fonseca*

Seca Films
Los Angeles, CA 90026
Tel 213-484-6141
Email ....secafilms@hotmail.com

Victoria Fraasa*

Miramar, FL
Tel 954-963-6321
Fax 954-962-9110
Email....................filmservices@aol.com
Web ....www.FilmProductionServices.com

Production Facilities & Services

Cris Franco

Cris Franco Entertainment (CFE)
Sherman Oaks, CA 91411-4060
Tel 818-642-0935
Email ....me@crisfranco.com
Web ....www.crisfranco.com

Producer, CAFÉ CALIFORNIA CLASSICS
Producer, THE CRIS FRANCO SHOW

Germaine Franco

Staff
Independently Thinking Music
Los Angeles, CA 90034
Tel 310-836-8499
Cell 310-985-8423
Email.......germainefranco@hotmail.com

Composer, CROSSINGS, 2003, Loyola
    Marymount University, Short
Production Assistant, GIGLI, 2003,
    Sony
Production Assistant, THE ITALIAN JOB,
    2003, Paramount, Feature
Composer, REVELACCIONES, 1996,
    Cornell University, Documentary
Composer, LA CARPA, 1992, American
    Playhouse Theatre, TV Movie

William Franco*

Speckled Gekko Productions
Glendale, CA 91206
Tel 818-240-7416
Email.................spgekko@earthlink.net

Sound

Danielle Frankl*
Los Angeles, CA 90034
Tel 310-244-3358
Email ....dfrankl@attbi.com

Rami Frankl*
DVD Producer
Hoboken Entertainment, Inc.
Los Angeles, CA 90066
Tel 310-979-0010
Email.................rami@hobokenent.com

Production Facilities & Services

John Carlos Frey*
Gatekeeper Productions
Los Angeles, CA 90069
Tel 323-656-1355
Fax 323-656-1619
Email ....Gatekeeperfilm@aol.com

Director, GATEKEEPER , 2002, Feature
Writer, GATEKEEPER, 2002, Feature

Efrain Fuentes
VP, Diversity
Walt Disney Studios
Burbank, CA 91521
Tel 818-560-1000
Email ....efrain.fuentes@disney.com

Lillian Fuentes
Tel 818-368-8080
Fax 818-368-7010
Email ....lillijo7010@aol.com

Associate Director, OSCARS 1999,
   1999, NBC, Awards Show
Associate Director, OSCARS 1998,
   1998, NBC, Awards Show

Reinardo Funez
Eyekunstler
Santa Fe Springs, CA 90670
Tel 909 961 1524
Cell 909-961-1524
Email ....rei@taosinternetcafe.com
Web ....eyekunstler.com

Art Department

Donna Gaba
Agent
David Shapira & Associates
Encino, CA 91436
Tel 818-906-0322
Fax 818-783-2562

Nino Gabaldon*
Mexikan Films
Los Angeles, CA 90004
Tel 323-855-4416
Cell 323-856-8677
Fax 818-954-9942
Email ....mknfilms@earthlink.net

Actor, AMERICAN LION

Evy Ledesma Galán*
Festival Director
Cinesol
Austin, TX 78746
Tel 512-327-1333
Email ....info@galaninc.com
Web ....www.galaninc.com

Hector Galán*

Galán Productions, Inc.
Austin, TX 78746
Tel 512-327-1333
Fax 512-327-1547
Email ....galan@galaninc.com
Web ....www.galaninc.com

Executive Producer, VISIONES:LATINO
ART & CULTURE, 2004, PBS,
Documentary
Producer, ACCORDION DREAMS, 2001,
PBS, Documentary
Producer, THE FORGOTTEN
AMERICANS, 2000, PBS,
Documentary
Producer, CHICANO! THE HISTORY OF
THE MEXICAN/AMERICAN CIVIL
RIGHTS MOVEMENT, 1996, PBS,
Documentary
Producer, AMERICAN EXPERIENCE,
1993, PBS
Producer, FRONTLINE (VARIOUS),
1982-1994, PBS, Documentary

Kathryn F. Galán*

Executive Director
NALIP
Santa Monica, CA 90406
Tel 310-457-4445
Fax 310-589-9997
Email.....................nalip_kfg@msn.com
Web ....www.nalip.org

Executive Producer, EARLY BIRD
SPECIAL, 2001, Early Bird Special
LLC, Feature
Producer, FRENCH KISS, 1995,
Twentieth Century Fox, Feature
Producer, SQUANTO, 1994, Walt Disney
Company, Feature
Executive Producer, BECOMING
COLETTE, 1992, CANAL+, Feature
Executive Producer, DAYBREAK, 1992,
HBO, Feature

Nely Galán

President-CEO
Galán Entertainment
Venice, CA 90291
Tel 310-823-2822
Fax 310-823-7361
Email ....ngalan@galanent.com
Web ....www.galanent.com

Agent: William Morris Agency,
310-859-4000

Producer, LA CENICIENTA, 2003,
Telemundo Network, TV Series
Producer, VIVA VEGAS, 2000,
Telemundo Network, TV Series
Producer, LOS BELTRAN, 1999,
Telemundo Network, TV Series

Ricardo Gale

Shades of Grey
Miami, FL 33186
Tel 305-233-8611
Tel 305-310-9777
Fax 305-310-9777
Email ....ricardogale@yahoo.com

Production Manager

Felipe Galindo*

FEGGO
New York, NY 10025
Tel 212-864-6648
Fax 212-316-1645
Email ....feggo@mail.com

Dennis Gallegos

Tepper Gallegos Casting
Los Angeles, CA 90004
Tel 323-469-3577
Fax 323-469-3577

Casting Director, THE GLASS JAR,
1999, Sterling Pacific Films, Feature
Casting Director, TEAM KNIGHT RIDER,
1997, Universal, TV
Casting Director, TWO BITS & PEPPER,
1995, PM Entertainment, Feature

Philip J. Gallegos
Studio City, CA 91604
Tel 818-769-8180
Tel 415-648-5390
Email ....jukeboxphd@aol.com

2nd Assistant Director, TIME OF YOUR LIFE, 1999, 20th Century Fox, TV Series
2nd Assistant Director, ALMOST HEROES, 1998, Warner Bros., Feature
2nd Assistant Director, WILD SIDE, 1995, Evergreen Video, Feature
2nd Assistant Director, WEDLOCK / DEADLOCK ??, 1991, HBO, TV Movie
2nd Assistant Director, DEEP SPACE 9, 1987, TWE Home Video, TV Series
2nd Assistant Director, KNOTS LANDING, CBS, TV Series

Denise Galvao*
San Diego, CA
Tel 858-581-9318
Email ....dedelna@hotmail.com

Alegria Garcia*
San Antonio, TX 78249
Tel 210-493-5460
Email ....cuerazola@hotmail.com

Alejandro Garcia
Telemundo
Hialeah, FL 33010
Tel 305-884-8200
Web ....www.telemundo.com

Alexis Garcia*
Attorney
O'Melveny & Myers LLP
Los Angeles, CA 90067
Tel 310-246-6861
Fax 310-246-6779
Email ....AGarcia@omm.com

Alexis Garcia
Attorney
O'Melveny & Myers LLP
Los Angeles, CA 90067
Tel 310-592-8859
Fax 310-246-6779
Email.....................acargica@omm.com

Ana Maria Garcia
Bayamon, PR
Tel 787-731-7237
Email ....anamaria@yunque.net

Producer, LA OPERACIÓN, 1982, Cinema Guild, Documentary

Andy Garcia
CineSon
Sherman Oaks, CA 91423
Tel 818-501-8246
Tel 818-501-3647
Web ....www.cineson.com

Agent: Paradigm, Clifford Stevens, 212-703-7540

Actor, OCEAN'S TWELVE, 2004, Warner Bros., Feature
Actor, THE LAZARUS CHILD, 2004, Warner Bros., Feature
Producer, THE LOST CITY, 2004, Platinum Equity, Feature
Actor, THE LOST CITY, 2004, Platinum Equity, Feature
Producer, THE MAN FROM THE ELYSIAN FIELDS, 2001, Samuel Goldwyn Films, Feature
Executive Producer, THE TIES THAT BIND, 2001, Universal Studios Home Video, Feature
Producer, THE UNSAID, 2001, Universal Studios Home Video, Feature
Executive Producer, THE ARTURO SANDOVAL STORY, 2000, HBO, Feature
Executive Producer, SWING BOAT, 1999, ABC, TV Movie

Eddie Garcia
Email ....eddman22@aol.com

Producer, SHATTERED, 2002, Feature

Elena Maria Garcia*
Hot Mama Productions
Plantation, FL 33317
Tel 954-327-9159
Email..................imajin@ix.netcom.com

Erick Garcia*
Office Manager
Maya Pictures
Los Angeles, CA
Tel 310-281-3770
Fax 310-281-3777
Email ....erickgarcia@hotmail.com
Web ....www.maya-pictures.com

Jesus Garcia*
Austin, TX 78702
Fax 512-478-9438
Email ....jesu52@yahoo.com

Jose Jesus JJ Garcia*
Bellaire, TX 77402
Tel 713-774-1292
Email ....hollywoodtexas@aol.com

Josie Garcia*
Los Angeles, CA 90015
Tel 213-368-8832
Email..........................josiemg@aol.com

Producer

Julissa Garcia
Agent
William Morris Agency
Beverly Hills, CA 90212
Tel 310-859-4000

Lino Garcia
General Manager
ESPN Deportes
San Jose, CA 95127
Tel 212-916-9200
Email ....taraiza@hotmail.com

Mike Garcia
Director of Drama Development
HBO Original Programming
Los Angeles, CA 90067
Tel 310-201-9300
Web ....www.hbo.com

Oswaldo Garcia*
Pasadena, CA 91106
Email ....ogarcia@eiconline.org

Rodrigo Garcia
La Banda Films
Beverly Hills, CA 90210
Tel 310-858-7203

*Agent: Endeavor, Adriana Alberghetti,
310-248-2000*

Director, FATHERS AND SONS, 2004,
Feature
Director, CARNIVALE, 2003, HBO, TV
Series
Director, TEN TINY LOVE STORIES,
2001, Lios Gate Films Home
Entertainment, Feature
Director of Photography, BODY SHOTS,
1999, New Line Cinema, Feature
Director of Photography, GIA, 1998,
HBO, TV Movie
Director of Photography, FOUR ROOMS
"THE MISSING INGREDIENT", 1995,
Miramax, Feature
Director of Photography, INDICTMENT:
THE MCMARTIN TRIAL, 1995,
Mediacs AG, TV Movie
Director of Photography, MI VIDA LOCA,
1994, Sony Pictures Classics, Feature
Director of Photography, EL VERANO DE
LA SENORA FORBES, 1988, Radio
Television Espanola (RTVE), TV Movie

Romualdo Garcia*
San Antonio, TX 78221
Tel 210-846-3447
Fax 210-222-6040
Email ....gartpro@swbell.net

Victor Garcia*
Los Angeles, CA 90036
Tel 818-560-1681
Email ....victoreligarcia@yahoo.com

Producer, EROSION, 2003, Dark Lantern
  Entertainment, Feature
Producer, THE LEGEND OF DIABLO,
  2003, Spartan Entertainment ,
  Feature
Producer, TEA WITH GRANDMA, 2002,
  Short
Producer, GIANT ROBO EPISODE II,
  Manga Entertainment
Producer, THE BOY IN THE BOX, Short

William Garcia*
Pembroke Pines, FL 33024
Tel 954-437-6886
Cell 305-582-1122
Email ....dp4261@aol.com
Web ....www.movingpic.com/camera.html

Director of Photography, AREA 305
  "DONDE ESTARA", 2003, Univision
  Records, Music Video
Director, LENNY KRAVITZ, 2003, Virgin
  Records, EPK
Director, OBIE "ANTE", 2003, Emi
  Latin, Music Video
Director of Photography, RED BIRD,
  2003, Andromeda Productions, Short
Director, THE SOLDIER, 2003, Film
  Festival, Short
Director of Photography, MICHAEL
  JACKSON, 2002, Epic Records,
  Documentary

Georgina Garcia Riedel*
Loosely Based Pictures, LLC
Silverlake, CA 90026
Tel 323-953-9635
Email ....griedel@hotmail.com

Director, HOW THE GARCIA GIRLS
  SPENT THEIR SUMMER, 2004,
  Loosely Based Pictures, LLC, Feature
Writer, HOW THE GARCIA GIRLS
  SPENT THEIR SUMMER, 2004,
  Loosely Based Pictures, LLC, Feature

Carolina Garcia-Aguilera
Miami Beach, FL
Tel 305-695-1060
Tel 305-695-0640
Email ....4cubans@bellsouth.net

Novelist, LUPE SOLANO SERIES

Diego Garcia-Moreno
Lamaraca Productions
Boston, MA 02134
Tel 473-772-7808

Anne Garcia-Romero*
Santa Monica, CA 90405
Tel 310-314-1633
Email ....agaro@aol.com

Manager: Marilyn Atlas Management,
310-278-5047

Writer, DESERT LONGING OR LAS
  AVENTURERAS, 2002, South Coast
  Repertory, Stage Play
Writer, SANTA CONCEPCION, 1998,
  NYSF/Public Theater, Stage Play

filmmakers

Irma Garcia-Sinclair*

SYNGARNICITY
Alameda, CA 94501
Tel 510 864-3221
Fax 510-864-3222
Email ....newagecurandera@earthlink.net

Agent: SYNGARNICITY, 510-864-3221

ADR Looping, CARNIVALE, 2003, HBO,
   TV Series
Actor, FIDEL, 2002, Showtime, Feature
Dialect Coach, ALL THE PRETTY
   HORSES, 2001, MCA/Universal,
   Feature
ADR Looping, MASK OF ZORRO, 2001,
   MCA/Universal, Feature
Dialect Coach, 1997, 20th Century Fox,
   Feature
ADR Looping, DANCES WITH WOLVES,
   1992, Warner Bros., Feature
Actor, JURY OF ONE, 1992, ABC, TV
   Series
Actor, AMERICAN ME, 1991,
   MCA/Universal/Warner Bros., Feature
Dialect Coach, THE BIG FIX, 1978,
   MGM, Feature

Belinda Gardea

Los Angeles, CA
Tel 323-896-2353
Email ....bgardea@aol.com

Casting Director, HOW THE GARCIA
   GIRLS SPENT THEIR SUMMER,
   2004, Loosely Based Pictures, LLC,
   Feature
Casting Director, QUALITY OF LIFE,
   2004, Quality of Film LLC, Feature
Casting Director, LIVING THE LIFE,
   2000, Richs Productions, Feature
Casting Director, STAR MAPS, 1997,
   20th Century Fox, Feature

Lisa Garibay*

Los Angeles, CA 90027
Tel 213-840-3517
Fax 310-453-5258
Email ....lyg@thenitmustbetrue.com
Web ....www.thenitmustbetrue.com

*Agent: ICM, Eddie Borgas,
310-550-4000*

Writer, Feature

Marcy Garriot

La Sonrisa Productions, Inc.
Email ....info@sonrisa.com

Producer, SPLIT DECISION, 2001, First
   Run Features, Documentary

Eddie Garza*

Dinuba, CA 93618
Tel 559-591-3446
Email...............erasmo19@hotmail.com

Juan Garza

Together Brothers Production
Los Angeles, CA 90042
Tel 323-478-9505
Fax 323-478-9505
Email.............juancarlosgarza@usa.com

Editor, SOUL FOOD, 2003, Showtime,
   TV Series
Director, NEVER TRUST A SERIAL
   KILLER, 2002, Feature
Editor, RESURRECTION BLVD., 2000,
   Showtime, TV Series
Editor, THE PRINCESS AND THE
   BARRIO BOY, 2000, Showtime, TV
   Movie
Editor, NY UNDERCOVER, 1996, Fox
   Television, TV Series
Editor, SWIFT JUSTICE, 1996, TV
   Series
Director, REYES Y REY, 1995,
   Telemundo Network, TV Series

Mario Garza*

San Marcos, TX 78666
Tel 512-974-9778
Email ....Mario.Garza@ci.austin.tx.us

Ani Gasti

HBO
New York, NY 10036
Tel 212-512-1000

Michael Gavino*

Michael Gavino Productions
Lighthouse Point, FL 33064
Tel 954-941-1334
Cell 754-235-4170
Fax 954-941-1334
Email...............meangavine@yahoo.com

Agent: Stellar Talent Agency, Cindy
Freed, 305-672-2217,
stlrtalent@aol.com

Actor, 4 FAMILY, 2003, Genuine Studio,
   Feature
Writer, BOYS VERSUS THE STAR, 2003,
   Short
Actor, MURDER BY THE BOOK, 2003,
   MIU, Short
Actor, THE FOUR HORSEMEN, 2003,
   Meridian Entertainment, Feature
Writer, HOMER'S HOT AIR, 2002, TV
   Series
Producer, THE ENCOUNTER, 2002,
   Short
Writer, ADIOS, 2000, Stage Play

Digna Gerena*

Boston, MA 02128
Tel 617-653-2389
Fax 617-353-3611
Email ....digna262@nalip.info

Executive Producer, BOSTON LATINO,
   2003, Boston Neighborhood Network
   TV, TV Special
Media Advocate, CONTRIBUTOR, 2003,
   Candela Magazine, Website
Media Advocate, THE LATINO FILM
   CONSORTIUM, 2003, Strand Theatre
   Boston, Film Series

Mauricio Gerson

Telemundo
Hialeah, FL 33010
Tel 305-884-8200
Fax 202-296-7908
Web ....www.telemundo.com

Marta Gibbons*

WNET/Thirteen
New York, NY
Tel 212-560-2972
Email ....gibbons@thirteen.org

Monica Gil

Community Relations Executive
Telemundo
Glendale, CA 91201
Tel 818-502-5700
Email.......................v4m@hotmail.com

Luna Gilbert*

Santa Barbara, CA 93101
Tel 805-680-6360

filmmakers

Guido Giordano
Agent
International Creative Management
Beverly Hills, CA 90211
Tel 310-550-4000
Email ....ggiordano@icmtalent.com
Web ....www.icmagency.com

Michela Giorelli
Supervising Producer
Discovery Networks Latin America/Iberia
Miami, FL 33126
Tel 305-507-1700
Email ....michela_giorelli@discovery.com

Jeff Gipson*
Cine las Americas
Austin, TX 78767
Tel 512-841-5930
Email ....jeff@cinelasamericas.org
Web ....www.cinelasamericas.org

Sergio Giral
Giral Media
Bay Harbor Island, FL 33154
Tel 305-864-8567
Email....................giralmedia@aol.com

Polita Glynn*
Tropicultura Productions
Surfside, FL 33154
Tel 305-868-0100
Fax 305-868-5010
Email....................polita@the-beach.net

Producer, DRUM OF TIME, 2000, Short
Producer, BISCAYNE NATIONAL PARK:
  LEGACY OF ENVIRONMENTAL
  PIONEERS, 1997, PBS, Documentary

Vanessa Gocksch
Miami Lakes, FL 33014
Tel 305-556-1250
Email ....intermundos@yahoo.com

Director, Documentary

Alix Gomez
Manager
San Juan, PR
Tel 787-765-2266

Angel Gomez
Los Angeles, CA 90068
Tel 323-481-5044
Email..............angelgomez@earhlink.net

Director, UN HOGAR COMO TODOS

Devora Gomez*
Dar Luz Films
Bellflower, CA 90706
Tel 562-804-4516
Fax 562-804-4573
Email ....dandevmole@aol.com

Eduardo Gomez*
Aztec NW Media
Tukwila, WA 98188
Tel 206-243-5941
Email ....egomez@aztecnw.com

Greg Gomez*
Creative Development
Maya Pictures
Los Angeles, CA 90004
Tel 310-281-3770
Fax 310-281-3777
Email.........................goretti@azteca.net
Web ....www.maya-pictures.com

Producer, THE WEDDING, 2004

Marisol Gomez*
E. Elmhurst, NY 11370
Email ....marisolgomez@earthlink.net

Mike Gomez
Los Angeles, CA 90004
Tel 626-443-1837

Agent: Zanuck, Passon & Pace,
818-783-4890

Actor, LUMINARIAS, 2000, New Latin
 Pictures, Feature
Actor, THE BIG LEBOWSKI, 1998,
 Gramercy Pictures, Feature
Actor, THE MILAGRO BEANFIRLD WAR,
 1988, Universal Pictures, Feature
Actor, EL NORTE, 1984, Atisan
 Entertainment, Feature

Patricia Gomez
WMVS
Milwaukee, WI 53233
Tel 414-271-1036

Yvonne Gomez
Label Manager
Surco Records
Los Angeles, CA 90038
Tel 323-661-7289
Email ....yvonne@surconet.com

Lorena Gomez-Barris*
Oakland, CA 94609
Tel 510-601-9335
Email ....lologb@hotmail.com

Antonio Gomez-Orodea
Discovery Networks
New York, NY 10028
Tel 786-273-4571
Email ....
antonio_gome_ordea@discovery.com

Diana E. Gonzales
Staff
E! Entertainment
Los Angeles, CA 90066
Tel 310-709-6783
Email ....dgonzales@eentertainment.com

Production Facilities & Services,
 ACADEMY AWARDS 2003, 2003, E!
 Entertainment, TV Episode
Producer, E! COMPANY MEETING,
 2003, E! Entertainment
Production Facilities & Services,
 GOLDEN GLOBES, 2003, E!
 Entertainment, TV Episode
Producer, COMCAST MEETING, E!
 Entertainment

Vincent George Gonzales
Burbank, CA
Tel 310-497-7793

2nd Assistant Director, MELVIN GOES
 TO DINNER, 2003, Sundance
 Channel, Feature
2nd Assistant Director, PEARL
 HARBOR, 2001, Buena Vista
 International, Feature
2nd Assistant Director, RUSTIN, 2001,
 Vanguard Cinema, Feature
2nd Assistant Director, SIX FEET
 UNDER, 2001, HBO, TV Series
2nd Assistant Director, THE MYSTIC
 MASSEUR, 2001, Columbia TriStar
 Home Entertainment, Feature
2nd Assistant Director, THE KID, 2000,
 Buena Vista, Feature
1st Assistant Director, A NIGHT AT
 SOPHIE'S, 1999, Grange Hall
 Productions, Feature

A.P. Gonzalez
Los Angeles, CA 90068
Tel 323-957-1936
Fax 323-957-1938

Director, SILENT CRISIS:DIABETES
  AMONG US, 2002, Discovery Health,
  Documentary
Director, FOTO NOVELAS: MANGAS,
  1997, ITVS, TV Series
Director, TOGETHER AGAINST ABUSE,
  1990, PBS, Documentary

Carolina Gonzalez*
Daily News
Brooklyn, NY 11238
Tel 212-210-2205
Fax 212-643-7828
Email...................cgonza@earthlink.net

David Gonzalez*
Wildman Productions
Palm City, FL
Tel 954-427-2522
Tel 772-288-4381
Fax 954-427-3233
Email.....................gonzalezdj@aol.com

Director of Photography, FOR THE
  RECORD, GUAM IN WWII, 2004,
  ITVS, Documentary
Director of Photography, LOUIE: A
  SERIOUS COMEDY, 2004, Feature
Director of Photography, THE STATE OF
  THE TERRITORY: US-PUERTO RICO
  RELATIONS AT THE CROSSROADS,
  2004, Polymorphous Pictures,
  Documentary

Elizabeth Gonzalez
Burbank, CA 91504
Tel 818-618-7533
Email ....liz200go@hotmail.com

Gabriel Gonzalez
Los Angeles, CA 90004
Tel 310-673-9065
Email.....................bikabur@yahoo.com

Hector Gonzalez
Executive Producer
PBS KUAT-TV
Tucson, AZ 85721
Tel 520-621-7368
Fax 520-621-3360
Email ....gonzalez@u.arizona.edu
Web................................www.kuat.org

Producer, REFLEXIONES, 2003, PBS
  KUAT-TV, TV Series
Producer, ARIZONA ILLUSTRATED ,
  1980-2003, PBS KUAT-TV, TV Series

Janet Gonzalez*
San Antonio, TX 78232
Email ....janetmg@directvinternet.com

Jesus Gonzalez
ZRecordz/Sony Discos
Los Angeles, CA 90015
Tel 310-714-3050
Email ....malverde@malverde.com

Attorney: James Blancarte,
310-788-2760

Joseph Julian Gonzalez
Bakersfield, CA 93311
Tel 661-665-2226
Fax 661-665-2226
Email ....Jjgonzalez@earthlink.net

Composer, RESURRECTION BLVD.,
  2002, Showtime, TV Series
Composer, PRICE OF GLORY, 2000,
  New Line Cinema, Feature
Composer, CURDLED, 1996, Miramax,
  Feature

Lisa Gonzalez*
Urban Latino
N. Bergen, NJ 07046
Tel 201-453-0694
Fax 201-869-7548
Email ....writebeat@aol.com

Marybel Gonzalez*
Los Angeles, CA 90011
Tel 213-749-8231
Fax 310-281-3777
Email ......gonzalexmarybel@hotmail.com

Meredith Gonzalez*
San Antonio, TX 78202
Email ....NinoPeter@aol.com

Omar Gonzalez
Calo Cine
Los Angeles, CA 90048
Tel 213-204-0782
Email ....cineloco@yahoo.com

Writer, EN LA DULCE SENSACION DE
   UN BESO MORDELON, 1994, Short
Educator

Peter Gonzalez*
San Antonio, TX 78202
Email ....ninopeter@cs.com

Rosa Gonzalez
Culver City, CA
Tel 310-559-3928
Email...............prrosagonzalez@aol.com

Line Producer, ASTHMA: FIGHTING TO
   BREATHE, 2003, Discovery Health,
   Documentary
1st Assistant Director, BUBBA HO-TEP,
   2003, Vitagraph Films, LLC, Feature
Line Producer, SILENT CRISIS:
   DIABETES AMONG US, 2002,
   Discovery Health, Documentary

Production Manager, PHANTASM IV:
   OBLIVION, 1998, Orion Home Video,
   Feature
Production Manager, OUT 2 LUNCH,
   1988, King's Road, Feature

Sonia Gonzalez*
Los Angeles, CA 90026
Tel 213-250-3889
Email ....lasone189@aol.com

Director, BRAGGING RIGHTS, 2004,
   Documentary
Editor, NUYORICANS, 2002,
   PBS/Glazen Creative, Documentary
Writer, BODEGA DREAMS, 2000, Fox
   Searchlight, Feature
Director, DEBUTANTE, 2000, Short
Editor, EL CIRCULO VICIOSO, 1998,
   Ground Zero Entertainment, Feature
   Film
Editor, Assistant, THE DEVIL'S OWN,
   1997, Columbia Pictures, Feature
Editor, DESTINATION UNKNOWN,
   1996, Ground Zero Entertainment,
   Feature Film
Editor, Assistant, MALCOLM X, 1992,
   Warner Bros., Feature

Victor Gonzalez
West Covina, CA
Tel 626-858-9013
Email..............vgonzalez3@earthlink.net

Producer, VIVIR INTENTANDO, 2003,
   Buena Vista International, Feature
Director, CIUDAD DE DIOS, 1999,
   Feature

Alejandro Gonzalez Iñarritu

21 Films
Los Angeles, CA 90232
Tel 310-838-4036
Fax 310-838-3823
Email ....backshopla@aol.com

Agent: Endeavor, John Lesher,
310-248-2000

Director, 21 GRAMS, 2003, Focus
Features, Feature
Director, AMORES PERROS, 2000,
Lions Gate Films, Feature
Writer, AMORES PERROS, 2000, Lions
Gate Films, Feature

Jackie Gonzalez-Carlos*

GonCa Entertainment Productions
Culver City, CA 90232
Tel 310-309-0901
Email ....GonCaProductions@Mail.com

Producer, 2FAST 2FURIOUS VOD, 2003,
Universal/Def Jam Recordings
Producer, 8 MILE VOD, 2003,
Universal/Aftermath/Shady Records,
DVD
Executive Producer, INNER HEART,
2003, GonCa Entertainment
Productions, Documentary
Director, INNER HEART, 2003, GonCa
Entertainment Productions,
Documentary
Executive Producer, MORNING SHOW,
2003, GonCa Entertainment
Productions, Documentary
Director, MORNING SHOW (IN
PROGRESS), 2003, GonCa
Entertainment Productions,
Documentary
Producer, WINDTALKERS DVD SPECIAL
FEATURES, 2002, MGM, DVD
Executive Producer, THE COMPLAINER,
2001, GonCa Entertainment
Productions, TV Series
Director, UNITED WE STAND, 2001,
GonCa Entertainment Productions,
PSA

Maria Gonzalez-Palmier*

TexMex Tales, LLC
Los Angeles, CA 90068
Tel 323-969-1499
Fax 323-962-1377
Email ....whitelikethemoon@aol.com
Web ....www.whitelikethemoon.com

Actor, THREAT MATRIX, 2003, TV
Special
Director, WHITE LIKE THE MOON,
2002, AFI, Short
Writer, WHITE LIKE THE MOON, 2002,
AFI, Short

Roberto F. Gonzalez-Rubio

Pasadena, CA 91103
Tel 626-791-6880
Cell 818-406-3095
Fax 626-791-7996

2nd Assistant Director, ALMOST A
WOMAN, 2001, PBS, TV Movie
2nd Assistant Director, RESURRECTION
BLVD., 2001, Showtime, TV Series
2nd Assistant Director, PRISON LIFE,
2000, Incarcerated Entertainment
Productions, Short
2nd 2nd Assistant Director,
RESURRECTION BLVD., 2000,
Showtime, TV Series
2nd Assistant Director, THE BROTHERS
GARCIA, 2000, Nickelodeon, TV
Series
2nd 2nd Assistant Director, DON'T DO
IT, 1994, Triboro Entertainment
Group, Feature

Veronica Gonzalez-Rubio

Simi Valley, CA
Tel 818-548-5877

1st Assistant Director, EVERYBODY
LOVES RAYMOND, 1999, CBS, TV
Series
1st Assistant Director, KATIE JOPLIN,
1999, Warner Bros., TV Series
2nd Assistant Director, HOPE &
GLORIA, 1996, NBC, TV Series

2nd Assistant Director, NAKED GUN 2 1/2, 1991, Paramount Pictures, Feature

2nd Assistant Director, THE LUCKY DAY, 1991, CBS, TV Movie

2nd Assistant Director, THE ABYSS, 1989, 20th Century Fox, Feature

Maureen Gosling*

Intrepidas Productions
Oakland, CA 94609
Tel 510-595-7926
Email ....mgosling@igc.org
Web...............www.maureengosling.com

Producer, CHULAS FRONTERAS / DEL MERO CORAZON, 2003, Arhoolte Records, Feature

Editor, A DREAM IN HANOI, 2002, Moira Productions, Feature

Director, BLOSSOMS OF FIRE, 2000, Intrepidas Production, Feature

Editor, BOYS WILL BE MAN, 2000, Moira Productions, Feature

Director, A SKIRT FULL OF BUTTERFLIES, 1993, Intrepidas Production, Short

Editor, BURDEN OF DREAMS, 1982, Flower Films, Feature

Alan Grazioso

Chicago, IL 60623
Tel 781-306-1892
Email............alan@graziosopictures.com

Erika Grediaga*

Los Angeles, CA 90004
Tel 323-856-9253
Fax 323-856-9253
Email ....egrediaga@hotmail.com

Director, CLOISTERS, 2003, AFI, Short
Writer, CLOISTERS, 2003, AFI, Short

Evangeline Griego*

About Time Productions
Los Angeles, CA 90041
Tel 323-982-1635
Fax 323-221-4825
Email.....................abouttyme@aol.com

Producer, ROSA'S BOYS, 2004, Documentary

Director, BORDER VISIONS/VISIONES FRONTERIZOS, 2003, PBS, Documentary

Producer, BORDER VISIONS/VISIONES FRONTERIZOS, 2003, PBS, Documentary

Director, PAÑO ARTE: IMAGES FROM INSIDE, 1997, PBS, Documentary

Producer, PAÑO ARTE: IMAGES FROM INSIDE, 1997, PBS, Documentary

Javier Grillo Marxuach

Los Angeles, CA 90048
Tel 323-782-4548

Agent: Broder • Webb • Chervin • Silbermann Agency, Chris Silberman, 310-281-3400

Writer, JAKE 2.0, 2003, UPN, TV Series

Producer, JAKE 2.1, 2003, UPN, TV Series

Writer, BOOMTOWN, 2002, NBC, TV Series

Producer, BOOMTOWN, 2002, UPN, TV Series

Writer, THE DEAD ZONE, 2002, UPN and SciFi Channel, TV Series

Writer, LAW AND ORDER, 2001, NBC, TV Series

Producer, THE CRONICLE, 2001, The Sci-Fi Channel, TV Series

Writer, CHARMED, 1998, Warner Bros. Network, TV Series

Writer, THREE, 1997, TV Series

filmmakers

Junior Guapo*

Impresario Enterprises, LLC
Los Angeles, CA 90007
Tel 323-414-2295
Email ....jguapo@onebox.com

Producer, PEPSI, AMERICAN EAGLE
CLOTHING, 2003, Paradigm
Independent, Commercial
Executive Producer, SCOUT, 2003,
MGM, Feature-Animation
Producer, SCOUT, 2002, MGM, Feature
Producer, TRAUCO'S DAUGHTER, 2002,
Short

Eddie Guerra

Los Angeles, CA
Tel 323-933-1201
Agent: CAA, Peter Micelli,
310-288-4545

Writer, CSI MIAMI, 2002-2003, Buena
Vista Television, TV series

Jay Guerra

San Pedro, CA
Tel 310-548-5026
Fax 310-548-0432
Email ....jayguerra@earthlink.net

2nd Assistant Director, DRAGNET, 2003,
ABC, TV Series
1st Assistant Director, RECYCLING SLO,
2003, AFI, Feature
1st Assistant Director, CRAZY
BEAUTIFUL, 2001, Buena Vista
Pictures, Feature
2nd Assistant Director, MURDER IN
SMALL TOWN X, 2001, Fox Network,
TV Series
2nd Assistant Director, STOLEN FROM
THE HEART, 2000, CBS, TV Movie
1st Assistant Director, THE ROCK,
Hollywood Pictures, Feature

Lucas Guerra

Principal, Creative Director
ARGUS
Boston, MA 02210
Tel........................617-423-0822 x205
Fax 617-423-2181
Web ....www.thinkargus.com

Luis Guerra*

Austin, TX 78704
Tel 512-443-0587

Sergio Guerra*

Chicano/Latino Film Club
Los Angeles, CA 90065
Tel 323-254-4954
Email ....sergio_j_g@yahoo.com

Victor Guerra*

Austin, TX 78704
Tel 512-443-0587

Dan Guerrero

Los Angeles, CA 90036
Tel 323-822-1278
Email ....dan@daguerrero.com

Manager: Mark Sendroff,
2112-840-6400

Writer, GOLDEN EAGLE AWARDS,
2003, Award Shows
Writer, ALMA AWARDS, 2002, Award
Shows
Producer, AL DIA CON MARIA
CONCHITA, 1998, Telemundo
Network

Luis Guerrero

Executive Assistant
Maya Pictures
Los Angeles, CA 90038
Tel 310-281-3770
Fax 310-281-3777
Web ....www.maya-pictures.com

Sergio Guerrero
Indieye Productions
Los Angeles, CA 90042
Tel 310-444-9909
Email ....sergiogg@earthlink.net

Writer, A DAY WITHOUT A MEXICAN, 2004, Alta Vista, Feature

Adrian Guillen*
Poetic Pictures
Palmdale, CA 93550
Tel 661-305-5807
Fax 661-947-3743
Email ....poeticpictures01@aol.com

Producer, HOMIES GRAVEYARD SHIFT, 2003, Belle Vista Pictures, Feature
Producer, ROUND TWO, 2003, Feature

Inez Guillen*
Image Group Post, LLC
New York, NY 10025
Tel 212-316-0567
Email...............tainaqt71@earthlink.net

HOW BIG IS IT, 2002, Independent Short

Joseph Guillen*
Poetic Pictures
Palmdale, CA 93550
Tel 661-305-5807
Fax 661-947-3743

Magdalena Guillen*
Paramount, CA 90723
Tel 562-272-4331
Email...............bluegirl076@yahoo.com

Costume Designer
LAST CHANCE

Maritza Guimet*
Creative Power Enterprises
N. Miami Beach, FL 33160
Tel 305-305-1949
Email.........maritza@cpeproduction.com

Producer

Carla Gutierrez*
Silver Spring, MD 20901
Email ....cgutierrezny@earthlink.net

Charlotte Gutierrez
Cine Acción
San Francisco, CA 94103
Tel 415-553-8135
Fax 415-553-8137
Email ....info@CineAccion.com

Diego Gutierrez
Los Angeles, CA
Agent: CAA, Chris Harbert, 310-288-4545

Writer, JUDGING AMY, 2003, TV Series
Writer, KINGPIN, 2003, NBC/ Lions Gate Films, TV Movie
Writer, THE SHIELD, 2003, FX, TV Series
Writer, BUFFY THE VAMPIRE SLAYER, 2001, UPN/20th Century Fox, TV Series
Writer, DAWSON'S CREEK, 2001, Warner Bros./Columbia Pictures, TV Series
Writer, DAWN OF THE DEAD

Gary Michael Gutierrez
San Francisco, CA 94707
Tel.......................415-788-7500 x235

Agent: The Peter Turner Agency, Peter Turner, 310-315-4772

Special/Visual Effects, THE LIZZIE MCGUIRE MOVIE, 2003, Buena Vista Pictures, Feature
Special/Visual Effects, MAX Q, 1998, Buena Vista Television, TV Movie
Special/Visual Effects, JACK, 1996, Buena Vista Pictures, Feature
Special/Visual Effects, DRACULA, 1992, Columbia Pictures, Feature
Special/Visual Effects, THE SERPENT AND THE RAINBOW, 1988, Universal Pictures, Feature
Special/Visual Effects, THE RUNNING MAN, 1987, TriStar Pictures, Feature

Vincent Gutierrez*
Aizada Productions
North Hills, CA 91343
Tel 818-895-0639
Fax 818-895-9433
Email ....vincent.gutierrez@csun.edu

Wendy Gutierrez*
Vista, CA 92083
Email ....chicanadesigns@yahoo.com

Johnathan Gwyn*
Motion Pixel
Austin, TX 78758
Tel 713-953-7587
Cell 310-663-6557
Email ....plusfilm@hotmail.com
Web ....www.motionpixel.net

Agent: Blvd. Talent, Cynthia Robbins, 512-458-2583

Director, CONFESSION INVASION, 2003, Much Luvv Records, Music Video
Actor, LA TAQUERIA, 2003, York Entertainment, Feature

Director, COTTON MOUTH, 2002, Madison Home Video, Feature
Actor, THUG LIFE, 2002, York, Feature
Director, FRESH WATER, 2001, Univesity of Houston, Short
Actor, KILLING THE BADGE, 1999, Ventura Distribution, Feature

Bernardo Hajdenberg
Sound Dimensions
Albuquerque, NM 87102
Tel 212-757-5147

Shelli Hall*
Executive Director
Tucson Film Office
Tucson, AZ 85701
Tel 520-770-2126
Fax 520-884-7804
Email ....shall@mtcvb.com

Janet Hamann*
Accounts Manager
San Diego State University, President's Office
San Diego, CA 92182
Tel 619-594-3491
Email ....jhamann@mail.sdsu.edu

Matthew Handal*
Handalm With Care Productions
New York, NY 10009
Tel 212-260-7702
Tel 212-505-5268
Cell 917-209-4242
Fax 212-260-7702
Email ....handalm@aol.com

Editor, LIZARD LICK, 2003, MTV, TV Series
Producer, ROCCO MORETTI: 1ST DAY; D-DAY, 2003, Short
Writer, VIAGRA SPOT, 2003, Commercial
Editor, WOMANDOCS, 2001, True Ent., Documentary

144

Writer, NOWHERE MAN, 2000, Feature
Writer, BIRDS OF PREY, 1997, Feature
Editor, PARA VIVIR O MORIR, 1996, de
   la nada prods., Feature

Shayla Harris*

Brooklyn, NY 11205
Tel 212-664-3067
Email ....shayjoy@yahoo.com

Salma Hayek

Ventana Rosa Productions
Los Angeles, CA

*Agent: William Morris Agency, Michelle
Bohan, 310-859-4000*

Actor, AFTER THE SUNSET, 2004, New
   Line Cinema, Feature
Actor, MURPHY'S LAW, 2004, Feature
Producer, MURPHY'S LAWS, 2004,
   Feature
Producer, FRIDA, 2002, Miramax Films,
   Feature
Director, THE MALDONADO MIRACLE,
   2002, Showtime Networks Inc.,
   Feature

Salma Hayek

Senior Executive Producer
Ventanarosa Productions
Los Angeles, CA

THE MALDONADO MIRACLE, 2003,
   Showtime Networks, Feature
FRIDA, 2002, Miramax Films, Feature
IN THE TIME OF THE BUTTERFLIES,
   2001, MGM Home Entertainment,
   Feature
NO ONE WRITES TO THE COLONEL,
   1999, Keyfilms Roma, Feature
THE VELOCITY OF GARY, 1998,
   Columbia TriStar Home Video, Feature

Jamie Hayes*

SDSU
San Diego, CA 92116
Tel 619-283-3895
Email ....jchayes@hotmail.com

Christy Heady*

Winston Harlee Productions
Deerfield Beach, FL 33442
Tel 786-417-8538
Fax 954-428-2783
Email ....Christy@winstonharlee.com

Director, Documentary

Andres Heidenreich

Director, PASSWORD: UNA MIRADA EN
   LA OBSCURIDAD, 2002, Feature
Editor, PASSWORD: UNA MIRADA EN
   LA OBSCURIDAD, 2002, Feature

Mikaila Henderson*

Los Angeles, CA 90041
Email ....tink1124@hotmail.com

Eric W. Henriquez

New York, NY 10128
Cell 917-374-2048
Email ....yohebaby@aol.com

2nd Assistant Director, IT RUNS IN THE
   FAMILY, 2003, MGM, Feature
2nd Assistant Director, BAD COMPANY,
   2002, Buena Vista Pictures, Feature
2nd Assistant Director, HACK, 2002,
   CBS, TV Series
2nd 2nd Assistant Director, BOILER
   ROOM, 2000, New Line Cinema,
   Feature
2nd Assistant Director, DEADLINE,
   2000, NBC, TV Series
2nd 2nd Assistant Director, JUST
   LOOKING, 1999, Sony Pictures
   Classics, Feature
2nd 2nd Assistant Director, LIBERTY
   HEIGHTS, 1999, Warner Bros.,
   Feature

filmmakers

Rosie Henriquez*
San Diego, CA 92126
Email ....row_z@hotmail.com

Paula Heredia
Mamboreta, Inc.
New York, NY 10006
Tel 212-953-3564

Agent: Larry Garvin Management

Editor, IN MEMORIAM: NEW YORK
   CITY, 2002, HBO, Documentary
Director, THE PARIS REVIEW: EARLY
   CHAPTERS, 2001, Checkerboard
   Foundation, Documentary
Editor, I REMEMBER ME, 2000,
   Zeitgeist Films, Documentary
Director, THE COUPLE IN THE CAGE,
   1997, Maraboreta, Documentary
Editor, UNZIPPED, 1995, Miramax
   Films, Documentary

Angel Hernandez
Station Manager
WLRN: Public Radio and Television
Miami, FL 33128
Tel 305-995-2154

Bel Hernandez*
Executive Director
Latin Heat
West Covina, CA 91793
Tel 626-917-2160
Fax 818-846-9419
Email........................bel@latinheat.com

Eugene Hernandez
Editor
Indiewire
New York, NY 10019
Email ....eug@firedrill.net

Francisco Hernandez*
Smokin' Mirrors Productions
Los Angeles, CA 90027
Tel 323-906-2937
Email ....fran2k@pacbell.net

Director, JAROCHO ELEGUA, 2002,
   Vangarde Records, Music Video
Producer, PACO'S SUITCASE BOMB,
   2002, Fox Searchlab, Short

Georgina Hernandez*
Son del Barrio Music
Santa Clara, CA 95050
Tel 408-554-9036
Fax 650-725-6487
Email ....gmedia@pacbell.net

Hector Hernandez
La Fabrica Films
Mexico, DF 06140 Mexico
Tel 52-55-2119656
Fax 52-55-2866345
Email........scavengers@lafabrica.com.mx

Helen Hernandez
President
Imagen Foundation
Washington, DC 20006
Tel 323-644-7965
Email ....intllegacy@aol.com

Lou Hernandez*

Fiddler Productions, Inc
Naples, FL 34104
Tel 239-435-1818
Cell 239-248-2493
Fax 239-649-4965
Email ....fiddlerpro@comcast.net
Web ....www.fiddlerproductions.com

Director, ONE EVENING, 2003, Fiddler
  Productions Inc, Feature
Executive Producer, ONE EVENING,
  2003, Fiddler Productions Inc,
  Feature
Director, BLACK, 2000, Fiddler
  Productions Inc, Short
Director, TACKLEBOX, 2000, Fiddler
  Productions Inc., Short

Marc Hernandez

Manager
Crescendo Entertainment Group
Los Angeles, CA 90036
Tel 323-937-9700
Email marchernandez@crescendo-la.com

Peggy Hernandez*

Queen of Hearts Productions
Beverly Hills, CA 90210
Tel 310-385-8487
Fax 310-914-1490
Email ....peggy_hernandez@msn.com

Regina Hernandez

Cine las Americas
Austin, TX 78705
Tel 512-374-1562
Email...................regina_dez@jump.net

Roberto Hernandez

Latin Zone Productions
San Francisco, CA 94110
Tel 415-206-0577
Fax 415-206-0499
Email ....latinzoneprod@aol.com

Roger Hernandez*

En Caliente Productions
San Antonio, TX 78205
Tel 210-223-8830
Fax 210-223-9900
Email ....encalientepro@msn.com

Sandra Hernández*

Simi Valley, CA 93094
Email ....shernan@earthlink.net

Rudy Hernandez, Jr.*

First Flight Pictures LTD
Key Biscayne, FL 33149
Tel 305-606-2129
Fax 305-261-8861
Email ..firstflightpictures2@hotmail.com

Producer, ASÍ FUE, BABY, 2002, FFP,
  Documentary
Director, ASÍ FUE, BABY, 2002, FFP,
  Documentary
Associate Producer, BABY FACE
  NELSON, 2000, A&E
  Biography/Towers Productions, TV
Associate Producer, DOOMSDAY, 2000,
  Discovery Channel / Tower
  Productions, TV
Associate Producer, FRAMED, 2000,
  A&E American Justice / Towers
  Productions, TV
Director, ROPE BURN, 1998, Columbia
  College, Short
Producer, FR. BROWN, Columbia
  College, Documentary
Director, FR. BROWN, Columbia College,
  Documentary

Allison Herrera*

San Antonio, TX 78201
Email......allison.herrera@randolph.af.mil

Catherine Herrera*

Malinche Films
San Francisco, CA 94112
Tel 415-885-2723
Tel 408-295-7422
Email............mayanmx@worldnet.att.net
Web ....www.gamerrera.com/transition

*Attorney: Brooke Oliver, 415-641-1116,
Brooke@artemama.com*

Director, FROM THE SAME FAMILY: AN
   INTIMATE VIEW OF GLOBALIZATION,
   2004, Festival Distribution - BAVC,
   Experimental
Director, TRANSITION, 2003, Film Arts
   Foundation, Documentary
Producer, SHORT NEWS PROGRAMS,
   1998, Canadian Broadcast
   Corporation, Documentary
Director, ALPHABET PEOPLE, 1992,
   Self-Distributed, Documentary Short

Fernando Herrera*

Downey, CA 90242
Email ....nandofmvh@hotmail.com

Gloria Herrera

Ex-Bo Productions
New York, NY

Producer, WASHINGTON HEIGHTS,
   2002, Mac Releasing, LLC, Feature
Production Manager, WASHINGTON
   HEIGHTS, 2002, Mac Releasing. LLC,
   Feature
Writer, DETAILS, 2000, Short

Mike Higuera

Cacho-Cacho Entertainment
La Tuna Canyon, CA 91352
Tel 818-504-0554
Fax 818-504-0556
Email ....mafigtree@cs.com

Director, VIVA VEGAS, 2000, Telemundo,
   TV Series
Director, LOS BELTRAN, 1999,
   Telemundo, TV Series

Director, HANG TIME, 1995, NBC, TV
   Series
Director, SAVED BY THE BELL, 1993,
   NBC, TV Series
Director, SOLO EN AMERICA

Yesenia Higuera

Miami, FL 33145
Tel 310-926-4932
Email ....yesifilm@yahoo.com

Barbara Holguin*

New York, NY 10276
Tel 917-317-0170
Email ....santab2000@aol.com

Manuel Huerta*

Los Angeles, CA 90034
Tel 310-434-0275
Email ....manuelhuerta1@yahoo.com

Cynthia Huerta Paloma*

Austin, TX 78734
Tel 512-773-1046
Fax 512-216-9402
Email ....cahuerta17@yahoo.com

Debra Hurd*

Creative Makeup
Miramar, FL 33023
Tel 954-981-3510
Cell 954-980-6596
Fax 954-989-7396
Email ....creativemakeup@aol.com
Web ....www.CreativeMakeup.com

Make-up & Hair, MAXIMILLION MUSIC
   VIDEO, 2003, Illucid Productions,
   Music Video
Make-up & Hair, OFF THE CHAIN,
   2003, Illucid Productions, Feature
Special/Visual Effects, TRIGGER HAPPY,
   2003, Comedy Central, TV episode

Special/Visual Effects, HUNTING FOR HERSCHEL, 2002, Bride of Hamlet, Feature

Special/Visual Effects, DARK WOODS, 2001, Berlinghoff Productions, Feature

Make-up & Hair, 531, 1998, Goodman/Brown Productions, Feature

Claire Hurtubise*
Luna Media Group
Miami Beach, FL 33140
Tel 786-258-6883
Email ....c_hurtubise@hotmail.com

Lena Hyde*
San Francisco, CA 94110
Email............................Lhyde@aol.com

Adriana Ibanez
Senior VP Scheduling
Telemundo
Hialeah, FL 33010
Tel 305-884-8200
Web ....www.telemundo.com

Cristina Ibarra*
Subcine
New York, NY 10012
Tel 917-447-4498
Email.............cristinaibarra@yahoo.com
Web ....www.subcine.com

Director, THE LAST CONQUISTADOR, 2004, PBS/LPB, Documentary

Producer, THE LAST CONQUISTADOR, 2004, PBS/LPB, Documentary

Director, LUPE + JUANDI ON THE BLOCK, 2003, Fulana, Short

Director, GRANDMA'S HIP HOP, 2002, Latino Public Broadcasting, Interstitial

Director, DIRTY LAUNDRY: A HOMEMADE TELENOVELA, 2000, Subcine, Short

Leon Ichaso
Los Angeles, CA
Tel 818-753-9545

Agent: Innovative Artists, Jim Stein, 310-656-0400

Director, PINERO, 2001, Miramax, Feature

Writer, PINERO, 2001, Miramax, Feature

Director, ALI: AN AMERICAN HERO, 2000, Fox Network, TV Movie

Director, HENDRIX, 2000, MGM & Showtime, TV Movie

Director, EXECUTION OF JUSTICE, 1999, Showtime, TV Movie

Director, FREE OF EDEN, 1999, Showtime, TV Movie

Writer, AZUCAR AMARGA, 1996, First Look Pictures Releasing, Feature

Henry Iglesias
Be In the Now Productions
Tarzana, CA 91356
Tel 818-344-3229
Tel 818-688-3142
Email ....shasta26@pacbell.net
Web ....www.beinthenow.com

Composer, LUCKY PENNY, Short

Kathy Im*
Program Officer
The MacArthur Foundation
Chicago, IL 60603
Tel 312-726-8000
Email ....kim@macfound.org

Jorge Insua
Agent
Creative Artists Agency
Beverly Hills, CA 90212
Tel 310-288-4545
Fax 310-288-4800
Email ....jinsua@caa.com

filmmakers

Arturo Interian
VP, Production
Lifetime Networks
Los Angeles, CA
Tel 310-556-7500
Email ....ainterian@lifetimetv.com

Yvan Iturriaga*
Oakland, CA 94609
Tel 213-952-7652
Email ....cacique03@earthlink.net

Producer, CONTINUITY OF PATHWAYS,
    2003, Occidental College, LA, Short
Director, CONTINUITY OF PATHWAYS,
    2003, Occidental College, LA, Short
Writer, CONTINUITY OF PATHWAYS,
    2003, Occidental College, LA, Short
Producer, OFFSIDES, 2003, Occidental
    College, LA, Short
Director, OFFSIDES, 2003, Occidental
    College, LA, Short
Writer, OFFSIDES, 2003, Occidental
    College, LA, Short

Richard Izarra
Produccion Y Distribucion
Miami, FL 33186
Tel 305-256-6774

Veronica Jacuinde
TV Host
Mun2/Telemundo
Hialeah, FL 33010
Tel 305-884-8200
Email ....bdbaca@gte.net
Web ....www.telemundo.com

Ed Jaime
Festival Director
LA Chicano Film Festival
Tel 626-289-5407

Jorgiania Jake*
University of Arizona
Tucson, AZ 85746
Tel 520-312-6666
Email...............texmexpix@hotmail.com

Stan Jakubowicz*
Aventura, FL 33180
Tel 305-606-0412
Fax 305-692-5006
Email ....jak7711@aol.com

Director
Writer

David Jalquel*
Fremont, CA 94536
Tel 510-791-5056
Email ....gucumatz@aol.com

Linda Jaquez
Account Administrator
Cable Entertainment
Sacramento, CA 85719
Tel 310-829-0033
Email ....linda@brivideo.com

Susan Jasso*
Yierba Buena Productions
Austin, TX 78704
Tel 512-587-6391
Email ....sjasso13@aol.com

Producer, PAINFLOWER, 1996,
    Independent, Feature

Bill Jersey*

CEO/Director-Producer
Quest Productions
Berkeley, CA 94710
Tel 510-548-0854
Fax 510-548-1824
Email ....bjersey@questprod.com

Producer, THE MAKING OF AMADEUS,
  2002, Saul Zaentz Company,
  Documentary
Director, THE MAKING OF AMADEUS,
  2002, Saul Zaentz Company,
  Documentary
Producer, THE RISE AND FALL OF JIM
  CROW - "DON'T SHOUT TOO SOON",
  2002, PBS, Documentary
Director, THE RISE AND FALL OF JIM
  CROW - "DON'T SHOUT TOO SOON",
  2002, PBS, Documentary
Producer, EVOLUTION - "WHAT ABOUT
  GOD?", 2001, PBS, Documentary
Director, EVOLUTION - "WHAT ABOUT
  GOD?", 2001, PBS, Documentary

Jorge Jiménez*

An Eagle Tribute Productions
Sherwood, CA 97140
Tel 503-925-9107
Fax 503-925-1747
Email ....jorgej9@gte.net

Producer, ABRIENDO CAMINO, 2004,
  Latino Educational Media Center,
  Documentary

Lillian Jiménez*

Latino Educational Media Center
Bronx, NY 10451
Tel 781-401-9020
Fax 646-328-0415
Email ....Lilpiri@aol.com

Producer, ABRIENDO CAMINO, 2004,
  Latino Educational Media Center,
  Documentary

Sandy Jiménez*

New York, NY 10034
Tel 212-304-4777
Email ....sjimenez@rcn.com

Judi Jordan*

Divine Horizons Entertainment, Inc.
Venice, CA 90291
Tel 310-301-6618
Fax 310-876-2425
Email ....goldenfeather2000@yahoo.com
Web ....www.clubvidaloca.com

Producer, CLUB LA VIDA LOCA, 2004,
  Echelon Ent. Inc., Feature
Producer, TWIN FLAMES, 2002, Short

Joel Juarez*

Venice, CA 90291
Tel 310-823-5293
Email ....juarezfilms@aol.com

Robert Julian*

New York, NY 10031
Tel 718-753-7524
Email ......goonproductions@hotmail.com

Cheryl Kanekar*

SDSU
San Diego, CA 92119
Tel 619-303-8304
Email ....c-k@cox.net.

filmmakers

Betty Kaplan

Luzadero, LLC
Los Angeles, CA 90004
Tel 323-654-8809
Fax 323-654 9179
Web ....www.bettykaplan.org

Agent: Suzanna Camejo, 310-449-4064

Director, ALMOST A WOMAN, 2002,
  PBS, TV Movie
Director, THE DIVISION, 2001, Lifetime,
  TV Series
Director, DONA BARBARA, 1998,
  Universal Pictures, Feature
Writer, DONA BARBARA, 1998,
  Universal Pictures, Feature
Director, OF LOVE AND SHADOWS,
  1994, Miramax, Feature
Writer, OF LOVE AND SHADOWS, 1994,
  Miramax, Feature
Director, BOLIVAR, 1990, Venezolana de
  Television, TV Movie
Director, THE VIOLINIST, PBS, Short
Writer, THE VIOLINIST, PBS, Short

Michelle Katz*

Espiritus Productions
Culver City, CA 90232
Tel 310-836-9673
Fax 310-559-5319
Email ....michkatz@pacbell.net

Gary Keller*

Hispanic Research Center
Tempe, AZ 85287
Tel 480-965-5388
Fax 480-965-8309
Email ....gary.keller@asu.edu

Director

Diego Kenneth

Washington Township, NJ 07676
Tel 201-664-2198
Fax 201-358-2560
Email.......................kenakmd@aol.com

Associate Director, 2000 SUPERBOWL
  HALFTIME SHOW, 2000, ABC, TV
  Special
Director, OUT OF THE BOX, 1998, Walt
  Disney Pictures, TV Series
Associate Director, DANCE IN AMERICA:
  "FOSSE"
Associate Director, DAYTIME EMMY
  AWARDS, TV Special
Associate Director, LIVE BY REQUEST,
  A&E
Associate Director, MISS AMERICA
  PAGEANT, TV Special
Director, SESAME STREET, PBS, TV
  Series
Director, SQUARE ONE TV, TV Special
Associate Director, THE MAN WHO
  CAME TO DINNER, PBS

Robert Kircher*

Bonita Springs, FL 34135

Rolando Klein*

Pasadena, CA 91104
Tel 626-797-0808
Email ....roseweb@earthlink.net

Joleen Koehly*

Chairperson
Digital Media Art College
Boca Raton, FL 33431
Tel ....561-391-1148 ext. 215
Fax 561-391-2489
Email ....jkoehly@dmac-edu.org

Production Designer, BAKER'S MEN,
2002, Hyahr Films, Short
Production Designer, SLING SHOT,
2000, IFAC, Short
Production Designer, YOUR EYES, 2000,
Namascar Films, Music Short
Educator
Writer

Leticia Konisberg*

Houston, TX 77004
Tel 713-523-3451
Email ....l_konisgberg@hotmail.com

Cristina Kotz Cornejo

Assistant Professor
Emerson College
Cambridge, MA 02138
Tel 617-824-8816
Fax 617-824-8803
Email ....info@wildwimminfilms.com
Web ....www.wildwimminfilms.com

Director, ERNESTO, 2000, Short
Director, THE APPOINTMENT, 1999,
Short

Lili Kristan*

ManJon Productions
San Antonio, TX 78238
Tel 210-523-7748
Fax 210-523-2696

Pamela S. Kuri

Film Navigator
Sierra Madre, CA
Tel 626-836-2024
Tel 818-288-5874
Fax 626-355-8523
Email ....pamkuri@aol.com

1st Assistant Director, CARNIVALE,
2003, HBO, TV Series
1st Assistant Director, TREMORS 3,
2001, Universal Home Entertainment,
Feature
1st Assistant Director, FROM THE
EARTH TO MOON, 1998, HBO, TV
Movie
2nd Assistant Director, CRIME OF THE
CENTURY, 1996, HBO, Feature
Producer, DEVOTION, 1995, Aunti Em
Productions, Feature
2nd Assistant Director, EARTH 2, 1994,
Universal TV, TV Movie
Producer, CLAIRE OF THE MOON,
1992, Strand Releasing, Feature
Producer, IRONHEART, 1992, Imperial
Video, Feature
2nd Assistant Director, TEENAGE
MUTANT NINJA TURTLES, 1990,
New Line Cinema, TV Series

Gloria LaMorte

Ex-Bo Productions, Inc.
New York, NY 10018
Tel 646-366-0018
Fax 212-921-0456
Email.......................exboprod@aol.com
Web ....www.exbofilms.com

Co-Producer, WHAT'S FOR DINNER?,
2003, Short
Co-Producer, WASHINGTON HEIGHTS,
2001, MAC Releasing, Feature
Co-Producer, DETAILS, 2000, HBO,
Short

filmmakers

Mary Lampe*
Executive Director
Southwest Alternative Media Project
Houston, TX 77006
Tel 713-522-8592
Fax 713-522-0953
Email ....mmlampe@swamp.org

Media Advocate

Luis Lassen*
Los Angeles, CA 90048
Tel 323-769-5764
Email ....lumalas@aol.com

Frances Lausell*
Isla Films
San Juan, PR 00913
Tel 787-977-0229
Fax 787-977-0229
Email ....islafilms@coqui.net

Producer, EL BESO, 2000, RGH
    Lions/Vanguard Int., Feature
Producer, Documentary

Ryan Law
4 Element Entertainment
Los Angeles, CA 90034
Tel 310-980-8906
Email ....shawnabaca@hotmail.com
Web ....www.shawnabaca.com

Writer, ROSE'S GARDEN, Impersonal
    Impression
Producer, ROSE'S GARDEN, Impersonal
    Impression

Anita Lawson*
Afterwords Ink
Washington, DC 20013
Tel 202-723-1292
Fax 413-702-3875
Email ....anitamlawson@hotmail.com

Producer, GIRL!, 2000, Stage Play
Writer, GIRL!, 2000, Stage Play
Writer, A DONATION PLEASE, 1991,
    Stage Play
Producer, A DONATION PLEASE, 1991,
    Stage Play
Producer, IF JESUS WAS A HOMEBOY,
    Feature

Robert Leach*
Publisher
SCREEN Magazine
Chicago, IL 60610
Tel 312-640-0800
Fax 312-640-1928
Email ....publisher@screenmag.com

Media Advocate

Rick Leal*
Grand Prairie, TX 75050
Tel 214-740-9372
Email ....rickleal60@aol.com

Director, FRIDAY NIGHT UNDER THE
    LIGHTS, 1990, Short

David Leal-Cortez*
Baltimore, MD
Tel 301-564-4499

Andy Lebron*
Bronx, NY 10475
Cell 917-544-0766
Fax 509-267-1841
Email...............lebron1112@yahoo.com
Web ....www.latinoextra.com

Writer

John Leguizamo

Lower East Side Films
New York, NY 10014
Tel 212-966-0111
Email ....lesf@aol.com

Agent: William Morris Agency, Scott Lambert

Director, UNDEFEATED, 2003, HBO, TV Movie

Executive Producer, UNDEFEATED, 2003, HBO, TV Movie

Writer, UNDEFEATED, 2003, HBO, TV Movie

Writer, SEXAHOLIC: A LOVE STORY, 2002, Cream Cheese Films, TV Special

Executive Producer, KING OF THE JUNGLE, 2001, Urbanworld Films, Feature

Executive Producer, PIÑERO, 2001, Miramax, Feature

Writer, FREAK, 1998, HBO, TV Special

Dennis Leoni*

Patagonia House
Chatsworth, CA 91311
Tel 661-254-0979
Fax 661-253-1763
Email..............PatagoniaHouse@aol.com

Agent: The Rothman Agency, Rob Rothman, 310-247-9898

Executive Producer, RESURRECTION BLVD., 2000, Showtime, TV Series

Director, RESURRECTION BLVD., 2000, Showtime, TV Series

Executive Producer, MCKENNA, 1994, ABC, TV

Writer, COVINGTON CROSS, 1992, Thames Television, TV Series

Writer, THE COMMISH, 1991, ABC, TV Special

Executive Producer, THE GUARD, 1990, Showtime, TV

Writer, ANGEL OF MERCY, TV Series

Luisa Leschin

Los Angeles, CA

Agent: William Morris, Aaron Kaplan, Cori Wellins, Sam Haskell, 310-274-7451

Co-Producer, GEORGE LOPEZ, 2003, ABC, TV Series

Writer, RESURRECTION BLVD., 2000, Viacom Productions Inc., TV Series

Diana Lesmez

VP, Production and Development
Arenas Group
Beverly Hills, CA 90210
Tel 310-385-4401
Fax 310-385-4402
Email..............dianaL@arenasgroup.com
Web ....www.arenasgroup.com

Vivien Lesnik Weisman

Guerilla Gaze Pictures
Santa Monica, CA 90402
Tel 310-920-8402
Email ....vivienwe@aol.com

Director, DINE AND SHINE, 2002, Guerrila Gaze Pictures, Feature

Producer, DINE AND SHINE, 2002, Guerrilla Gaze Pictures, Feature

Writer, DINE AND SHINE, 2002, UCLA School of Film and TV, Short

Director, MARIA CRISTINA, 2000, UCLA School of Film and TV, Short

Writer, MARIA CRISTINA, 2000, UCLA School of Film and TV, Short

Producer, MARIA CRISTINA, 1999, UCLA School of Film and TV, Short

Director, LINDA, 1998, UCLA School of Film and TV, Short

Producer, LINDA, 1998, UCLA School of Film and TV, Short

Writer, LINDA, 1998, UCLA School of Film and TV, Short

Roxanne Rodriguez Lettman
Director of International Format
Development
Columbia/TriStar International Television
Culver City, CA 90232
Tel 310-244-5546
Tel 310-244-0546

Melissa Levine*
Los Angeles, CA 90024
Tel 310-594-5503
Email ....Melissacandace@yahoo.com

Daniel Levy*
Latino Magazine
New York, NY 10025
Tel 212-865-1383
Fax 212-865-1383
Email ....janadaniel@hotmail.com

Diane Librizzi*
La Loca Entertainment, Inc.
New York, NY 10001
Email ....Latmedia@aol.com

James Lima
Los Angeles, CA

*Agent: ICM, Cal Boyington,
310-550-4000*

Attorney: Matthew Saver, 310-820-0202

Executive Producer, JOE MILLIONAIRE
  1, 2003, NBC, TV Series
Executive Producer, JOE MILLIONAIRE
  2, 2003, NBC, TV Series
Director, THE SCARIEST PLACES ON
  EARTH, 2001, Fox Family Channel, TV
  Series
Co-Producer, THE SCARIEST PLACES
  ON EARTH, 2001, Fox Family
  Channel, TV Series
Director, BEHIND THE SCENES, 2000,
  Lions Share Pictures, Feature

Co-Producer, TAKEN, 2000,
  Dreamworks, TV Movie
Director, THE OTHERS, 2000, ABC, TV
  Series

José Lima*
Miami Shores, FL 33150
Email ....joselima2@yahoo.com

Carolina Liu
Los Gatos, CA 95032
Tel 408-367-5959
Email ....cmrl@yahoo.com

Producer, BLOCO AFRO AND AFOXE,
  2002, Short
Producer, FESTIVE LAND: CARNAVAL
  IN BAHIA, 2001, CMIL
Director, FESTIVE LAND: CARNAVAL IN
  BAHIA, 2001, CMIL

Ruth Livier*
Livier Productions, Inc.
Stevenson Ranch, CA 91381
Tel 213-445-3441
Email ....V57khp126@aol.com

*Agent: CAA, Michael Wimer,
310-288-4545*

Manager: Ellen Travis, 310-459-7274

Actor, RESURRECTION BLVD.,
  2001-2002, Showtime

Luis Llosa
Coastal Desert
Miami, FL 33149
Email ....lucholl@terra.com.pe

*Agent: CAA, Michael Wimer,
310-288-4545*

Director, ANACONDA, 1997, Columbia
  TriStar, Feature
Writer, EL ANGEL VENGADOR, 1994,
  TV
Producer, NEW CRIME CITY, 1994,
  Iguana Films, Feature

Director, THE SPECIALIST, 1994,
Warner Bros., Feature

Producer, WATCHERS III, 1994,
Concorde-New Horizons

Producer, EIGHT HUNDRED LEAGUES
DOWN THE AMAZON, 1993,
Concorde-New Horizons, Feature

Director, SNIPER, 1993, Tri Star
Pictures, Feature

Benjamin Lobato*

Tucson, AZ 85712
Tel 520-325-3586
Email ....bdlobato@earthlink.net

Director, MARIPOSA CANYON, 2002,
Short

Efrain Logreira*

Corte Hispana
Santa Monica, CA 90402
Tel 310-458-6998
Email ....efrem@cortehispana.com
Web...................www.cortehispana.com

Attorney: John Levine, 310-899-9408

Writer, MIRANDA'S RIGHTS, 2002,
Independent, Edutainment

Producer, VIOLENCIA EN EL TRABAJO,
2001, Independent,
Educational/Industrial

Producer, BASTA YA DE ACOSARME,
2000, Independent,
Educational/Industrial

Writer, NO... STOP HARASSING ME!,
2000, Industrial film, Edutainment

Composer, CENTILNELAS DEL
SILENCIO, Independent, Short

Diana Logreira Campos*

Hispanic Information and
Telecommunication Network
New York, NY 10002
Tel 212-966-5660
Tel 212-677-6604
Cell 347-531-8547
Fax 212-966-5725
Email....................brujadilc@yahoo.com

Producer
Director, VERDAD EN EL JAIRE

Rick Lombardo

Valencia, CA 91355
Tel 213-498-9468
Email ....rlombardo@mindspring.com

Producer, VIVIR INTENTANDO, 2003,
Buena Vista International, Feature

Director, PLACES OF MYSTERY, 2000,
The Discovery Network, TV Series

Producer, ACCESS HOLLYWOOD, TV
Series

Producer, REAL TV, Paramount, TV
Series

Julian Londono*

Austin, TX 78759
Tel 512-231-8618
Email ....julian_londono@hotmail.com

Writer, FAILING TO ADJUST, 2002,
Texas A&M University, Short

Director, FAILING TO ADJUST, 2002,
Texas A&M University, Short

Writer, THE EAGLE: LEARNING TO FLY
AGAIN, 2001, Texas A&M University,
Short

Director, THE EAGLE: LEARNING TO
FLY AGAIN, 2001, Texas A&M
University, Short

filmmakers

Gilda Longoria*

GBL PRODUCTIONS
San Antonio, TX 78217
Tel 210-650-9836
Tel 210-650-9836
Cell 210-887-0449
Fax 210-650-9836
Email ....longmag@sbcglobal.net

2nd Assistant Director, BROKEN SKY, 2003, PBS, TV Series
2nd Assistant Director, JUNK YARD SAINTS, 2003, PBS, TV Series
Producer, TEJANO MUSIC AWARDS, 2003, TTMA - PBS, TV Special
Production Manager, THE POND, 2003, GBL Productions, Short
Producer, FAITH PLEASES GOD, 2002, La Familia Television, TV Series
Production Manager, GOD PLEASER, 2002, La Familia Television, TV Series
2nd Assistant Director, GUTTER BALL, 2002, Jack Hailey Production, Short
Production Manager, LATINO LAUGH FEST, 2002, SI TV, TV Special
Producer, MARKET SQUARE "WHERE TOURISTS GO", 2002, GBL Productions, Commercial

Marcie Longoria*

Austin, TX 78741
Tel 512-797-6224
Email ....marsea32@yahoo.com

Adam Lopez*

San Fernando, CA 91340
Tel 310-699-5444
Email ....adamlopez@nalip.info

Director, REAL WISDOM, 2003, Independent, Short
Writer, REAL WISDOM, 2003, Indpendent, Short
Director, SOUL FOOD, 2000, Independent, Short
Writer, SOUL FOOD, 2000, Independent, Short
Producer

Angel Dean Lopez

Los Angeles, CA 90048
Tel 323-782-4548

Agent: APA, Marc Parisar,
310-888-4268

Writer, JUDGING AMY, 1999-2002, CBS, TV Series
Writer, BRIMSTONE, 1998, Fox Network, TV Series
Writer, NEW YORK UNDERCOVER, 1994, Fox Network, TV Series

Anthony Lopez*

Miami Lakes, FL 33018
Tel 305-467-3912
Email ....tone001_x@hotmail.com

Benjamin Lopez

Tucson, AZ 85748
Tel 520-247-5520
Tel ....520-881-3300 ext. 111
Email ....blopez@volunteertucson.org

Actor, BORDER BULLET, 2003, Waiting for distribution, Independent Film
Producer, 500 YEARS OF CHICANO HISTORY, 1998, Short
Writer

Cynthia Lopez*

Communications Director
P.O.V./American Documentary Inc.
New York, NY 10004
Tel 212-989-7425
Fax 212-989-8230
Email ....clopez@pov.org

Eduardo Lopez*

Whittier Union High School District
Whittier, CA 90604
Tel 562-692-9194

Edwin René López*
New York, NY 10040
Tel 212-781-3347
Email ....latinfilms@juno.com

Director

Fabian Lopez*
Los Angeles, CA 90063
Tel 323-447-9388
Email ....fabianlakers@sbcglobal.net

Fernando Lopez
Telemundo Corp.
Glendale, CA
Tel 818-502-0029
Email.......................v4m@hotmail.com

George Lopez*
Brooklyn, NY 11216
Tel 718-388-6799
Email ....glopez7688@yahoo.com

George Lopez*
Encanto Enterprises, Inc.
Los Angeles, CA 90038
Tel 818-954-3332
Fax 323-933-0633
Web ....www.georgelopez.com

Agent: Jonas Public Relations, Jeff Abraham, 310-656-3355

Manager: Ron Deblasio, 323-933-9977

Producer, GEORGE LOPEZ SHOW, 2003, ABC, TV Series
Writer, THE GEORGE LOPEZ SHOW, 2003, ABC, TV Series
Actor, TORTILLA HEAVEN, 2003, Feature
Actor, FRANK MCKLUSKY, C.I., 2002, Buena Vista Pictures, Feature
Actor, REAL WOMEN HAVE CURVES, 2002, HBO, Feature

Josefina Lopez*
Chispas Productions
Los Angeles, CA 90033
Tel 323-263-7684
Fax 323-263-7681
Email ....superchingona@hotmail.com
Web ....www.josefinalopez.com

Manager: Marilyn Atlas, 310-278-5047

Writer, AND BABY MAKES THREE, 2003, CBS/Atlantic Alliance, TV Movie
Writer, LOTERIA FOR JUAREZ, 2003, HBO, Feature
Writer, MACARTHUR PARK, 2003, Showtime, Feature
Writer, REAL WOMEN HAVE CURVES, 2002, HBO, Feature

Louis Lopez*
Zepol Productions
Pembroke Pines, FL 33026
Tel 954-431-5700
Fax 954-432-2266
Email.....................lgl39@bellsouth.net

Ramón López*
Cedar Park, TX 78613
Tel 512-633-7546
Fax 512-331-3154
Email ....lopez13@slb.com

Sal Lopez
Beverly Hills, CA

Manager: Arenas Entertainment, 310-385-4401

Actor, BATMAN: MYSTERY OF SPIDER WOMAN, 2004, Warner Bros., Feature
Actor, EL PADRINO, 2003, El Padrino. LLC, Feature
Actor, BANGER SISTERS, 2002, Fox Searchlight, Feature
Executive Producer, LUMINARIAS, 2000, New Latin Pictures, Feature

Tania Lopez

Agent
International Creative Management
Beverly Hills, CA 90211
Tel 310-550-4322
Tel 310-540-4100
Email ....tlopez@icmtalent.com
Web ....www.icmagency.com

Tery Lopez*

Creative Development
Maya Pictures
Los Angeles, CA 90038
Tel 310-281-3770
Fax 310-281-3777
Email.................rockenvivo@yahoo.com
Web ....www.maya-pictures.com

Producer

Victoria Lopez

HBO
New York, NY 10036
Tel 212-512-1000

Lalo Lopez Alcaraz

Pocho Productions
Los Angeles, CA 90063
Tel 562-907-1996
Email.......................pocho@pocho.com

Writer, PACO'S SUITCASE BOMB, 2002,
  Fox Searchlab, Short
Writer, TACO TRUCK: THE MOVIE,
  2002, New Line, Feature

Alfredo Lopez-Brignoni*

Coral Gables, FL 33114
Tel 305-444-7031
Fax 305-444-7031
Email ....elopezbrignoni@bellsouth.net

Kamala Lopez-Dawson

Blind Ambition Films
Venice, CA 90291
Tel 323-460-2846
Email ....BAF@ureach.com

*Agent: William Morris Agency, Scott
Lambert, 310-859-4000*

Producer

Madeleine Lopez-Silvero

VP, Acquisitions
A&E Mundo History Channel
Miami, FL
Tel 305-260-7577

Frank Loreta

Los Angeles, CA
Tel 213-467-1244

Editor

Jorge Lozano

Festival Director
Alucine Toronto Film Festival
Toronto, Canada
Tel 416-986-4989
Email ....info@alucinefestival.com
Web ....www.alucinefestival.com

Karla Lozano

HBO Latino
New York, NY 11036
Tel 212-512-1750
Email ....karla.lozano@hbo.com

Monica Lozano

President
La Opinion
Los Angeles, CA 90028
Tel 213-896-2153
Email ......monica.lozano@laopinion.com

Tana Lucero-Colin
Blue Pocha Productions
Denver, CO 80211
Tel 303-480-9041
Email.........................hanajov@aol.com

Elmo Lugo*
Aventura, FL 33160
Tel 305-932-3643
Email ....astrid_creative_endeavors@
                                    yahoo.com

Elba Luis Lugo
MUVI Films
San Juan, PR
Tel 787-729-9180

Producer, SIAN KA'AN, 2004, Feature
Writer, SIAN KA'AN, 2004, Feature
Producer, 12 HORAS, 2001, Manhattan
    Pictures International, Feature

Facundo Lujan*
San Francisco, CA 94107
Tel 415-546-3832
Fax 415-546-3832
Email............................fac-rev@usa.net

Gilbert Luna*
Santa Barbara, CA 93101
Tel 805-680-6360
Email ....gilbertluna@yahoo.com

Lupe Luna*
Lynwood, CA 90262
Email......................lpitajames@aol.com

Rocio Luquero*
Seattle, WA 98144
Tel 206-860-7891
Email ....rocioln@hotmail.com

Paco Madden*
Washington, DC 20009
Tel 202-387-9173
Email ....Screen_Scribe@hotmail.com

Elsa Madrigal
Chicago, IL 60615
Tel 312-543-5495
Email ....elsamadrigal@aol.com

Producer, CALLA LA BOCA, 2003,
    Columbia College, Documentary Short

Immanuel Maes*
Santa Fe, NM 85705
Email ....imaes@excite.com

Melanie Magisos*
Sr. Project Developer, Digital Initiatives
Arizona State University
Tempe, AZ 85287
Tel 480-965-3990
Fax 480-965-0315
Email ....Melanie.Magisos@asu.edu

Yuri Makino*
Asst. Professor, Univ. of Arizona, Dept.
of Media Arts
Borderline Films
Tucson, AZ 85705
Tel 520-621-8974
Fax 520-621-9662
Email ....ymakino@u.arizona.edu
Web ....www.borderlinefilms.com

Kisha Maldonado
Executive Assistant
Ground Zero Entertainment
Los Angeles, CA 90045
Tel 310-410-3030
Email ....kisha@ground-zero-ent.com

filmmakers

Sonia Malfa-Clements*

Programs Director
AIVF
Brooklyn, NY 11215
Tel 718-809-6080
Email ....soniamalfa@earthlink.net

Juan Mandelbaum

Writer, Director
Geovision
Watertown, MA 02472
Tel....................617-926-5454 ext 104
Fax 617-926-5411
Email ....juanm@geovisiononline.com
Web ....www.geovisiononline.com

Director, A TASTE OF PASSOVER, 1999,
  PBS, TV Special
Director, POETRY HEAVEN, 1998, WNET
  & WNJN, TV Series
Producer, A NEW WORLD OF MUSIC,
  1996, APS, TV
Director, ANTI-SMOKING CAMPAIGN,
  1994-2002, State of Massachusetts,
  PSA
Producer, CAETANO IN BAHIA, 1994,
  WGBH, TV
Producer, BUILDERS OF IMAGES,
  1993, PBS, TV
Writer, BUILDERS OF IMAGES, 1993,
  PBS, TV Series
Writer, IN WOMEN'S HANDS, 1993,
  PBS, TV Series

Luis Mandoki

Santa Barbara, CA

*Agent: William Morris Agency, Mike
Simpson, 310-274-7451*

Producer, HEART OF THE ATOM, 2004,
  Wild at Heart Films, Feature
Director, ONE MORE DAY FOR
  HIROSHIMA, 2004, Azucar
  Entertainment, Feature
Producer, ONE MORE DAY FOR
  HIROSHIMA, 2004, Azucar
  Entertainment, Feature

Producer, UTOPIA, 2003, SciFi
  Channel, TV Series
Director, TRAPPED, 2002, Sony
  Pictures Entertainment, Feature
Director, ANGEL EYES, 2001, Warner
  Bros., Feature
Director, AMAZING GRACE, 2000,
  Trimark Pictures, Feature
Director, MESSAGE IN A BOTTLE,
  1999, Warner Bros., Feature
Director, WHEN A MAN LOVES A
  WOMAN, 1994, Buena Vista Pictures,
  Feature

Jose Carlos Mangual*

Magia Uno, Inc.
Santa Monica, CA 90403
Tel 310-393-8636
Fax 310-899-1598
Email ....mangual1@msn.com

Producer, HOW THE GARCIA GIRLS
  SPENT THEIR SUMMER, 2004,
  Loosely Based Pictures, LLC, Feature
Producer, ANIMA, 2003, AFI, Short
Production Coordinator, RAICES, 2000,
  Documentary
Production Coordinator, GUITARRA MIA,
  1999, Documentary
Production Coordinator, LOS DIAZ DE
  DORIS, 1998, HBO Latino, Feature
Production Manager, DESPUES DEL
  ADIOS, 1997, Telemundo

Pancho Mansfield

Sr. VP Development, Original
Programming
Showtime Networks
Los Angeles, CA 90024
Tel 310-234-5262

Raul Marchand Sanchez

San Juan, PR 00909
Tel 787-724-0762
Fax 787-723-4562
Email....................barrero@earthlink.net

Director, 12 HORAS

Poli Marichal*

Los Angeles, CA 90036
Tel 323-655-1275
Email ....rocopolis@earthlink.net

Animator, AMERICAN FAMILY, 2002,
PBS, TV Series
Director, SON AFROCARIBENO, 1998,
Documentary
Producer, SON AFROCARIBENO, 1998,
Documentary
Writer, TODO CAMBIA, 1994, Universal
Pictures, Short
Producer, TODO CAMBIA, 1994,
Universal Pictures, Short

Cheech Marin

*Agent: Paradigm Talent Agency,
310-277-4400*

Actor, SILVER CITY, 2004, IFC
Productions, Feature
Actor, THE UNDERCLASSMAN, 2004,
Miramax, Feature
Actor, THE ORTEGAS, 2003, Fox
Network, TV Series
Writer, LAUGHING OUT LOUD:
AMERICA'S FUNNIEST COMEDIENS,
2001, TV Special
Director, BORN IN EAST LA, 1987,
Universal Pictures, Feature
Writer, BORN IN EAST LA, 1987,
Universal Pictures, Feature
Director, GET OUT OF MY ROOM, 1985,
Feature
Writer, CHEECH AND CHONG'S THE
CORSICAN BROTHERS, 1984, MGM,
Feature

Octavio Marin*

Signature Programs Director
NALIP
Los Angeles, CA 90024
Tel 310-208-1919
Cell 310-429-8351
Fax 310-453-5258
Email ....octavio@nalip.org
Web ....www.nalip.org

*Agent: Arlene Thorton & Associates,
818-760-6688*

Production Consultant, AMERICA 101,
2003, Fobia Films, Feature
Production Manager, HOW THE GARCIA
GIRLS SPENT THEIR SUMMER,
2003, Loosely Based Pictures, LLC.,
Feature
Production Consultant, TEXAS
RANGERS, 2001, Dimension
Miramax, Feature
Production Consultant, ONE MAN'S
HERO, 1999, MGM - Orion, Feature
Associate Producer, CAFÉ ARGENTINA,
1997, Crome Pictures, Short

Ingrid Marquez*

Laguna Niguel, CA 92677
Tel 949-887-7088
Fax 949-249-2413
Email ....imarquez@cox.net

Julio Martha*

San Ysidro, CA 92173
Tel 619-428-3440

Ivy Martin

Marketing Executive
Time Warner Cable
Torrance, CA 90505
Tel 310-974-1440
Fax 310-618-1049
Email...............ivy.martin@twcable.com

Alfredo Martinez*

Red Scarlet Productions
Montebello, CA 90640
Tel 323-887-0529
Email..don_al_2000_90640@yahoo.com

Alma Martinez*

New York, NY 10016
Tel 831-423-0360
Fax 831-459-4908
Email...............almamar@cats.ucsc.edu

Anna Martinez

S. W. Videographics
Tucson, AZ 85721
Tel 214-748-2225
Email ....amartinez@sw-video.com

Benito Martinez

Burbank, CA 91501
Tel 818-558-5677

Agent: SDB Partners, 310-785-0060

Actor, NEW SUIT, 2002, Trillon
   Entertainment, Feature
Actor, THE SHIELD, 2002, Columbia
   TriStar, TV Series
Actor, MI FAMILIA/MY FAMILY, 1995,
   New Line, Feature
Actor, OUTBREAK, 1995, Warner Home
   Video, Feature

Chuck Martinez

True Friend Productions
Santa Monica, CA 90406
Tel 310-230-1020
Tel 310-230-9667
Email ....trufrn@aol.com

Director, THE EFFECTS OF MAGIC,
   1998, The Discovery Network
Director, SUPERBOY, 1988 - 1992,
   Viacom, TV Series
Director, NICE GIRLS DON'T EXPLODE,
   1987, New World Home Video,
   Feature

Emanuel Anthony Martinez*

Round Rock, TX 78681
Email ....emanuel@segundobarrio.com

Ernesto Martínez*

Los Angeles, CA 90016
Tel 323 935-0605
Email ....esmarti@ucla.edu

Jose Martinez*

Hallandale, FL 33009
Tel 954-359-3255
Fax 954-458-8421
Email ....jamd313@hotmail.com

Ruben Martinez

Associate Editor
Pacific News Service
Washington, DC 20045
Tel 323-428-2193

Sebastian Martinez*

Calabasas, CA 91302
Email ....sebastianmrtnz@aol.com

Yvette Martinez

Television Race Initiative
San Francisco, CA 94110
Tel 415-553-2841
Fax 415-553-2848
Email ....highimpacttv@pov.org

Barbara Martinez-Jitner
El Norte Productions
Los Angeles, CA 90071
Tel 213-253-0825
Fax 213-625-2492
Email ....bmjelnorte@hotmail.com

Producer, AMERICAN FAMILY, 2002, Fox
   Television/PBS, TV Series
Producer, THE 20TH CENTURY: IN THE
   MELTING POT, 1999, Showtime, TV
   Special
Director, WHY DO FOOLS FALL IN LOVE,
   1998, Warner Bros., Feature

Carmen Martinez-Bergum*
Marina Del Rey, CA 90295
Tel 310-821-0713

Jessica Martinez-Puga
Safada y Sano Productions LLC.
LaPuente, CA 91747
Tel 323-445-0939
Tel 714-225-9535
Email ....info@safadaysano.com
Web ....www.safadaysano.com

Miguel Mas
Mas & More Entertainment
Los Angeles, CA 90026
Tel 213-250-9162
Cell 323-365-5610
Fax 213-250-9162
Email ....mimas@prodigy.net

Manager: The Levin Agency,
323-653-7073

Director, CIRCULOS, 2004, Feature
I WITNESS, 2002, Feature

Daniel Matas*
Indivox Films
New York, NY 10034
Tel 212-567-2910
Email ....indivox@yahoo.com
Web ....indivox.net

Director of Photography, RURAL
   AMERICA, 2003, NAACHO/Kellogg
   Foundation, Documentary
Director of Photography, CHAOS IN THE
   STREETS: WORLD TRADE TRAGEDY,
   2002, Indivox Films, Documentary
Director, NO LONG GOODBYES, 2001,
   INDIVOX FILMS, Feature
Producer, NO LONG GOODBYES, 2001,
   Indivox Films, Feature

Bienvenida Matias*
New York, NY 10009
Tel 212-529-3928
Email ....beni_matias@earthlink.net

Producer, ABRIENDO CAMINO, 2004,
   Latino Educational Media Center,
   Documentary
Producer, FOR THE RECORD: GUAM IN
   WW II, 2004, Polymorphous Pictures,
   Inc., Documentary
Educator, HUNTER COLLEGE, 2002,
   Film & Media Studies Dept., Portable
   Video Production
Director, HEART OF LOISAIDA, 1979,
   Reaven / Matias Productions,
   Documentary

Laala Matías*
New York, NY 10025
Tel 212-941-7720
Email ....laavida@yahoo.com

Jeff Maynor*
San Dimas, CA 91773
Tel 909-305-6773
Email ....jmaynor@yahoo.com

filmmakers

Talía Maynor*
San Dimas, CA 91773
Tel 909-305-6773
Email ....talia_o@yahoo.com

Alonso Mayo*
Manzana Azul (Blue Apple)
Los Angeles, CA 90039
Tel 323-309-1036
Email ....afmayo@mac.com

Director, SILENCIO, 2002, Manzana
    Azul, Short
Director, WEDNESDAY AFTERNOON,
    2002, American Film Institute, Short
Director, ALAS HUMANAS (HUMAN
    WINGS), 2001, Manzana Azul, Short

Jennifer Maytorena Taylor
Specific Pictures
Tel 415-552-5856
Email ......jennifer@specificpictures.com

Producer, BRAVE NEW VALLEY, 2004,
    LPB, Documentary
Director, BRAVE NEW VALLEY, 2004,
    LPB, Documentary
Producer, MY COMRADE YANKEE,
    2003, Documentary Short
Director, HOMEFRONT, 2002, KQED,
    Documentary
Producer, INDEPENDENT VIEW,
    2001-2002, KQED, TV Series

Madeline Mazzaira
Festival Coordinator
Miami Latin Film Festival
Miami, FL 33176
Tel 305.279.1809
Email ....mmazaira@hispanicfilm.com

Leonor McCall-Rodriguez
Mira Promo, Inc.
Redondo Beach, CA 90278
Tel 310-937-2789
Tel 310-379-4486
Cell 310-710-3824
Fax 310-937-8721
Email ....leonor@mirapromo.com
Web ....www.mirapromo.com

Publicist

Eren McGinnis*
Dos Vatos Productions
Lexington, KY 40508
Tel 859-254-3928
Fax 859-254-3928
Email ....erenmcginnis@hotmail.com
Web...........................www.dosvatos.com

Producer, IMPRESARIO, 2002, Dos
    Vatos/KET, Documentary
Producer, BEYOND THE BORDER,
    2001, Dos Vatos/ITVS/LPBP,
    Documentary
Producer, THE GIRL NEXT DOOR,
    2000, Café Sisters/Indican, Feature
Producer, TOBACCO BLUES, 1998,
    Café Sisters/ITVS, TV

Andres Medina
WGN Television Chicago
Ventura, CA 93006
Tel 773-883-3475

Editor

Augustine Medina
Attorney
Beltran & Medina
Los Angeles, CA 90012
Tel 213-580-0125

Daniel Medina*
South Pasadena, CA 91030
Email ....monster613@aol.com

Diane Medina
Director, Community Relations
KABC-TV
Glendale, CA 91201
Tel 818-863-7231
Email ....diane.medina@disney.com

Joey Medina*
Spank Monkey Productions
Tel 818-415-4434
Fax 626-797-5539
Email ....SpankMonkeyFilms@aol.com
Web ....www.elmatadorthemovie.com

Director, EL MATADOR, 2001, Feature
Producer, GAME SHOW NETWORK, 2000, Game Show Network, TV
Actor

Laura Medina
Santa Monica, CA
Fax 310-392-0533
Email ....medinalj@aol.com

Co-Producer, THE WONDERFUL ICE CREAM SUIT, 1998, Walt Disney Pictures, Feature
Production Manager, RACE THE SUN, 1996, TriStar Pictures, Feature
Director, WOMEN AT RISK, 1994, Women in Film
Production Manager, FRANKENSTEIN UNBOUND, 1990, 20th Century Fox, Feature
Production Manager, BORN TO BE WILD
Co-Producer, THE TICKET

Nellie Medina*
Futuri Entertainment, Inc.
W. Hempstead, NY 11552
Tel 516-505-9536
Email ....futurientertainment@yahoo.com

Production Manager, CONCERT FOR BANGLADESH, 2003, Apple Corps LTD. UK., Documentary
Line Producer, FESTIVAL EXPRESS, 2003, Giant Films UK, Feature
Line Producer, GULLY, 2002, Short
Producer, HUNG-UP, 2002, Short
Producer, AUTOPSY SERIES, 2001, HBO, TV Special
Producer, CONFESSIONS OF A MAFIA HITMAN, 2001, HBO, TV
Production Manager, ROLL OF THE DICE: THE CAPEMAN ON BROADWAY, 1998, Channel 4 UK, Documentary

Louis Mejia
President
CEO TV News
Miami, FL 33143
Tel 786-268-2723
Fax 305-888-5161
Email ....lmejia@the-beach.net
Web ....ceotvnews.com

Attorney: Ozzie Torres

Executive Producer, TIMELESS SOUL, 2001, BKWSU, Short
Writer, TIMELESS SOUL, 2001, BKWSU, Short

Andrea Melendez*
Buda, TX 78610
Tel 512-312-2512
Email ....gaealies@hotmail.com

Jose Oscar Melendez

Blind Ambition Films
Venice, CA 90291
Tel 323-460-2846
Email ....BAF@ureach.com

*Agent: William Morris Agency, Scott
Lambert, 310-859-4000*

Jaime Mendez*

Seattle, WA 98109
Tel 206-286-8526
Email.........................jems1@msn.com

Ricardo Mendez Matta

Los Angeles, CA
Tel 323-655-1275
Fax 323-655-8343
Email ....rocopolis@earthlink.net

*Agent: The Stone Manners Agency,
Michael Sheehy, 323-655-1313*

Director, THE DISTRICT, 2003, CBS, TV
   Series
Director, TOUCHED BY AN ANGEL,
   2002, CBS, TV Series
Director, NASH BRIDGES, 2001, CBS,
   TV Series
1st Assistant Director, BREAD AND
   ROSES, 2000, Lions Gate Films,
   Feature
1st Assistant Director, PRICE OF GLORY,
   2000, New Line Cinema, Feature
WEIRD SCIENCE, 1994, USA
   Network/Viacom, TV Series
1st Assistant Director, TRADE WINDS,
   1993, NBC, TV Movie

Jim Mendiola*

Hollywood, CA
Tel 323-876-8093
Email ....hidalgo12@aol.com

Writer, SPEED KILLS, 2003, Badass
   Pictures, Feature
Director, SPEED KILLS, 2003, Badass
   Pictures, Feature

Director, COME AND TAKE IT DAY,
   2001, ITVS, Feature
Writer, COME AND TAKE IT DAY, 2001,
   ITVS, Feature
Producer, COME AND TAKE IT DAY,
   2001, ITVS, Feature

Alex Mendoza*

Mendoza & Associates
Temple City, CA 91780
Tel 626-447-0469
Fax 626-447-0469
Email ....alexmend@aol.com

Production Facilities & Services,
   Printing
Graphic Designer

Ashley Mendoza

New York, NY 10025
Tel 212-865-9227
Cell 917-859-6017
Email ....amfilm@mac.com

Writer, DORA THE EXPLORER, 2001,
   Nickelodeon, TV Series, Animated
Associate Producer, DORA THE
   EXPLORER, 2001, Nickelodeon, TV
   Series, Animated

Bernard Mendoza*

Redwood City, CA 94063
Tel 650-274-3561
Email ......mendozabernard@hotmail.com

Edy Mendoza

CBS
Los Angeles, CA 90035
Tel 323-575-4025
Email..........edith.mendoza@tvc.cbs.com

Linda Mendoza

Sherman Oaks, CA
Tel 818-981-4288
Agent: CAA, Andy Elkin, 310-288-4545

Director, CHASING PAPI, 2003, 20th
  Century Fox, Feature
Director, THE ORTEGAS, 2003, Fox
  Network, TV Series
Director, GROUNDED FOR LIFE, 2001,
  Fox Network, TV Series
Director, THE BERNIE MAC SHOW,
  2001, Fox Network, TV Series
Director, ALMA AWARDS, 2000, TV
  Special
Director, THE CHRIS ROCK SHOW,
  1997, HBO, TV Series
Director, KENAN & KEL, 1996,
  Nickelodeon, TV Series
Director, MAD TV, 1995, Fox Network,
  TV Series

Minerva Mendoza*

Yuma, AZ 85365
Email ....mendozaminerva@aol.com

Angel Meneces

Staff
Bolivia al Dia
N. Miami Beach, FL 33162
Tel 305-948-6118
Tel 305-948-6118
Fax 305-945-6611
Email..........angelmeneces@hotmail.com

Producer, BOLIVIA AL DIA, 2001,
  WLRN, TV
Writer, VIERNES, 2000
Writer, GIROS, 1999, La Raza
  Newspaper, TV Guide
Producer, MAS DEPORTE, 1993, Red
  ATB, TV
Producer, CONCEPTO, 1987,
  TeleAndina, TV
Writer, TELEGUIA, 1987, Ultima Hora
  Newspaper, TV Guide

Joe Menendez

Studio City, CA
Tel 818-990-0305
Email ....menendezjoe@hotmail.com
Web ....www.sonrisa.com
*Agent: Preferred Artists, Brad Rosenfeld,
818-990-0305*

Writer, HUNTING OF MAN, 2003,
  Feature
Director, THE HUNTING OF MAN,
  2003, Feature
Director, LORDS OF THE BARRIO,
  2002, Spectrum Films, Feature
Writer, LORDS OF THE BARRIO, 2002,
  Spectrum Films, Feature
Director, THE BROTHERS GARCIA,
  2001, Nickelodeon, TV Series
Director, TAINA, 2000, Nickelodeon, TV
  Series
Director, VIVA VEGAS, 2000,
  Telemundo, TV Series
Director, LOS BELTRAN, 1999,
  Telemundo, TV Series
Writer, LOS BELTRAN, 1999,
  Telemundo, TV Series

Ramon Menendez

Los Angeles, CA
*Agent: Innovative Artists, Nancy Nigrosh,
310-656-5142*
*Attorney: Mark Kalmansohn,
310-553-8833*

Director, GOTTA KICK IT UP, 2002, The
  Disney Channel, TV Movie
Director, PERVERSIONS OF SCIENCE,
  1997, HBO, TV Series
Director, TALES FROM THE CRYPT: THE
  BRIBE, 1994, HBO, TV Series
Director, MONEY FOR NOTHING, 1993,
  Hollywood Pictures, Feature
Writer, MONEY FOR NOTHING, 1993,
  Hollywood Pictures, Feature
Director, STAND AND DELIVER, 1988,
  Warner Bros., Feature
Writer, STAND AND DELIVER, 1988,
  Warner Bros., Feature

filmmakers

Juan Menzor-Rivera*
Oakland, CA 94612
Tel 501-628-0601
Fax 415-978-9635

Claudia Mercado*
Los Angeles, CA
Tel 323-276-0322
Email ....coatluchxic@yahoo.com

Jon Mercedes*
Fiesta Communications
Los Angeles, CA 90028
Tel 323-314-5647

Rafael Merino*
Cine Huracan
New York, NY 10029
Email ....rmerino@cinehuracan.com

Deana Mesa*
Yorba Linda, CA 92886
Email ....Deana_Mesa@excite.com

Joaquin Mesa*
Exposure Plus
Los Angeles, CA 90004
Tel 323-461-5031
Fax 831-515-3068

Roland Mesa
The Cimarron Group
Los Angeles, CA 90038
Tel 323-936-6162

Director, THE REVENGE OF THE NERDS
  3, 1992, 20th. Century Fox, Feature
Director, TALES FROM THE CRYPT,
  1989, HBO, Feature

Jake Meyers*
Pasadena, CA 91107
Tel 323-993-5724
Email ....jakeameyers@yahoo.com

Humberto Meza*
Meza Productions
Los Angeles, CA 90005
Tel 213-381-1245
Email....................dazlomel@yahoo.com

Jean Meza*
Los Angeles, CA 90063
Email....................jmeza1@hotmail.com

Omar Meza*
Agent Assistant
William Morris Agency
Los Angeles, CA 90007
Tel 213-765-4986
Email ....rsiasst@wma.com
Web ....www.usc-eisa.com

Producer, SINK OR SWIM

Philip Meza*
Vista, CA 92084
Email ....MezaPhilip@hotmail.com

Patricia Migliori Farnes*
HDE Prods
New York, NY 10024
Tel 212-362-8055
Email ....HistoriasDeEllas@aol.com

Adriana Millan*
Millan Enterprises
La Mirada, CA 90638
Tel 562-944-3590
Email ....ambastet@aol.com

Elisha Miranda*

Chica Luna Productions, Inc
New York, NY 10032
Tel 201-814-0925
Cell 201-832-2894
Fax 201-814-1327
Email...............chicalunafilms@aol.com
Web ....www.chicaluna.com

Attorney: Innes Smolansky, Esq.,
Innes@filmlegal.com

Director, BLIND DATE, 2003, Chica Sol
  Films, LLC/Student Academy Award
  Grant, Short
Writer, FOR THE LOVE OF PATRIA,
  2003, Women Make Movies, Short
Producer, A-ALIKE, 2002, New Heritage
  Films/Middle Passage Filmworks, Short
Director, BAPTISM BY FIRE, 2002,
  Women Make Movies, Documentary
  Short
Producer, BAPTISM BY FIRE, 2002,
  Women Make Movies, Documentary
  Short
Director, CORPORATE DAWGZ, 2002, DV
  Republic.com, Short
Producer, CORPORATE DAWGZ, 2002,
  DV Republic.com, Short

Nestor Miranda

Mira Productions
Los Angeles, CA 90045
Tel 310-410-3030
Fax 310-410-3003
Email ....mirafilms@msn.com
Web ....www.mirafilms.com

Director, AVENUE A, 2004, Fox
  searchlight, Feature
Writer, AVENUE A, 2003, Fox
  Searchlight, Feature
Director, SHIVER, 2003, Ground Zero
  Entertainment, Feature
Writer, SHIVER, 2003, Ground Zero
  Entertainment, Feature
Producer, ONCE UPON A RIDE, 2001,
  Black Filmmakers Foundation, TV
  Series

Producer, BLAZIN', 1999, Ground Zero
  Entertainment, Feature
Producer, DESTINATION UNKNOWN,
  1997, Ground Zero Entertainment,
  Feature
Director, DESTINATION UNKNOWN,
  1997, Ground Zero Entertainment,
  Feature
Writer, DESTINATION UNKNOWN,
  1997, Ground Zero Entertainment,
  Feature

Teresa Mireles

The Bravo Group
New York, NY 10003
Tel 212-780-5800

Rhonda L. Mitrani*

The Florida Room
Miami Beach, FL 33139
Tel 305-582-7191
Fax 305-610-4564
Email ....rhonda@thefloridaroom.com
Web ....cubamiathefilm.com

Editor, THE SUITOR, 2001, Gigantic
  Pictures, TV Movie
Editor, HIT AND RUNWAY, 1999, Lot
  47, Feature
Producer

Lucila Moctezuma*

New York, NY 10016
Tel 212-889-9515
Email ....lmoctezuma@hotmail.com

Lilia Molina*

Westminster, CA
Tel 818-469-2714
Email..................molinalilis@yahoo.com

Sergio Molina
Los Angeles, CA

Executive Producer, MI FAMILIA/MY FAMILY, 1995, New Line Cinema, Feature
Writer, HOY NO CIRCULA, 1993, TV Series
Writer, EL JINETE DE LA DIVINA PROVIDENCIA, 1988, Feature
Writer, LOS PIRATAS, 1986, Feature

Rene Moncivais*
Ft. Worth, TX 76137
Email ....rmoncivais@hotmail.com

Julie Monroy*
Film Club/CSNU
Los Angeles, CA 90065
Tel 323-277-0421
Cell 323-350-2163
Email...........julie_monroy@hotmail.com

Director, CENTRAL AMERICANS, FIRST GENERATIONS, 2001, Documentary
Executive Producer, SALVADORAN WOMEN AND THEIR RELIGION, 2001, Documentary
Director, HOMMIES UNIDOS, 2000, CSU Northridge, Documentary

Ricardo Montalban
Nosotros
Hollywood, CA 90004
Tel 323-466-8566
Fax 323-466-8540
Email ....velascojjv@aol.com
Web...........................www.nosotros.org

Agent: Velasco and Associates, Jerry Velasco, 323-466-8566

Actor, SPY KIDS 3, 2003, Miramax, Feature
Actor, SPY KIDS 2, 2002, Miramax, Feature
Actor, CANNONBALL RUN 2, 1984, Warner Bros., Feature

Sara Monteagudo*
deFelix Productions
Coral Springs, FL 33076
Tel 954-575-9221
Email ....sara@defelix.com

Richard Montes*
Safada y Sano Productions LLC.
LaPuente, CA 91747
Tel 323-445-0939
Email..................info@safadaysano.com
Web ....www.safadaysano.com

Roberto Monticello*
New York, NY 10014
Tel 212-229-8390

John Montoya
His Panic Endeavors
Lancaster, CA 93534
Tel 661-886-0967
Email ....johnmontoya55@yahoo.com

Attorney: Leif Reinstein/Bloom, Hergott and Diemer, 310-859-6800, lwr@bhdllp.com

Director, BORN 2B GANGSTAZ?, 2003, Documentary Short
Director, INTRODUCING LEANDRO FELIPE, 2003, Pending, Documentary Short
Director of Photography, INTRODUCING LEANDRO FELIPE, 2003, Pending, Documentary Short
Producer, BOOK WARS, 2000, Avatar, Documentary
Producer, LIVE NUDE GIRLS UNITE!, 2000, First Run Features, Documentary
Director of Photography, LIVE NUDE GIRLS UNITE!, 2000, First Run Features, Documentary
Director, OUR OWN ROAD, 2000, Neta/Aquarius, Documentary Short

Director of Photography, OUR OWN
ROAD, 2000, Neta/Aquarius,
Documentary Short
Producer, JUST A GAME?, 1996, New
Dimensions Media, Documentary Short

Richard Montoya
Los Angeles, CA
Tel 213-447-0538
Web ....www.cultureclash.com

*Manager: Ivan de Paz, Arenas
Entertainment, 310-385-4401*

Actor, CHAVEZ RAVINE, 2003, Mark
Taper Forum, Stage Play
Writer, CHAVEZ RAVINE, 2003, Mark
Taper Forum, Stage Play
Actor, NUYORICAN STORIES, 1999,
INTAR, Stage Play
Writer, NUYORICAN STORIES, 1999,
INTAR, Stage Play
Actor, FALLING DOWN, 1993, Warner
Bros., Feature
Actor, RADIO MAMBO, 1993, INTAR,
Stage Play
Writer, RADIO MAMBO, 1993, INTAR,
Stage Play
Actor, HERO, 1992, Columbia Pictures,
Feature

Danny Mora
Tel 323-936-5299
Email ....drsusane@msn.com

Actor, CORONADO, 2003, Uncharted
Territory, Feature
Actor, BROWN'S REQUIEM, 1998,
Avalanche Releasing, Feature
Actor, ROAD ENDS, 1997, New City
Releasing, Feature

Analuisa Morales*
Tempe, AZ 85281
Tel 480-329-2269
Fax 480-423-6077
Email ....analuixa@msn.com

Iris Morales*
New York, NY 10025
Tel 212-222-3448
Email ....imorales@fcny.org

Michael Morales
Attorney
Los Angeles, CA 90069
Tel 310-278-0066
Fax 310-887-1875
Email....................michael@entatty.com

Robert Morales*
Canopus
Hollywood, FL 33024
Tel 408-944-9558
Fax 408-944-9558
Email ....darktangos@hotmail.com

Robert Morales*
Zepol Productions
Pembroke Pines, FL 33026
Tel 954-431-5700
Fax 954-432-2266
Email ....rob@zepolvideo.com

Rosalinda Morales
FarMore Casting and Prod.
Los Angeles, CA
Tel 213-840-4738
Fax 530-325-4738

Casting Director, EL PADRINO, 2003, El
Padrino, LLC, Feature
Casting Director, BREAD AND ROSES,
2000, Lions Gate Films, Feature
Casting Director, REYES Y REY, 1998,
TV Series

Sylvia Morales*
Los Angeles, CA
Tel 310-391-0070
Email.......................smorales@attbi.com

Agent: Contemporary Artists Ltd.,
310-395-1800

Director, RESURRECTION BLVD., 2000,
   Showtime, TV Series
Producer, TELL ME AGAIN...WHAT'S
   LOVE, 1998, PBS, TV Series
Director, REYES Y REY, 1995,
   Telemundo Network, TV Series
Producer, CHICANO! THE MEXICAN
   AMERICAN CIVIL RIGHTS
   MOVEMENT, 1994, PBS, TV Series
Producer, THE FAITH EVEN TO THE
   FIRE, 1990, PBS, TV Series

Alessandra Morales-Gunz*
Tustin, CA 92780
Email ....algunz@yahoo.com

Nelson Moran*
Bronx, NY 10474
Tel 212-744-4328
Fax 212-535-5299
Email ....ceenm@aol.com

Oscar Moreas*
Cine las Americas
Austin, TX 78753
Web ....www.cinelasamericas.org

Alex Moreno
Vice President
Creative Industry Handbook
Toluca Lake, CA 91602
Tel 818-752-3200
Cell 818-968-9444
Fax 818-752-3221
Email ....alex@creativehandbook.com
Web ....www.creativehandbook.com

Media Advocate

Dorinda Moreno*
Hitec Aztec Communications
Los Angeles, CA 90089
Tel 925-676-6241

Eduardo Moreno
Producer
KCET
Tel 323-953-5320
Email ....emoreno@kcet.org

Fernando Moreno*
It's TV Productions
Studio City, CA 91603
Email.......................itstvmedia@aol.com

Mylene Moreno*
Souvenir Pictures
Los Angeles, CA 90046
Tel 323-512-4678
Fax 323-512-4679
Email ....mylenem@earthlink.net

Director, TRUE HEARTED VIXENS,
   2001, POV, Documentary
Producer, CORMAC'S TRASH, 1999,
   Short
Director, CHICANO! EPISODE, 1996,
   PBS/KCET, Documentary
Producer, CHICANO! EPISODE, 1996,
   PBS/KCET, Documentary

Pepe Moreno
Computer Games Designer
Digital Fusion, Inc.
Tel 310-274-5110
Email ....pepe@fusiongames.com

Bob Morones

Universal City, CA 91602
Tel 323-465-8110

Casting Director, KINGPIN, 2003, NBC,
   TV Series
Casting Director, RESURRECTION
   BLVD., 2002, Showtime, TV Series
Casting Director, DEAD IN THE WEST,
   2000, Razorwire Pictures, Feature
Casting Director, ROMERO, 1989, Four
   Square, Feature
Casting Director, PLATOON, 1986, MGM
   Entertainment, Feature
Casting Director, SALVADOR, 1986,
   Imagine Entertainment, Feature

Marcelo Mosenson*

Brooklyn, NY 11213
Tel 718-735-3528
Fax 718-735-3528
Email ....nomadefilms@yahoo.com

Marcela Moya*

Costa Mesa, CA 92627
Tel 949-646-8908
Email ....marcela5@hotmail.com

Mariana Mucci*

Los Angeles, CA 90034
Tel 310-876-3081
Email.........marianamucci@hotmail.com

Juan Miguel Muñiz

CNN en Español
Los Angeles, CA 90028
Tel 323-993-5042
Fax 323-993-5188
Email ....juan.muniz@turner.com

Cynthia Muñoz

Muñoz Public Relations
San Antonio, TX 78207
Tel 210-225-3353
Email ..cynthia@munozpublicrelations.com

Maria Muñoz*

Ph.D. Candidate
UCLA's Critical Studies Program in the
Film, TV and Digital Media Dept.
San Pedro, CA 90731
Tel 310-548-0894
Email ....munozchacon@hotmail.com

Robert Muñoz

Director of Business Development
New Line Cinema
Los Angeles, CA 90048
Tel 310-854-5811
Web ....www.newlinecinema.com

Maria Murillo*

Cine Chatota
Los Angeles, CA 90021
Tel 213-627-7573
Email ....lachatota@earthlink.net

Peter Murrieta

Los Angeles, CA
Tel 818-954-4255
Email ....candyb32@yahoo.com

Agent: CAA, Ted Miller, 310-288-4545

Producer, ALL ABOUT THE
   ANDERSONS, 2003, Warner Bros.
   Television Network, TV Series
Writer, R3, 2003, Sony Pictures
   Entertainment, Feature
Writer, GREETINGS FROM TUCSON,
   2002, Warner Bros. Television
   Network, TV Series
Producer, GREETINGS FROM TUCSON,
   2002, Warner Bros., TV Series
Writer, THREE SISTERS, 2001, NBC,
   TV Series

Kimberly Myers*
Development Executive
Maya Pictures
Los Angeles, CA 90065
Tel 310-281-3770
Fax 310-281-3777
Web ....www.maya-pictures.com

Producer, PASSION, 1996, PBS, TV
Producer, JACOB, 1994, TNT, TV
Producer, MIDNIGHT'S CHILD, 1992,
   The Polone Company

Lesa Myers*
Michael's Productions
Pearland, TX 77581
Tel 281-482-8496
Email ....lesa.myers@puffer.com

Monica Nanez*
San Francisco, CA 94112
Tel 415-846-6938
Email...............monanez@sbcglobal.net

Producer, DIRTY LAUNDRY, 2000, Short

Gerardo Naranjo
Perro Negro Productions
Los Angeles, CA 90007
Tel 323-661-0977

Director, MALA CHANCE, 2003, Perro
   Negro Productions, Feature
Director, THE LAST ATTACK OF THE
   BEAST, 2002, AFI, Short

Miguel Naranjo Caballero*
Los Angeles, CA 90034
Tel 310-621-2827
Email..........Unexxpected1@hotmail.com

Michael Narvaez*
Managing Partner
I Believe in America Productions, LLC.
Bronx, NY 10463
Tel 917-519-9600
Fax 718-432-2827
Email ....michael.narvaez@verizon.net

Manager: LaSalle Management Group,
212-541-4444, lillian@lasallemange-
mentgroup.com

Producer, I BELIEVE IN AMERICA,
   2004, IBIA, LLC, Feature
Writer, I BELIEVE IN AMERICA, 2004,
   Feature
Actor, FUNNY VALENTINE, 2003,
   Feature
Actor, MAID IN MANHATTAN, 2002, US
   Studio, Feature
Writer, BLAZIN, 2001, Feature
Producer, HE'S COMING AND NOBODY
   CARES!, 2000, Short
Writer, HE'S COMING AND NOBODY
   CARES!, 2000, Short

Gregory Nava
El Norte Productions
Los Angeles, CA 90071
Tel 213-253-0825
Fax 213-625-2492
Email ....bmjelnorte@hotmail.com

Agent: ICM, Martha Luttrell,
310-550-4000

Producer, KILLING PABLO, 2004,
   Dreamworks Distribution, Feature
Director, AMERICAN FAMILY, 2002,
   PBS, TV
Producer, AMERICAN FAMILY, 2002,
   PBS, TV Series
Writer, AMERICAN FAMILY, 2002, PBS,
   TV Series
Writer, FRIDA, 2002, Miramax, Feature
Producer, 20TH CENTURY: IN THE
   MELTING POT, 1999, Showtime, TV
   Movie

Director, THE 20TH CENTURY: IN THE MELTING POT, 1999, Showtime, Documentary

Director, SELENA, 1997, Warner Bros., Feature

Writer, SELENA, 1997, Warner Bros., Feature

Lisa Navarrete

Communications Director
National Council of La Raza
Washington, DC 20036
Tel 202-785-1670
Fax 202-776-1792
Email ....lnavarrete@nclr.org

Roberto Navarro*

Montebello, CA 90640
Tel 323-722-7573
Email ....roberto_navarro@yahoo.com

Jesus Nebot

Zokalo Entertainment
Santa Monica, CA 90403
Tel 310-478-0770
Fax 310-496-2772
Email ....jesus@zokalo.com
Web ....www.zokalo.com

Agent: BKI, Joel Kleinman, 323-874-9800

Manager: David Gardner, 310-2744622

Actor, BOOM TOWN, 2003, NBC, TV Series

Actor, NO TURNING BACK, 2002, Zenpix, Universal, Feature

Producer, NO TURNING BACK, 2002, Zenpix, Universal, Feature

Director, NO TURNING BACK, 2001, Zenpix, Universal, Feature

Actor, NYPD BLUE, 2000, ABC, TV Series

Hector Negrete*

Los Angeles, CA 90034
Email ....hectorious@hotmail.com

Frances Negron-Muntaner*

Polymorphous Pictures
Plantation, FL 33324
Tel 305-672-0322
Fax 305 673-1665
Email ....bikbaporub@aol.com

Producer, FOR THE RECORD, GUAM IN WWII, 2004, ITVS, Documentary

Director, FOR THE RECORD, GUAM IN WWII, 2004, ITVS, Documentary

Producer, THE STATE OF THE TERRITORY: US-PUERTO RICO RELATIONS AT THE CROSSROADS, 2004, Polymorphous Pictures, Documentary

Director, THE STATE OF THE TERRITORY: US-PUERTO RICO RELATIONS AT THE CROSSROADS, 2004, Polymorphous Pictures, Documentary

Producer, BRINCANDO EL CHARCO, 1994, Women Make Movies, Documentary

Director, BRINCANDO EL CHARCO, 1994, Women Make Movies, Documentary

Dan Neira*

Cineira Entertainment Corp.
Pasadena, CA 91103
Tel 626-432-7446
Fax 626-432-7495
Email ....cineiro@earthlink.net
Web..........cineiraentertainmentcorp.com

Damian Nelson*

Tucson, AZ 85719
Tel 520-795-3306
Email ....damian4@mindspring.com

filmmakers

Jennifer Nelson*
Bronx, NY 10475
Email ....imimy_jn@hotmail.com

Johnny Ray Nelson*
Los Angeles, CA 90036
Email ....ryxingstar@yahoo.com

Heather Nichols*
Carson, CA 90745
Email.....................hmn3@hotmail.com

Andres Nicolini*
New York, NY 10040
Tel 212-928-0097
Email ....andresnicolini@yahoo.com

Gustavo Nieto-Roa*
Centauro Comunicaciones
Miami, FL 33166
Tel 305-436-1159
Fax 305-433-0974
Email.................gustavo@centauro.com

Bill Nieves
New York, NY 10024
Tel 212-724-2087
Fax 212-724-2111
Email........muchovideo@mindspring.com

Director, ENTERTAINMENT TONIGHT,
2001, NBC, TV Series

Yvette Nieves Cruz*
New Rochelle, NY 10805
Email..............ynievescruz@hotmail.com
Web ....www.evc.org

Karine Nissim*
Broken Legs Productions
Miami, FL 33131
Tel 305-377-0202
Email ....karnissim@aol.com

Alex Nogales*
President
National Hispanic Media Coalition
Los Angeles, CA 90007
Tel 213-384-8494
Tel 213-746-6988
Fax 213-746-1305
Email ....nhmc@azteca.net
Web ....www.nhmc.com

Media Advocate

Dr. Chon Noriega*
Executive Director
UCLA Chicano Studies Research Center
Los Angeles, CA 90095
Tel 310-206-0714
Fax 323-660-9302
Email ....Cnoriega@tft.ucla.edu
Web ....www.sscnet.ucla.edu/csrc/

Media Advocate
Educator

Julio Noriega
Film & Video Division Director
Venevision International/Cisneros Group
Coral Gables, FL 33134
Tel 305-442-3411
Fax 305-448-4762
Web ....www.venevisionintl.com

Distributor

Jennifer Nowotny*
Cal State University
San Marcos, CA 92096
Tel 760-750-8663
Email ....jnowtny@csusm.edu

Web Developer

Emanuel Nuñez
Agent
Creative Artists Agency
Beverly Hills, CA 90212
Tel 310-288-4545
Fax 310-288-4800

Frank Nuñez*
Little Boyz Dreams
Vista, CA 92084
Tel 760-758-7389
Fax 760-758-7389
Email ....nunezfrank@hotmail.com

Director, 187 SHADOW LANE, 2003,
   Spartan/El Matador, Feature
Producer, 187 SHADOW LANE, 2003,
   Spartan/El Matador, Feature
Director, DIABLO, 2003, Feature
Producer, DIABLO, 2003, Feature
Writer, JAIL CELL, Short

Roque Nuñez*
New York, NY 10031
Tel 212-234-4492
Email ....rockynunez@yahoo.com

Lorenzo O'Brien
Copal Productions
Pasadena, CA 94011
Tel 213-709-0527
Email ....lobrien@gte.net

Producer, AMERICAN FAMILY, 2003,
   PBS, TV Series
Writer, AMERICAN FAMILY, 2003, PBS,
   TV Series
Producer, NEVER TRUST A SERIAL
   KILLER, 2002, Feature
Producer, PILGRIM, 2000, Lions Gate
   Films Home Entertainment, Feature
Producer, DEATH AND THE COMPASS,
   1997, Together Brothers Productions,
   Feature
Producer, DEATH AND THE COMPASS,
   1996, Anchor Bay Entertainment,
   Feature

Producer, HIGHWAY PATROLMAN,
   1993, First Look Pictures, Feature
Writer, HIGHWAY PATROLMAN, 1993,
   First Look Pictures, Feature

Ruben Obregon*
Los Angeles, CA 90036
Tel 323-651-1050
Email ....robregon@ucla.edu

Clemen Ochoa
Santa Fe, NM
Tel 505-466-2311

2nd 2nd Assistant Director, GHOSTS OF
   MARS, 2001, Screen Gems, Inc.,
   Feature
2nd 2nd Assistant Director, EMMA'S
   WISH, 1998, Citadel Entertainment,
   TV Movie
2nd 2nd Assistant Director, VAMPIRES,
   1998, Sony Pictures Entertainment,
   Feature
2nd 2nd Assistant Director, F.T.W.,
   1994, Nu Image, Feature
2nd Assistant Director, GETTYSBURG,
   1993, New Line Cinema, Feature

Kaaren Ochoa
Los Angeles, CA
Tel 310-727-3300

1st Assistant Director, WHILE
   OLEANDER, 2002, Warner Bros.,
   Feature
Production Manager, PROOF OF LIFE,
   2000, Warner Bros., Feature
1st Assistant Director, SELENA, 1997,
   Warner Bros., Feature
1st Assistant Director, GETTYSBURG,
   1993, New Line Cinema, Feature

filmmakers

Antonio Ogaz*
New Vista Productions
Duarte, CA 91010
Tel 626-305-5194
Email.....................aogaz@earthlink.net

Paul Ohnersorgen*
Topanga, CA 90290
Tel 310-435-4201
Email ....ajnaone@netzero.net

Ibon Olaskoaga
Global Vision Media
Los Angeles, CA 90037
Tel 818-842-4479
Email ....ibonolas@yahoo.com

Producer
Editor

Jorge Oliver
Professor, SFSU
Cherubim Productions
San Francisco, CA
Tel 415-255-2454
Email ....joliver_stl@yahoo.com

Editor, LA PASPORTO AL LA TUTA
  MONDO, 2002, Montell and
  Associates, TV
Editor, TIMBRELS AND TORAHS, 2000,
  Montell and Associates, Documentary
  Short
Director, PRIDE IN PUERTO RICO,
  1999, Frameline Distribution,
  Documentary Short
Director, WRITTEN, 1998, Cherubim
  Productions, Short
Director, URANUS IN THE SEVENTH
  HOUSE, 1996, Cherubim Productions,
  Short

Javier Olivera
Pachamama Films, LLC.
Los Angeles, CA 90068
Tel 323-871-1055
Cell 323-447-7185
Email ....pachamamafilms@aol.com

Agent: ICM, Eddie Borges,
310-550-4266, eborges@icmtalent.com

Director, EL CAMINO, 2000, Tercer
  Milenio, Feature
Writer, EL CAMINO, 2000, Condor
  Media (USA), Feature
Director, EL VISITANTE, 1999, Tercer
  Milenio, Feature
Writer, EL VISITANTE, 1999, Tercer
  Milenio, Feature
Director, LAURA Y ZOE, 1998,
  Aries/Artear (Argentina), TV Series
Writer, TODAVIA EXISTIMOS, 1998,
  INAI, Documentary

Edward James Olmos
Olmos Productions
Burbank, CA 91521
Tel 818-560-8651
Fax 818-560-8655

Agent: CAA, Steve Tellez,
310-288-4545

Actor, BATTLE STAR GALACTICA, 2003,
  SciFi Channel, TV Series
Actor, AMERICAN FAMILY, 2002, PBS,
  TV Series
Actor, JACK AND MARILYN, 2002,
  Olmos Productions, Feature
Director, JACK & MARILYN, 2002,
  Florida Studios, Feature
Producer, JACK& MARILYN, 2002,
  Florida Studios, Feature
Producer, AMERICANOS: LATINO LIFE
  IN THE UNITED STATES, 2000,
  Olmos Productions, Documentary
Director, AMERICAN ME, 1992,
  Universal Pictures, Feature
Producer, AMERICAN ME, 1992,
  Universal Pictures, Feature
Director, MIAMI VICE, 1984, NBC, TV
  Series

Daniela Ontiveros*
Tucson, AZ 85705
Email ....danielao@email.arizona.edu

Jose Luis Orbegozo*
Brooklyn, NY 11215
Tel 718-399-3116
Cell 917-622-8907
Fax 718-399-3116
Email......................jlorbe@hotmail.com
Web ....www.orbeworld.com

Director, MARYANN, 2002, NYU, Short
Producer, MARYANN, 2002, NYU, Short
Writer, MARYANN, 2002, Short
Producer, THE CLOSED DOOR, 1997, Short

Andre Orci
Creative Development
Maya Pictures
Los Angeles, CA 90038
Tel 310-281-3770
Fax 310-281-3777
Web ....www.maya-pictures.com

Sierra Ornelas*
Tucson, AZ 85712
Tel 520-327-3852
Email ....jetagarlo@aol.com

Production Assistant, HOW THE GARCIA GIRLS SPENT THEIR SUMMER, 2003, Loosely Based Pictures, LLC., Feature

Salavador Orofina*
Miami Beach, FL 33139
Email.....................scorofino@msn.com

Paulette Orona*
North Hills, CA 91343

Roberta Orona-Cordova*
Professor
CSUN
Alzada Productions
Winnetka, CA 91306
Tel 818-677-6818
Email...............roberta.orona@csun.edu

Educator

Lourdes Ortega*
Publicist
Ortega Public Relations
Redondo Beach, CA 90277
Tel 310-316-3313
Cell 310-592-8530
Email ....ortegapr@hotmail.com

Alfredo Ortega-Trillo*
National City, CA 91950
Tel 619-791-2608
Email............................trillo@telnor.net

Arianna Ortiz*
Santa Monica, CA 90403
Tel 310-795-8994
Email ....gazpacha@yahoo.com

David Ortiz*
Creative Executive
Warner Bros.
Burbank, CA 91522
Tel 818-954-6223
Cell 310-994-6306
Email ....David.Ortiz@warnerbros.com

Luis Ortiz
Program Manager
Latino Public Broadcasting
Los Angeles, CA
Tel 323-466-7110
Email ....elhuicholin@yahoo.com

Monica Ortiz*
Los Angeles, CA 90027
Email ....monicao@mail.com

Paul Ortiz*
New York, NY 10027
Tel 212-222-9965
Email......Humblegladiator@netscape.net

Rolando Ortiz*
Fiesta Studios
Los Angeles, CA 90026
Tel 213-384-5069
Email............fiestastudios@hotmail.com

Yazmin Ortiz
Blind Ambition Films
Venice, CA 90291
Tel 323-460-2846
Email ....BAF@ureach.com

Agent: William Morris Agency, Scott Lambert, 310-859-4000

Director, EL BAILE, 2003, Short
Producer

Fernando Oubina*
Orlando, FL 32807
Tel 407-257-2977
Email ..FernandoUSA2003@hotmail.com

George Ozuna*
Head of Digital Cinema Department
Northeast School for the Arts
San Antonio, TX 78221
Tel 210-669-9935
Email....................gozun001@neisd.net

Educator

Carolina Pacheco
Researcher, Documentary
Greystone Television
North Hollywood, CA 91601
Tel 818-762-2900

Adriana E. Padilla
Cuentos del Pueblo Productions
Beverly Hills, CA 90212
Email..cuentos_del_pueblo@hotmail.com

Writer, PAN DULCE Y CHOCOLATE,
   Short
Producer, PAN DULCE Y CHOCOLATE,
   Short

Antone Pagan*
Silent Warrior Productions
New York, NY 10108
Tel 212-459-1910
Email ....familywarrior@aol.com

Edwin Pagan*
PaganImages, Inc.
New York, NY 10009
Tel 917-653-2273
Fax 212-967-0390
Email ....paganimage@aol.com

Director of Photography

Antonio Palaez*
MediaQuest
Zapopan, Jalisco 45019 Mexico
Fax 011-52-33-3832-0497
Email ....apelaez@cybercable.net.mx

Laura Palaez*
MediaQuest
Zapopan, Jalisco 45019 Mexico
Tel 011-52-33-3832-0497
Tel 011-52-33-3944-5197
Fax 011-52-33-3832-0497
Email ....xplorando@yahoo.com

Producer, XPLORANDO, 2001,
   Mediaquest, TV Series
Producer, EL MILAGRO DE LAS ROSAS,
   1999, Mediaquest, Short

Mercedes Palomo

President
Pigeon Productions
Miami, FL 33145
Tel 305-856-2929
Fax 305-858-0357
Web ....www.pigeonprod.com

Production Facilities & Services

Ari Palos*

Dos Vatos Productions
Tucson, AZ 85719
Tel 520-325-0307

Director, IMPRESSARIO, 2001, PBS,
  Documentary
Director, KENTUCKY THEATER, 2000,
  Dos Vatos Productions, Documentary
Director of Photography, OKIE
  NOODLING, 2000, Little League
  Pictures, Documentary

Pedro Pano*

Los Angeles, CA 90042

Robert Parada

Angelinos Productions
Pacoima, CA 91331
Tel 818-796-1779
Cell 818-216-8323
Fax 818-686-6009
Email ....Angelinosprods@cs.com

Producer, THE BLUES, 2002, Ground
  Zero Entertainment, Feature
Producer, HUSTLAS, 2000, Maverick
  Entertainment, Feature
HUSTLAS, 1999, Maverick
  Entertainment, Feature

Rey Parla*

First Flight Pictures
Miami, FL 33172
Tel 305-225-8808
Email ....firstflightpictures@hotmail.com
Web ....indieparla@worldnet.att.net

DIABLO, ifilm.com / apple.com
Producer, EMPUJANDO UN BOTON,
  Sonic Habitat
Producer, SPORADIC GERMINATION,
  Miami Film Festival

George Parra

Malibu, CA 90265
Email.......................h2oparra@aol.com

1st Assistant Director, LEGALLY BLOND
  2: RED, WHITE & BLONDE, 2003,
  MGM, Feature
1st Assistant Director, MALIBU'S MOST
  WANTED, 2003, Warner Bros.,
  Feature
1st Assistant Director, ABOUT
  SCHMIDT, 2002, New Line Cinema,
  Feature
1st Assistant Director, XXX, 2002,
  Columbia TriStar, Feature
1st Assistant Director, THE FAST AND
  THE FURIOUS, 2001, Universal
  Pictures, Feature
1st Assistant Director, ANY GIVEN
  SUNDAY, 1999, Warner Bros., Feature
1st Assistant Director, THE MASK OF
  ZORRO, 1998, TriStar Pictures,
  Feature
1st Assistant Director, JINGLE ALL THE
  WAY, 1996, 20th Century Fox,
  Feature
1st Assistant Director, THE ROCK,
  1996, Buena Vista Pictures, Feature

Jonathan Parra*

San Francisco, CA 94110
Tel 415-621-3178
Email ....jonathanparra@hotmail.com

filmmakers

183

Jose Luis Partida*

Producer
Grupo Vida
Dallas, TX 75219
Tel 214-478-8619
Fax 469-621-1412
Email..............Joseluis@grupovida-tv.org
Web ....www.grupovida-tv.org

Producer, AIDS NATIONAL, PSA
Producer, DENNY'S NATIONAL
  COMMERCIAL SPOTS, Commercial
Producer, DENNY'S NATIONAL
  PROMOTION, Commercial
Executive Producer, LAS VEGAS HEALTH
  (CERO HUMO CAMPAIGN)
Director, MI HIJO MI HIJA AMOR,
  Documentary

Lionel Pasamonte

Executive Producer, Co-
LATV
Venice, CA 90270
Tel 310-745-1575
Email ....maxpasa1@aol.com

Producer, LATV LIVE, 2003, LATV, TV
Award Shows, ALMA AWARDS, 2002,
  ABC, TV Special

Dagoberto Patlan*

KLRN TV
San Antonio, TX 98215
Tel 210-270-9000
Email ....Dpatlan@KLRN.ORG

Edward Paulino*

John Jay College of Criminal Justice
New York, NY 10038
Email.................guacherno@yahoo.com

Carlos Pelayo*

SDSU
San Diego, CA 92116
Tel 619-516-4626
Email ....clos98@yahoo.com

Jaime Pelayo*

Los Angeles, CA 90048
Tel 323-651-2697
Email ....jaimepelayo@hotmail.com

Jose Antonio Pelayo*

Cliffside Park, NJ 07010
Email ....jantonio@mindspring.com

Bill Peña*

Armstrong Insurance
San Antonio, TX 78201
Tel 210-614-3044
Fax 210-614-4333
Email ....arminsur@swbell.net

Deana Peña*

Armstrong Insurance
San Antonio, TX 78202
Tel 210-614-3045
Fax 210-614-4334
Email ....arminsur@swbell.net

Dina Peña*

San Antonio, TX 78237
Email......................ernie811@msn.com

Dora Peña*

San Antonio, TX 78249
Tel 210-694-4677
Email ....doralpena@hotmail.com

Elizabeth Peña

Fletcher and Phil Inc.
Los Angeles, CA 90025
Fax 310-455-3439

Agent: Paradigm, Susie Tobin,
310-277-4400

Actor, HOW THE GARCIA GIRLS SPENT THEIR SUMMER, 2004, Loosely Based Pictures LLC., Feature
Actor, THE DEAD HOLLYWOOD MOMS SOCIETY, 2004, Hallmark, TV Movie
Actor, TORTILLA SOUP, 2001, Samuel Goldwyn Films, Feature
Director, RESURRECTION BLVD., 2000, Showtime, TV Series
Actor, RESURRECTION BLVD., 2000, Showtime, TV Series
Director, THE BROTHERS GARCIA, 2000, Nickelodeon, TV Series
Actor, RUSH HOUR, 1998, New Line Cinema, Feature
Actor, LA BAMBA, 1987, Columbia Pictures, Feature

Manuel Peña*

San Antonio, TX 78249
Tel 210-699-4677
Email...............manjpena@hotmail.com

Sandra Peña*

Pocha Productions
Santa Ana, CA 92701
Tel 714-972-0073
Fax 714-245-9710
Email.......................pochioux@aol.com

Jeff Penichet*

President
Hispanic Film Project
Los Angeles, CA 90025
Tel 213-746-6988

Louis Pepiton*

SDSU
El Cajon, CA 92020
Tel 619-444-1074
Email ....mcpepiton@hotmail.com

Nina Perales*

Austin for Argentina
Austin, TX 78758
Email ....na_perales@yahoo.com

Luiz Peraza

Senior VP, Acquisitions
HBO Latin America
Coral Gables, FL 33134

Louis E. Perego Moreno*

Skyline Features
New York, NY 10036
Tel 212-956-7771
Fax 212-956-3115
Email ....SkyFeature@aol.com

Sylvia Perel

Festival Director
Latino Film Festival of Marin
San Rafael, CA 94901
Tel 415-454-4039
Email ....info@latinofilmfestival.org

Rene Pereya

Los Angeles, CA 90064
Tel 310-397-1656
Email...................palmiro200@aol.com

Director, PEDRO PARAMO, 2003, Mexican Embassy, Stage Play
Director, REGRESO A CASA, 2000, Short
Director, KENNEDY'S CHILDREN, 1998, Actors Studio NY, Stage Play
Acting Coach

Nelson Pereyra*
Elizabeth, NJ 07201
Tel 908-354-2075

Annie Perez
Mayor's Office for Film & Entertaimment
Miami, FL 33128
Tel 305-375-3288

Anthony Perez
CEO
Ground Zero Entertainment
Los Angeles, CA 90045
Tel 310-410-3030
Email ....tony@ground-zero-ent.com

Distributor

Emily Perez*
Los Angeles, CA 90064
Tel 310-804-7479
Fax 310-446-6258
Email ....em_perez@comcast.net

Producer, COMODYNES, 2003, Rebel
  Zone Films, Commercial
Producer, POWERADE: BOY BATTLE,
  2003, Xeno Films, Commercial, Spec
Producer, THE AFFIDAVIT, 2003, Blue
  Fox Media, Short
COPPER WOMAN, 1994, IFP Project
  Involve, Feature

Jack Perez
Los Angeles, CA

Manager: Ilan Breil, 310-446-1466

Director, MONSTER ISLAND, 2003, MTV
  Films, Feature
Writer, MONSTER ISLAND, 2003, MTV
  Films, Feature
Director, WILD THINGS 2, 2003,
  Columbia Pictures, Feature
Director, THE BIG EMPTY, 2001,
  Hollywood Home Video, Feature
Director, UNAUTHORIZED BRADY
  BUNCH: THE FINAL DAYS, 2000, Fox
  Film Corp., TV Movie

Director, LA CUCARACHA, 1998,
  Atmosphere Films, Feature
Director, HERCULES / XENA "THE
  GAUNTLET", 1997, Universal TV, TV
  Series

Juan Carlos Perez*
Valley Village, CA 91607
Tel 818-761-5016
Email ....jcarlosperez@sbcglobal.net

Writer
Director

Leo Perez*
Chief Operating Officer
Si TV
Los Angeles, CA 90038
Tel 323-256-8900
Email ....lperez@sitv.com
Web ....www.sitv.com

FUNNY IS FUNNY, 1998-2001,
  Syndication, TV
LATINO LAUGH FESTIVAL, 1997-2000,
  Showtime, TV
THE BROTHERS GARCIA, 1997-2000,
  Nickelodeon, TV

Marilyn Perez*
Studio 1101
New York, NY 10011
Tel 212-353-1111
Cell 917-538-2276
Fax 212-995-0426
Email ....mperez@marilynperez.com

Producer, PEACE IN THE 21ST
  CENTURY-AN IMPERATIVE FOR
  SURVIVAL, 2003, Third World
  Newsreel, Educational/Industrial
Writer, SMOKESCREEN (TRAILER),
  2002, Studio 1101, Promotional
  Trailer
Producer, THE RETURN OF THE DIVAS,
  2002, The Gabriel Project,
  Documentary Short

Producer, WOES, FOES & HEROES, 2001, LAVA,The Gabriel Project, Documentary Short

Director, WOES, FOES & HEROES, 2001, LAVA, The Gabriel Project, Documentary Short

Writer, WOES, FOES & HEROES, 2001, LAVA, The Gabriel Project, Documentary Short

Director, JULIA VALDEZ-ONE CUBAN ARTIST, 1999, The Gabriel Project, Documentary Short

Writer, JULIA VALDEZ-ONE CUBAN ARTIST, 1999, The Gabriel Project, Documentary Short

Director, VIRTUAL REALITIES/ REALIDADES VIRTUALES, 1997, The Gabriel Project, Documentary Short

Patrick Perez*

Los Angeles, CA 90029
Tel 323-660-3437
Cell 213-926-6571
Fax 323-664-0908
Email ....pperez2000@yahoo.com

Editor, INNER CITY PSA, 2003, Sundance Channel, PSA

Producer, JUMPER, 2003, Sphere Entertainment, Short

Director, BENNY THE MUTE, 2002, Indie, Short

Editor, PACO'S SUITCASE BOMB, 2001, Fox Searchlab, Short

Director, SHORT CHANGED, 2000, Independent, Short

Director, LA BOLSA, 1998, Independent, Short

Paul Perez*

Advent Entertainment
Pasadena, CA 91107
Tel 626-575-7176

Script Supervisor, PEOPLES, 2003, Strictly Kings Productions, Feature

Rachel Perez*

Monterey Park, CA 91755
Tel 323-459-4235
Email ....rachelperez@earthlink.net

Sandra Perez*

Bronx, NY 10475
Tel 718-379-7675
Email.............sperez262@optonline.net
Web ....www.latinoarts.org

Severo Perez

Script & Post Script
Los Angeles, CA 90026
Tel 323-662-0265
Fax 323-662-2249
Email ....spfilms@aol.com

Maria Perez Brown*

Dorado Entertainment, Inc.
New York, NY 10019
Tel 212-654-6716
Email ....maria.perez@nick.com

Executive Producer, TAINA, 2000, Nickelodeon, TV Series

Director, TAINA, 2000, Nickelodeon, Feature

Executive Producer, GULLAH, GULLAH ISLAND, 1994, Nickelodeon, TV Series

Ivonne Perez Montijo*

Frog Girl Productions
Valley Village, CA 91607
Tel 818-509-8856
Fax 818-509-0248
Email ....IvonnePMontijo@aol.com

Writer, JUAN Y ROSA, LA VIRGEN &
FLAN, 2001, Stage Play
Producer, JUAN Y ROSA, LA VIRGEN &
FLAN, 2001, Stage Play
Producer, SKIP TRACER, 1997,
Maverick Arts
Writer, DESEO, Coqui Productions, Short
Producer, DESEO, Coqui Productions,
Short

Luis Perez Tolon

Director of Production and Development
Discovery Networks/Latin America/Iberia
Miami, FL 33126
Tel 305-507-1700
Fax 305-507-1560
Email ....luis_perez-tolon@discovery.com

Fernando Perez Unda

Mexico

Editor, AMORES PERROS, 2000, Lions
Gate Films, Feature

Lisandro Perez-Rey*

Gato Media
Miami, FL 33137
Tel 305-724-6373
Email ....gatoflix@yahoo.com

Director, HIP HOP HAVANA, 2004,
Documentary
Producer, HIP HOP HAVANA, 2004,
Documentary
Director, BEYOND THE SEA, 2003,
Documentary
Producer, BEYOND THE SEA, 2003,
Documentary

Rafael Pérez-Torres*

Santa Barbara, CA 93101
Tel 805-966-1165
Fax 805-966-2154
Email ....perezt@humnet.ucla.edu

Cesar Peschiera*

Film Production Coordinator
Packair Airfreight, Inc.
Los Angeles, CA 90045
Tel 310-337-0529
Tel 310-337-9993
Cell 310-261-7629
Fax 310-337-0669
Email ....filmlocations@packair.com
Web...........................www.packair.com

International Forwarding/Customs Broker
Production Facilities & Services

Elizabeth Peters*

Executive Director
AIVF
New York, NY 10013
Tel 212-807-1400
Fax 212-463-8519
Email ....elizabeth@aivf.org

MG Pimienta*

Miami Beach, FL 33140
Tel 305-673-9940
Email...................mgpimienta@aol.com

Rachel Pineda*

Staff
ESPN
Bristol, CT 06010
Tel 860-766-2000
Email ....reedsucker@yahoo.com

Production Assistant, THIS IS SPORTS
CENTER, 2003, ESPN, TV Series

Carlos F. Pinero
Burbank, CA
Email...............tyranny2k@earthlink.net

1st Assistant Director, SWEET FRIGGIN' DAISIES, 2002, Feature

2nd Assistant Director, BARB WIRE, Feature

2nd Assistant Director, CLEAR AND PRESENT DANGER, Feature

1st Assistant Director, FRIENDS, NBC, TV Series

2nd Assistant Director, HUDSON STREET, TV Series

2nd Assistant Director, LOVE AND WAR, TV Series

2nd Assistant Director, MURPHY BROWN, TV Series

2nd Assistant Director, TRAFFIC, Feature

1st Assistant Director, VERONICA'S CLOSET, TV Series

Jorge Pinos
Agent
William Morris Agency
Beverly Hills, CA 90212
Tel 310-859-4000
Tel 310-859-4231

Felix Pire*
Hollywood, CA 90068
Tel 323-882-6523
Cell 323-823-1971
Email.............................fpire@aol.com

Writer, THE ORIGINS OF HAPPINESS IN LATIN, 2003, Arizona Theatre Company & Off-Off B'way, Stage Play

Director, NEW MILLENNIUM PROJECT, 2001, Perfomed at L.A.'s Levantine Center, Stage Play

Actor, DEAR GOD, 1996, Paramount Pictures, Feature

Actor, IT'S MY PARTY, 1996, MGM/UA, Feature

Actor, 12 MONKEYS, 1995, Universal Studios, Feature

Writer, HURRICANE NENA, Feature

Suzan Pitt*
Los Angeles, CA 90065
Tel 323-227-5345
Email ....suzanpitt@earthlink.net

Tony Plana
Hollywood, CA

Agent: Paradigm, Debbie Kline, 310-277-4400

Actor, FIDEL, 2002, Showtime, TV Movie

Director, GREETINGS FROM TUCSON, 2002, Warner Bros., TV Series

Actor, HALF PAST DEAD, 2002, Sony Pictures Entertainment, Feature

Actor, VEGAS, CITY OF DREAMS, 2001, DMG Entertainment, Feature

Director, PRINCESS AND THE BARRIO BOY, 2000, Showtime, TV Movie

Director, RESURRECTION BLVD., 2000, Showtime, TV Series

Director, THE BROTHERS GARCIA, 2000, Nickelodeon, TV Series

Director, A MILLION TO JUAN, 1994, Sam Goldwyn Entertainment, Feature

Connie Ponce*
Chino, CA 91710
Tel 909-464-2249

Ximena Ponce*
Bay Harbor, FL 33154
Tel 305-866-5247
Cell 786-252-6607
Email...................xime999@yahoo.com

Director, BESAME MUCHO, 2002, NYU Tisch Film Production Program, Short

Writer, BESAME MUCHO, 2002, NYU Tisch Film Production Program, Short

Producer, BESAME MUCHO, 2002, NYU Tisch Film Production Program, Short

filmmakers

Aric Porro*
Los Angeles, CA 90078
Tel 323-806-5123
Email ....aricporro@hotmail.com

Lourdes Portillo
Xochitl Film and Video
San Francisco, CA 94110
Tel 415-642-1614
Email........................lportillo@mac.com
Web..................www.lourdesportillo.com

Director, SENORITA EXTRAVIADA, 2001,
  Balcony Releasing, Documentary
Director, CORPUS, 1999, Xochitl Film
  and Video, Documentary
Director, EL DIABLO NUNCA DUERME,
  1996, Documentary
Director, SOMETIMES MY FEET GO
  NUMB, 1996, Frame Line,
  Documentary

David Portorreal*
Tallahassee, FL 32310
Fax 850-644-2626
Email ....dportorreal@yahoo.com

Carolina Posse
Programming Manager
Latino Cultural Center
Chicago, IL 60605
Tel 773-855-5188
Email ....cposse@latinoculturalcenter.org

Santiago Pozo
CEO
Arenas Group
Beverly Hills, CA 90210
Tel 310-385-4410
Tel 310-385-4401
Fax 310-385-4402
Email...........santiago@arenasgroup.com

Producer, IMAGINING ARGENTINA,
  2003, Arenas Entertainment, Feature
Producer, EMPIRE, 2002, Arenas
  Entertainment, Feature

Francesca Prada
Diana Films
San Francisco, CA 94110
Tel 415-826-2444
Tel 415-378-8658
Fax 415-824-7385
Email ....Dianafilms@aol.com

Producer
Director
Writer

Anayansi Prado*
Impacto Films
Los Angeles, CA 90026
Tel 323-251-7787
Email ....impactofilms@hotmail.com

Producer, MAID IN AMERICA, Impacto
  Films, Documentary
Director, MAID IN AMERICA, Impacto
  Films, Documentary
Writer, MAID IN AMERICA, Impacto
  Films, Documentary

Henry K. Priest
Boricua Films
W. Hollywood, CA 90046
Tel 323-850-2650
Email..............Henry@BoricuaFilms.com
Web ....www.BoricuaFilms.com

Producer, UNDERDOG, 2003, AFI Fest,
  Short
Producer, URBAN GRAFFITI, 2003, TV
Producer, I CAME HERE FOR LOVE,
  2002, Latino American Filmmakers
  Showcase - National Broadcast, TV
  Series

Rodrigo Prieto

Los Angeles, CA
Email ....rpstame@aol.com

Director of Photography, ALEXANDER, 2004, Warner Bros., Feature
Director of Photography, 21 GRAMS, 2003, Focus Features, Feature
Director of Photography, PERSONA NON GRATA, 2003, Rule 8, Documentary
Director of Photography, 25TH HOUR, 2002, Touchstone Pictures, Feature
Director of Photography, 8 MILE, 2002, Universal Pictures, Feature
Director of Photography, FRIDA, 2002, Miramax Films, Feature
Director of Photography, ORIGINAL SIN, 2001, MGM, Feature
Director of Photography, AMORES PERROS, 2000, Lions Gate Films, Inc., Feature
Director of Photography, RICKY 6, 2000, The Shooting Gallery, Feature

Michael Pryfogle*

Terrapin Pictures / Mi Cine
San Francisco, CA 94110
Tel 415-826-8254
Fax 415-642-1609
Email ....terrapin@pobox.com
Web..............................www.Micine.net

Producer

David Puente

Producer, Field
ABC News
New York, NY 10023
Tel 212-456-6312
Email ....David.Puente@abc.com

Nick Puga

Agent
Arts & Letters Management
Los Angeles, CA 90046
Tel 323-883-1070
Fax 323-883-1067

Raul Puig

Miami, FL
Tel 305-670-9859
Email................raulapuig@bellsouth.net

Producer, CURDLED, 1996, Miramax Films, Feature

Maria Pulice*

Hot Mama Productions
Ft. Lauderdale, FL 33301
Tel 917-669-5312
Tel 954-764-8133
Email................mariapulice@yahoo.com

Production Accountant

Georgia Quiñones*

Sologaistoa
Oakland, CA 94610
Tel 510-663-8959
Email ....quinones20007@cs.com

Rogelio Quiñones*

RQ Productions
El Paso, TX 79902
Tel 915-533-3254
Fax 915-533-3254
Email ....rqprods@htg.net

Ernesto Quintero*

Four Brown Hats
Los Angeles, CA 90031
Tel 323-343-9037
Fax 323-225-1353
Email ....fbrownhats@aol.com

Fabian Quintero*

Woodside, NY 11377
Email ....stewartx@hotmail.com

Sofia Quintero*
Bronx, NY 10472
Tel 212-352-4436
Email ....poderlatina@hotmail.com

Susan Racho*
Glendale, CA 91206
Tel 818-551-9619
Fax 818-551-9619
Email ....sracho@msn.com

Director, THE BRONZE SCREEN: 100
    YEARS OF THE LATINO IMAGE IN
    AMERICAN CINEMA, 2002,
    Documentary
Producer, THE BRONZE SCREEN: 100
    YEARS OF THE LATINO IMAGE IN
    AMERICAN CINEMA, 2002,
    Documentary

Mike Racioppo*
WebCasting Media Productions, Inc.
Staten Island, NY 10310
Tel 973-258-1781
Fax 973-258-1781
Email ....mraci@webcastingmedia.com

Faith Radle*
Badass Pictures
San Antonio, TX 78201
Tel 210-226-5225
Tel 210-367-6970
Email ....FaithRadle@aol.com

Producer, SPEEDER KILLS, 2003,
    Badass Pictures, Feature
Associate Producer, VOICES FROM
    TEXAS, 2003, Cinema Guild,
    Documentary
Post Production Supervisor, COME AND
    TAKE IT DAY, 2001, ITVS, Feature

Alexander Ramirez*
Chica Sol Films, LLC
Ridgefield Park, NJ
Tel 201-814-0925
Fax 201-814-1327
Email ....mile1072@msn.com
Web ....www.chicasolfilms.com

Fernando Ramirez*
New York, NY 10033
Tel 212-923-4973
Email ....framirez1@hotmail.com

Maria Elena Ramirez*
Austin, TX 78753
Tel 512-832-6732
Email ....ramirez@klru.pbs.org

Mario Ramirez
Jackmar Entertainment
Universal City, CA 91618
Tel 818-761-5725
Fax 818-761-5725
Email ....jackmar@marioramirez.com

Director
Writer
Producer

Max Ramirez*
CineAccion
San Francisco, CA 94110
Email ....max@maxramirez.com

Rebecca Ramirez
Chief Administrator
AHA
New York, NY
Tel 212-727-7227
Fax 212-727-0549
Email ....ahanews@latinoarts.org

Rick Ramirez*
Burbank, CA 91505
Tel 818-599-9655
Email ....ramireztv@hotmail.com

Producer

Steven Ramirez*
Berkeley, CA 94707
Email ....srinfo2000@aol.com

Victoria Ramirez*
Porcelain Angels Productions
Los Angeles, CA 90026
Tel 323-769-7059
Email ....vrramirez1@aol.com

Victoria Ramirez*
Crookston, MN 56716
Tel 218-281-2130

Margarita Ramon*
Terra Incognita Productions
Toronto, Ontario MSA2L2 Canada
Tel 416-920-8319
Tel 416-929-6484
Fax 416-929-6575
Email ....mramon@ionsys.com

Director, MARIA DEL MAR BONET,
　　2003, CBC Canada, Radio
　　Documentary
Director, POWER MAPPING, 1998,
　　Telelatino TV, Documentary
Writer, ABORIGINAL VOICES
　　MAGAZINE, 1997, National
　　Distribution, Magazine Articles
Writer, GIOCCO LOCO, 1992, Telelatino
　　Network TV, Game Show
Writer, NOVEDADES, 1992, CFMTV, TV
　　Series
Director, CHINA AFTER TIANNOMEN
　　SQUARE, 1991, BCTV, TV Series
Writer, ULTIMA HORA, 1988, CFMTV -
　　Ontario/New York State, TV Series

Agustin Gus Ramos*
Sparrow Hawk Productions
Encino, CA 91316
Tel 213-479-0341
Fax 818-881-2034
Email ......sparrowhawkdelta@yahoo.com

Alfredo Ramos
Tel 213-262-0051

Director, ROAD DOGZ, Shooting Star
　　Partners, Feature

Ana Ramos*
WNET
New York, NY 10001
Tel 212-560-2984
Email ....ramosa@thirteen.org

Marc Ramos*
Exposure Plus
Santa Cruz, CA 95060
Tel 831-459-8025
Fax 831-515-3068
Email ....boricua@cats.ucsc.edu
Web ......www.soar.ucsc.edu/exposureplus

P. Ramos*
San Francisco, CA 94114
Email ....cocktail@pobox.com

Ralph Rangel*
Brea, CA 92821
Tel 714-671-3053
Email ....rangelralph@hotmail.com

Karen Ranucci
Latin American Video Archives
New York, NY 10014
Tel 212-463-0108
Fax 212-243-2007
Email...............................imre@igc.org
Web ....www.latinamericanvideo.org

filmmakers

Ruth L. Ratny*
Chicago, IL 60611
Tel 312-274-9985
Email ....RuthLRatny@hotmail.com
Web ....www.screenzine.com

Stephanie Rauber*
Rauber Filmworks
New York, NY 10019
Tel 212-529-9711

Director, DEMYSTIFYING THE DEMON, 2004, Documentary

William Recinos*
Los Angeles, CA 90029
Tel 323-864-6649
Email...................citywalkr2@attbi.com

Ray Reveles
President
Latino Talent Network
Los Angeles, CA 90004
Tel 626-331-1318

Marcelo Rey
Entertainment Editor
La Opinion
Los Angeles, CA 90013
Tel 213-896-2024

Nicolas Rey
Agent
Alvarado Rey Agency
Los Angeles, CA 90048
Tel 323-655-7978
Fax 323-655-2777

Frank Reyes
Loiza Films
New York, NY

Agent: William Morris Agency, Ramses Ishak, 310-274-7451

Director, CERAMIC LIFE, 2004, Universal Pictures, Feature
Writer, CERAMIC LIFE, 2004, Universal Pictures, Feature
Director, EMPIRE, 2002, Universal Pictures, Feature
Writer, EMPIRE, 2002, Universal Pictures, Feature

Jorge Reyes
Los Angeles, CA

Agent: ICM, 310-550-4000

Writer, RESURRECTION BLVD., 2000, Viacom Production Inc., TV Series

Marvin Reyes*
Arlington, VA 22201
Tel 202-267-7478
Email...................marvin.reyes@faa.gov

Quinto Reyes
North Hollywood, CA 91606
Tel 818-509-1743
Email ....qreyes@pacbell.net

Writer, MAD TV, Spec Script (Fox)
Writer, MY WIFE AND KIDS, Spec Script (ABC)
Writer, SCRUBS, Spec Script (Fox)
Writer, THE GEORGE LOPEZ SHOW, Spec Script (ABC)
Writer, THE SIMPSONS, Spec Script (Fox)

Ruben Reyes
Pima College
Tucson, AZ 85713
Tel 520-624-7313
Fax 520-884-1152
Email ....rreyes@exchange.co.pima.az.us

Ruperto Reyes*
Artistic Director
Teatro Vivo
Austin, TX 78703
Tel 512-970-7016
Fax 512-474-7848
Email ....rupertreyes@yahoo.com

Ramon Ricard
New York, NY 10040
Tel 646-515-1142
Fax 212-567-5766
Email.................sabadofilms@mac.com

Director, SABADO MORNING, 2002,
  Sabado Films, Short
Line Producer, THE GOTHIC LINE,
  2001, Hit and Run, Feature
Director, COJUNTOS ANTIBALAS MUSIC
  VIDEO, 1999, The Family Productions,
  Music Video
Line Producer, TIMES UP!, 1999, The
  Family, Feature
Line Producer, SUNSHINE DELI AND
  GROCERY, 1998, Feature

Charles Rice-Gonzalez*
Rice-Gonzalez Public Relations
Bronx, NY 10474
Tel 718-542-0267
Email ....Rice-Gonzalez@usa.net

Gizella Richardson*
Stockton, CA 95209
Tel 209-478-8619
Email ....richardson2n2@cs.com

Diana Rico*
Mermaid Moon Productions
Venice, CA 90291
Tel 310-823-9496
Fax 310-823-9496
Email ....dianarico@earthlink.net

Producer, HOW DO I LOOK?, 2004,
  Style Network, TV Series
Writer, HOW DO I LOOK?, 2004, Style
  Network, TV Series
Producer, IT'S GOOD TO BE ..., 2003,
  E! Entertainment Television, TV Series
Writer, IT'S GOOD TO BE ..., 2003, E!
  Entertainment Television, TV Series
Producer, E! TRUE HOLLYWOOD STORY,
  2002, E! Entertainment Television, TV
  Series
Writer, E! TRUE HOLLYWOOD STORY,
  2002, E! Entertainment Television, TV
  Series
Producer, ROYALTY A-Z, 2002, E!
  Entertainment Television

Concetta Rinaldo-Williams
Kilauea, HI
Tel 808-828-6861
Email ....crinwil2@yahoo.com

1st Assistant Director, FIVE HOUSES,
  1998, Fox Television Network, TV
  Movie
1st Assistant Director, TIL THERE WAS
  YOU, 1997, Paramount Pictures,
  Feature
1st Assistant Director, MY SO-CALLED
  LIFE, 1994, ABC, TV Series
1st Assistant Director, ROSWELL, 1994,
  Showtime, TV series
2nd Assistant Director, UNSPEAKABLE
  ACTS, 1990, ABC, TV Movie
1st Assistant Director, PROVIDENCE, TV
  Series

filmmakers

Jewels Rio*
San Antonio, TX
Tel 210-365-7854
Email ....jrio@telemundo.com

Diana Rios*
Asst. Professor of Communication
Sciences Dept.
University of Connecticut
Storrs, CT
Tel 860-486-2000
Fax 860-486-2906
Email ....diana.rios@uconn.edu

Ed Rios
Albuquerque, NM
Tel 505-699-2786

Director of Photography

Jonisha Rios*
Hollywood, CA 90078
Tel 323-244-1737
Tel 212-769-6989
Email ....baezent@yahoo.com

Producer, CHICLE, 2002, Baez
   Entertainment, TV Special
Producer, NUDE IN NEW YORK, 2000,
   Producers' Club, Stage Play

Marcial Rios*
Santa Ana, CA 92701
Tel 714-227-6080
Email ....marcialrios@hotmail.com

Writer, LA TIERRA DEL DOLOR, 2003,
   Chapman University, Short
Director, LA TIERRA DEL DOLOR, 2003,
   Chapman University, Short
Producer, LA TIERRA DEL DOLOR,
   2003, Chapman University, Short
Writer, UNFORGIVING DREAM, 2002,
   Chapman University, Short
Director, UNFORGIVING DREAM, 2002,
   Chapman University, Short

Writer, ICE CREAM MAKES THINGS
   BETTER, 2001, Chapman University,
   Short
Director, ICE CREAM MAKES THINGS
   BETTER, 2001, Chapman University,
   Short

Manuel Rivas*
Watsonville, CA 95076
Tel 831-722-6096
Email.................manuelrivas@mac.com

Pascui Rivas
Cordoba, NY 5000 Argentina
Tel 11-54-351-4815677
Email ....pascui@argentina.com
Web ....www.el-sereno.com.ar

Director, EL SERENO, 2004, Short
Sound, LA CIUDAD DE LOS HOMBRES
   LACTANTES, 2001, Universidad
   Nacional de Cordoba, Short
Sound, EL MEDICO RURAL, 2000,
   Universidad Nacional de Cordoba,
   Short

Ramon Rivas
Rivas Film Associates
Valley Glen, CA 91401
Tel 818-782-4510
Email ....ramonrayrivas@aol.com

Director of Photography, CUENTOS POR
   SOLITARIOS, USA Network, TV Series
Director, EL MONOSABIO, Feature
Director, GHETTO DOCTOR, TV Movie
Director of Photography, HEART OF
   MIDNIGHT
Director, UFO: PAST, PRESENT AND
   FEATURE, TV Movie

Alex Rivera*

Journeyman Productions
New York, NY 10012
Tel 212-253-6273
Fax 212-253-6284
Email.....................alex@alexrivera.com
Web ....arivera@interport.net

Producer, TV Series, VISIONES, 2004,
    PBS, Documentary
Director, THE SIXTH SECTION, 2003,
    POV/American Documentary,
    Documentary
Producer, THE SIXTH SECTION, 2003,
    POV/American Documentary,
    Documentary
Director, ANIMAQUILADORA/WHY
    CYBRACEROS?, 1997, Third World
    News reel, Mockumentary
Director, PAPAPAPA, 1997, Third World
    Newsreel, Documentary
Producer, PAPAPAPA, 1997, Third World
    Newsreel, Documentary

Angel Rivera

Affirmative Action and Diversity
Department Director
Screen Actors Guild
Hollywood, CA 90036
Tel 323-954-1600
Email ....arivera@sag.org

Isabel Rivera

RiverFish Productions
New York, NY
Tel 212-489-9781
Email....irivera@riverfishproductions.com
Web.........www.riverfishproductions.com

Executive Producer, LATIN ACCESS,
    2002, NBC, TV Series
Creator, LATIN ACCESS, 2002, NBC, TV
    Series
Executive Producer, NEW YORK
    MAGAZINE AWARDS SHOW, 2001,
    NBC, TV Special
Executive Producer, PUERTO RICAN DAY
    PARADE, 2000, NBC, TV Special
Producer, REGIS & KATHIE LEE, ABC,
    TV Series

Jose Rivera

Los Angeles, CA

Agent: Rick Berger, 310-824-6300

Writer, THE MOTORCYCLE DIARIES,
    2004, Southfork Pictures, Feature
Writer, SHADOW REALM, 2002, TV
    Series
Writer, NIGHT VISIONS, 2001, Warner
    Bros. Television, TV Series
Producer, EERIE, INDIANA, 1992, NBC,
    TV Series
Writer, EERIE, INDIANA, 1992, NBC,
    TV Series
Creator, EERIE, INDIANA, 1992, NBC,
    TV Series

Marisol Rivera*

Panin Pictures
Bronx, NY 10456
Tel 718-538-8881
Email..........nyricanwoman@hotmail.com

Ralph Rivera

VP, Business Product Management
AOL Entertainment
Dulles, VA 20166
Tel 703-265-1000

Ray Rivera*

Los Angeles, CA 90033
Tel 323-769-5250
Email ....rayray_rivera@yahoo.com

Roberto Rivera*

San Diego, CA 92102
Tel 619-232-0354

Alicia Rivera Frankl*

Maya Cinemas Holding Co.
Los Angeles, CA 90024
Tel 310-281-3770
Fax 310-281-3777
Email ....aliciar@mayacinemas.com

Production Manager, ASTHMA:
  FIGHTING TO BREATHE, 2003,
  Discovery Health, Documentary
Production Manager, CRISIS DIABETES
  AMONG US, 2002, Discovery Health,
  Documentary
Production Manager, D.R.E.A.M TEAM,
  1999, Fremantle Group, Documentary
Production Manager, THE MASK OF
  ZORRO, 1998, Columbia Pictures,
  Feature
Line Producer, THE MASK OF ZORRO,
  1998, Columbia Pictures, Feature
Production Accountant

Teodoro Rivera III*

Los Gatos, CA 95032
Tel 408-395-3548
Email ....tedr.ra@earthlink.net

Rafael Rivera-Viruet

RJR Asociados
New York, NY 10465
Tel 718.794.6484
Fax...............................718.794.6484
Email...............rrivera111540@aol.com

Producer, WILKINS - PIONERO DEL
  ROCK EN ESPANOL, 2003,
  Documentary
Distributor, HARLOW - 35TH
  ANNIVERSARY MUSIC SPECIAL,
  2002, Music Special
Producer, SAN JUAN - CIUDAD DE
  TODOS, 2000, Museum City of San
  Juan, PR, Documentary
Producer, THROUGH THE EYES OF
  LARRY HARLOW - EL JUDIO
  MARAVILLOSO, 1998, Cinema Guild,
  Documentary

Jonathan Robinson*

When in Doubt Productions
New Haven, CT
Tel 203-777-1690
Fax 203-777-1698
Email ....
whenindoubtproductions@yahoo.com

Director, EVERY CHILD IS BORN A
  POET, 2003, Documentary

Henry Robles*

Los Angeles, CA 90019
Tel 323-936-3656
Fax 323-931-3523
Email................texmex12@earthlink.net

*Agent: United Talent Agency, Jay
Gassner, 310-273-6700*

Writer, TV Series

Veronica Robles*

Orale con Veronica
Chelsea, MA 02150
Tel 617-884-2136
Tel 727-944-5544
Email.........contact@veronicarobles.com
Web.................www.veronicarobles.com

Producer, ORALE CON VERONICA,
  2002, Cuenca Vision & Public Access
  TV, TV Series
Producer, MARIACHI / CONTINENTE,
  1999, Cuenca Vision MA, TV Special
Producer, MEXICO MAGIA Y PASION,
  1999, Thalia Spanish Theater, Stage
  Play

Zasha Robles

Post Production Services
Etcetera Group
Miami, FL 33172
Tel 305-594-3000

Production Facilities & Services

Christopher Rodarte*
La Llorona Productions
Tucson, AZ 85711
Tel 520-326-7163

Alex Rodriguez*
Public Relations
VirtualHispanic.com
Santa Barbara, CA 93105
Tel 805-964-9393
Fax 805-964-9398
Email ....alex@virtualhispanic.com
Web ....www.VirtualHispanic.com

Publicist

Alfredo Rodriguez*
Westlake Village, CA 91361
Email ....alrod_la@hotmail.com

Carlos Rodriguez*
S & Q Films
Miami, FL 33138
Tel 305-759-2777
Email ....crodrigmia@aol.com

Daniel Rodriguez
Director Latin Acquisitions
Ground Zero Latino
Los Angeles, CA 90045
Tel 310-410-3030
Fax 310-410-3003
Email ....groundzerolatino@aol.com

Distributor

Horacio Rodriguez*
FLX Entertainment
Burbank, CA 91505
Tel 818-954-7419
Email ....habanaman@aol.com

Horacio "Lacho" Rodriguez
Jaguar Films
Los Angeles, CA
Tel 310-968-3758
Email ....horaciordz@mac.com

Producer
Writer

Hunter Rodriguez*
Glendale, CA 91208
Email ....hunter@ffi.com

Joel Rodriguez*
Miami, FL 33165
Tel 305-218-6661
Fax 305-598-0293
Email ....joelrod@bluechipco.com

Jorge Rodriguez*
Los Angeles, CA 90006
Tel 323-734-2309
Fax 323-734-2309
Email..........jdrgonzalezzzz@hotmail.com

Marcel Rodriguez
Executive Director
Llano Grande Center
Elsa, TX 78538
Tel 956-262-4474
Email ....info@llanogrande.org

Maria Rodriguez*
Philadelphia, PA 19147
Tel 215-467-4417
Fax 215-898-9804
Email ....marite001@aol.com

filmmakers

filmmakers

Molly Robin Rodriguez
Northridge, CA 91325
Tel 818-320-0123
Email.................mollyrobin@yahoo.com

2nd 2nd Assistant Director, 15
  MINUTES
2nd Assistant Director, CSI, TV Series
2nd Assistant Director, ER, TV Series
2nd 2nd Assistant Director, GILMORE
  GIRLS, TV Series
2nd 2nd Assistant Director, KINGPIN, TV
  Series
2nd Assistant Director, MALCOLM IN
  THE MIDDLE, TV Series
2nd Assistant Director, RESURRECTION
  BLVD., TV Series
2nd Assistant Director, SOLDIER OF
  FORTUNE, Feature
2nd Assistant Director, THE DR. QUINN
  MOVIE, TV Movie

Nestor N. Rodriguez*
Avant Garde Entertainment, LLC
Riverdale, NY 10463
Tel 718-543-9238
Email ....RainmakerNYC@aol.com

Producer, MALEDETTA PRIMAVERA,
  2001, Film Festivals, Short
Postproduction Supervisor

Pablo Rodriguez*
Los Angeles, CA
Email ....paulvato@yahoo.com

Paul Rodriguez*
Los Angeles, CA

*Agent: David Shapira & Associates,
949-262-3422*

Producer, THE ORIGINAL LATIN KINGS
  OF COMEDY, 2002, Paramount
  Pictures, TV Special
Director, A MILLION TO JUAN, 1994,
  Samuel Goldwyn Company, Feature
Writer, BELZER BEHIND BARS, 1983,
  TV Special

Paul Rodriguez*
Senior VP
Wilshire Stages
Los Angeles, CA 90048
Tel 323-951-1700
Fax 323-951-1710
Email......prodriguez@wilshirestages.com
Web ....www.wilshirestages.com

Production Facilities & Services

Pedro Rodriguez
Sound Stages
Tel 525-532-4500

Producer

Richard Rodriguez*
Kenrod Associates
San Antonio, TX 78250
Tel 210-680-5754
Fax 210-680-5755
Email ....richard@kenrod.biz

Web Developer

Robert Rodriguez
Los Hooligans Production
Austin, TX
Tel 512-443-3713

*Agent: ICM, Robert Newman,
310-550-4000*

*Publicist: Sandra Condito,
323-822-4336*

Director, ONCE UPON A TIME IN
  MEXICO, 2003, Sony Pictures
  Entertainment, Feature
Writer, ONCE UPON A TIME IN
  MEXICO, 2003, Sony Pictures
  Entertainment, Feature
Director, SPY KIDS 3-D: GAME OVER,
  2003, Miramax, Feature
Writer, SPY KIDS, 2001, Miramax,
  Feature

Executive Producer, FROM DUSK TILL
   DAWN 3: THE HANGMAN'S
   DAUGHTER, 2000, Buena Vista Home
   Video, Feature
Executive Producer, FROM DUSK TILL
   DAWN 2: TEXAS BLOOD MONEY,
   1999, Dimension Films, Feature
Executive Producer, FROM DUSK TILL
   DAWN, 1996, Dimension Films,
   Feature
Writer, DESPERADO, 1995, Columbia
   Pictures, Feature
Director, EL MARIACHI, 1992, Columbia
   Pictures, Feature

Steve Rodriguez
Manager
Rodriguez Management
Los Angeles, CA
Tel 310-273-0051
Email ..paulo@rodriguezmanagement.com

Teresa Rodriguez*
Miami, FL 33155
Tel 305-663-0507
Email ....terirod1@aol.com

Roxanne Rodriguez Lettman
Director of International Format
Development
Columbia/TriStar International Television
Culver City, CA 90232
Tel 310-244-5546
Tel 310-244-0546

Pilar Rodriguez-Aranda*
Anarca Films
Santa Fe, NM 87505
Tel 505-986-0642
Cell 505-501-0277
Email ....pilar@anarcafilms.com
Web ....anarcafilms.com

Director, BORDER SHE IS, 2001, Iron
   Communications, Canada, Short,
   Experimental
Director, EL GUAJOLOTE, 2000, Iron
   Communications, Canada, Short
Director, THE IDEA WE LIVE IN, 1991,
   Women Make Movies, Experimental

Veronica Rodriguez-Brett*
Tucson, AZ 85737
Tel 520-408-3078
Email ....sakura@cox.net

Sandra Roggemann*
SDSU
La Jolla, CA 92037
Tel 858-551-5834
Email ....sandra_roggemann@gmx.net

Claudia Rojas
Univision
Los Angeles, CA 90045
Tel 310-348-3565
Email ....crojas@univision.net

Ingrid Rojas*
Brooklyn, NY 11238
Tel 917-592-7481
Email ....indierojas@yahoo.com

Producer, Documentary
Director, Documentary

Evelyn Rojo*
Email..............crashdowncafe@msn.com

filmmakers

Sylvie Rokab

In the Light Productions, Inc.
Coral Gables, FL 33146
Tel 305-663-4647
Email..sylvie@in-the-lightproduction.com
Web ....www.in-the-light.com

Producer, IN THE LIGHT, 2003,
Innermotion, Documentary
Director, IN THE LIGHT, 2003,
Innermotion, Documentary
Director of Photography, IN THE LIGHT,
2003, Innermotion, Documentary
Director of Photography
Director of Photography, COMMERCIALS

Phil Roman*

Phil Roman Entertainment
Burbank, CA 91505
Tel 818-985-1200
Email.....................phil@romanent.com
Web ....www.philromanent.com

Executive Producer, GRANDMA GOT
RUN OVER BY A REINDEER, 2000,
Warner Home Video, TV Movie,
Animated
Director, GRANDMA GOT RUN OVER BY
A REINDEER, 2000, Warner Home
Video, TV Movie, Animated
Executive Producer, KING OF THE HILL,
1997, 20th Century Fox, TV Series,
Animated
Executive Producer, THE MAGIC PEARL,
1997, ABC Television, TV Movie,
Animated
Executive Producer, BRUNO THE KID,
1996, Vitello Productions, TV Series,
Animated
Executive Producer, C-BEAR AND
JAMAL, 1996, Xenon Entertainment
Group, TV Series, Animated
Director, TOM AND JERRY - THE MOVIE,
1993, Miramax, Feature, Animated
Executive Producer, GARFIELD'S
THANKSGIVING, 1989, CBS, TV
Movie, Animated
Director, GARFIELD'S THANKSGIVING,
1989, CBS, TV Movie, Animated

Aldo Romero*

Ozone Park, NY 11416
Tel 718-296-5617
Email.............................ar826@att.net

Elaine Romero*

Tucson, AZ 85705
Tel 520-884-8210
Tel 520-624-7669
Cell 917-640-7027
Fax 520-624-7669
Email.........................erome1@aol.com
Web....................www.elaineromero.com

Writer, THE FAMILY JEWEL, 2002
Co-Producer, DREAM FRIEND, 2001,
Dream Friend Productions, Short
Writer, DREAM FRIEND, 2001, Dream
Friend Productions, Short
Writer, Stage Play

Felix Romero*

Bronx, NY 10465
Tel 718-822-7951
Fax 718-822-1245
Email ....felixromero@msn.com

Writer, Stage Play

Ross Romero*

Anaheim, CA 92805
Tel 714-917-2045
Email ....ltnent@yahoo.com

Gabriela Ronseg*

Pasadena, CA 91116
Email ....bcronseg@cs.com

Victor Rosa*

Bag of Beans Productions
Burlington, NJ 08016
Tel 609-387-2386
Email ....vrosa@rcn.com

Rafael Rosado*

Worthington, OH 43085
Tel 614-841-9203
Email.................rrosado@ameritech.net

Storyboard Artist, BABY LOONEY
  TUNES, 2002, Warner Bros.
  Animation, TV Series, Animated
Storyboard Artist, STUART LITTLE,
  2002, Sony Animation, TV Series,
  Animated
Storyboard Artist, TEENAGE MUTANT
  NINJA TURTLES, 2002, 4 Kids
  Productions, TV Series, Animated
Director, THE TORTURED CLOWN,
  2001, Sundance Channel, Short
Producer, THE TORTURED CLOWN,
  2001, Sundance Channel, Short
Director, MEN IN BLACK: THE
  ANIMATED SERIES, 1998, Sony
  Animation/Columbia, TV Series,
  Animated
Producer, MEN IN BLACK: THE
  ANIMATED SERIES, 1998, Sony
  Animation/Columbia, TV Series,
  Animated
Director, EXTREME GHOSTBUSTERS,
  1997, Sony Animation/Columbia, TV
  Series, Animated
Producer, EXTREME GHOSTBUSTERS,
  1997, Sony Animation/Columbia, TV
  Series, Animated

Monica Rosales*

Film Industry Depot
Miami, FL 33173
Tel 305-348-2768
Email ....mozart1936@aol.com

Adriana Rosas-Walsh*

Film Arts Foundation
San Francisco, CA 94103
Tel 415-552-8760
Fax 415- 552-0882
Email.................adrianarw@filmarts.org

Robert Rose*

Manager
Artist and Idea Management
New York, NY 10003
Tel 212-253-6153
Fax 212-253-7007
Email.................rob@artistandidea.com

Benjamin Rosen*

New York, NY 10016
Email ....acentos@concentric.net

Cyn Rossi*

Partner
Cynalex Productions, LLC
New York, NY 10021
Tel 212-207-4740
Fax 212-207-4709
Email ....ccanel@aol.com
Web ....www.cynalexproductions.com

Producer, A NIGHT TO FORGET, 2003,
  Stage Play
Producer, CHOPPING, 2002, Stage Play
Writer, RHYTHM OF THE SAINTS,
  Sundance Film Festival, Feature
Producer, RHYTHM OF THE SAINTS,
  Sundance Film Festival, Feature

Fernanda Rossi

New York, NY
Tel 212-249-2017
Email ....info@documentarydoctor.com
Web ....www.documentarydoctor.com

Writer, INVENTING A GIRL, 2000,
  Documentary
Producer, INVENTING A GIRL, 2000,
  Documentary
Writer, ON THE EDGE, 2000,
  Documentary
Producer, ON THE EDGE, 2000,
  Documentary

filmmakers

Pablo Luis Rovito

FIPCA
Buenos Aires,   Argentina
Tel 54-11-4306-1916
Email ....pablorovito@fibertel.com.ar

Producer, Feature

Andres Rubalcava

Elusive Minds Productions
Tel 818-470-4068
Email ....rubandres@aol.com

Bernardo Ruiz*

Roja Productions/ Matters of Race
New York, NY
Tel 646-373-9068
Email............bernardo@bernardoruiz.net

Writer, THE DEVIL'S TWILIGHT, 2003,
   WNET, Short
Director, THE DEVIL'S TWILIGHT, 2003,
   WNET, Short
Co-Producer, THE SIXTH SECTION,
   2003, POV, Documentary Short

David Ruiz*

Culver City, CA 90230
Tel 310-337-1443
Email ....druiz99@ucla.edu

Diana Ruiz*

Michael's Productions
Friendswood, TX 77546
Tel 281-482-8494
Email ....diana.ruiz@puffer.com

Jose Luis Ruiz

Steam
Los Angeles, CA
Tel 310 636 4620

Director, UNA MUJER PROHIBIDA,
   1974, Imperial Films, Feature
Producer, CRIMEN DE DOBLE FILO,
   1965, C.B. Films, Feature

Michael Ruiz*

Michael's Productions
Friendswood, TX 77546
Tel 281-483-8169
Email ....maruiz@ems.jsc.nasa.gov

Rosalva Ruiz

Channel 22 / Our People Our Town
San Antonio, TX 78212

Yessica Ruiz*

Hollywood, CA 33021
Tel 954-989-0646

Actor

George Rush*

Station Manager
Wilson & Rush, LLP
San Francisco, CA 94122
Tel 415-759-4201
Email ....george@wilsonrush.com

Citlali Saenz

Radio Bilingüe
San Francisco, CA 94123
Tel 415-674-0926
Fax 415-771-5466
Web ....www.radiobilingue.org

Monica Saenz

Latina Style Magazine
Los Angeles, CA
Tel 213-629-2512

Stephanie Saenz*
KSCI-TV
Venice, CA 90291
Tel 310-392-4378
Email ....ssaenz@kscitv.com

Jennifer Safira*
Hot Mama Productions
Ft. Lauderdale, FL 33301
Tel 954-817-3386
Fax 954-761-1617
Email ....safgrl@aol.com

Gustavo Sagastume*
VP, Programming
PBS
Hollywood, FL 33020
Tel 954-929-0993
Fax 954-929-8440
Email ....gsagastume@pbs.org

Stephanie Saint Sanchez
Chicago, IL 60622
Tel 713-868-9827

Richard Saiz*
Programming Manager
ITVS
San Francisco, CA 94110
Tel 415-356-8383
Fax 415-356-8391
Email ....richard_saiz@itvs.org

Abel Salas*
Membership Coordinator
NALIP
Los Angeles, CA 90022
Tel 323-888-9660
Tel 310-857-1657
Email ....abel@nalip.org

Writer

Tomas Salas*
Austin, TX 78704
Tel 512-461-7889
Email ....tomasjosesalas@hotmail.com

Producer, Stage Play

Michelle Salcedo*
Brooklyn, NY 11201
Tel 718-246-8180
Cell 917-842-6415
Email ......michellesalcedo@earthlink.net

Editor, A BABY STORY, 2003, TLC, TV Movie

Director, A DONDE VA VICENTE? WHERE IS VINCENT GOING?, 2003, Documentary

Editor, MAKING THE BAND 2, 2003, MTV Networks, TV Series

Editor, WHAT NOT TO WEAR, 2003, The Learning Channel, TV Special

Ana Saldaña*
San Antonio, TX 78212
Email ....anasaldana@hotmail.com

Ric Salinas
Los Angeles, CA
Web ....www.cultureclash.com

Manager: Ivan de Paz, Arenas Entertainment, 310-385-4401

Actor, CHAVEZ RAVINE, 2003, Mark Taper Forum, Stage Play

Writer, CHAVEZ RAVINE, 2003, Mark Taper Forum, Stage Play

Actor, NUYORICAN STORIES, 1999, INTAR, Stage Play

Writer, NUYORICAN STORIES, 1999, INTAR, Stage Play

Actor , MI VIDA LOCA, 1994, Sony Pictures, Feature

Actor, RADIO MAMBO, 1993, INTAR, Stage Play

Writer, RADIO MAMBO, 1993, INTAR, Stage Play

filmmakers

Calogero Salvo*
CS Productions, LLC
New York, NY 10011
Tel 212-691-8305
Fax 212-691-8305
Email ....call4cs@aol.com

Valerie Samaniego-Finch*
San Antonio, TX 78232
Email ....mauitx@hotmail.com

Carlos San Miguel
Los Angeles, CA 90066
Tel ....310-391 -7623
Email ....latinoactor@hotmail.com
Web homepage.mac.com/csm1

Agent: The Samantha Group, Samantha Botana, 626-683-2444

Actor, MOST WANTED, 2003, L.A. Film School, Short
Actor, SWALLOW, 2003, HBO, Short
Actor, ESPIRITU, 2000, USC - Maria Elena ChAve.z, director, Short
Writer
Director

Alex Sanchez*
Arlington, VA 22209
Tel 703-516-4395
Email ....ahitzsanchez@yahoo.com

Carlos Sanchez
Marketing Director, Latin America
Warner Home Video
Burbank, CA
Tel 818-954-6000
Web ....www.warnerbros.com

Felix Sanchez
Executive Director
National Hispanic Fdn. for the Arts
Washington, DC 20007
Tel 202-293-8330
Fax 202-965-5252
Web ....www.HispanicArts.org

Marta Sanchez*
Kalpullitlal Teca Medra Projects
San Francisco, CA 94112
Tel 415-307-3397
Fax 415-587-3492
Email ....marzinasanchez@msn.com

Martha Sanchez
Women Make Movies
New York, NY 10013
Tel 212-925-0606
Web ....www.wmm.org

Misael Sanchez*
Bronx, NY 10463
Tel 212-854-7516
Fax 212-854-7702
Email ....ms589@columbia.edu

Ralph Sanchez
Executive
Nickelodeon Animation Development
Burbank, CA 91502
Tel 818-736-3656

Rodolfo Sanchez*
Solstream Media
San Diego, CA 92116
Tel 619-280-6655
Email ....jones_sanchez@yahoo.com

Veronica Sanchez
Commerce City, CO 80022
Tel 303-668-9325
Cell 303-668-9325
Email.................sanchezvp@yahoo.com

Production Manager, SEX & ALCOHOL, 2003, CU Boulder, Short
Producer, SEX & ALCOHOL, 2003, CU Boulder, Short
1st Assistant Director, SEX & ALCOHOL, 2003, CU Boulder, Short
Producer, YOUR MOVE, 2003, CU Boulder, Short
1st Assistant Director, YOUR MOVE, 2003, CU Boulder, Short
Producer, LIMBO, 2002, CU Denver, Short
Production Manager, LOVE WON'T DIE, 2002, CU Denver, Music Video
Production Manager, ON THE CAROUSEL, 2002, CU Denver, Short
1st Assistant Director, ON THE CAROUSEL, 2002, CU Denver, Short

Carlos Sandoval
Camino Bluff Productions, Inc.
New York, NY 10025
Tel 631-267-6565

Director, FARMINGVILLE, 2004, POV, Documentary
Producer, FARMINGVILLE, 2004, POV, Documentary

George Sandoval*
West End Productions
Oxnard, CA 93030
Tel 805-240-9496
Fax 805-240-9464
Email.............geosand@W.endprod.com
Web ....www.W.endprod.com

Director, THE MOMENT

Jorge Sandoval*
Long Beach, CA 90804
Tel 310-880-7376
Email ....jorge_vs@yahoo.com

Dario Sanmiguel*
Archangel Films
San Francisco, CA 94117
Tel 415-255-8723
Fax 415-255-8723
Email ....dariodirdp@earthlink.net

Director of Photography

Elena Santaballa
Culver City, CA 90231
Tel 310-839-3349
Tel 310-576-3252
Fax 310-839-0525
Email ....esantaballa@zworg.com

1st Assistant Director, EVERYBODY LOVES RAYMOND, 1998, CBS, TV Series
2nd Assistant Director, SPORTSNIGHT, 1998, ABC, TV Series
1st Assistant Director, FIRED UP, 1997, NBC, TV Series
2nd Assistant Director, THE SINGLE GUY, 1995, NBC, TV Series
2nd Assistant Director, PICKET FENCES, 1994, CBS, TV Series
1st Assistant Director, BLUEBIRD
1st Assistant Director, ENGLISH ONLY, Universal, Feature
1st Assistant Director, JULIE LYDECKER

Guillermo Santana*
Wasco, CA 93280
Tel 661-758-8048
Fax 661-322-7590
Email.................gsantana1@yahoo.com

Marta Santana*
Wasco, CA 93280
Tel 661-758-8048

filmmakers

Paul Santana

Agent
APA
Los Angeles, CA 90069
Tel 310-273-0744
Fax 310-888-4242

Susan Santiago Kerin*

Arlington, VA 22207
Tel 703-536-5234
Email ....santiago1121@yahoo.com

Ray Santisteban*

Nantes Films
San Antonio, TX 78210
Tel 210-534-1919
Email ....nantes67@aol.com

Director, VOICES FROM TEXAS, 2003, Cinema Guild, Documentary

Editor, VOICES FROM TEXAS, 2003, Nantes Films, Documentary

Editor, MY WEST SIDE, 2001, Nantes Films, Documentary Short

Director, TEXAS CONJUNTO: MUSIC OF THE PEOPLE, 2000, Guadalupe Cultural Arts Center, Documentary Short

Associate Producer, CHICANO: HISTORY OF THE MEXICAN AMERICAN CIVIL RIGHTS MOVEMENT, 1996, Galán Productions, Documentary

Director, NUYORICAN POETS CAFE, 1994, Nantes Films, Documentary Short

Associate Producer, PASSIN' IT ON, 1992, First Run/Icarus Films, TV Series

John Phillip Santos*

The Ford Foundation
New York, NY 10017
Tel 212-573-4914
Fax 212-351-3649
Email ....j.santos@fordfound.org

Writer

Manny Santos

MIKAVI Productions, Inc
New York, NY 10128
Tel 212-348-9419
Cell 347-524-5345
Email ....mikavi@mikavi.com
Web ....www.mikavi.com

Director, NOTICIAS 41 UNIVISION, 2001, Univision Network, TV Series

Producer, AQUI Y AHORA, 2000, Univision Network, TV Series

Producer, DE LA SALLE, 2000, NBC, Feature

Producer, HISPANIC BUSINESS TODAY, 2000, NBC, TV Series

Producer, FIGHTING THE TIDE, 1999, PBS, Documentary

Producer, NEW YORK CROSS ROADS, 1999, PBS, TV Series

Director, SCIENCE QUEST, 1998, PBS, TV Series

Producer, REDISCOVERING A LOST WORLD, 1996, PBS, Documentary

Director, REDISCOVERING A LOST WORLD, 1996, PBS, Documentary

Aurora Sarabia*

Berkeley, CA 94704
Email ......filmgoddess2001@yahoo.com

Cristina Saralegui

Blue Dolphin Productions
Miami, FL 33172
Tel 305-538-9074
Agent: CAA, Jorge Insua, 310-288-4545

Executive Producer, A QUE NO TE ATREVES, 1999, Univision Network, TV Series

Executive Producer, EL SHOW DE CRISTINA, 1989-2004, Univision Network, TV Series

Talk Show Host, EL SHOW DE CRISTINA, 1989-2004, Univision Network, TV Series

Stephen Sariñana-Lampson*
Cine Coyote Films
Pasadena, CA 91105
Tel 626-405-1500
Fax 626-399-7788
Email ......stephen@thecoyotestudio.com

Producer, FOUR DAYS IN
   BARRANQUILLA, CineCoyote Films
Director, FOUR DAYS IN
   BARRANQUILLA, CineCoyote Films

Paul Saucido
The Back Porch Company
Universal City, CA 91618
Tel 310-822-6526
Email ....backporch@earthlink.net
Web ....www.paulsaucido.tv

Adam Schlachter*
Los Angeles, CA 90068
Tel 323-851-0968
Email................adimafilm@hotmail.com

Writer, DEEP BREATH
Writer, LOST BULLET, Feature
Writer, TOP TEN, Feature

Mark Schreiber*
Venice, CA 90291
Tel 310-396-2144
Email ....markschreiber@excite.com

Laurel Scott*
SDSU
Santee, CA 92071
Tel 619-258-7207

Julia Segrove-Jaurigui
San Francisco, CA
Tel 415-821-0775
Email ....jsegrovee@earthlink.net

Writer, FREQUENCY OF OCCURENCES,
   2004, Feature
Producer, FREQUENCY OF
   OCCURENCES, 2004, Feature
Producer, L'ARMOIRE, 2004

Dianne Segura*
Segue Enterprises
Los Angeles, CA 90028
Tel 310-226-7018
Email ....seguebiz@mindspring.com

Francesca Seiden*
Miami, FL 33138
Tel 305-899-1630
Cell 786-200-2986
Email ....franceasca@aol.com

Jose Sepulveda*
San Francisco, CA 94110
Email ....sepulveda_jose@hotmail.com

Monica Serafin*
Brooklyn, NY
Tel 917-407-8816
Email ....chachavez8@hotmail.com

Patricio Serna

Pakidermo Films
San Pedro Garza Garcia,, CA 66297
Mexico
Tel 52-8183035470760
Cell 310-819-2925
Fax 52-8183035470
Email ....patricio@pakidermo.com
Web ....www.pakidermo.com

Agent: Endeavor, Elyse Scherz

Writer, BAILEN 58, 2003, Pakidermo,
   Short
Director, MATING CALL, 2003, NYU,
   Short
Writer, MATING CALL, 2003, NYU, Short
Actor, MATING CALL, 2003,
   NYU/Pakidermo, Short
Director, TROMBA D'ORO, 2002,
   Pakidermo, Short
Writer, TROMBA D'ORO, 2002,
   Pakidermo, Short
Actor, TROMBA D'ORO, 2002,
   Pakidermo, Short
Director, CHUPACABRAS, 1999,
   Pakidermo, Short
Actor, CHUPACABRAS, 1999,
   Pakidermo, Short

Celeste Serna-Williams*

Austin, TX
Tel 917-458-1058
Email ....serna@io.com

Ernesto Serrano*

San Antonio, TX 78228
Email..........................ernie@811.com

Gustavo Serrano*

Seaford, NY 11783
Email ....wgustv@yahoo.com

Joan Shigekawa*

Program Officer
The Rockefeller Foundation
New York, NY 10018
Tel 212-869-8500
Fax 212-764-3468
Web ....www.rockfound.org

Jesús Sifuentes*

Gato Negro Films
San Antonio, TX 78223
Tel 210-337-8110
Cell 210-715-0511
Email.........elgatonegro13@netzero.com

Herbert Siguenza

Culture Clash
Los Angeles, CA
Tel 323-662-2575
Web ....www.cultureclash.com

*Manager: Ivan de Paz, Arenas
Entertainment, 310-385-4401*

Actor, CHAVEZ RAVINE, 2003, Mark
   Taper Forum, Stage Play
Writer, CHAVEZ RAVINE, 2003, Mark
   Taper Forum, Stage Play
Producer, THE MOVIE PITCH, 2003,
   Arekita Productions, Feature
Writer, THE MOVIE PITCH, 2003,
   Arekita Productions, Feature
Actor, NUYORICAN STORIES, 1999,
   INTAR, Stage Play
Writer, NUYORICAN STORIES, 1999,
   INTAR, Stage Play
Actor, STAR MAPS, 1997, 20th Century
   Fox, Feature
Actor, RADIO MAMBO, 1993, INTAR,
   Stage Play
Writer, RADIO MAMBO, 1993, INTAR,
   Stage Play

Gail Silva*

Executive Director
Film Arts Foundation
San Francisco, CA 94103
Tel ....415-552-8760 ext. 315
Fax 415-552-0882
Email ....gails@filmarts.org

Debbie Silverfine*

NYSCA
New York, NY 10014
Tel 212-627-7778
Email....................dsilverfine@nysca.org

Samantha Smith*

Georgetown, TX 78626
Tel 512-841-5930
Fax 512-385-2398
Email ....cine@texas.net

Graphic Designer

Jimmy Smits

Los Angeles, CA

Agent: CAA, 310-288-4545

Actor, STAR WARS II: ATTACK OF THE
    CLONES, 2002, 20th Century Fox,
    Feature
Actor, PRICE OF GLORY, 2000, New
    Line Cinema, Feature
Actor, MI FAMILIA/MY FAMILY, 1995,
    New Line, Feature
Actor, NYPD BLUE, 1994-98, 20th
    Century Fox, TV Series
Actor, LA LAW, 1986-91, 20th Century
    Fox, TV Series

Roberto Sneider

La Banda Films
Beverly Hills, CA 90211
Tel 310-858-7204
Email ....roberto@labandafilms.com
Web....................www.labandafilms.com

Producer, FRIDA, 2002, Miramax,
    Feature
Director, DOS CRIMENES, 1995,
    Behavior, Feature
Producer, DOS CRIMENES, 1995
Writer, DOS CRIMENES, 1995

Enrique Soberanes*

Montebello, CA 90640

Juan Sola*

Los Angeles, CA 90036
Tel 323-936-8432
Email ....juanelesola@yahoo.com

Actor

Helena Solberg*

Radiant Films, Inc.
New York, NY 10025
Tel 212-678-6529
Email..........radiantefilmes@terra.com.br

Antonio Solis*

Athena Film
Costa Mesa, CA 92626
Tel 714-343-3225
Email..................solis@athenafilms.com
Web ....www.athenafilms.com

Manuel Solis*

San Antonio, TX 78228
Tel 210-434-5631
Email ....solizm@hotmail.com

filmmakers

Eric Soliz*
Poetic Pictures
Palmdale, CA 93550
Tel 661-305-5807
Fax 661-947-3743

Michael Solomon*
Castnet.com
Orlando, FL 32809
Web...........................www.castnet.com

Betsy Solorzano*
Los Angeles, CA 90016
Tel 323-932-0473

Antonio Sosa
VP, Distribution & Acquisition
Fox Home Entertainment
Los Angeles, CA 90067
Tel 310-369-4661
Tel 310-969-0562
Email ....antonios@fox.com

Distributor

Irene Sosa*
Jersey City, NJ 07302
Tel 201-792-5004
Email ....IreneSosa@aol.com

Rosario Sotelo*
San Francisco, CA 94108
Tel 415-260-7903
Email.................sotelo24@hotmail.com

Production Assistant, PIMPIN' FRUIT,
2003, Bandido Productions, Short

Luis Soto
Cool Moss, Inc.
Los Angeles, CA
Tel 323-969-9313

*Manager: Nick Mechanic,
310-741-1966*

Producer, VIETNAM WAR STORY: THE
LAST DAYS, 1989, HBO, Feature
Producer, THE HOUSE OF RAMON
IGLESIA, 1986, PBS, TV Movie
Producer, THE EQUALIZER, 1985, CBS,
TV Series
Director, FAME, 1982, NBC, TV Series

Martha Soto*
Brooklyn, NY 11206
Email ....soto__perez@hotmail.com

Alison Sotomayor*
Los Angeles, CA 90007
Cell 310-901-5939
Fax 562-402-8701
Email ....fiztek@aol.com
Web ....nhmc.org

Producer, HEROES IN THE HOOD: E.
LA'S HOMEBOY IDUSTRIES, 2003,
National Hispanic Media Coalition, TV
Series
Producer, MAOF: A FOUNDATION'S
VISION & MISSION, 2003, Mexican
American Opportunity Foundation,
Documentary
Producer, LIFE & TIMES NEWS &
PUBLIC AFFAIRS PROGRAM, 2001,
KCET-TV Public Television, TV Series
LIFE & TIMES NEWS & PUBLIC
AFFAIRS PROGRAM, 1997-2001,
KCET Public Television, TV Series

Gustavo Stebner*
Staff
Aveneaux Films
Bronx, NY 10463
Tel 210-683-9955
Email................gustavo@Ave.neaux.com

Writer, FEMMES DE BERLIN, 2004,
   Feature
Writer, WATER & DANTE, 2004, Feature
Producer, THE DARK MAGIC SHOW,
   2003-2004, The Magic of Rolando
   Medina, Documentary
Producer, A SU SALUD, 2003,
   Univision, TV Series
Producer, BREAKING BARRIERS:
   LIVING WITH ASTHMA, 2003,
   University of Texas Health Science
   Center, TV Series
Director, CHAQUETA, 2003, Aveneaux
   Films, Short
Director, THE AIR HOCKEY AFFAIR,
   2002, Aveneaux Films, Short
Director, MICHAEL BASTARD, 2000,
   Tavan Entertainment, Short

Susan Stoebner*
Los Angeles, CA 90036
Email ....sstoebner@aol.com

Beatriz Stotzer*
Los Angeles, CA 90017
Tel 213-483-2060
Fax 213-483-7848
Email ....email4new@aol.com
Web ....www.neweconomicsforwomen.org

Pinky Suavo
Pretty Vacant Productions
Austin, TX 78715
Tel 512-280-3983
Email ....pinkeesuavo@yahoo.com

Traci Swain*
New York, NY 10025
Tel 888-838-1474
Fax 212-866-3666
Email ....tswain27@aol.com

Angelique Szeman*
Encino, CA 91316
Tel 818-694-6818
Email ....angieszeman@yahoo.com

Gabriela Tagliavini
Los Angeles, CA 90201
Tel 310-717-1907
Email ....gabbo_t@yahoo.com

*Agent: Don Buchwald, Sheryl Petersen,
323-602-2346*

Manager: Todd Sharp, 323-512-7300

Director, 30 DAYS UNTIL I'M FAMOUS,
   2003, VH1, TV Movie
Director, LADIES NIGHT, 2003,
   Disney/Buena Vista International,
   Feature
Director, THE WOMAN EVERY MAN
   WANTS, 2001, Independent, Feature
Writer, THE WOMAN EVERY MAN
   WANTS, 2001, Independent, Feature

Dalia Tapia*
Columbia College Chicago
Chicago, IL 60608
Tel 773-847-3278
Fax 773-671-7979
Email ....daliatapia@hotmail.com

Kelly Taylor*
Beverly Hills, CA 90212
Tel 800-915-1545
Email ....adventure@hot-shot.com

Rick Tejada-Flores

Paradigm Productions
Berkeley, CA 94702
Tel 510-883-9814
Fax 510-848-5795
Email ......grtf@paradigmproductions.org
Web ....www.paradigmproductions.com

Producer, THE GOOD WAR AND THOSE
   WHO REFUSED TO FIGHT, 2000,
   ITVS, Documentary
Writer, THE GOOD WAR AND THOSE
   WHO REFUSED TO FIGHT, 2000,
   ITVS, Documentary
Director, THE GOOD WAR AND THOSE
   WHO REFUSED TO FIGHT, 2000,
   ITVS, Documentary
Producer, THE FIGHT IN THE FIELDS,
   1997, ITVS, Documentary
Writer, THE FIGHT IN THE FIELDS,
   1997, ITVS, Documentary
Director, THE FIGHT IN THE FIELDS,
   1997, ITVS, Documentary

Marianne Teleki*

Santa Monica, CA 90404
Tel 510-883-9527
Email ....quepasion@yahoo.com

Producer

Ray Telles

Paradigm Productions
Berkeley, CA 94702
Tel 510-883-9814
Fax 510-848-5795
Email........................Rto2900@aol.com
Web ....www.paradigmproductions.com

Producer, THE GOOD WAR AND THOSE
   WHO REFUSED TO FIGHT, 2000,
   ITVS, Documentary
Director, THE GOOD WAR AND THOSE
   WHO REFUSED TO FIGHT, 2000,
   ITVS, Documentary
Producer, THE FIGHT IN THE FIELDS,
   1997, ITVS, Documentary
Director, THE FIGHT IN THE FIELDS,
   1997, ITVS, Documentary

Rick Telles

Los Angeles, CA
Tel 818-288-1072
Email ....rdtelles@aol.com

*Agent: Don Buchwald & Associates,
323-655-7400*

Executive Producer, HITCHHIKER
   CHRONICLES, 2003, FX, TV Series
Executive Producer, NEXT ACTION
   STAR, 2003, NBC, TV Series
Executive Producer, SURF GIRLS,
   2003, MTV, TV Series
Director, CONQUEST, 2002, History
   Channel, TV Series
Executive Producer, SURREAL LIFE,
   2002, Warner Bros., TV Series
Director, CANNONBALL RUN, 2001,
   USA Networks, TV Series
Director, FEAR, 2001, MTV, TV Series

Steve Tellez

Agent
Creative Artists Agency
Beverly Hills, CA 90212
Tel 310-288-4545
Fax 310-288-4800
Email ....stellez@caa.com

Mitch Teplitsky*

Marketing/Fundraising Consultant
New York, NY 10024
Tel 212-721-6016
Email ....mitch@soyandina.com

Producer, SOY ANDINA, Documentary
Director, SOY ANDINA, Documentary

Conrado Terrazas*

Los Angeles, CA 90026
Email..............mexicatene@hotmail.com

Marketing/Fundraising Consultant

Janie Terrazas

Mun2/Telemundo
Hialeah, FL 33010
Tel 305-884-8200
Fax 305-525-8919
Email ....bolex@pobox.com
Web ....www.telemundo.com

Martin Terrones*

Los Angeles, CA 90019
Tel 323-931-0953
Fax 323-931-0953
Email ....mterrone@tft.ucla.edu

Max Terronez*

Exposure Plus @ UCSC
Santa Cruz, CA 95062
Tel 831-476-6066
Fax 831-515-3068
Email ....MTerronez@exposureplus.org
Web ....http://soar.ucsc.edu/exposureplus

David Ticotin

Calabasas, CA 91301
Tel 818-889-7768
Fax 818-889-7768
Email ....dnaticotin@aol.com

1st Assistant Director, ALIAS, Feature
1st Assistant Director, COLLATERAL DAMAGE, Feature
1st Assistant Director, ERASER, Feature
1st Assistant Director, FIRST CONTACT
1st Assistant Director, LAST ACTION HERO, Feature
1st Assistant Director, MIGHTY JOE YOUNG, Feature
1st Assistant Director, ROUGH RIDERS, Feature
1st Assistant Director, STAR TREK, Feature
1st Assistant Director, WILD WILD WEST, Feature

Lawrence Toledo*

Hope Street Productions
Tucson, AZ 85719
Tel 520-319-2613
Fax 520-327-7672
Email.................hsp2@mindspring.com
Web ....www.runninatmidnite.com

Pablo Toledo*

Hope Street Productions
Tucson, AZ 85719
Tel 520-319-2613
Fax 520-327-7672
Email ....diesel601@earthlink.net
Web ....www.runninatmidnite.com

Director, RUNNING AT MIDNIGHT, 2003, Feature
Writer, RUNNING AT MIDNIGHT, 2003, Feature

Maria Topete*

Brooklyn, NY 11234
Tel 718-252-1272
Email.............maria_topete@yahoo.com

Michael Toribio*

Rockaway Park, NY 11694
Tel 917-662-1286
Email ....Bambinotoribio@hotmail.com

Armando Torres*

Bondage Music
Alhambra, CA 91803
Tel 626-281-3621
Email...........bondagemusic@yahoo.com
Web ....armando-torrres.com

filmmakers

Benjamin Torres*
MTI Productions
Beverly Hills, CA 90212
Tel 310-390-9907
Fax 310-390-9107
Email ....btorres@mtiproductions.com
Web ....www.MTIProductions.com

Promotion/Event Producer

Esteban Torres
Los Angeles, CA
Tel 626-917-0910

Media Advocate

Fabiola Torres*
Associate Professor
CSUN Chicano Studies
Northridge, CA 91330
Tel 818-240-1000
Fax 818-677-7578
Email ....fabiola.torres@csun.edu

Educator

Jackie Torres
Jackmar Entertainment
Universal City, CA 91618
Tel 818-761-5725
Fax 818-761-5725
Email ....jackmar@jackietorres.com

Director
Writer
Producer

Jay Torres
Tel 818-506-6776

*Agent: Innovative Artists, Jack Leighton,
310-656-5130*

Director, Second Unit, KINGPIN, 2003,
  NBC, TV Series

Jose Torres*
J Train Audio Productions
New York, NY 10033
Tel 212-543-2407
Email ....soundguy@jtrainaudio.com

Sound

Marco Torres*
Sylmar, CA 91342
Tel 818-833-3128
Fax 818-833-3128
Email ....torres21@azteca.net

Educator, New Media

Robert Torres*
New York, NY 10018
Tel 212-673-9502
Fax 212-239-7156
Email ....urbansite@aol.com

Producer

Thomas Torres*
Newark, NJ 07105
Tel 973-207-5296
Email ....Soullive@earthlink.net

Writer, WHITE SOUND, 1999, Short
Director, WHITE SOUND, 1999, Short

Joseph Tovares
WGBH-TV
Belmont, MA 02478
Tel 617-300-5965
Tel 617-489-3710
Cell 617-803-3176
Fax 617-254-7535
Email ..joseph_tovares@latinonation.com

Director, REMEMBER THE ALAMO,
  2004, PBS, Documentary
Executive Producer, LA PLAZA, 2003,
  PBS, TV Series
Director, THE ZOOT SUIT RIOTS, 2002,
  PBS, Documentary

Writer, THE ZOOT SUIT RIOTS, 2002,
    PBS, Documentary
Director, BREAKTHROUGH: THE
    CHANGING FACE OF SCIENCE IN
    AMERICA, 1996, PBS, Documentary
Writer, BREAKTHROUGH: THE
    CHANGING FACE OF SCIENCE IN
    AMERICA, 1996, PBS, Documentary

Jose-Luis Trassens*
Sherman Oaks, CA 91423
Tel 818-907-6924
Email ....JOLTG@aol.com

Producer

Jesus Salvador Trevino*
Barrio Dog Productions
Los Angeles, CA 90041
Fax 323-257-4347
Email ....chuytrevino@earthlink.net
Web......................www.chuytrevino.com

*Agent: William Morris Agency, Jeffrey
Wise, 310-859-4126*

Director, MIRACLES, 2003, Buena Vista
    Television, TV Series
Director, THE O.C., 2003, Fox Network,
    TV Series
Director, THE COURT, 2002, ABC, TV
    Series
Director, CROSSING JORDAN, 2001,
    NBC, TV Series
Director, RESURRECTION BLVD., 2000,
    Showtime, TV Series
Director, CRUSADE, 1999, TNT &
    Warner Bros., TV Series
Director, THIRD WATCH, 1999, NBC, TV
    Series
Director, DAWSON'S CREEK, 1998,
    Columbia Tristar, TV Series
Director, THE PRACTICE, 1997, ABC, TV
    Series

Carmelita Tropicana*
New York, NY 10009
Tel 212-979-9225
Fax 212-979-0135
Email ....atropix@aol.com

Ela Troyano*
New York, NY 10009
Tel 212-979-0135
Email ....etroyano@aol.com

Director, LA LUPE, 2004, ITVS,
    Documentary
Producer, LA LUPE, 2004, ITVS,
    Documentary
Director, DELTA, 1997, Strand
    Releasing, Feature
Director, LATIN BOYS GO TO HELL,
    1997, Strand Releasing, Feature
Writer, LATIN BOYS GO TO HELL,
    1997, Strand Releasing, Feature

Charley Trujillo
San Jose, CA 95112
Tel 408-947-0958
Fax 408-279-6381
Email ....chusmahouse@earthlink.net

Director, 3 SOLDADOS: CHICANOS IN
    VIETNAM, 2002, PBS, Documentary

Rafael Trujillo*
Thirteen/WNET
New York, NY 10001
Tel 212-560-2902
Email ....trujillo@thirteen.org

filmmakers

Susana Tubert*
New York, NY 10011
Tel 212-691-3587
Cell 917-292-2361
Fax 212-229-2379
Email....................susanat725@aol.com
Web ..www.susanatubertproductions.com

Attorney: Roger Arar, Loeb & Loeb,
212-407-4906, rarar@loeb.com

Director, GYPSY GIRL, 2003, Short
Writer, GYPSY GIRL, 2003, Short
Producer, GYPSY GIRL, 2003, Short
Director, 4 GUYS NAMED JOSE... AND UNA MUJER NAMED MARIA!, 2000, Stage Play
Director, THE GUIDING LIGHT, SEGMENT DIR., 2000, CBS, TV Series
Writer, THE ART OF SWINDLING, 1996, Alliance Theater, Stage Play
Writer, A DAY IN THE LIFE OF A ROBOT, 1986, Don Quijote Children's Theatre, Stage Play

Donna Umali*
Sampaguita Productions
Orange, CA 92867
Tel 206-818-6176
Email ....lildonna@hotmail.com

Director, REALITY CHECK, Chapman University School of Film and Television, Short

Monica Uribe
Executive
Discovery Channel Digital Network
Miami, FL
Tel 305-507-4094

Pepe Urquijo*
Bandido Productions
Oakland, CA 94606
Tel 415-550-9093
Email ....pepe@pepelicula.com
Web ....www.pepelicula.com

ATREVATE, 2003, Music Video
Producer, FRUIT OF LABOR, 2003, Bandido Productions, Feature
PIMPIN FRUIT, 2003, Bandido Productions, Short
Producer, EVERYDAY EASTLAKE, 2001, Bandido Productions, Short
Producer, BECA DE GILAS: REBECA'S STORY, 1999, Subcine.com, Documentary Short
ALGUN DIA, 1998, Subcine.com, Short

Dawn Valadez*
Vaquera Productions
San Leandro, CA 94577
Tel 510-326-0309
Email ....dawn@agirlslife.org

John Valadez*
Kitchen Sync
Dix Hills, NY 11746
Tel 516-810-7238
Email ....johnjvaladez@aol.com

Producer, THE HEAD OF JOAQUIN MURRIETA, 2004, LPB, Documentary
Director, THE HEAD OF JOAQUIN MURRIETA, 2004, LPB, Documentary
Producer, THE LAST CONQUISTADOR, 2004, PBS, Documentary
Producer, MATTERS OF RACE: THE DIVIDE, 2003, PBS, Documentary

David C. Valdes*
Tarzana, CA

Attorney: Michael Adler, 310-205-6999

Producer, OPEN RANGE, 2003, Buena Vista Pictures, Feature

Producer, TIME MACHINE, 2002, Warner Bros., Feature

Producer, THE GREEN MILE, 1999, Warner Bros., Feature

Producer, TURBULENCE, 1997, MGM, Feature

Producer, STARS FELL ON HENRIETTA, 1995, Warner Bros., Feature

Executive Producer, IN THE LINE OF FIRE, 1993, Columbia TriStar, Feature

Executive Producer, UNFORGIVEN, 1992, Warner Home Video, Feature

Producer, THE ROOKIE, 1990, Warner Bros., Feature

Executive Producer, WHITE HUNTER, BLACK HEART, 1990, Warner Bros., Feature

Leslie Valdes
Cell 646-263-8476
Email...............alphabest@earthlink.net

Writer, THE BACKYARDIGANS, 2004, Nickelodeon, TV Series, Animated

Writer, DORA THE EXPLORER "THE CITY OF LOST TOYS", 2003, Nickelodeon Live, Stage Play

Writer, DORA THE EXPLORER, 2000, Nickelodeon, TV Series, Animated

Blanca Valdez
Blanca Valdez Casting
West Hollywood, CA 90046
Tel 323-876-5700
Fax 323-876-5297

Casting Director, VIVA VEGAS, 2000, Telemundo Network, TV Series

Casting Director, LOS BELTRAN, 1999, Telemundo Networks, TV Series

David Armando Valdez*
Austin, TX 78751
Tel 512-294-6061
Email ....homieknomes@yahoo.com

Jeff Valdez
President & CEO
SiTV
Los Angeles, CA 90065
Tel 323-256-8900
Fax 323-467-5544

Executive Producer, THE BROTHERS GARCIA, 2000, Nickelodeon, TV Series

Writer, THE BROTHERS GARCIA, 2000, Nickelodeon, TV Series

Producer, CAFE OLE', 1997, SiTV, TV Series

Writer, CAFE OLE', 1997, SiTV, TV Series

Producer, FUNNY IS FUNNY, 1997, Galavision Television, TV Series

Writer, FUNNY IS FUNNY, 1997, Galavision Television, TV Series

Producer, LATINO LAUGH FESTIVAL, 1997, Showtime & Comedy Central, TV Special

Karina Valdez*
Los Angeles, CA 90078
Tel 310-714-5238
Email ....Karina@zebra.net

filmmakers

Luis Valdez

El Teatro Campesino
San Juan Bautista, CA 95045
Tel 831-623-2444
Email ....info@elteatrocampesino.com
Web ....www.elteatrocampesino.com

*Agent: Writers & Artists Agency,
323-866-0900*

Director, THE CISCO KID, 1994,
    Esparza/ Katz Productions, Feature
Writer, THE CISCO KID, 1994, Esparza/
    Katz Productions, Feature
Director, LA PASTORELA, 1991, Richard
    Soto Productions, TV Movie
Writer, LA PASTORELA, 1991, Richard
    Soto Productions, TV Series
Director, LA BAMBA, 1987, Columbia
    Pictures, Feature
Writer, LA BAMBA, 1987, Columbia
    Pictures, Feature
Director, ZOOT SUIT, 1982, Universal
    Pictures, Feature

Maria Valdez*

Soul-Stirring Productions
Los Angeles, CA 90027
Tel 818-980-0203
Email................maria@mariavaldez.com

Producer, MOMMY, HOW MUCH DO YOU
    MAKE AN HOUR?
Actor, MOMMY, HOW MUCH DO YOU
    MAKE AN HOUR?

Mabel Valdiviezo

Bay Area Video Coalition
San Francisco, CA 94109
Tel 415-614-9697
Email.....................haikufilms@aol.com
Web.................www.soledadforever.com

Editor, FRUIT OF LABOR, 2003,
    Bandido Productions, Documentary
Editor, GOOD MORNING MS. KELLEY!,
    2001, Hybrid Productions,
    Documentary

Editor, THE WATER'S MUSE, 2000,
    Matahari Films, Short
Director, THE WATER'S MUSE, 2000,
    Matahari Films, Short
Educator

Maribel Valdiviezo*

Matahari Post
San Francisco, CA 94133
Tel 415-788-2230
Email.................mataharipost@aol.com

Jose Luis Valenzuela

Sleeping Giant Productions
Los Angeles, CA 90022
Tel 323-887-0665
Fax 323-887-9600
Email............SleepingGiantPro@aol.com

Director, LUMINARIAS, 2000, New
    Latin Pictures, Feature
Producer, LUMINARIAS, 2000, New
    Latin Pictures, Feature

Yvette Valenzuela*

San Diego, CA 92101
Tel 619-851-5627
Email ......valenzuelayvette@hotmail.com

Yolanda Valle*

North Highlands, CA 95660
Email ....yvalle@ucdavis.edu

Gabriel Vallejo*

South Gate, CA 90280
Tel 323-564-6164
Email ....gvallejo@ucla.edu

Jorge Vallejo*
Earth2mars
New York, NY 10010
Tel 212-545-8545
Fax 212-545-7728
Email.................jorge@earth2mars.com

COLUMBIA HOUSE, Commercial
MENNEN, TV Commercial
RED LOBSTER, Commercial

Julio Vallejo
Maya Cinema
Los Angeles, CA 90065
Tel 310-384-5411
Fax 310-281-3777
Email ....vallejoc@hotmail.com

Production Manager, ALL THE KING'S
　MEN, 1999, BBC, TV Movie
Production Manager, HOT BLOOD,
　1991, Sunshine Films Production,
　Feature

Victor A. Vallejo*
Los Angeles, CA 90027
Tel 323-660-6373
Email......................vavle.1@pacbell.net

Ethan Van Thillo
Festival Director
San Diego Latino Film Festival
San Diego, CA 92101
Tel 619-230-1938
Email............ethan@mediaartscenter.org

Domingo Vara*
Los Angeles, CA 90036
Tel 323-939-3715
Fax 323-939-3715
Email............domingovara@hotmail.com

Laura Varela*
San Antonio, TX 78224
Tel 210-226-5307
Email ....ixcheli@aol.com

Rosa Varela*
La Sirena Productions
Mesa, AZ 85213
Tel 480-655-0377
Email ....real2realmusic@yahoo.com

Sandra Varela*
Alan Ett Creative Group
Los Angeles, CA 90039
Tel 818-508-3311
Email................sansal_varela@msn.com

Adolfo Vargas*
Cal Poly University Pomona
Diamond Bar, CA 91765
Tel 909-869-3916
Fax 909-869-3933
Email..............arvargas@csupomona.edu

Emily Vargas*
New York, NY
Tel 646-489-3484
Email..........emily_vargas5@hotmail.com

Jacob Vargas
Los Angeles, CA
Agent: Paradigm, 310-277-4400

Actor, TRAFFIC, 2000, USA Films,
　Feature
Actor, SELENA, 1997, Warner Bros.,
　Feature

filmmakers

Pepe Vargas

Festival Director
Chicago International Latino Film
Festival
Chicago, IL 60605
Tel 312-413-1330
Tel 312-344-8030
Web ....www.latinoculturalcenter.org

Blanca Vasquez*

New York, NY 10025
Tel 212-274-8080
Fax 212-222-1156
Email...............blancav105@yahoo.com

Henry Vasquez Pelayo*

Brown Boyz Films
Burbank, CA 91502
Tel 818-563-4263
Fax 323-933-4662
Email........brownboyzfilms@hotmail.com

Regina Vater*

Austin, TX 78751
Tel 512-451-1674
Email ....hydie@mail.utexas.edu

Paul Vato

Barrio Speedwagon
North Hills, CA 91343
Tel 323-377-8286
Email.................paulvato@hotmail.com
Web ....paulvato.com

*Agent: Susan Nathe and Associates,
Steve Cummins, 323-653-7573*

Actor, CEDRIC THE ENTERTAINER
   PRESENTS:2003, Fox/Stan Lathan,
   TV Special
Actor, DODGE CARAVAN COMMERCIAL,
   2003, Global Hue, Commercial
Actor, THE BOLD AND THE BEAUTIFUL,
   2003, CBS / Bell - Phillip Television,
   TV Series
Actor, BARRIO SPEEDWAGON, 2002,
   Barrio Speedwagon, Stage Play

Actor, CRICKET CELLULAR, 2002,
   Strom Magallon, Commercial
Actor, DEL TACO, 2001, Squeak
   Productions, Commercial

Gabriela Vazquez

Los Angeles, CA
Tel 310-313-5515

Production Manager, MEN IN BLACK II,
   2002, Sony Pictures, Feature
Production Manager, THE TICK, 2001,
   Fox Networks, TV Series
2nd Assistant Director, SENSELESS,
   1998, Miramax, Feature
2nd Assistant Director, CONTACT, 1997,
   Warner Bros., Feature
2nd Assistant Director, MEN IN BLACK,
   1997, Columbia Pictures, Feature
2nd Assistant Director, NINE MONTHS,
   1995, 20th Century Fox, Feature
2nd Assistant Director, TERMINAL
   VELOCITY, 1994, Buena Vista
   Pictures, Feature
2nd Assistant Director, BUGSY, 1991,
   TriStar Pictures, Feature

Gustavo Vazquez*

San Francisco, CA 94112
Tel 415-585-6984
Email ....gustavo@exploratorium.org

Jose Antonio Vazquez

Executive Director
Stooppix
London, SE41QX England
Tel 011-44-0208-699-6700
Email ....sarumsircle@yahoo.com
Web.......................www.stooppix.free.fr

Producer, CHARCOAL, 2000, UB
   Productions, Short

Luis Vazquez Gomez*
Arroz Y Frijoles Productions
San Francisco, CA 94110
Tel 415-587-7892
Email ....luvasquez@aol.com

Antonio Vega*
Nosotros
Los Angeles, CA 90026
Tel 323-769-7059

Astrid M. Vega*
Aventura, FL 33160
Tel 305-932-3643
Email ....
astrid_creative_endeavors@yahoo.com

Carmen Vega*
Los Angeles, CA 90006
Email ....Cvpoema@hotmail.com

Gilberto Vega*
Tucson, AZ 85714
Tel 520-889-7713
Email ....ghost_face_tito@hotmail.com

Mirtha Vega*
Aeria-Vega Productions, LLC
Sausalito, CA 94966
Tel 415-892-4790
Fax 415-892-4790
Email ....eaglesoar_prod@hotmail.com

Director, TRYST, 2003, Feature

Yvette Vega*
Yvette Vega Productions
Island Park, NY 11558
Tel 516-526-3077
Email ....reelcelebrities@aol.com
Web ....www.reelcelebrities.tv

Producer, IN SEARCH OF MY
    CULTURAL HEROES, 2003, Latin
    USA Film Festival, Documentary
Producer, REEL CELEBRITIES, 2003,
    www.reelcelebrities.tv, TV Special
Producer, MY ANGEL ANGELICA, 2002,
    Tribeca Film Center, Short
Actor, LA CHICA FITNESS, USA - Tape
    worm, Home Video
Actor, LA MACARENA, Anchor Bay

Jerry Velasco*
President
Nosotros
Hollywood, CA 90004
Tel 323-466-8566
Fax 323-466-8540
Email ....velascojgv@aol.com

Award Shows
Publicist
Management

Aram Velazquez*
Miami, FL 33186
Email.....................eramix@eramix.com

Alejo Velez*
Institute of Texan Cultures
San Antonio, TX 78205
Tel 210-458-2273
Email ....avelez@utsa.edu

Laura Velez
Executive Director
Puerto Rico Film Commision
San Juan, PR 00918
Tel 787-756-5706
Fax 787-756-5706
Email ....lavelez@preda.com

Lorna Ventura*
Stepsister Production
Jackson Heights, NY 11372
Tel 212-462-9284
Email ....lornaventura@nyc.rr.com

Christina Vergara*
Ozark Productions
Los Angeles, CA 90034
Tel 310-836-6356
Email......vergara_christina@hotmail.com

Actor

Jorge Vergara*
Apuesta Pictures
Los Angeles, CA 90048
Tel 323-936-2110
Fax...............................323.525.2721
Email ....victorguerra@earthlink.net

Producer, THE ASSASSINATION OF
   RICHARD NIXON, 2003, Focus,
   Feature
Producer, THE DEVIL'S BACKBONE,
   2001, Columbia TriStar Home
   Entertainment, Feature

Jose Vicuña
President
Plural Entertainment
Madrid, 28013 Spain
Tel 34-91-515-9280
Fax 34-91-515-9140
Email.................jvicuna@pluralent.com

Victoria Vieira*
Festival Director
Latino Film Festival
Sausalito, CA 94965
Tel 415-331-2502
Fax 415-331-5572
Email ....sperel@linex.com
Web ....www.cuisineperel.com

Camilo Vila
Venice, CA
Tel 310-396-4301
Email ....olimac@comcast.net

Director, 18 WHEELS OF JUSTICE,
   2000, Stu Segall Productions Inc., TV
   Series
Director, RESURRECTION BLVD., 2000,
   Showtime, TV Series
Director, UNLAWFUL PASSAGE, 1994,
   Seban Entertainment, Feature
Director, OPTIONS, 1988, Vestron
   Pictures, Feature
Director, THE UNHOLY, 1988, Vestron
   Pictures, Feature
Producer, AMIGOS, 1985, Hargrove
   Entertainment Inc., Feature
Producer, ME OLVIDE DE VIVIR, 1980
Director, LOS GUISANOS, 1978, South
   American Shorts, Feature

Jose Antonio Villacis*
N. Hollywood, CA 91606
Tel 323-356-0856
Email ....antonio_ny@hotmail.com

Juan Miguel Villafane*
JKL Films
San Juan, PR 00901
Tel 787-753-1881
Email ....jmv333@aol.com

Ligiah Villalobos

Jalapeno Films
W. Hollywood, CA 90046
Tel 310-826-8671

Writer
Producer

Michael Villalobos

Mr. Latino America
Los Angeles, CA 90042
Tel 818-766-0784

Executive Producer

Reynaldo Villalobos

Santa Barbara, CA
Tel 805-745-8784
Fax 805-745-8804
Email ....debsamuel@aol.com

Director of Photography, JACK AND
 MARILYN, 2002, Focus Institute of
 Film, Feature
Director of Photography, NOT ANOTHER
 TEEN MOVIE, 2001, Columbia TriStar
 Films, Feature
Director of Photography, LOVE &
 BASKETBALL, 2000, New Line
 Cinema, Feature
Director of Photography, L.A. DOCTORS,
 1998-99, CBS Productions, TV Series
Director, HOLLYWOOD CONFIDENTIAL,
 1997, Paramount Home Video, TV
 Movie
Director, SOLDIER OF FORTUNE, 1997,
 Rysher Entertainment, TV Series

Luis Villanueva

President
Venevision International
Miami, FL
Tel 305-442-3411

Distributor

Raymond Villareal*

San Antonio, TX 78245
Email ....RV11111@yahoo.com

Jerry Villarreal

Nuesion
Houston, TX 77266
Tel 800-870-3721
Email ....info@nuesion.com
Web ....www.nuesion.com

Producer, POR NO SABER, 2002,
 Nuesion, Short
Director, POR NO SABER, 2002,
 Nuesion, Short

Maria Christina Villasenor*

Guggenheim Museum
New York, NY 10012
Tel 212-423-3839
Email ....mvillasenor@guggenheim.org

Eric Volz*

San Diego, CA 92102
Tel 619-239-2284
Email..................ericsvolz@hotmail.com

Tania Waisberg*

San Francisco, CA 94107
Tel 415-546-3832
Fax 415- 546-3832
Email...........................wtania@usa.net

Kristine Wallis

Agent
The Wallis Agency
Burbank, CA 91505
Tel 818-953-4848
Fax 818-845-2437
Email..................info@wallisagency.com
Web ....www.wallisagency.com

Jean Watson*
City of Sunny Isles Beach
Sunny Isles Beach, FL 33160

Pamela Wells*
Toluca Lake, CA 91602
Email ....jada60@hotmail.com

Kirk Whisler*
Latino Print Network
Carlsbad, CA 92008
Tel 760-434-7474
Fax 760-434-7476
Email.........................kirk@whisler.com
Web ....www.latinoprintnetwork.com

Media Advocate

Robin Wilson*
Pfunkshun Productions
Converse, TX 78109
Tel 210-854-3252
Email...........................rlwilson@wt.net

Michael Wimer
Agent
Creative Artists Agency
Beverly Hills, CA 90212
Tel 310-288-4545
Fax 310-288-4800

Peggy Wintermute*
Agent
Wintermute Talent Agency
Beverly Hills, CA 90210
Tel 310-385-8487
Email ....pwintermute@arrow.com

Alex Wolfe*
Brooklyn, NY 11211
Tel 718-388-0350
Fax 718-302-9481
Email ....mambomedia@yahoo.com

Ginny Wolnowicz*
Cosmoflix
Sunny Isles Beach, FL 33316
Tel 786-286-6669
Fax 305-947-4549
Email ....Ginnydom@aol.com

Vivian Wu
President
MARdeORO Film Inc.
San Marino, CA 91108
Tel 626-799-1388
Fax 626-799-2388
Email ....mardeoro@earthlink.net

Crystina Wyler*
Hawkli Productions
Miami, FL 33176
Tel 305-596-5150
Fax 305-279-4393
Email ....info@hawkli.com
Web ....www.hawkli.com

Writer

Juan Carlos Zaldivar*
90 Miles, LLC
Miami, FL 33139
Tel 305-532-8110
Email ....jucamaza@aol.com

Director, 90 MILES, 2003, POV,
  Documentary
Producer, 90 MILES, 2003, POV,
  Documentary

David Zamora*
Los Angeles, CA
Tel 213-580-9018

Del Zamora
Los Angeles, CA
Tel 213-387-1315
Fax 213-380-0378
Email ....delzamora@hotmail.com

Director, CHANNEL 0, 1999, Pocho
　Productions, TV Series
Writer, CHANNEL 0, 1999, Pocho
　Productions, TV Series
Director, FRIDA KAHLO IN THE CASA
　AZUL, 1996, Rampage Productions,
　Short
Writer, FRIDA KAHLO IN THE CASA
　AZUL, 1996, Rampage Productions,
　Short
Producer, I'LL BE HOME FOR
　CHRISTMAS, 1991, Universal Studios,
　Short

Patricia Zapata*
San Antonio, TX 78229
Tel 210-615-6540
Email.............pzapata@mindspring.com

Katynka Zazueta Martinez*
UC San Diego
San Diego, CA 92116
Tel 619-291-4970
Email ....kmartine@weber.ucsd.edu

Nicole Zepeda*
Austin, TX 78705
Tel 956-460-4095
Email ....blackunicorn12@aol.com

Jaime Zesati*
Walnut Creek, NY 94596
Tel 925-930-9811
Email................ace77@mindspring.com

Monica Zevallos
Account Executive Latin Market
Ascent Media
Santa Monica, CA 91404
Tel 310-434-6529
Cell 323-547-0337
Fax 310-434-6511
Email ....mzevallos@ascentmedia.com

Esteban Zul*
Pocho Productions
Los Angeles, CA 90027
Fax 213-380-0378
Email ....badoso@aol.com

Writer, PACO'S SUITCASE BOMB,
　2002, Fox Searchlab, Short
Writer, TACO TRUCK: THE MOVIE,
　2002, New Line, Feature

Frank Zuñiga*
Executive Director
New Mexico Film Office
Santa Fe, NM 87504
Tel 505-827-9286
Fax 505-827-9799
Email ......frank.zuniga@edd.state.nm.us
Web............................www.nmfilm.com

Pedro Zurita
Videoteca del Sur
New York, NY 10003
Tel 212-674-5405
Fax 212-614-0464
Email.............videlsur@mindspring.com

filmmakers

National Association of Latino Independent Producers

production
resources

courtesy of
Hollywood Creative Directory

STUDIOS

Walt Disney Company, The
500 S. Buena Vista St.
Burbank, CA 91521
Phone   818-560-1000
www.disney.com

DreamWorks SKG
1000 Flower St.
Glendale, CA 91201
Phone   818-695-5000
www.dreamworks.com

Metro-Goldwyn-Mayer (MGM)
10250 Constellation Blvd.
Los Angeles, CA 90067
Phone   310-449-3000
www.mgm.com

Miramax Films
375 Greenwich St.
New York, NY 10013-2338
Phone   212-941-3800
www.miramax.com

New Line Cinema
116 N. Robertson Blvd., Ste. 200
Los Angeles, CA 90048
Phone   310-854-5811
www.newline.com

Paramount Pictures
5555 Melrose Ave.
Los Angeles, CA 90038-3197
Phone   323-956-5000
www.paramount.com

Sony Pictures Entertainment
10202 W. Washington Blvd.
Culver City, CA 90232-3195
Phone   310-244-4000
www.sony.com

Twentieth Century Fox
10201 W. Pico Blvd.
Los Angeles, CA 90035
Phone   310-369-1000
www.fox.com

Universal
100 Universal City Plaza
Universal City, CA 91608-1085
Phone   818-777-1000
www.universalstudios.com

Warner Bros.
4000 Warner Blvd.
Burbank, CA 91522-0001
Phone   818-954-6000
www.warnerbros.com

NETWORKS AND MAJOR CABLE CHANNELS

ABC
500 S. Buena Vista St.
Burbank, CA 91521
Phone   818-460-7777
www.abc.com

CBS
7800 Beverly Blvd.
Los Angeles, CA 90036-2188
Phone   323-575-2345
www.cbs.com

Fox
10201 W. Pico Blvd.
Los Angeles, CA 90035
Phone   310-369-1000
www.fox.com

HBO
1100 Avenue of the Americas
New York, NY 10036
Phone   212-512-1000
www.hbo.com

NBC
3000 W. Alameda Ave.
Burbank, CA 91523-0001
Phone   818-840-4444
www.nbc.com

production resources

Showtime
1633 Broadway
New York, NY 10019
Phone   212-708-1600
www.sho.com

UPN
11800 Wilshire Blvd.
Los Angeles, CA 90025
Phone   310-575-7000
www.upn.com

WB Television Network, The
4000 Warner Blvd., Bldg. 34-R
Burbank, CA 91522-0001
Phone   818-977-5000
www.thewb.com

STATE FILM COMMISSIONS

ALABAMA

Alabama Film Office
Alabama Center for Commerce
401 Adams Ave., Ste. 630
Montgomery, AL 36104
Phone   334-242-4195
         800-633-5898
Fax   334-242-2077
www.alabamafilm.org
Brenda Hobbie – Film Office Coordinator

ALASKA

Alaska Film Program
550 W. Seventh Ave., Ste. 1770
Anchorage, AK 99501-3510
Phone   907-269-8190
Fax   907-269-8125
www.alaskafilm.org
Margy Johnson - Director

ARIZONA

Arizona Film Commission
3800 N. Central Ave., Bldg. D
Phoenix, AZ 85012
Phone   602-771-1193
         800-523-6695
Fax   602-771-1211
www.azcommerce.com
Robert Detweiler - Director

ARKANSAS

Arkansas Film Office
One Capitol Mall, Ste. 4B-505
Little Rock, AR 72201
Phone   501-682-7676
Fax   501-682-3456
www.1800arkansas.com/film
Joe Glass - Film Commissioner

CALIFORNIA

California Film Commission
7080 Hollywood Blvd., Ste. 900
Hollywood, CA 90028
Phone   323-860-2960
         800-858-4749
Fax   323-860-2972
www.film.ca.gov
www.cinemascout.com
www.filmcafirst.com
Karen R. Constine - Director

COLORADO

Colorado Film Commission
1625 Broadway, Ste. 1700
Denver, CO 80202
Phone   303-620-4500
         800-SCOUTUS
Fax   303-620-4545
www.coloradofilm.org
Stephanie Two Eagles - Contact

CONNECTICUT

Connecticut Film, Video & Media Office
805 Brook St., Bldg. 4
Rocky Hill, CT 06067
Phone   860-571-7130
         800-392-2122
Fax   860-721-7088
www.ctfilm.com
Guy Ortoleva - Exec. Director

DELAWARE

Delaware Film Office
Delaware Tourism Office
99 Kings Highway
Dover, DE 19901
Phone   302-739-4271, x6823
Fax   302-739-5749
www.state.de.us/dedo
Cheryl Heiks - Film Office Coordinator

DISTRICT OF COLUMBIA

**Office of Motion Picture &
TV Development**
441 Fourth Street NW, Ste. 760 North
Washington, DC 20001
Phone   202-727-6608
Fax   202-727-3246
www.film.dc.gov
Crystal Palmer - Director

FLORIDA

**Governor's Office of Film &
Entertainment**
Executive Office of the Governor
400 S. Monroe St., Ste. 2002
Tallahassee, FL 32399-0001
Phone   850-410-4765
         877-352-3456
         818-508-7772
         (LA Office)
Fax   850-410-4770
www.filminflorida.com
Susan Albershardt – Film Commissioner

GEORGIA

**Georgia Department of Film,
Video & Music**
285 Peachtree Center Ave., Ste. 1000
Atlanta, GA 30303
Phone   404-656-3591
         877-746-6842
Fax   404-656-3565
www.filmgeorgia.org
Greg Torre - Director

HAWAII

**Hawaii Film Office
(State of Hawaii)**
250 S. Hotel St., 5th Fl.
Honolulu, HI 96813
Phone   808-586-2570
Fax   808-586-2572
info@hawaiifilmoffice.com
www.hawaiifilmoffice.com
Donne Dawson – Film Commissioner

**Maui County Film Office
(Islands of Maui, Molokai, Lanai)**
200 S. High St., 6th Fl.
Wailuku, HI 96793
Phone   808-270-7415
Fax   808-270-7995
info@filmmaui.com
www.filmmaui.com
Benita Brazier - Film Commissioner

**Honolulu Film Office
(Island of Oahu)**
530 S. King St., Rm. 306
Honolulu, HI 96813
Phone: 808-527-6108
Fax: 808-527-6102
info@filmhonolulu.com
www.filmhonolulu.com
*Walea Constantinau – Film
Commissioner*

production resources

Kauai Film Commission
(Island of Kauai)
4444 Rice St., Ste, 200
Lihue, HI 96766
Phone   808-241-6386
Fax   808-241-6399
info@filmkauai.com
www.filmkauai.com
Tiffani Lizama – Film Commissioner

Big Island Film Office
(Island of Hawaii)
25 Aupuni St., Rm 219
Hilo, HI 96720
Phone   808-326-2663
Fax   808-935-1205
film@bigisland.com
www.filmbigisland.com
Marilyn Killeri – Film Commssioner

IDAHO
Idaho Film Bureau
700 W. State St.
PO Box 83720
Boise, ID 83720-0093
Phone   208-334-2470
             800-942-8338
Fax   208-334-2631
www.filmidaho.com
Peg Owens - Director

ILLINOIS
Illinois Film Office
100 W. Randolph, Ste. 3-400
Chicago, IL 60601
Phone   312-814-3600
Fax   312-814-8874
www.filmillinois.state.il.us
Brenda Sexton – Film Commissioner

INDIANA
Indiana Film Commission
Indiana Department of Commerce
1 N. Capitol Ave., Ste. 700
Indianapolis, IN 46204-2288
Phone   317-232-8829
Fax   317-233-6887
www.filmindiana.com
Jane Rulon - Director

IOWA
Iowa Film Office
200 E. Grand Ave.
Des Moines, IA 50309
Phone   515-242-4726
Fax   515-242-4809
www.state.ia.us/film
Wendol Jarvis - Contact

KANSAS
Kansas Film Commission
1000 SW Jackson, Ste. 100
Topeka, KS 66612
Phone   785-296-2178
Fax   785-296-3490
www.filmkansas.com
Peter Jasso - Film Commissioner

KENTUCKY
Kentucky Film Commission
500 Mero St.
2200 Capitol Plaza Tower
Frankfort, KY 40601
Phone   502-564-3456
             800-345-6591
Fax   502-564-7588
www.kyfilmoffice.com
Jim Toole - Director

production resources

LOUISIANA

Louisiana Film Commission
PO Box 94185
Baton Rouge, LA 70804-4320
Phone   225-342-8150
          888-655-0447
Fax   225-342-5349
www.lafilm.org
Mark Smith - Film Commissioner

MAINE

Maine Film Office
59 State House Station
Augusta, ME 04333
Phone   207-624-7631
Fax   207-287-8070
www.filminmaine.com
Lea Girardin - Director

MARYLAND

Maryland Film Office
217 E. Redwood St., 9th Fl.
Baltimore, MD 21202
Phone   410-767-6340
          800-333-6632
Fax   410-333-0044
www.marylandfilm.org
Jack Gerbes - Director

MASSACHUSETTS

Massachusetts Film Bureau
198 Tremont St.
PMB #135
Boston, MA 02116
Phone   617-523-8388
www.massfilmbureau.com
Robin Dawson – Exec. Director

MICHIGAN

Michigan Film Office
702 W. Kalamazoo St.
Lansing, MI 48915
Phone   517-373-0638
          800-477-3456
Fax   517-241-2930
www.michigan.gov/hal
Janet Lockwood - Director

MINNESOTA

Minnesota Film & TV Board
401 N. Third St., Ste. 460
Minneapolis, MN 55401
Phone   612-332-6493
Fax   612-332-3735
www.mnfilm.org
Craig Rice - Exec. Director

MISSISSIPPI

Mississippi Film Office
PO Box 849
Jackson, MS 39205
Phone   601-359-3297
Fax   601-359-5048
www.visitmississippi.org/film
Ward Emling - Manager

MISSOURI

Missouri Film Commission
301 W. High St., Ste. 720
PO Box 118
Jefferson City, MO 65102
Phone   573-751-9050
Fax   573-522-1719
www.missouridevelopment.org/film
Jerry Jones - Director

MONTANA

Montana Film Office
301 S. Park Ave.
Helena, MT 59620
Phone 406-841-2876
       800-553-4563
Fax   406-841-2877
www.montanafilm.com
Sten Iversen - Director

NEBRASKA

Nebraska Film Office
PO Box 94666
301 Centennial Mall South, 4th Fl.
Lincoln, NE 68509-4666
Phone 402-471-3680
       800-228-6505
Fax   402-471-3365
www.filmnebraska.org
Laurie J. Richards - Nebraska Film Officer

NEVADA

Nevada Film Office
555 E. Washington Ave., Ste. 5400
Las Vegas, NV 89101
Phone 702-486-2711
       877-638-3456
Fax   702-486-2712
www.nevadafilm.com
Charles Geocaris - Director

NEW HAMPSHIRE

New Hampshire Film & Television Office
172 Pembroke Rd.
PO Box 1856
Concord, NH 03302-1856
Phone 603-271-2665
Fax   603-271-6870
www.filmnh.org
Jay Brenchick - Director

NEW JERSEY

New Jersey Motion Picture & Television Commission
153 Halsey St., 5th Fl.
PO Box 47023
Newark, NJ 07101
Phone 973-648-6279
Fax   973-648-7350
www.njfilm.org
Joseph Friedman - Exec. Director

NEW MEXICO

New Mexico Film Office
1100 St. Francis Dr., Ste. 1200
Santa Fe, NM 87505
Phone 505-827-9810
       800-545-9871
Fax   505-827-9799
www.nmfilm.com
Frank Zuniga - Director

NEW YORK

New York State Governor's Office for Motion Picture and Television Department
633 Third Ave., 33rd Fl.
New York, NY 10017
Phone 212-803-2330
Fax   212-803-2339
www.nylovesfilm.com
Pat Swinney Kaufman - Deputy Commissioner/Director

New York City Mayor's Office of Film, Theatre & Broadcasting
1697 Broadway, Ste. 602
New York, NY 10019
Phone 212-489-6710
Fax   212-307-6237
www.nyc.gov/film
Katherine Oliver - Commissioner

NORTH CAROLINA

North Carolina Film Office
4324 Mail Service Center
Raleigh, NC 27699
Phone   919-733-9900
          800-232-9227
Fax   919-715-0151
www.ncfilm.com
Bill Arnold – Film Commissioner

NORTH DAKOTA

North Dakota Film Commission
1600 E. Century Ave., Ste. 2
Bismarck, ND 58503
Phone   701-328-2525
Fax   701-328-4878
www.ndtourism.com
Sara Otte Coleman – Film Commissioner

OHIO

Ohio Film Commission
77 S. High St., 29th Fl.
Columbus, OH 43215
Phone   614-466-2284
          800-230-3523
Fax   614-466-6744
www.ohiofilm.com
Steve Cover - State Film Commissioner

OKLAHOMA

Oklahoma Film Commission
15 N. Robinson, Ste. 802
Oklahoma City, OK 73102
Phone   405-522-6760
          800-766-3456
Fax   405-522-0656
www.oklahomafilm.org
Dino Lalli - Director

OREGON

Oregon Film & Video Office
One World Trade Center
121 SW Salmon St., Ste. 1205
Portland, OR 97204
Phone   503-229-5832
Fax   503-229-6869
www.oregonfilm.org
Veronica Rinard - Exec. Director

PENNSYLVANIA

Pennsylvania Film Office
Commonwealth Keystone Bldg., 4th Fl.
Harrisburg, PA 17120-0225
Phone   717-783-3456
Fax   717-787-0687
www.filminpa.com
Brian Kreider - Director

PUERTO RICO

Puerto Rico Film Commission
355 F.D. Roosevelt Ave., Ste. 106
Hato Rey, PR 00918
Phone   787-754-7110
          787-758-4747, x2251
Fax   787-756-5706
www.puertoricofilm.com
Laura A. Velez - Exec. Director

RHODE ISLAND

Rhode Island Film & TV Office
RI Economic Development Corporation
One W. Exchange St.
Providence, RI 02903
Phone   401-222-2601
Fax   401-273-8270
www.rifilm.com
Rick Smith - Director

production resources

SOUTH CAROLINA

South Carolina Film Office
1201 Main St., Ste. 1750
Columbia, SC 29201
Phone   803-737-0490
Fax   803-737-3104
www.scfilmoffice.com
Jeff Monks – Director, Business Development

SOUTH DAKOTA

South Dakota Film Office
711 E. Wells Ave.
Pierre, SD 57501
Phone   605-773-3301
Fax   605-773-3256
www.filmsd.com
Chris Hull - Manager

TENNESSEE

Tennessee Film, Entertainment and Music Commission
312 Eighth Avenue N.,
Tennessee Tower, 9th Fl.
Nashville, TN 37243
Phone   615-741-3456
            877-818-3456
Fax   615-741-5554
www.filmtennessee.com
David Bennett - Exec. Director

TEXAS

Texas Film Commission
PO Box 13246
Austin, TX 78711
Phone   512-463-9200
Fax   512-463-4114
www.texasfilmcommission.com
Tom Copeland - Director

UTAH

Utah Film Commission
324 S. State St., Ste. 500
Salt Lake City, UT 84111
Phone   801-538-8740
            800-453-8824
Fax   801-538-8746
www.film.utah.org
Leigh von der Esch - Exec. Director

VERMONT

Vermont Film Commission
10 Baldwin St., Drawer #33
Montpelier, VT 05633-2001
Phone   802-828-3618
Fax   802-828-0607
www.vermontfilm.com
Danis Regal - Exec. Director

VIRGINIA

Virginia Film Office
901 E. Byrd St.
Richmond, VA 23219-4048
Phone   804-371-8204
            800-854-6233
Fax   804-371-8177
www.film.virginia.org
Rita McClenny - Director

WASHINGTON

Washington State Film Office
2001 Sixth Ave., Ste. 2600
Seattle, WA 98121
Phone   206-256-6146
Fax   206-256-6154
www.filmwashington.com
Suzy Kellett - Director

WEST VIRGINIA
West Virginia Film Office
c/o West Virginia Division of Tourism
90 MacCorkle Ave. SW
South Charleston, WV 25303
Phone   304-558-2200
           800-225-5982
Fax   304-558-0108
www.wvdo.org
Denise Allen - Contact

WISCONSIN
Wisconsin Film Office
201 W. Washington Ave., 2nd Fl.
Madison, WI 53703
Phone   800-345-6947
Fax   608-266-3403
www.filmwisconsin.org
Sarah Klavas - Director, Marketing

WYOMING
Wyoming Film Office
214 W. 15th St.
Cheyenne, WY 82002-0240
Phone   307-777-3400
           800-458-6657
Fax   307-777-2838
www.wyomingfilm.org
Michell Phelan - Manager

INTERNATIONAL FILM COMMISSIONS

AUSTRALIA
Melbourne Film Office
GPO Box 4361
Melbourne, Victoria 3001
Australia
Phone   61-3-9660-3240
Fax   61-3-9660-3201
www.film.vic.gov.au/info
Louisa Coppel – Director

New South Wales Film & Television Office
GPO Box 1744
Sydney, New South Wales 2000
Australia
Phone   61-2-9264-6400
Fax   61-2-9264-4388
www.fto.nsw.gov.au
Kingston Anderson – Film Commissioner

Pacific Film & Television Commission
PO Box 94, Albert St.
Brisbane, Queensland 4002
Australia
Phone   61-7-3224-4114
Fax   61-7-3224-6717
www.pftc.com.au
Robin James – Film Commissioner

South Australian Film Corporation
3 Butler Dr., Hendon Common
Hendon, South Australia 5014
Australia
Phone   61-8-8348-9300
Fax   61-8-8347-0385
www.safilm.com.au
Judith Crombie – CEO

CANADA
Alberta Film Commission
5th Fl., Commerce Pl.
10155 – 102 St.
Edmonton, Alberta
T5J 4L6 Canada
Phone   780-422-8584
Fax   780-422-8582
www.albertafilm.ca
Dan Chugg – Film Commissioner

British Columbia Film
2225 W. Broadway,
Vancouver, British Columbia
V6K 2E4 Canada
Phone   604-736-7997
Fax   604-736-7290
www.bcfilm.bc.ca
Rob Egan – President/CEO

Thompson-Nicola Film Commission
300-465 Victoria St.
Kamloops, British Columbia
V2C 2A9 Canada
Phone   250-377-8673
Toll Free BC 1-877-377-8673
Fax   250-372-5048
Cell   250-319-6211
vweller@tnrd.bc.ca
www.tnrd.bc.ca
*Victoria Weller – Exec. Director
of Film*

Montréal Film and TV Commission
303 Notre-Dame Street East,
Level 2
Montréal, Québec H2Y 3Y8 Canada
Phone   514-872-2883
Fax   514-872-3409
www.montrealfilm.com
André Lafond – Film Commissioner

Toronto Film and Television Office
100 Queen Street West,
Main Fl., West Side
Toronto, Ontario M5H 2N2 Canada
Phone   416-392-7570
Fax   416-392-0675
www.torontofilm.com
*Rhonda Silverstone – Film
Commissioner*

FRANCE

Commission Nationale du Film France
30, Avenue de Messine
Paris 75008 France
Phone   33-1-5383-9898
Fax   33-1-5383-9899
www.filmfrance.com
Benoit Caron – Exec. Director

GERMANY

Berlin Brandenburg Film Commission
August-Bebel-Str. 26-53
Potsdam-Babelsberg D-14482 Germany
Phone   49-331-743-8730
Fax   49-331-743-8799
www.filmboard.de
Christiane Raab – Film Commissioner

ITALY

Italian Film Commission
Via Forcella, 13
Milan 20144 Italy
Phone   39-02-8940-3372
Fax   39-335-837-2876
www.filminginitaly.com
Francesco Campi – Film Commissioner

UNITED KINGDOM

British Film Commission
10 Little Portland St.
London W1W 7JG UK
Phone   44-020-7861-7860
Fax   44-020-7861-7864
www.bfc.co.uk
*Steve Norris – British Film
Commissioner*

London Film Commission
20 Euston Centre
London NW1 3JH UK
Phone   44-020-7387-8787
Fax   44-020-7387-8788
www.london-film.co.uk
Sue Hayes – Film Commissioner

GUILDS, UNIONS, AND ASSOCIATIONS

Academy of Motion Picture Arts and Sciences (AMPAS)

www.oscars.org
Honorary organization of motion picture professionals founded to advance the arts and sciences of motion pictures.
8949 Wilshire Blvd.
Beverly Hills, CA 90211-1972
Phone   310-247-3000
Fax   310-859-9351
         310-859-9619

Academy of Television Arts & Sciences (ATAS)

www.emmys.tv
Nonprofit corporation for the advancement of telecommunications arts and sciences.
5220 Lankershim Blvd.
North Hollywood, CA 91601
Phone   818-754-2800
Fax   818-761-2827

Academy Players Directory

www.playersdirectory.com
Print and online casting directories.
1313 N. Vine St.
Hollywood, CA 90028
Phone   310-247-3058
Fax   310-550-5034

Actors' Equity Association (AEA)

www.actorsequity.org
Labor union representing US actors and stage managers working in the professional theater.
Chicago
125 S. Clark St., Ste. 1500
Chicago, IL 60603
Phone   312-641-0393
Fax   312-641-6365

Los Angeles
Museum Square
5757 Wilshire Blvd., Ste. 1
Los Angeles, CA 90036
Phone   323-634-1750
Fax   323-634-1777

Orlando
10319 Orangewood Blvd.
Orlando, FL 32821
Phone   407-345-8600
Fax   407-345-1522

New York
National Headquarters
165 W. 46th St., 15th Fl.
New York, NY 10036
Phone   212-869-8530
Fax   212-719-9815

San Francisco
350 Sansome St., Ste. 900
San Francisco, CA 94104
Phone   415-391-3838
Fax   415-391-0102

Actors' Fund of America

www.actorsfund.org
Nonprofit organization providing for the social welfare of entertainment professionals.
Chicago
203 N. Wabash Ave., Ste. 2104
Chicago, IL 60601
Phone   312-372-0989
Fax   312-372-0272

Los Angeles
5757 Wilshire Blvd., Ste. 400
Los Angeles, CA 90036
Phone   323-933-9244
Fax   323-933-7615

New York
729 Seventh Ave., 10th Fl.
New York, NY 10019
Phone   212-221-7300
Fax   212-764-0238

production resources

Actors' Work Program
www.actorsfund.org
Career counseling for members of the Actors' Fund of America.
Los Angeles
5757 Wilshire Blvd., Ste. 400
Los Angeles, CA 90036
Phone   323-933-9244
Fax   323-933-7615

New York
729 Seventh Ave.
New York, NY 10019
Phone   212-354-5480
Fax   212-921-4295

Alliance of Canadian Cinema, Television & Radio Artists (ACTRA)
www.actra.ca
Labor union founded to negotiate, safeguard, and promote the professional rights of Canadian performers working in film, television, video, and all recorded media.
625 Church St., 3rd Fl.
Toronto, Ontario M4Y 2G1 Canada
Phone   800-387-3516
         416-489-1311
Fax   416-489-8076

Alliance of Motion Picture & Television Producers (AMPTP)
www.amptp.org
Trade association involved with labor issues within the motion picture and television industries.
15503 Ventura Blvd.
Encino, CA 91436
Phone   818-995-3600
Fax   818-382-1793

American Cinema Editors (ACE)
www.ace-filmeditors.org
Honorary society made up of editors deemed to be outstanding in their field.
100 Universal City Plaza,
Bldg. 2282, Rm. 234
Universal City, CA 91608
Phone   818-777-2900
Fax   818-733-5023

American Cinematheque at the Egyptian Theatre
www.egyptiantheatre.com
www.americancinematheque.com
Nonprofit cultural arts organization programming specialty film series at the Egyptian Theatre.
1800 N. Highland Ave., Ste. 717
Hollywood, CA 90028
Phone   323-461-2020
         323-466-3456
         (24-hour recorded information)
Fax   323-461-9737

American Federation of Film Producers (AFFP)
www.filmfederation.com
Trade organization of creative professionals committed to excellence in filmmaking.
3000 W. Alameda Ave., Ste. 1585
Burbank, CA 91523
Phone   818-840-4924

American Federation of Musicians (AFM)
www.afm.org
Labor union representing professional musicians.
Los Angeles
3550 Wilshire Blvd., Ste. 1900
Los Angeles, CA 90010
Phone   213-251-4510
Fax   213-251-4520

1501 Broadway, Ste. 600
New York, NY 10036
Phone   212-869-1330
Fax   212-764-6134

American Federation of Television & Radio Artists (AFTRA)

www.aftra.org
Labor organization representing broadcast performers.

Los Angeles
5757 Wilshire Blvd., Ste. 900
Los Angeles, CA 90036
Phone   323-634-8100
Fax   323-634-8194

New York
260 Madison Ave., 7th Fl.
New York, NY 10016
Phone   212-532-0800
Fax   212-532-2242

American Film Institute (AFI)

www.afi.com
Organization dedicated to preserving and advancing the art of the moving image through events, exhibitions, and education.

Los Angeles
2021 N. Western Ave.
Los Angeles, CA 90027
Phone   323-856-7600
Fax   323-467-4578

Washington, DC
The John F. Kennedy Center for the Performing Arts
Washington, DC 20566
Phone   202-833-2348
Fax   202-659-1970

American Film Market (AFMA)

www.afma.com
www.americanfilmmarket.com
Trade association for the independent film and television industries.
10850 Wilshire Blvd., 9th Fl.
Los Angeles, CA 90024-4321
Phone   310-446-1000
Fax   310-446-1600

American Guild of Musical Artists (AGMA)

www.musicalartists.org
Union representing classical artists, opera singers, ballet dancers, stage managers, and stage directors.
1430 Broadway, 14th Fl.
New York, NY 10018
Phone   212-265-3687
Fax   212-262-9088

American Guild of Variety Artists (AGVA)

Labor union representing performers in Broadway, off-Broadway, and cabaret productions, as well as theme park and nightclub performers.

Los Angeles
4741 Laurel Canyon Blvd., Ste. 208
North Hollywood, CA 91607
Phone   818-508-9984
Fax   818-508-3029

New York
363 Seventh Ave., 17th Fl.
New York, NY 10001
Phone   212-675-1003
Fax   212-633-0097

production resources

American Humane Association (AHA)

www.ahafilm.org

Watchdog organization dedicated to preventing cruelty to animal actors performing in films and television.

Western Regional Office
Film and Television Unit
15366 Dickens St.
Sherman Oaks, CA 91403
Phone   818-501-0123
         800-677-3420
         (Hotline)
Fax   818-501-8725

American Screenwriters Association (ASA)

www.goasa.com

Nonprofit organization promoting and encouraging the art of screenwriting as well as the support and advancement of screenwriters.

269 S. Beverly Dr., Ste. 2600
Beverly Hills, CA 90212-3807
Phone   866-265-9091

American Society of Cinematographers (ASC)

www.theasc.com

Union representing professional cinematographers, dedicated to improving the quality of motion picture presentation.

1782 N. Orange Dr.
Hollywood, CA 90028
Phone   323-969-4333
         800-448-0145
Fax   323-882-6391

American Society of Composers, Authors & Publishers (ASCAP)

www.ascap.com

Performing rights organization representing composers, lyricists, songwriters, and music publishers.

Los Angeles
7920 W. Sunset Blvd., 3rd Fl.
Los Angeles, CA 90046
Phone   323-883-1000
Fax   323-883-1049

Nashville
2 Music Square West
Nashville, TN 37203
Phone   615-742-5000
Fax   615-742-5020

New York
One Lincoln Plaza
New York, NY 10023
Phone   212-621-6000
Fax   212-724-9064

American Society of Journalists & Authors (ASJA)

www.asja.org

Organization of independent nonfiction writers.

1501 Broadway, Ste. 302
New York, NY 10036
Phone   212-997-0947
Fax   212-768-7414

American Society of Media Photographers (ASMP)

www.asmp.org

Trade organization dedicated to protecting and promoting the interests and high professional standards of photographers whose work is for publication.

150 N. Second St.
Philadelphia, PA 19106
Phone   215-451-2767
Fax   215-451-0880

production resources

American Women in Radio & Television, Inc. (AWRT)

www.awrt.org
National organization supporting the advancement of women in the communications industry.
8405 Greensboro Dr., Ste. 800
McLean, VA 22102
Phone   703-506-3290
Fax   703-506-3266

Art Directors Guild & Scenic, Title and Graphic Designers

www.ialocal800.org
Organization representing Production Designers, Art Directors, Assistant Art Directors and Scenic, Title and Graphic Designers.
Local 800 I.A.T.S.E.
11969 Ventura Blvd., Ste. 200
Studio City, CA 91604
Phone   818-762-9995
Fax: 818-762-9997

Association of Film Commissioners International (AFCI)

www.afci.org
Organization providing representation and support to member film commissions.
314 N. Main, Ste. 307
Helena, MT 59601
Phone   406-495-8040
(LA)   323-462-6092
Fax   406-495-8039
(LA)   323-462-6091

Association of Independent Video and Filmmakers (AIVF)

www.aivf.org
Nonprofit membership organization serving local and international film and videomakers, including documentarians and experimental artists.
304 Hudson St., 6th Fl.
New York, NY 10013
Phone   212-807-1400
Fax   212-463-8519

Association of Independent Commercial Producers (AICP)

www.aicp.com
Organization representing interests of US companies that specialize in producing commercials in various media (film, video, Internet, etc.) for advertisers and agencies.

Los Angeles
650 N. Bronson Ave., Ste. 223B
Los Angeles, CA 90004
Phone   323-960-4763
Fax   323-960-4766

New York
3 W. 18th St., 5th Fl.
New York, NY 10011
Phone   212-929-3000
Fax   212-929-3359

Association of Talent Agents (ATA)

www.agentassociation.com
Nonprofit trade association for talent agencies representing clients in the motion picture and television industries, as well as literary, theater, radio, and commercial clients.
9255 Sunset Blvd., Ste. 930
Los Angeles, CA 90069
Phone   310-274-0628
Fax   310-274-5063

Authors Guild, The

www.authorsguild.org
Society dedicated to advocacy for fair compensation, free speech, and copyright protection for published authors.
31 E. 28th St., 10th Fl.
New York, NY 10016
Phone   212-563-5904
Fax   212-564-5363

production resources

Black Filmmaker Foundation (BFF), The

www.dvrepublic.com
Nonprofit organization of emerging Black filmmakers.
670 Broadway, Ste. 300
New York, NY 10012
Phone   212-253-1690
Fax   212-253-1689

Breakdown Services

www.breakdownservices.com
Communications network and casting system providing integrated tools for casting directors and talent representatives, as well as casting information for actors.

Los Angeles
2140 Cotner Ave.
Los Angeles, CA 90025
Phone   310-276-9166

New York
Phone   212-869-2003

Vancouver
Phone   604-943-7100

Broadcast Music, Inc. (BMI)

www.bmi.com
Nonprofit performing rights organization of songwriters, composers, and music publishers.

Los Angeles
8730 Sunset Blvd., 3rd Fl. West
West Hollywood, CA 90069-2211
Phone   310-659-9109
Fax   310-657-6947

Nashville
10 Music Square East
Nashville, TN 37203-4399
Phone   615-401-2000
Fax   615-401-2707

New York
320 W. 57th St.
New York, NY 10019
Phone   212-586-2000
Fax   212-489-2368

California Arts Council (CAC)

www.cac.ca.gov
State organization encouraging artistic awareness, expression, and participation reflecting California's diverse cultures.
1300 I St., Ste. 930
Sacramento, CA 95814
Phone   916-322-6555
            800-201-6201
Fax   916-322-6575

Casting Society of America (CSA)

www.castingsociety.com
Trade organization of professional film and television casting directors.

Los Angeles
606 N. Larchmont Blvd., Ste. 4B
Los Angeles, CA 90004-1309
Phone   323-463-1925
Fax   323-463-5753

New York
c/o Bernard Telsey
145 W. 28th St., Ste. 12F
New York, NY 10001
Phone   212-868-1260
Fax   212-868-1261

Caucus for Television Producers, Writers & Directors

www.caucus.org
Organization protecting and promoting the artistic rights of producers, writers and directors in the film and television industries.
PO Box 11236
Burbank, CA 91510-1236
Phone   818-843-7572
Fax   818-846-2159

Cinewomen

www.cinewomen.org
Nonprofit organization dedicated to supporting the advancement of women within the motion picture industry.

Los Angeles
9903 Santa Monica Blvd., Ste. 461
Beverly Hills, CA 90212
Phone   310-855-8720

New York
PO Box 1477, Cooper Station
New York, NY 10276
Phone   212-604-4264

Clear, Inc.

www.clearinc.org
*Organization of clearance and research
professionals working in the film,
television, and multimedia industries.*
PO Box 628
Burbank, CA 91503-0628
Fax   413-647-3380

Commercial Casting Directors Association (CCDA)

*Organization dedicated to providing a
level of professionalism for casting
directors within the commercial industry.*
Attn: Jeff Gerrard
c/o Loud Mouth Studios
13261 Moorpark St.
Sherman Oaks, CA 91423
Phone   818-782-9900

Costume Designers Guild (CDG)

www.costumedesignersguild.com
*Union representing motion picture,
television, and commercial costume
designers. Promotes research, artistry,
and technical expertise in the field of
film and television costume design.*
4730 Woodman Ave., Ste. 430
Sherman Oaks, CA 91423
Phone   818-905-1557
Fax   818-905-1560
        818-501-5228

Directors Guild of America (DGA)

www.dga.org
*Labor union representing film and
television directors, unit production
managers, first assistant directors,
second assistant directors, technical
coordinators, tape associate directors,
stage managers, and production
associates.*

Chicago
400 N. Michigan Ave., Ste. 307
Chicago, IL 60611
Phone   888-600-6975
        312-644-5050
Fax   312-644-5776

Los Angeles
7920 Sunset Blvd.
Los Angeles, CA 90046
Phone   800-421-4173
        310-289-2000
        (Main Line)
        323-851-3671
        (Agency Listing)
Fax   310-289-2029

New York
110 W. 57th St.
New York, NY 10019
Phone   800-356-3754
        212-581-0370
Fax   212-581-1441

Dramatists Guild of America, Inc., The

www.dramaguild.com
*Professional association of playwrights,
composers, and lyricists.*
1501 Broadway, Ste. 701
New York, NY 10036
Phone   212-398-9366
Fax   212-944-0420

Filmmakers Alliance

www.filmmakersalliance.com
*Nonprofit collective of independent
filmmakers.*
453 S. Spring St.
Los Angeles, CA 90013
Phone   213-228-1152
Fax   213-228-1156

Hispanic Organization of Latin Actors (HOLA)
www.hellohola.org
Arts service organization committed to projecting Hispanic artists and their culture into the mainstream of Anglo-American industry and culture.
107 Suffolk St., Ste. 302
New York, NY 10002
Phone   212-253-1015
Fax   212-253-9651

Hollywood Radio & Television Society (HRTS)
www.hrts-iba.org
Nonprofit organization made up of West Coast executives from the entertainment (and ancillary) industries, providing mentoring and scholarship programs as well as networking opportunities.
Sponsors The International Broadcasting (& Cable) Awards.
13701 Riverside Dr., Ste. 205
Sherman Oaks, CA 91423
Phone   818-789-1182
Fax   818-789-1210

Horror Writers Association
www.horror.org
Worldwide organization of horror and dark fantasy writers and publishing professionals.
PO Box 50577
Palo Alto, CA 94303
Phone   650-322-4610

Humanitas Prize, The
www.humanitasprize.org
Prestigious prizes awarded to film and television writers whose produced scripts communicate values which most enrich the human person.
17575 Pacific Coast Highway
PO Box 861
Pacific Palisades, CA 90272
Phone   310-454-8769
Fax   310-459-6549

Independent Feature Project (IFP)
www.ifp.org
Not-for-profit service organization providing resources and information for independent filmmakers and industry professionals.

Chicago
33 E. Congress Parkway, Ste. 505
Chicago, IL 60605
Phone   312-435-1825
Fax   312-435-1828

Los Angeles (IFP/W)
8750 Wilshire Blvd., 2nd Fl.
Beverly Hills, CA 90211
Phone   310-432-1200
Fax   310-432-1203

Miami
210 Second St.
Miami Beach, FL 33139
Phone   305-538-8242

Minneapolis
401 N. Third St., Ste. 450
Minneapolis, MN 55401
Phone   612-338-0871
Fax   612-338-4747

New York
104 W. 29th St., 12th Fl.
New York, NY 10001-5310
Phone   212-465-8200
Fax   212-465-8525

International Alliance of Theatrical Stage Employees (IATSE)
www.iatse.lm.com
Union representing technicians, artisans and craftpersons in the entertainment industry including live theater, film and television production, and trade shows.

Los Angeles
10045 Riverside Dr.
Toluca Lake, CA 91602
Phone   818-980-3499
Fax   818-980-3496

New York
1430 Broadway, 20th Fl.
New York, NY 10018
Phone   212-730-1770
Fax   212-730-7809
          212-921-7699

International Press Academy
www.pressacademy.com
Association of professional
entertainment journalists.
9601 Wilshire Blvd., Ste. 620
Beverly Hills, CA 90210
Phone   310-271-7041
Fax   310-550-0420

Latino Filmmakers Association
cinemaadrian@hotmail.com
c/o Adrian Rodriguez
10612 Shoreline Dr.
Norwalk, CA 90650
Phone   562-863-7832

Motion Picture Association of America (MPAA)
www.mpaa.org
Trade association for the US motion
picture, home video, and television
industries.
15503 Ventura Blvd.
Encino, CA 91436
Phone   818-995-6600
Fax   818-382-1799

Motion Picture Editors Guild
www.editorsguild.com
Union representing motion picture,
television, and commercial editors,
sound technicians and projectionists,
and story analysts.

Chicago
6317 N. Northwest Highway
Chicago, IL 60631
Phone   773-594-6598
          888-594-6734
Fax   773-594-6599

Los Angeles
7715 Sunset Blvd., Ste. 200
Hollywood, CA 90046
Phone   323-876-4770
Fax   323-876-0861

New York
165 W. 46th St., Ste. 900
New York, NY 10036
Phone   212-302-0700
Fax   212-302-1091

Multicultural Motion Picture Association (MMPA)
www.diversityawards.org
Association promoting and encouraging
diversity of ideas, cultures, and
perspectives in film; sponsor of the
annual Diversity Awards.
8601 Wilshire Blvd., Ste. 700
Beverly Hills, CA 90212
Phone   310-358-8300
Fax   310-358-8304

Music Managers Forum (MMF)
www.mmfus.org
Organization dedicated to furthering the
interests of managers and their artists in
all fields of the music industry including
live performance, and recording and
publishing matters.
PO Box 444, Village Station
New York, NY 10014
Phone   212-213-8787
Fax   212-213-9797

production resources

Music Video Production Association (MVPA)

www.mvpa.com

Nonprofit trade organization made up of music video production and post production companies, as well as editors, directors, producers, cinematographers, choreographers, script supervisors, computer animators, and make-up artists involved in the production of music videos.

201 N. Occidental Blvd.,
Bldg. 7 Unit B
Los Angeles, CA 90026
Phone   213-387-1590
Fax   213-385-9507

Mystery Writers of America (MWA)

www.mysterywriters.org

Organization of published mystery authors, editors, screenwriters, and other professionals in the field. Sponsors symposia, conferences, and The Edgar Awards.

17 E. 47th St., 6th Fl.
New York, NY 10017
Phone   212-888-8171
Fax   212-888-8107

Nashville Association of Talent Directors (NATD)

www.n-a-t-d.com

Professional entertainment organization comprised of industry professionals involved in all aspects of the music and entertainment industries.

PO Box 23903
Nashville, TN 37202-3903
Phone   615-662-2200 (x*410)

National Academy of Recording Arts & Sciences (NARAS)

www.grammy.com

Organization dedicated to improving the quality of life and cultural condition for musicians, producers, and other recording professionals. Provides outreach, professional development, cultural enrichment, education, and human services programs. Sponsors The Grammy Awards.

The Recording Academy
3402 Pico Blvd.
Santa Monica, CA 90405
Phone   310-392-3777
Fax   310-399-3090

National Association of Latino Independent Producers (NALIP)

www.nalip.org

Organization of independent Latin film producers.

Los Angeles
PO Box 1247
Santa Monica, CA 90406
Phone   310-457-4445
Fax   310-589-9997

New York
250 W. 26th St., 4th Fl.
New York, NY 10001
Phone   646-336-6333
Fax   212-727-0549

National Association of Television Program Executives (NATPE)

www.natpe.org
www.natpeonline.com

Nonprofit association of business professionals who create, develop and distribute content.

2425 Olympic Blvd., Ste. 600E
Santa Monica, CA 90404
Phone   310-453-4440
Fax   310-453-5258

National Conference of Personal Managers (NCOPM)

www.ncopm.com
Association for the advancement of personal managers and their clients.

Palm Desert
PO Box 609
Palm Desert, CA 92261-0609
Phone   760-200-5892
Fax   760-200-5896

New York
41 W. 56th St.
New York, NY 10019
Phone   212-582-1940
Fax   212-582-1942

National Council of La Raza (NCLR)

www.nclr.org
Private, nonprofit, nonpartisan, tax-exempt organization dedicated, in part, to promoting fair, accurate, and balanced portrayals of Latinos in film, television, and music. Sponsor of the ALMA Awards.
1111 19th St., Ste. 1000
Washington, DC 20036
Phone   202-785-1670
Fax   202-785-7620

National Music Publishers Association (NMPA)

www.nmpa.org
Organization dedicated to interpreting copyright law, educating the public about licensing, safeguarding the interests of American music publishers, and protecting music copyright across all media and national boundaries.
475 Park Avenue South, 29th Fl.
New York, NY 10016-6901
Phone   646-742-1651
Fax   646-742-1779

Nosotros

www.nosotros.org
Organization established to improve the image of Latinos/Hispanics as they are portrayed in the entertainment industry, both in front of and behind the camera, as well as to expand employment opportunities within the entertainment industry. Sponsor of The Golden Eagle Awards.
650 N. Bronson Ave., Ste. 102
Hollywood, CA 90004
Phone   323-466-8566
Fax   323-466-8540

Organization of Black Screenwriters, Inc., The

www.obswriter.com
Nonprofit organization developing and supporting Black screenwriters.
1968 W. Adams Blvd.
Los Angeles, CA 90018
Phone   323-735-2050
Fax   323-735-2051

PEN

www.pen.org
Nonprofit organization made up of poets, playwrights, essayists, novelists, television writers, screenwriters, critics, historians, editors, journalists, and translators. Dedicated to protecting the rights of writers around the world, to stimulate interest in the written word, and to foster a vital literary community.
Pen American Center
568 Broadway, 4th Fl.
New York, NY 10012-3225
Phone   212-334-1660
Fax   212-334-2181

production resources

Producers Guild of America (PGA)
www.producersguild.org
Organization representing the interests of all members of the producing team.
8530 Wilshire Blvd., Ste. 450
Beverly Hills, CA 90211
Phone   310-358-9020
Fax   310-358-9520

Recording Musicians Association (RMA)
www.rmala.org
Nonprofit organization of studio musicians and composers.
817 Vine St., Ste. 209
Hollywood, CA 90038-3716
Phone   323-462-4762
Fax   323-462-2406

Romance Writers of America (RWA)
www.rwanational.org
National nonprofit genre writers' association providing networking and support to published and aspiring romance writers.
16000 Stuebner Airline, Ste. 140
Spring, TX 77379
Phone   832-712-5200
Fax   832-717-5201

Screen Actors Guild (SAG)
www.sag.org
Union representing actors in feature films, short films, and digital projects.

Los Angeles
5757 Wilshire Blvd.
Los Angeles, CA 90036
Phone   323-954-1600
  (Main Line)
      323-549-6858
  (Commercial/Infomercials/Industrial/Education)
      323-549-6811
  (Production Services-Extras)
      323-549-6864
  (Singers' Reps.)
      323-549-6835
  (Television Contracts)

323-549-6828
  (Theatrical Motion Pictures)
323-549-6737
  (Actors to Locate)
323-549-6644
  (Affirmative Action)
323-549-6745
  (Agency/Agent Contracts)
323-549-6755
  (Dues Information)
323-549-6773
  (Emergency Fund)
323-549-6627
  (Legal Affairs)
323-549-6778
  (Membership Services)
323-549-6769
  (New Memberships)
323-549-6505
  (Residuals)
800-205-7716
  (Residuals)
323-549-6869
  (Signatory Records)
818-954-9400
  (SAG Pension & Health)
323-549-6855
  (Stunts/Safety)
323-549-6023
  (SAG Jobs Hotline)
Fax   323-549-6603

New York
360 Madison Ave., 12th Fl.
New York, NY 10017
Phone   212-944-1030
  (Main Line)
      212-944-6715
  (TTY Line)
Fax   212-944-6774

Scriptwriters Network
www.scriptwritersnetwork.com
Organization providing information and career counseling for film and television writers.
11684 Ventura Blvd., Ste. 508
Studio City, CA 91604
Phone   323-848-9477

SESAC

www.sesac.com
Nonprofit performing rights organization of songwriters, composers, and music publishers.

Los Angeles
501 Santa Monica Blvd., Ste. 450
Santa Monica, CA 90401-2430
Phone   310-393-9671
Fax   310-393-6497

Nashville
55 Music Square East
Nashville, TN 37203
Phone   615-320-0055
Fax   615-329-9627

New York
152 W. 57th St., 57th Fl.
New York, NY 10019
Phone   212-586-3450
Fax   212-489-5699

Society of Children's Book Writers & Illustrators (SCBWI)

www.scbwi.org
Professional organization of writers and illustrators of children's books.
8271 Beverly Blvd.
Los Angeles, CA 90048
Phone   323-782-1010
Fax   323-782-1892

Society of Composers & Lyricists

www.filmscore.org
Nonprofit volunteer organization advancing the professional interests of lyricists and composers of film and television music.
400 S. Beverly Dr., Ste. 214
Beverly Hills, CA 90212
Phone   310-281-2812
Fax   310-284-4861

Society of Illustrators (SOI)

www.societyillustrators.org
Society made up of professional illustrators, art directors, art buyers, creative supervisors, instructors, and publishers, dedicated to the well-being of individual illustrators and the industry of illustration.
128 E. 63rd St.
New York, NY 10021-7303
Phone   212-838-2560
Fax   212-838-2561

Society of Operating Cameramen (SOC)

www.soc.org
Organization promoting excellence in the fields of camera operation and the allied camera crafts.
PO Box 2006
Toluca Lake, CA 91610
Phone   818-382-7070

Society of Stage Directors & Choreographers (SSDC)

www.ssdc.org
Union representing directors and choreographers of Broadway national tours, regional theater, dinner theater, and summer stock, as well as choreographers for motion pictures, television, and music videos.
1501 Broadway, Ste. 1701
New York, NY 10036-5653
Phone   212-391-1070
Fax   212-302-6195

Stunts-Ability, Inc.

www.stuntsability.com
Nonprofit organization training amputees and other disabled persons for stunts, acting, and effects for the entertainment industry.
PO Box 600711
San Diego, CA 92160-0711
Phone   619-785-6846

production resources

Talent Managers Association (TMA)

www.talentmanagers.org
Nonprofit organization promoting and encouraging the highest standards of professionalism in the practice of talent management.
4804 Laurel Canyon Blvd., Ste. 611
Valley Village, CA 91607
Phone   310-205-8495
Fax   818-765-2903

Women In Film (WIF)

www.wif.org
Organization dedicated to empowering, promoting, and nurturing women in the film and television industries.
8857 W. Olympic Blvd., Ste. 201
Beverly Hills, CA 90211
Phone   310-657-5144
Fax   310-657-5154

Women's Image Network (WIN)

www.winfemme.com
Not-for-profit corporation encouraging positive portrayals of women in theater, television, and film.
PO Box 69-1774
Los Angeles, CA 90069
Phone   310-229-5365

Writers Guild of America (WGA)

Union representing writers in the motion pictures, broadcast, cable, and new technologies industries.

Los Angeles (WGAW)
www.wga.org
7000 W. Third St.
Los Angeles, CA 90048-4329
Phone   323-951-4000
        (Main Line)
        323-782-4502
        (Agency Listing)
Fax   323-782-4800
        (Main Fax)

New York (WGAE)
www.wgaeast.org
555 W. 57th St., Ste. 1230
New York, NY 10019
Phone   212-767-7800
Fax   212-582-1909

LIBRARIES AND MUSEUMS

Academy of Motion Picture Arts & Sciences - Margaret Herrick Library

www.oscars.org
Extensive and comprehensive research and reference collections documenting film as an art form and an industry.
333 S. La Cienega Blvd.
Beverly Hills, CA 90211
Phone   310-247-3000
        (Main Line)
        310-247-3020
        (Reference)
Fax   310-657-9351

American Museum of Moving Images

www.ammi.org
Permanent collection of moving image artifacts.
35th Ave. At 36th St.
Astoria, NY 11106
Phone   718-784-4520
Fax   718-784-4681

Library of Moving Images, Inc., The

www.libraryofmovingimages.com
Independent film archives including 19th Century experimental film footage, silent film footage, 20th Century newsreel footage, short subjects, education and industrial films, classic documentaries, vintage cartoons, and home movies.
6671 Sunset Blvd., Bungalow 1581
Hollywood, CA 90028
Phone   323-469-7499
Fax   323-469-7559

Los Angeles Public Library – Frances Howard Goldwyn/ Hollywood Regional Branch Library

www.lapl.org
Extensive collection documenting the entertainment industry including scripts, posters, and photographs.
1623 N. Ivar Ave.
Los Angeles, CA 90028
Phone　323-856-8260
Fax　　323-467-5707

Museum of Television & Radio

www.mtr.org
Extensive collection of television and radio programming.

Los Angeles
465 N. Beverly Dr.
Beverly Hills, CA 90210
Phone　310-786-1000
Fax　　310-786-1086

New York
25 W. 52nd St.
New York, NY 10019
Phone　212-621-6600
Fax　　212-621-6700

New York Public Library for the Performing Arts

www.nypl.org
Extensive combination of circulating, reference, and rare archival collections in the performing arts.
40 Lincoln Center Plaza
New York, NY 10023-7498
Phone　212-870-1630

Writers Guild Foundation - James R. Webb Memorial Library

www.wga.org
Collection dedicated to the art, craft, and history of writing for motion pictures, radio, television, and new media. Open to the public and Guild members.
7000 W. Third St.
Los Angeles, CA 90048-4329
Phone　323-782-4544
Fax　　323-782-4695

production resources

National Association of Latino Independent Producers

index of
NALIP
members

Hunter Rodriguez
Joel Rodriguez 305-218-6661
Jorge Rodriguez.................................323-734-2309
Maria Rodriguez.................................215-467-4417
Nestor N. Rodriguez...........................718-543-9238
Pablo Rodriguez
Paul Rodriguez
Paul Rodriguez 323-951-1700
Richard Rodriguez..............................210-680-5754
Teresa Rodriguez...............................305-663-0507
Pilar Rodriguez-Aranda 505-986-0642
Veronica Rodriguez-Brett 520-408-3078
Sandra Roggemann 858-551-5834
Ingrid Rojas......................................917-592-7481
Evelyn Rojo
Phil Roman 818-985-1200
Aldo Romero.....................................718-296-5617
Elaine Romero...................................520-884-8210
Felix Romero.....................................718-822-7951
Ross Romero 714-917-2045
Gabriela Ronseg
Victor Rosa.......................................609-387-2386
Rafael Rosado..................................614-841-9203
Monica Rosales.................................305-348-2768
Adriana Rosas-Walsh........................415-552-8760
Robert Rose......................................212-253-6153
Benjamin Rosen
Cyn Rossi 212-207-4740
Bernardo Ruiz 646-373-9068
David Ruiz...310-337-1443
Diana Ruiz..281-482-8494
Michael Ruiz.....................................281-483-8169
Yessica Ruiz.....................................954-989-0646
George Rush.....................................415-759-4201
Stephanie Saenz...............................310-392-4378
Jennifer Safira..................................954-817-3386
Gustavo Sagastume..........................954-929-0993
Richard Saiz.....................................415-356-8383
Abel Salas..323-888-9660
Tomas Salas.....................................512-461-7889
Michelle Salcedo 718-246-8180
Ana Saldaña
Calogero Salvo 212-691-8305
Valerie Samaniego-Finch
Alex Sanchez 703-516-4395
Marta Sanchez 415-307-3397
Misael Sanchez 212-854-7516
Rodolfo Sanchez...............................619-280-6655

George Sandoval 805-240-9496
Jorge Sandoval.................................310-880-7376
Dario Sanmiguel 415-255-8723
Guillermo Santana 661-758-8048
Marta Santana..................................661-758-8048
Susan Santiago Kerin.......................703-536-5234
Ray Santisteban................................210-534-1919
John Phillip Santos...........................212-573-4914
Aurora Sarabia
Stephen Sariñana-Lampson...............626-405-1500
Adam Schlachter...............................323-851-0968
Mark Schreiber..................................310-396-2144
Laurel Scott......................................619-258-7207
Dianne Segura...................................310-226-7018
Francesca Seiden 305-899-1630
Jose Sepulveda
Monica Serafin 917-407-8816
Celeste Serna-Williams 917-458-1058
Ernesto Serrano
Gustavo Serrano
Joan Shigekawa 212-869-8500
Jesús Sifuentes 210-337-8110
Gail Silva ....415-552-8760 ext. 315
Debbie Silverfine 212-627-7778
Samantha Smith 512-841-5930
Enrique Soberanes
Juan Sola...323-936-8432
Helena Solberg 212-678-6529
Antonio Solis 714-343-3225
Manuel Solis.....................................210-434-5631
Eric Soliz 661-305-5807
Michael Solomon
Betsy Solorzano................................323-932-0473
Irene Sosa 201-792-5004
Rosario Sotelo 415-260-7903
Martha Soto
Alison Sotomayor
Gustavo Stebner...............................210-683-9955
Susan Stoebner
Beatriz Stotzer..................................213-483-2060
Traci Swain 888-838-1474
Angelique Szeman............................818-694-6818
Dalia Tapia.......................................773-847-3278
Kelly Taylor 800-915-1545
Marianne Teleki.................................510-883-9527
Mitch Teplitsky..................................212-721-6016
Conrado Terrazas
Martin Terrones 323-931-0953

National Association of Latino Independent Producers

index
by craft

1st Assistant Director
Fernando Alberto Castroman
Richard Espinoza
Vincent George Gonzales
Rosa Gonzalez
Veronica Gonzalez-Rubio
Jay Guerra
Pamela S. Kuri
Ricardo Mendez Matta
Kaaren Ochoa
George Parra
Carlos F. Pinero
Concetta Rinaldo-Williams
Veronica Sanchez
Elena Santaballa
David Ticotin

2nd Assistant Director
Fernando Alberto Castroman
Valintino Costa
Marisa Ferrey
Philip J. Gallegos
Vincent George Gonzales
Roberto F. Gonzalez-Rubio
Jay Guerra
Eric W. Henriquez
Pamela S. Kuri
Gilda Longoria
Clemen Ochoa
Carlos F. Pinero
Molly Robin Rodriguez
Elena Santaballa
Gabriela Vazquez

2nd 2nd Assistant Director
Valintino Costa
Marisa Ferrey
Roberto F. Gonzalez-Rubio
Eric W. Henriquez
Clemen Ochoa
Molly Robin Rodriguez

Acting Coach
Rene Pereya

Actor
Carlos Alberto
Antonio Banderas
Rick Barreras
Ana Marie de la Peña Portela
Dita de Leon
Hector Elizondo
Tonantzin Esparza
Nino Gabaldon
Andy Garcia
Irma Garcia-Sinclair
Michael Gavino
Mike Gomez
Maria Gonzalez-Palmier
Johnathan Gwyn
Salma Hayek
Ruth Livier
Benjamin Lopez
George Lopez
Sal Lopez
Cheech Marin
Benito Martinez
Joey Medina
Ricardo Montalban
Richard Montoya
Danny Mora
Michael Narvaez
Jesus Nebot
Edward James Olmos
Elizabeth Peña
Felix Pire
Tony Plana
Yessica Ruiz
Ric Salinas
Carlos San Miguel
Patricio Serna
Herbert Siguenza
Jimmy Smits
Juan Sola
Maria Valdez
Jacob Vargas
Paul Vato
Yvette Vega
Christina Vergara

ADR Looping
Irma Garcia-Sinclair

Agent
Carlos Alvarado
Eddie Borges
Michael Camacho
Carlos Carreras
Nancy Chaidez
Ivan de Paz
Donna Gaba
Julissa Garcia
Guido Giordano
Jorge Insua
Tania Lopez
Emanuel Nuñez
Jorge Pinos
Nick Puga
Nicolas Rey
Paul Santana
Steve Tellez
Kristine Wallis
Michael Wimer
Peggy Wintermute

Animator
Paris Bustillos
Marlon Cantillano
Poli Marichal
Pepe Moreno
Phil Roman
Rafael Rosado
Ralph Sanchez

Art Department
Reinardo Funez

Art Director
Elizabeth Calienes

Assignment Editor
Dolly Josette Espinal

Associate Director
Lillian Fuentes
Diego Kenneth

Associate Producer
Natalia Almada
Guillermo Arriaga
Jellybean Benitez
Nancy de los Santos
Roni Eguia Menendez
Rudy Hernandez, Jr.
Octavio Marin
Ashley Mendoza
Faith Radle
Ray Santisteban

Attorney
James Blancarte
Stephen Espinoza
Alexis Garcia
Augustine Medina
Michael Morales
Richard Rappaport

Audio Supervisor
Denise Dorn

Award Shows
Lionel Pasamonte
Jerry Velasco

Camera Assistant
Loreto Caro
Ernie Contreras
Alicia Flores

Camera Operator
Alicia Flores
Benny Flores

Casting Director
Carmen Cuba
Dennis Gallegos
Belinda Gardea
Adriana Millan
Rosalinda Morales
Bob Morones
Blanca Valdez

Caterer
Lori Cordova

Co-Producer
Isaac Artenstein
Jellybean Benitez
Gloria LaMorte
Luisa Leschin
James Lima
Laura Medina
Elaine Romero
Bernardo Ruiz

Composer
Germaine Franco
Joseph Julian Gonzalez
Henry Iglesias
Efrain Logreira

Coordinator
Sandra Avila

Costume Designer
Magdalena Guillen

Creator
Mike & Gibby Cevallos
Stephanie Fische
Isabel Rivera
Jose Rivera

Dialect Coach
Irma Garcia-Sinclair

Director
Shawn Baca
José Bayona
Juan Caceres
Patricia Cardoso
Carlos Castañeda
Jose Colomer
Tania Cuevas Martinez
Cecilia Domeyko
Edgar Endress
Daniel Faraldo

Edwin Figueroa
Angel Gomez
Mike Higuera
Stan Jakubowicz
Gary Keller
Carolina Liu
Diana Logreira Campos
Edwin René López
Raul Marchand Sanchez
Chuck Martinez
Laura Medina
Juan Carlos Perez
Francesca Prada
Mario Ramirez
Carlos San Miguel
George Sandoval
Stephen Sariñana-Lampson
Jackie Torres

Director, Commercial
Evelyn Badia
Ivan Cevallos

Director, Documentary
Maria Agui-Carter
Natalia Almada
Claudia Amaya
Emilia Anguita Huerta
Kary Antholis
Olga Arana
José Araujo
Luis Argueta
Eva S. Aridjis
Trina Bardusco
Marta Bautis
Alfredo Bejar
Ivonne Belen
Carlos Bolado
Frank Borres
Maria Bures
Rene Simon Cruz
Nancy de los Santos
Alfredo de Villa
Alberto Dominguez
Vanessa Gocksch
A.P. Gonzalez
Sonia Gonzalez

Jackie Gonzalez-Carlos
Evangeline Griego
Christy Heady
Paula Heredia
Rudy Hernandez, Jr.
Catherine Herrera
Cristina Ibarra
Bill Jersey
Poli Marichal
Bienvenida Matias
Jennifer Maytorena Taylor
Julie Monroy
Mylene Moreno
Gregory Nava
Frances Negron-Muntaner
Ari Palos
Jose Luis Partida
Lisandro Perez-Rey
Lourdes Portillo
Anayansi Prado
Susan Racho
Margarita Ramon
Stephanie Rauber
Alex Rivera
Jonathan Robinson
Ingrid Rojas
Sylvie Rokab
Michelle Salcedo
Carlos Sandoval
Ray Santisteban
Manny Santos
Rick Tejada-Flores
Ray Telles
Mitch Teplitsky
Joseph Tovares
Ela Troyano
Charley Trujillo
John Valadez
Juan Carlos Zaldivar

Director, Documentary Short
Natalia Almada
Loreto Caro
Rafael del Toro
Catherine Herrera
Elisha Miranda
John Montoya

Jorge Oliver
Marilyn Perez
Ray Santisteban

Director/Producer, EPK
Juan Carlos (JC) Duran
William Garcia

Director, Experimental
Loreto Caro
Catherine Herrera
Pilar Rodriguez-Aranda

Director, Feature
Alejandro Agresti
Alfonso Arau
Sergio Arau
José Araujo
Luis Argueta
Diego Arsuaga
Miguel Arteta
Carlos Avila
Michael Baez
Antonio Banderas
Norbeto Barba
Carlos Bolado
Juan Jose Campanella
Patricia Cardoso
Salvador Carrasco
Mike & Gibby Cevallos
Manny Coto
Alfonso Cuaron
Michael Cuesta
Tania Cypriano
Alfredo de Villa
Guillermo del Toro
Nelson Denis
Maria Escobedo
Natatcha Estebanez
John Carlos Frey
Rodrigo Garcia
Georgina Garcia Riedel
Juan Garza
Victor Gonzalez
Alejandro Gonzalez Iñarritu
Maureen Gosling
Johnathan Gwyn

Salma Hayek
Andres Heidenreich
Lou Hernandez
Leon Ichaso
Betty Kaplan
Vivien Lesnik Weisman
James Lima
Luis Llosa
Luis Mandoki
Cheech Marin
Chuck Martinez
Barbara Martinez Jitner
Miguel Mas
Daniel Matas
Joey Medina
Jim Mendiola
Linda Mendoza
Joe Menendez
Ramon Menendez
Roland Mesa
Nestor Miranda
Gerardo Naranjo
Gregory Nava
Jesus Nebot
Frank Nuñez
Javier Olivera
Edward James Olmos
Jack Perez
Maria Perez Brown
Tony Plana
Alfredo Ramos
Frank Reyes
Ramon Rivas
Paul Rodriguez
Robert Rodriguez
Jose Luis Ruiz
Roberto Sneider
Gabriela Tagliavini
Pablo Toledo
Ela Troyano
Luis Valdez
Jose Luis Valenzuela
Mirtha Vega
Camilo Vila

Director, Feature, Animated
Phil Roman

Director, Interstitial
Jorge Aguirre
Cristina Ibarra

Director, Mockumentary
Alex Rivera

Director, Music Video
Mario Avila
William Garcia
Johnathan Gwyn
Francisco Hernandez
Ramon Ricard

Director of Photography
Gonzalo Amat
Diego Arsuaga
José Bayona
Ricardo Crudo
Joao Fernandes
Rodrigo Garcia
William Garcia
David Gonzalez
Daniel Matas
John Montoya
Edwin Pagan
Ari Palos
Rodrigo Prieto
Ed Rios
Ramon Rivas
Sylvie Rokab
Dario Sanmiguel
Reynaldo Villalobos

Director, PSA
Jackie Gonzalez-Carlos
Juan Mandelbaum

Director, Radio Documentary
Margarita Ramon

Director, Second Unit
Jay Torres

Director, Short
Jorge Aguirre
Cruz Angeles
Sergio Arau
Eva S. Aridjis
Davah Avena
Mario Avila
Evelyn Badia
Michael Baez
Alfredo Bejar
Patricia Cardoso
Loreto Caro
Juliette Carrillo
Diana Contreras
Manuel de Seixas Correa
Angel David
Alfredo de Villa
Rafael del Toro
Andrew Delaplaine
Nelson Denis
Alejandro Diaz
Sonny Richard E. Espinoza
William Garcia
Sonia Gonzalez
Maria Gonzalez-Palmier
Maureen Gosling
Erika Grediaga
Johnathan Gwyn
Lou Hernandez
Rudy Hernandez, Jr.
Cristina Ibarra
Yvan Iturriaga
Betty Kaplan
Cristina Kotz Cornejo
Rick Leal
Vivien Lesnik Weisman
Benjamin Lobato
Julian Londono
Adam Lopez
Alonso Mayo
Elisha Miranda
Gerardo Naranjo
Jorge Oliver
Jose Luis Orbegozo
Yazmin Ortiz
Rene Pereya
Patrick Perez
Ximena Ponce

Ramon Ricard
Marcial Rios
Pascui Rivas
Pilar Rodriguez-Aranda
Rafael Rosado
Bernardo Ruiz
Patricio Serna
Gustavo Stebner
Thomas Torres
Susana Tubert
Donna Umali
Mabel Valdiviezo
Jerry Villarreal
Del Zamora

Director, Short, Experimental
Pilar Rodriguez-Aranda

Director, Stage Play
Juliette Carrillo
Angel David
Rene Pereya
Felix Pire
Susana Tubert

Director, Stage Play Festival
Juliette Carrillo

Director, TV
Emilia Anguita Huerta
Michael Baez
Jose Colomer
Alfredo de Villa
Sonny Richard E. Espinoza
Gregory Nava

Director, TV Movie
Alfonso Arau
Norbeto Barba
Oscar Luis Costo
Manny Coto
Nancy de los Santos
Leon Ichaso
Betty Kaplan
John Leguizamo
Ramon Menendez

Jack Perez
Tony Plana
Ramon Rivas
Gabriela Tagliavini
Luis Valdez
Reynaldo Villalobos

Director, TV Movie, Animated
Phil Roman

Director, TV Series
Jorge Aguirre
Felix Alcala
Rafael Andreu
Miguel Arteta
Carlos Avila
Evelyn Badia
Norbeto Barba
Juan Jose Campanella
Salvador Carrasco
Mike & Gibby Cevallos
Jose Colomer
Oscar Luis Costo
Alfonso Cuaron
Michael Cuesta
Ron de Moraes
Joao Fernandes
Richard Fernandes
Rodrigo Garcia
Juan Garza
A.P. Gonzalez
Mike Higuera
Betty Kaplan
Diego Kenneth
Dennis Leoni
James Lima
Rick Lombardo
Juan Mandelbaum
Chuck Martinez
Ricardo Mendez Matta
Linda Mendoza
Joe Menendez
Ramon Menendez
Sylvia Morales
Bill Nieves
Javier Olivera
Edward James Olmos

Elizabeth Peña
Jack Perez
Tony Plana
Margarita Ramon
Manny Santos
Luis Soto
Rick Telles
Jesus Salvador Trevino
Susana Tubert
Camilo Vila
Reynaldo Villalobos
Del Zamora

Director, TV Series, Animated
Rafael Andreu
Rafael Rosado

Director, TV Special
Frank Borres
Ron de Moraes
Diego Kenneth
Juan Mandelbaum
Linda Mendoza

Distributor
Julio Noriega
Anthony Perez
Rafael Rivera-Viruet
Daniel Rodriguez
Antonio Sosa
Luis Villanueva

Editor
Natalia Almada
Cruz Angeles
Eva S. Aridjis
Carlos Bolado
Salvador Carrasco
Carlos Castañeda
Rafael del Toro
Richard Fernandes
Juan Garza
Sonia Gonzalez
Maureen Gosling
Matthew Handal
Andres Heidenreich

Paula Heredia
Frank Loreta
Andres Medina
Rhonda Mitrani
Ibon Olaskoaga
Jorge Oliver
Patrick Perez
Fernando Perez Unda
Michelle Salcedo
Ray Santisteban
Mabel Valdiviezo

Editor, Assistant
Laura Cardona
Sonia Gonzalez

Educator
Abel Amaya
Roberto Arevalo
Daniel Bernardi
Sonny Richard E. Espinoza
George Fernandez
Omar Gonzalez
Fermin Herrera
Joleen Koehly
Cristina Kotz Cornejo
Yuri Makino
Bienvenida Matias
Dr. Chon Noriega
Jorge Oliver
Roberta Orona-Cordova
George Ozuna
Diana Rios
Fabiola Torres
Marco Torres
Mabel Valdiviezo

Executive
Bonnie Abaunza
Beatriz Acevedo
Diane Almodovar
Elizabeth Almonte
Claudia Amaya
Rafael Andreu
Abdiel Anglero
Jaime Angulo
Kary Antholis

Rene Anthony Torres
Bernadette Aulestia
Gabriel Barbarena
Frank Bennett Gonzalez
Luca Bentivoglio
Maria Bozi
Elizabeth Calienes
Walter Carasco
Gabriel Carmona
Calixto Chinchilla
George Cisneros
Ignacio Darnaude
Gilbert Davila
Deborah de la Torre
Marlene Dermer
Moctesuma Esparza
Alfonso Espinosa
Evy Ledesma Galan
Kathryn F. Galan
Nely Galan
Andy Garcia
Lino Garcia
Mike Garcia
Yvonne Gomez
Bel Hernandez
Helen Hernandez
Adriana Ibanez
Arturo Interian
Robert Leach
Diana Lesmez
Roxanne Rodriguez Lettman
Cynthia Lopez
Madeleine Lopez-Silvero
Jorge Lozano
Monica Lozano
Sonia Malfa-Clements
Pancho Mansfield
Octavio Marin
Ivy Martin
Diane Medina
Louis Mejia
Edy Mendoza
Alex Moreno
Robert Muñoz
Kimberly Myers
Lisa Navarrete
Alex Nogales
Dr. Chon Noriega
Julio Noriega

David Ortiz
Luis Ortiz
George Ozuna
Jeff Penichet
Luiz Peraza
Sylvia Perel
Anthony Perez
Leo Perez
Luis Perez Tolon
Elizabeth Peters
Carolina Posse
Santiago Pozo
Rebecca Ramirez
Ray Reveles
Ruperto Reyes
Angel Rivera
Ralph Rivera
Daniel Rodriguez
Paul Rodriguez
Gustavo Sagastume
Richard Saiz
Carlos Sanchez
Felix Sanchez
Ralph Sanchez
Gail Silva
Monica Uribe
Jeff Valdez
Ethan Van Thillo
Jerry Velasco
Laura Velez
Luis Villanueva
Frank Zuñiga

Executive Producer

Sergio Aguero
Juanita Anderson
Kary Antholis
Luis Argueta
Carlos Avila
Peter Bandera
Jellybean Benitez
Manny Coto
Moctesuma Esparza
Cari Esta Albert
Stephanie Fische
Hector Galan
Kathryn F. Galan
Andy Garcia

Digna Gerena
Jackie Gonzalez-Carlos
Junior Guapo
Lou Hernandez
John Leguizamo
Dennis Leoni
James Lima
Sal Lopez
Louis Mejia
Sergio Molina
Julie Monroy
Jose Luis Partida
Maria Perez Brown
Isabel Rivera
Robert Rodriguez
Phil Roman
Cristina Saralegui
Rick Telles
Joseph Tovares
David C. Valdes
Jeff Valdez
Michael Villalobos

Executive Producer, Co-
Natalie Chaidez

Graphic Designer
Alex Mendoza
Samantha Smith

International Forwarding/ Customs Broker
Cesar Peschiera

Line Producer
Victor Albarran
Deborah Calla
Alicia Flores
Rosa Gonzalez
Nellie Medina
Ramon Ricard
Alicia Rivera Frankl

Make-up & Hair
Debra Hurd

Manager
Marilyn Atlas
Jaime Baker
Piedad Bonilla
Carolyn Caldera
Alix Gomez
Marc Hernandez
Steve Rodriguez
Robert Rose
Jerry Velasco

Marketing/Fundraising Consultant
Mitch Teplitsky
Conrado Terrazas

Media Advocate
Magdalena Albizu
Eddie Arnold
Edgar Endress
Digna Gerena
Mary Lampe
Robert Leach
Alex Moreno
Alex Nogales
Dr. Chon Noriega
Esteban Torres
Kirk Whisler

Novelist
Carolina Garcia-Aguilera

Postproduction Supervisor
Faith Radle
Nestor N. Rodriguez

Producer
Magdalena Albizu
Russell Alexander-Orozco
Sabrina Avila
Sabrina Aviles
Jaime Baker
Gabriel Barbarena
Trina Bardusco
Frank Barrera
Luca Bentivoglio

Daniel Bernardi
Margarita Borda
Darlene Caamano-Loquet
Alberto Caballero
Juan Caceres
Gabriel Carmona
David Carrera
Lupe Casares
Rudy Casillas
Adrian Castagna
Al Castañeda
Carlos Castañeda
Teofilo Chacin
Natalie Chaidez
Maria Chavez
Dolores Colunga-Stawitz
Tania Cuevas Martinez
Dita de Leon
Cecilia Domeyko
Sandra Duque
Juan Carlos (JC) Duran
Alfonso Espinosa
Tom Flores
Cris Franco
Hector Galan
Josie Garcia
Victor Garcia
Greg Gomez
Diana E. Gonzales
Jackie Gonzalez-Carlos
Dan Guerrero
Maritza Guimet
Salma Hayek
Ryan Law
Carolina Liu
Luis Llosa
Diana Logreira Campos
Adam Lopez
Tery Lopez
Kamala Lopez-Dawson
Omar Meza
Rhonda L. Mitrani
Kimberly Myers
Ibon Olaskoaga
Yazmin Ortiz
Rey Parla
Ivonne Perez Montijo
Francesca Prada

Michael Pryfogle
Mario Ramirez
Rick Ramirez
Diana Rico
Horacio "Lacho" Rodriguez
Pedro Rodriguez
Julia Segrove-Jaurigui
Roberto Sneider
Marianne Teleki
Jackie Torres
Robert Torres
Jose-Luis Trassens
Maria Valdez
Camilo Vila
Ligiah Villalobos

Producer, Commercial
Evelyn Badia
Junior Guapo
Gilda Longoria
Jose Luis Partida
Emily Perez

Producer, Documentary
Maria Agui-Carter
Natalia Almada
Emilia Anguita Huerta
Kary Antholis
Olga Arana
José Araujo
Diego Arsuaga
Marta Bautis
Frank Borres
Pablo Bressan
Maria Bures
Deborah Calla
Pedro Celedon
Ileana Ciena
Rene Simon Cruz
Nancy de los Santos
Alberto Dominguez
Paul Espinosa
Sonny Richard E. Espinoza
Natatcha Estebanez
Hector Galan
Ana Maria Garcia
Marcy Garriot

Polita Glynn
Evangeline Griego
Rudy Hernandez, Jr.
Catherine Herrera
Cristina Ibarra
Bill Jersey
Jorge Jiménez
Lillian Jiménez
Frances Lausell
Poli Marichal
Bienvenida Matias
Jennifer Maytorena Taylor
Eren McGinnis
John Montoya
Mylene Moreno
Edward James Olmos
Lisandro Perez-Rey
Anayansi Prado
Susan Racho
Alex Rivera
Rafael Rivera-Viruet
Ingrid Rojas
Sylvie Rokab
Fernanda Rossi
Carlos Sandoval
Manny Santos
Alison Sotomayor
Gustavo Stebner
Rick Tejada-Flores
Ray Telles
Mitch Teplitsky
Ela Troyano
John Valadez
Yvette Vega
Juan Carlos Zaldivar

Producer, Documentary Short
Natalia Almada
Thomas Javier Castillo
Elsa Madrigal
Jennifer Maytorena Taylor
Elisha Miranda
John Montoya
Marilyn Perez
Pepe Urquijo

Producer, DVD
Jackie Gonzalez-Carlos

Producer, Educational/ Industrial
Efrain Logreira
Marilyn Perez

Producer, Feature
Marvin Acuña
Alejandro Agresti
Olga Arana
Alfonso Arau
José Araujo
Ishmael Arredondo Henriquez
Isaac Artenstein
Marilyn Atlas
Elizabeth Avellan
Mario Avila
Nelson Betancourt
Alberto Caballero
Carolyn Caldera
Deborah Calla
Laura Cardona
Pedro Celedon
Ivan Cevallos
Manuel de Seixas Correa
Rene Simon Cruz
Alfonso Cuaron
Michael Cuesta
Guillermo del Toro
Nelson Denis
Roni Eguia Menendez
Moctesuma Esparza
Cari Esta Albert
Natatcha Estebanez
Evelina Fernandez
Kathryn F. Galan
Andy Garcia
Eddie Garcia
Victor Garcia
Victor Gonzalez
Maureen Gosling
Junior Guapo
Adrian Guillen
Salma Hayek
Gloria Herrera

Susan Jasso
Judi Jordan
Pamela S. Kuri
Frances Lausell
Anita Lawson
Vivien Lesnik Weisman
Luis Llosa
Rick Lombardo
Elba Luis Lugo
Luis Mandoki
Jose Carlos Mangual
Daniel Matas
Eren McGinnis
Jim Mendiola
Nestor Miranda
Michael Narvaez
Gregory Nava
Jesus Nebot
Frank Nuñez
Lorenzo O'Brien
Edward James Olmos
Robert Parada
Santiago Pozo
Raul Puig
Faith Radle
Cyn Rossi
Pablo Luis Rovito
Jose Luis Ruiz
Manny Santos
Julia Segrove-Jaurigui
Herbert Siguenza
Roberto Sneider
Luis Soto
Pepe Urquijo
David C. Valdes
Jose Luis Valenzuela
Jorge Vergara
Camilo Vila

Producer, PSA
Jose Luis Partida

Producer, Short
Jorge Aguirre
Carlos Alberto
Claudia Amaya
Cruz Angeles

Emilia Anguita Huerta
Olga Arana
Roberto Arevalo
Ishmael Arredondo Henriquez
Marilyn Atlas
Mario Avila
Evelyn Badia
Deborah Calla
Octavio Carranza
Marisa Castañeda
Victor Garcia
Michael Gavino
Polita Glynn
Junior Guapo
Matthew Handal
Francisco Hernandez
Yvan Iturriaga
Judi Jordan
Vivien Lesnik Weisman
Carolina Liu
Benjamin Lopez
Jose Carlos Mangual
Poli Marichal
Nellie Medina
Elisha Miranda
Mylene Moreno
Monica Nanez
Michael Narvaez
Jose Luis Orbegozo
Adriana E. Padilla
Laura Palaez
Emily Perez
Patrick Perez
Ivonne Perez Montijo
Ximena Ponce
Henry K. Priest
Marcial Rios
Nestor N. Rodriguez
Rafael Rosado
Veronica Sanchez
Susana Tubert
Pepe Urquijo
Jose Antonio Vazquez
Yvette Vega
Jerry Villarreal
Del Zamora

Producer, Stage Play
Anita Lawson
Ivonne Perez Montijo
Jonisha Rios
Veronica Robles
Cyn Rossi
Tomas Salas

Producer, Stage Play Festival
Juliette Carrillo

Producer, TV
Laura Cardona
Pedro Celedon
Tania Cypriano
Alfredo de Villa
Benny Flores
Juan Mandelbaum
Eren McGinnis
Joey Medina
Nellie Medina
Angel Meneces
Kimberly Myers
Lionel Pasamonte
Henry K. Priest

Producer, TV Movie
Paul F. Cajero
Natalie Chaidez
Oscar Luis Costo
Gregory Nava
Luis Soto

Producer, TV Series
Paul F. Cajero
Deborah Calla
Laura Castañeda
Natalie Chaidez
Oscar Luis Costo
Rene Simon Cruz
Geno Escarrega
Dolly Josette Espinal
Paul Espinosa
Errol Falcon
Richard Fernandes

Ilse Fernandez
Nely Galan
Hector Gonzalez
Javier Grillo Marxuach
Rick Lombardo
Gilda Longoria
George Lopez
Luis Mandoki
Barbara Martinez Jitner
Jennifer Maytorena Taylor
Nestor Miranda
Sylvia Morales
Peter Murrieta
Gregory Nava
Lorenzo O'Brien
Laura Palaez
Henry K. Priest
Diana Rico
Alex Rivera
Isabel Rivera
Jose Rivera
Veronica Robles
Manny Santos
Luis Soto
Alison Sotomayor
Gustavo Stebner
Jeff Valdez

Producer, TV Series, Animated
Rafael Rosado

Producer, TV Special
Frank Borres
Gilda Longoria
Barbara Martinez Jitner
Nellie Medina
Jonisha Rios
Veronica Robles
Paul Rodriguez
Jeff Valdez
Yvette Vega

Production Accountant
Martin Alcala
Maria Pulice
Alicia Rivera Frankl

Production Assistant
Pauline Cashion
Carlos Espinoza
Germaine Franco
Sierra Ornelas
Rachel Pineda
Rosario Sotelo

Production Company
Laura Castañeda

Production Consultant
Octavio Marin

Production Coordinator
Fabio Alexandre da Silva
Jose Carlos Mangual

Production Designer
Elizabeth Calienes
Samuel Cordoba
Richard A. Fernandez
Joleen Koehly

Production Facilities & Services
Isaac Avila
Elika Crespo
Victoria Fraasa
Rami Frankl
Diana E. Gonzales
Rene Leda
Alex Mendoza
Mercedes Palomo
Cesar Peschiera
Zasha Robles
Paul Rodriguez
Dolly Rosell

Production Manager
Fabio Alexandre da Silva
Paul F. Cajero
Manuel de Seixas Correa
Claudia Cosio
Ricardo Gale

Rosa Gonzalez
Gloria Herrera
Gilda Longoria
Jose Carlos Mangual
Octavio Marin
Laura Medina
Nellie Medina
Kaaren Ochoa
Alicia Rivera Frankl
Veronica Sanchez
Julio Vallejo
Gabriela Vazquez

Promotion/Event Producer
Benjamin Torres

Publicist
Pauline Cashion
Ivan Cevallos
Dan del Campo
Leonor McCall-Rodriguez
Lourdes Ortega
Alex Rodriguez
Jerry Velasco

Researcher
Olga Arana

Script Supervisor
Paul Perez

Sound
Thomas Javier Castillo
William Franco
Pascui Rivas
Jose Torres

Special/Visual Effects
Gary Michael Gutierrez
Debra Hurd

Storyboard Artist
Rafael Rosado

Stunt Coordinator
Rocky Capella

Stunt Man
Rocky Capella

Supervising Producer
Martin Alcala
Loreto Caro
John Estrada

Supervisor, Cultural Content
Dolly Josette Espinal

Talk Show Host
Cristina Saralegui

Technical Director
Alberto Caballero

Web Developer
Jennifer Nowotny
Richard Rodriguez

Writer
Ricardo Acuña
Shawn Baca
José Bayona
Daniel Bernardi
Margarita Borda
Cynthia Buchanan
Vic Cabrera
Juan Caceres
Patricia Cardoso
Alfredo Cubiña
Maggie de la Cuesta
Cecilia Domeyko
Sandra Duque
Joseph Edo
Alfonso Espinosa
Daniel Faraldo
Edwin Figueroa
Diego Gutierrez
Stan Jakubowicz
Joleen Koehly

Ryan Law
Andy Lebron
Benjamin Lopez
Angel Meneces
Juan Carlos Perez
Marilyn Perez
Francesca Prada
Mario Ramirez
Quinto Reyes
Horacio "Lacho" Rodriguez
Elaine Romero
Abel Salas
Carlos San Miguel
John Phillip Santos
Adam Schlachter
Roberto Sneider
Jackie Torres
Ligiah Villalobos
Crystina Wyler

Writer, Award Shows
Dan Guerrero

Writer, Commercial
Matthew Handal

Writer, Documentary
Claudia Amaya
Emilia Anguita Huerta
José Araujo
Eva S. Aridjis
Ana Marie de la Peña Portela
Nancy de los Santos
Natatcha Estebanez
Javier Olivera
Anayansi Prado
Fernanda Rossi
Rick Tejada-Flores
Joseph Tovares

Writer, Documentary Short
Marilyn Perez

Writer, Edutainment
Efrain Logreira

Writer, Experimental
Ana Marie de la Peña Portela

Writer, Feature
Omonike Akinyemi
Sergio Arau
José Araujo
Luis Argueta
Guillermo Arriaga
Diego Arsuaga
Miguel Arteta
Mario Avila
Carlos Bolado
Juan Jose Campanella
Salvador Carrasco
Mike & Gibby Cevallos
Ernie Contreras
Manuel de Seixas Correa
Michael Cuesta
Ignacio del Moral
Guillermo del Toro
Nelson Denis
Katrina Elias
Maria Escobedo
Natatcha Estebanez
Evelina Fernandez
John Carlos Frey
Georgina Garcia Riedel
Lisa Garibay
Sonia Gonzalez
Alejandro Gonzalez Iñarritu
Sergio Guerrero
Matthew Handal
Leon Ichaso
Betty Kaplan
Josefina Lopez
Lalo Lopez Alcaraz
Elba Luis Lugo
Cheech Marin
Jim Mendiola
Joe Menendez
Ramon Menendez
Nestor Miranda
Sergio Molina
Peter Murrieta
Michael Narvaez
Gregory Nava
Lorenzo O'Brien

Javier Olivera
Jack Perez
Felix Pire
Frank Reyes
Jose Rivera
Robert Rodriguez
Cyn Rossi
Adam Schlachter
Herbert Siguenza
Gustavo Stebner
Gabriela Tagliavini
Pablo Toledo
Ela Troyano
Luis Valdez
Esteban Zul

Writer, Game Show
Margarita Ramon

Writer, Magazine Articles
Margarita Ramon

Writer, Short
Omonike Akinyemi
Cruz Angeles
Emilia Anguita Huerta
Guillermo Arriaga
Evelyn Badia
Patricia Cardoso
Octavio Carranza
Juliette Carrillo
Manuel de Seixas Correa
Claudia Cosio
Angel David
Ana Marie de la Peña Portela
Rafael del Toro
Alejandro Diaz
Michael Gavino
Omar Gonzalez
Erika Grediaga
Gloria Herrera
Yvan Iturriaga
Betty Kaplan
Vivien Lesnik Weisman
Julian Londono
Adam Lopez
Lalo Lopez Alcaraz

Poli Marichal
Louis Mejia
Elisha Miranda
Michael Narvaez
Frank Nuñez
Jose Luis Orbegozo
Adriana E. Padilla
Ivonne Perez Montijo
Ximena Ponce
Marcial Rios
Elaine Romero
Bernardo Ruiz
Patricio Serna
Thomas Torres
Susana Tubert
Del Zamora
Esteban Zul

Writer, Stage Play
Nilo Cruz
Angel David
Ana Marie de la Peña Portela
Katrina Elias
Evelina Fernandez
Anne Garcia-Romero
Michael Gavino
Anita Lawson
Richard Montoya
Ivonne Perez Montijo
Felix Pire
Elaine Romero

Felix Romero
Ric Salinas
Herbert Siguenza
Susana Tubert
Leslie Valdes

Writer, TV
Michael Baez
Luis Llosa

Writer, TV Movie
Natalie Chaidez
Nancy de los Santos
Diego Gutierrez
John Leguizamo
Josefina Lopez

Writer, TV Series
Carlos Avila
Julio Calderon
Mike & Gibby Cevallos
Natalie Chaidez
Manny Coto
Victor de Jesus
Nancy de los Santos
Michael Gavino
Javier Grillo Marxuach
Eddie Guerra
Diego Gutierrez
Dennis Leoni

Luisa Leschin
Angel Dean Lopez
George Lopez
Juan Mandelbaum
Joe Menendez
Sergio Molina
Peter Murrieta
Gregory Nava
Lorenzo O'Brien
Margarita Ramon
Jorge Reyes
Diana Rico
Jose Rivera
Henry Robles
Jeff Valdez
Luis Valdez
Del Zamora

Writer, TV Series, Animated
Jorge Aguirre
Ernie Contreras
Denise Dorn
Ashley Mendoza
Leslie Valdes

Writer, TV Special
John Leguizamo
Dennis Leoni
Cheech Marin
Paul Rodriguez

National Association of Latino Independent Producers

index
by state

Alaska
Rick Barreras

Arizona
Carlos Acuña
Alicia Barron
Daniel Bernardi
Barbara Bustillos-Cogswell
Rudy Casillas
Thomas Javier Castillo
Valintino Costa
Carlos Espinoza
Mario Esquer
Hector Gonzalez
Shelli Hall
Jorgiania Jake
Gary Keller
Benjamin Lobato
Benjamin Lopez
Melanie Magisos
Yuri Makino
Anna Martinez
Minerva Mendoza
Analuisa Morales
Damian Nelson
Daniela Ontiveros
Sierra Ornelas
Ari Palos
Ruben Reyes
Christopher Rodarte
Veronica Rodriguez-Brett
Elaine Romero
Lawrence Toledo
Pablo Toledo
Rosa Varela
Gilberto Vega

California
Bonnie Abaunza
Beatriz Acevedo
Marvin Acuña
Ricardo Acuña
Sergio Aguero
Margarita D. Aguirre
Valentin Aguirre
Victor Albarran
Carlos Alberto

Felix Alcala
Martin Alcala
Felipe Alejandro
Russell Alexander-Orozco
German Alonso
Roxana Altamirano
Carlos Alvarado
Gonzalo Amat
Abel Amaya
Abdiel Anglero
Fernando Anguita
Kary Antholis
Rene Anthony Torres
Richard Apodaca
Ruben Apodaca
Ray Aragon
Tania Araiza
Olga Arana
Jesse Aranda
Sergio Arau
Leida Arce
Alicia Arden
Lucero Arellano
Edward Arguelles
Catherine Armas-Matsumoto
Sergio Armendariz
Ishmael Arredondo Henriquez
Isaac Artenstein
Miguel Arteta
Marilyn Atlas
Davah Avena
Carlos Avila
Isaac Avila
José Avila
Sandra Avila
Shawn Baca
Michael Baez
Peter Bandera
Antonio Banderas
Norbeto Barba
Gabriel Barbarena
Alberto Barboza
Lisset Barcellos
Frank Barron
Frank Bennett Gonzalez
Luca Bentivoglio
Victoria Bernal
Enrique Berumen

James Blancarte
Carlos Bolado
Piedad Bonilla
Eddie Borges
Maria Bozzi
Dean Anthony Bradford
Carla Brandon
Abraham Brown
Sarah Brown-Gonzales
Cynthia Buchanan
Juan Carlos Buitron
Efraim Burdeinick
Darlene Caamano-Loquet
Agustin & Alicia Caballero
Alberto Caballero
Vic Cabrera
Paul F. Cajero
Roma Calatayud
Carolyn Caldera
Julio Calderon
Elizabeth Calienes
Deborah Calla
Michael Camacho
Juan Jose Campanella
Rocky Capella
Walter Carasco
Johnny Carbajal
Alejandro Cardenas
Patricia Cardoso
Gabriel Carmona
Carlos Caro
Michael Caro
Octavio Carranza
Salvador Carrasco
James Carrera
Carlos Carreras
Juliette Carrillo
Claudia Casillas
Adrian Castagna
Al Castañeda
Laura Castañeda
Laura Castañeda
Richard Castaniero
Jesús Castellanos
Ramon Castillo
Karina Castorena
Gabriel Castro
Fernando Alberto Castroman

index by state

index by state

Lucas Guerra
Cristina Kotz Cornejo
Juan Mandelbaum
Veronica Robles
Joseph Tovares

Maryland

Carla Gutierrez
David Leal-Cortez

Michigan

Deborah de la Torre

Minnesota

Victoria Ramirez

New Jersey

Angelo Bolaños
Dianet Colon
Ezequiel Colon-Rivera
Lisa Gonzalez
Diego Kenneth
Jose Antonio Pelayo
Nelson Pereyra
Alexander Ramirez
Victor Rosa
Irene Sosa
Thomas Torres

New Mexico

Marisa Castañeda
Arcie Chapa
Alex Flores
Bernardo Hajdenberg
Immanuel Maes
Clemen Ochoa
Ed Rios
Pilar Rodriguez-Aranda
Frank Zuñiga

New York

Luis Cady Abarca
Carolina Aguilera
Jorge Aguirre
Omonike Akinyemi
Magdalena Albizu

Natalia Almada
Juan Manuel Alvarado
Barbara Alvarez
Claudia Amaya
Cruz Angeles
José Araujo
Luis Argueta
Eva S. Aridjis
Rosa Arredondo
Bernadette Aulestia
Sabrina Avila
Evelyn Badia
Jaime Baker
Trina Bardusco
Frank Barrera
Marta Bautis
José Bayona
Richard Beaumont
Alfredo Bejar
Jellybean Benitez
Elisa Blatteis
Vanessa Braccini
Juan Caceres
Felix Leo Campos
David Capurso
Laura Cardona
Julissa Carmona
Elvira Carrizal
Angel Carrizosa
Raesha Cartagena
Lupe Casares
Liliana Castellanos
Juan Castillo
Raul Castillo
Calixto Chinchilla
Evelyn Collazo
Manuel de Seixas Correa
Nilo Cruz
Michael Cuesta
Tania Cypriano
Angel David
Carlos de Jesus
Maggie de la Cuesta
Rafael de la Uz
Perla de Leon
Rafael del Toro
Nelson Denis
Denise Dorn

Xochitl Dorsey
Sandra Duque
Eddy Duran
Ester Duran
Juan Carlos Escobedo
Maria Escobedo
Ilse Fernandez
Ivonne Fernandez-Jack
Drew Figueroa
Noemi Figueroa Soulet
Felipe Galindo
Ani Gasti
Marta Gibbons
Marisol Gomez
Antonio Gomez-Orodea
Carolina Gonzalez
Inez Guillen
Matthew Handal
Shayla Harris
Eric W. Henriquez
Paula Heredia
Eugene Hernandez
Gloria Herrera
Barbara Holguin
Cristina Ibarra
Lillian Jiménez
Sandy Jiménez
Robert Julian
Gloria LaMorte
Andy Lebron
John Leguizamo
Daniel Levy
Diane Librizzi
Diana Logreira Campos
Cynthia Lopez
Edwin René López
George Lopez
Victoria Lopez
Karla Lozano
Sonia Malfa-Clements
Alma Martinez
Daniel Matas
Bienvenida Matias
Laala Matías
Nellie Medina
Ashley Mendoza
Rafael Merino
Patricia Migliori Farnes

OUR SUPPORTERS

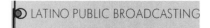

SAG – Producers' Industry
Advancement Cooperative Fund

DATA COLLECTION FORM

Dear NALIP members and friends,

We hope you enjoy the **Latino Media Resource Guide**™ and find it beneficial. Please help us make this book a powerful tool by updating and providing us with your most current credit and contact information on the questionnaire below. In addition to this invaluable book, NALIP brings to our community a state-of-the-art intranet site at http://my.nalip.info. This communication tool will give NALIP members and chapters their own website, email address, searchable directory, chat rooms, job boards and much more! For the time being, it is open to you, even if you are not yet a NALIP member—so hurry and visit us at http://my.nalip.info. You can even update all your information online! Employers can find you, members can contact you, and we can continue emailing you *Latinos in the Industry* and other important opportunities for your projects and careers.

First Name _____   Last Name _____

Company _____

Title/Position _____   Year of birth _____

Phone 1 _____   Phone 2 _____

Cell Phone _____   Fax _____

Email _____   Website _____

Address _____

City _____   State _____

Zip Code _____   Country _____

What is your primary job in the industry? (e.g. Writer, Producer, Editor, D.P., Agent, Executive, Publicist, etc.):
_____

Please list produced titles where you received that/those credit(s). Include year, distributor or production company, and type of project (e.g. feature, tv movie, documentary, short, etc.). Use back of form if needed.

_____
_____
_____
_____
_____
_____
_____

Are you a member of any of the following organizations?

❏ PGA   ❏ DGA   ❏ WGA   ❏ ASC   ❏ Other _____
❏ SAG   ❏ NALIP   ❏ IDA   ❏ AIVF

REPRESENTATION:

Agency _____   Contact _____

Phone _____   Email _____

Manager _____   Contact _____

Phone _____   Email _____

Attorney _____   Contact _____

Phone _____   Email _____

Please mail completed form to NALIP/LMRG, P.O. Box 1247, Santa Monica, CA 90406, or e-mail to LMRG@nalip.info or fax to 310.453.5258. Thank you.